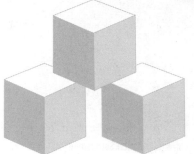

Hands On
SQL Server 7
with VB6

Send Us Your Comments:

To comment on this book or any other PRIMA TECH title, visit our reader response page on the Web at **www.prima-tech.com/comments**.

How to Order:

For information on quantity discounts, contact the publisher: Prima Publishing, P.O. Box 1260BK, Rocklin, CA 95677-1260; (916) 632-4400. On your letterhead, include information concerning the intended use of the books and the number of books you wish to purchase. For individual orders, visit PRIMA TECH's Web site at **www.prima-tech.com**.

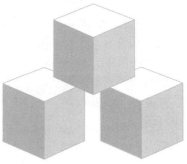

Hands On
SQL Server 7
with VB6

Wayne S. Freeze

PRIMA TECH

A DIVISION OF PRIMA PUBLISHING

A Division of Prima Publishing

Prima Publishing and colophon are registered trademarks of Prima Communications, Inc., Rocklin, California 95677.

Publisher: Matthew H. Carleson
Associate Publisher: Nancy Stevenson
Managing Editor: Dan J. Foster
Senior Acquisitions Editor: Deborah F. Abshier
Project Editor: Kevin W. Ferns
Technical Reviewer: John Paulsen
Copy Editor: Laura Gabler
Interior Layout: Marian Hartsough
Cover Design: Prima Design Team
Indexer: Sharon Hilgenberg

Microsoft, Windows, Windows NT, Internet Explorer, Visual Basic, and FrontPage are trademarks or registered trademarks of Microsoft Corporation.

Important: If you experience problems running Microsoft SQL Server, go to Microsoft's Web site at www.microsoft.com, or check the online help for technical support information. Prima Publishing cannot provide software support.

Prima Publishing and the author have attempted throughout this book to distinguish proprietary trademarks from descriptive terms by following the capitalization style used by the manufacturer.

Information contained in this book has been obtained by Prima Publishing from sources believed to be reliable. However, because of the possibility of human or mechanical error by our sources, Prima Publishing, or others, the Publisher does not guarantee the accuracy, adequacy, or completeness of any information and is not responsible for any errors or omissions or the results obtained from the use of such information. Readers should be particularly aware of the fact that the Internet is an ever-changing entity. Some facts may have changed since this book went to press.

ISBN: 0-7615-1385-X

Library of Congress Catalog Card Number: 98-68140

Printed in the United States of America

99 00 01 02 03 DD 10 9 8 7 6 5 4 3 2 1

To my father,
who taught me many things
over the years—including
that life is too short to rush through it.

About the Author

WAYNE S. FREEZE is a full-time computer book author, software developer, and technology consultant. Having worked with computers for over 25 years, Wayne has seen computers grow from room-sized machines to palm-top devices. His previous books have covered programming in Visual Basic, SQL, and the Internet. His titles have received favorable reviews from magazines such as Dr. Dobbs and have been featured on Microsoft's MSDN Web site. His lovely wife Jill is also a respected author in her own right, and they have collaborated on several titles together.

In his spare time, he likes to photograph war birds at airshows, read and write science fiction, play with his two children (Christopher and Samantha), tinker with his aquarium, and play with his collection of cars in various sizes. Wayne's formal education includes degrees in electrical engineering, computer science, and business management. You can visit his Web site at www.justpc.com or send him e-mail at wfreeze@justpc.com.

Acknowledgments

Nearly everyone thinks being an author is a wonderful job. You get to work at home, set your own hours, and have the freedom to do what you please. The only people who don't believe this are the authors, their family, and the people who take the recycled electrons and magically transform them in books. They know that writing is hard work, and the few minutes of joy in seeing the new book on the shelf doesn't always make up for the months of 16-hour days.

I want to thank Laura Belt for all her hard work. As long as you can keep finding new books, I'll keep writing them.

I also want to say thanks to my friends at Prima: Jenny Watson, thanks for giving me the opportunity to write the book I was supposed to write two years ago; Debbie Abshier, it was nice meeting you in person for the first time and it felt like coming home when I started writing this book; Kevin Ferns, thank you for being patient—I think it was worth the wait; John Paulsen, thanks for being the most thorough technical editor I've ever had; and Laura Gabler, thank you for making me sound literate.

Cherrie Chiu also deserves special recognition for all her hard work. While I'm sorry that things didn't work out as we'd planned, you gave me a lot more insight into the book industry.

One other aspect of writing is that it occupies so much time, I don't always find time to visit or even talk to my friends. Shaun, Elwyn, Rick, Bob W., Veronica, Scott, Bob K., and Ian, I'll be in touch soon. I promise. Thanks for your support. (Rick—I'll be over soon to do a little "shopping").

Life is never dull when Bucky and Goose are around. I wish you were around more often. We all miss you and can't wait for you to move east.

It seems like I never get to see my mother and father as often as I wish. I hope that changes in the future, since you are both very special people to me. I want to especially thank you for your support while writing this book. It was much appreciated.

You will find occasional references to Christopher, Samantha, and Jill throughout this book. Chris is just five years old and knows more about computers than some well-paid people I used to work with. And Samantha is only four, but she's not that far behind Chris in her ability to crash Windows on demand. I love both of you a whole lot. My lovely wife Jill is a very respected writer in her own right, having written books on Microsoft Office, Internet Explorer, and WebTV. Thanks for the Dum de-de dum-dum dum dum dum. If you believe in yourself, anything is possible! Also remember that no matter what happens, I love you.

Wayne S. Freeze
Beltsville, Maryland
January, 1999

Contents at a Glance

Contents

Introduction

Building a database application can be very difficult or very easy, depending on how you look at it. How hard it is depends on two main factors: choosing the right software and designing a good application. The combination of Visual Basic and SQL Server can't be beat for most applications, and this book will show you the easy way to build Visual Basic applications using SQL Server.

Microsoft SQL Server 7 is one of the leading database management systems available on the market today. It is easy to install and administer, and it comes with tools and wizards that make it easy to develop applications. The database server itself has been redesigned to automatically perform many tuning functions, leaving you free to focus on more important tasks.

Visual Basic 6 is Microsoft's strategic language for Rapid Application Development (RAD). It is easy to use, efficient, and flexible. I prefer this language because one can build a Windows program quicker and with less effort with VB6 than with any other programming language. It's a natural language for building database applications, owing to the level and sophistication of the tools included with the language.

This book is for the beginning to intermediate programmer who already has a working knowledge of Visual Basic. This means that you should know how to write and debug a Visual Basic program, be comfortable with the development environment, and know how to use most of the common controls, such as the **TextBox**, **Label**, and **CommandButton** controls. I also assume that you know how to use Windows and understand concepts such as files, directories, and overlapping windows. Additionally, you should have a basic knowledge of the Structured Query Language (SQL). A detailed understanding isn't necessary, but it will help you to do the examples.

What This Book Covers

This book shows you how to use SQL Server and Visual Basic to build a moderately complex application called WebBooks.com. It covers the creation of a database, from identifying the data elements to configuring automatic database backups. It also discusses several necessary tools, including the Enterprise Manager, the Data Transformation Services utilities, and the Query Analyzer.

In addition, this book addresses Visual Basic issues. It shows you a number of different approaches that you can use to create traditional Visual Basic client/server programs. It also covers how to use the new IIS Application feature to build a comprehensive Web site.

Furthermore, it demonstrates how to use many other technologies associated with SQL Server and Visual Basic, such as building an application server to hold your business logic, using DHTML Web pages, and creating reports with Microsoft Data Report.

ON THE CD

Nearly as important as the book is the CD-ROM, which provides the complete source code to the application, including sample data that you can use for testing the application. Additionally, an evaluation edition of SQL Server is included so you can install and try the various examples in this book.

What This Book Doesn't Cover

This book doesn't teach you how to build simple Visual Basic programs. If you don't know the difference between an event and a text box, come back after you've read another book such as Prima Tech's *Hands on Visual Basic 6*. Also, I assume that you have at least a passing knowledge of SQL, though I will rather quickly walk you through some of the basic information you need. Furthermore, the installation and configuration instructions for Windows NT, SQL Server, and Internet Information Server are not covered in this book.

Hardware and Software Requirements

It's possible to do your development and testing on a single system if necessary. However, make sure that you have a lot of memory (128 megabytes

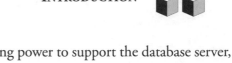

should be fine) and enough processing power to support the database server, the Web server, and Visual Basic (any Pentium II processor should be fine). If you want to use multiple machines, I suggest that the one with more memory be used for the database server. Performance of the database is controlled more by the amount of available memory than by any other factor.

I wrote this book using two computers: one (called Mycroft) for developing the application and the other (known as Athena) to run the database server. The development computer was a Gateway 9100 laptop with a Pentium 200 processor and 64 megabytes of main memory, along with Windows 98, Visual Basic 6, and SQL Server 7. The database server was a Gateway desktop computer with a Pentium 120 processor and 80 megabytes of main memory. It used Windows NT Server 4.0 with the NT Server Option Pack and Service Pack 4. Obviously SQL Server was installed, plus Internet Information Server (IIS) 4.0, and a copy of Visual Basic 6, though it wasn't really necessary. The two computers were connected using a 10 MHz Ethernet LAN. The combination was a little slower than I would have liked, but it worked for me.

Introducing WebBooks.com

In this book, you'll build an application called WebBooks.com. If you are familiar with Computer Literacy (www.clbooks.com) or Amazon.com (www.amazon.com), then you already have a good idea of what you're going to build. You aren't going to try to duplicate the complete functions offered by these Web sites. For one person, that could take years. But you'll finish the book with enough knowledge of how they work and how to apply those principles to your own database applications.

WebBooks.com has components that span both traditional client/server database programming and the Internet. Within this framework, the most important task is to help the customer purchase books. These people will access WebBooks.com exclusively through the Internet. It is also important to provide good support for the other people involved with WebBooks.com, such as the people who help customers over the telephone, the people who pack the books for shipment, and the people who maintain and operate the computers used by WebBooks.com. Most of these people will be accessing the system via the local area network installed at WebBooks.com and can take advantage of traditional client/server programs to access their data.

Database Project Roles

Every database project is the work of a number of people. Each person is responsible for a particular area of the project. The database administrator is responsible for the database server and each of the databases it contains. The systems analyst is responsible for determining the information that is stored in the database and the design of the functions the application will perform. The programmer is responsible for implementing and debugging the design from the systems analyst. The computer operator ensures that the routine processing required by the database server and the application is completed successfully and on schedule. The user is the person or persons who receive the benefit of the application, such as the WebBooks.com clerks who enter information and the customers who use the system to order their books.

When building this application, you need to be all of these people. You need to keep in mind how they will use it and what their distinct needs and wants are. Often these needs and wants will conflict among different people, and it is up to you to resolve them. You've heard the expression, *the customer is always right.* Since the majority of the users of the application are customers, their needs should come first, even if it means making the job of the systems analyst and the programmer more complicated.

Customer Information Subsystem

The Customer Information Subsystem (CIS) consists of a set of programs, database tables, and database utility jobs that manage information about WebBooks.com's customers. This includes such information as name, address, e-mail address, credit card information, etc. This first project is designed to get you comfortable with using the various tools available in SQL Server and Visual Basic. I begin by discussing how to determine the data elements needed, designing the database, creating the database, importing and exporting data, and building a simple client/server database program using the data control.

Inventory Information Subsystem

The Inventory Information Subsystem (IIS) continues the process of building the WebBooks.com application by adding information about the books available for sale. It then shows you how to design and build more complex databases and how to incorporate them into your Web site. I do this by

focusing on how to use the **DataEnvironment** feature to build more complex database programs and by introducing you to IIS Applications, with which you can easily build Web server applications.

Order Processing Subsystem

The Order Processing Subsystem (OPS) concludes the WebBooks.com application by adding the ability for customers to place orders and track their status. It also includes a utility that allows the clerks in the warehouse to print packing lists that will be included with a customer's order. It does this by introducing tools that allow you to distribute your business logic to other machines using ActiveX EXE programs. These programs allow you to create client-side programs using DHTML technology, which offers the benefits of using Microsoft Data Reporter to create printed reports.

The *Hands-On* Approach

In order to truly understand how to use SQL Server 7 with Visual Basic 6, you need to work through each of the subsystems. This means you shouldn't just read the material, but you should load the software from the CD-ROM and see it in action. Your job is to take this working example and add new functions and features to it. To get you started, at the end of each project, I include some ideas for features that you should implement. Also, I discuss some functions that I want you to implement on your own. By adding these features to the program, you'll avoid the frustrations that often accompany making a complex program run correctly and you'll get a better understanding of how the tools work.

Special Elements

At times, you'll be provided with information that supplements the discussion at hand. This special information is set off in easy-to-identify sidebars, so you can review or skip these extras as you see fit. You'll find the following types of special elements in this book:

Tips provide shortcuts to make your job easier, or better ways to accomplish certain tasks.

Notes provide supplemental information that might be of interest to you but is not essential to performing the task at hand.

 Cautions alert you to potential pitfalls or warn you when a particular operation is risky and might cause you to lose some of your work.

 This icon is used to refer you to items found on the CD that accompanies this book.

- **Code and items that appear onscreen.** Any code discussed in this book is presented in a special typeface to make it easy to distinguish from the rest of the text.

Visit My Web Site

I maintain a Web site at www.justpc.com with additional information about the books that my wife and I have written. You're also welcome to send me e-mail at wfreeze@justpc.com. I enjoy reading every note I get, and I try to respond to questions and comments as best as I can. If I can point you in the right direction to help you solve your own problem, I'll do that. If you find a bug or have an idea to improve any of the sample projects, please let me know. With your permission, I'd add it to my Web site so other readers could benefit from it. For more information on this book and others by PRIMA TECH, see PRIMA TECH's Web site at www.prima-tech.com.

CHAPTER 1

Features of SQL Server 7

Before you can build a database application, you need to understand a little about databases and database systems. This chapter introduces you to these concepts and explains how they are implemented in SQL Server 7.

You'll first learn the major characteristics of a database. Then you'll review SQL Server 7, including the platforms it runs on, the data types supported, and a couple utility programs you will use through the rest of this book.

Finally, the chapter concludes with a brief introduction to SQL, the language on which SQL Server is based. You'll tackle a few practical exercises that will introduce you to some important database concepts.

What Is a Database?

Simply stated, a database is a collection of related information organized in a manner that makes it easy to locate specific data. For example, a dictionary or an encyclopedia is considered a database. With the proliferation of computers, Database Management Systems (DBMS) not only allow the storage and retrieval of information, but also have the ability to handle issues of security, concurrency, and recovery.

At a minimum, a DBMS must be able to perform the following tasks:

- Create, modify, and delete databases
- Add, update, and delete data in a database
- Retrieve data from a database

However, most DBMSs also perform the following tasks:

- Manage database authorization and permissions
- Manage multiple users concurrently accessing data in a database
- Create backup files from data stored in a database
- Recover data from a backup file

SQL Server 7 Overview

This book is about the Microsoft SQL Server 7 relational database management system. It runs on Windows 95 and 98 and Windows NT 4.0 and 2000 (also known as NT 5.0) using the same code base. Thus you can build and test your database on a single Windows 9x workstation and migrate it to a Windows NT system when you have finished.

SQL Server Editions

SQL Server comes in three different editions: Desktop, Standard, and Enterprise (see Table 1-1). The Desktop edition is new in SQL Server 7 and is targeted at small databases that reside on a workstation. This edition might be useful for salespeople who use a laptop and need a database for processing orders or performing demonstrations. They can periodically link their system to the network and then use the database replication feature to synchronize their database with the corporate database. This edition would also be useful for applications programmers who want to test an application on a private database before migrating it to a much larger system.

Table 1-1 Features Supported by Each SQL Server Edition			
Feature	**Desktop**	**Standard**	**Enterprise**
Operating system Edition	All	NT Server	NT Server Enterprise
Maximum CPUs	2	4	32
Support more than 2GB of memory	No	No	Yes
Maximum database size	4GB	unlimited	unlimited

The Enterprise edition of SQL Server 7 is targeted at very large and/or very high-activity databases. It requires a special version of Windows NT Server called the Enterprise Edition, which supports more than two gigabytes (GB) of main memory and more than four processors.

The Standard edition of SQL Server 7 is the traditional version of SQL Server that has been in use for years. This edition requires a Windows NT Server system and should be used whenever you don't need the Enterprise edition or the Desktop edition.

All three editions of SQL Server 7 use the same set of code, so if your application runs properly on one of the editions, it should also run on the others unless you are using a special feature not available in them. Other database vendors use different sets of code for different databases, which can cause problems when you move your application from a small database installed on your workstation to a production database.

SQL Server Data Types

SQL Server 7 supports a wide range of data types (see Table 1-2). Not all of these data types can be used with Visual Basic, and in some cases you may lose precision when converting between the SQL Server data type and the Visual Basic data type.

When building a database, always allow a little extra space or more precision than you need when specifying a data type. Disk drives are cheaper than the cost of having to redo your application down the road.

Table 1-2   SQL Server Data Types

SQL Server Data Type	Visual Basic Data Type	Description
Binary	**Byte Array**	A fixed-length binary string up to 8,000 bytes long.
Bit	n/a	A single binary digit, either 0 or 1.
Char	**String**	A fixed-length non-Unicode string containing up to 8,000 characters.
Datetime	**Date**	A 64-bit value that can specify any date and time value from January 1, 1753, to December 31, 9999, with an accuracy of 3.33 milliseconds.
Decimal	n/a	A decimal value ranging from $-10^{38} - 1$ to $10^{38} - 1$.
Float	**Double**	A 64-bit floating point number ranging from $-1.79E + 308$ to $1.79E + 308$.
Image	**Byte Array**	A variable-length binary string up to $2^{31} - 1$ (2,147,483,647) bytes long.
Int	**Long**	A 32-bit integer ranging from -2^{31} ($-2,147,483,648$) to $2^{31} - 1$ (2,147,483,647).
Money	**Currency**	A dollar value ranging from -2^{63} ($-922,337,203,685,477.5808$) to $2^{63} - 1$ (922,337,203,685,477.5807) scaled to four decimal places.
Nchar	**String**	A fixed-length Unicode string containing up to 4,000 characters.
Ntext	**String**	A variable-length Unicode string containing up to $2^{30} - 1$ (1,073,741,823) characters.

Table 1-2	SQL Server Data Types	
SQL Server Data Type	**Visual Basic Data Type**	**Description**
Nvarchar	String	A variable-length Unicode string containing up to 4,000 characters.
Real	Single	A 32-bit floating number ranging from −3.40E + 38 to 3.40E + 38.
Smalldatetime	Date	A 32-bit value that can specify any date and time value from January 1, 1900, to June 6, 2079, with an accuracy of 1 minute.
Smallint	Integer	A 16-bit integer ranging from −215 (−32,768) to 215 − 1 (32,767).
Smallmoney	Currency	A dollar value ranging from −214,748.3648 to 214,748.3647.
Text	String	A variable-length non-Unicode string containing up to 231 − 1 (2,147,483,647) characters.
Timestamp	n/a	A 64-bit value that is guaranteed to be unique in a database. Each time a row is inserted or updated, this value will change.
Tinyint	Byte	An 8-bit integer ranging from 0 to 255.
Uniqueidentifier	n/a	A 128-bit Global Unique Identifier (GUID) value.
Varbinary	Byte Array	A variable-length binary string up to 8,000 bytes long.
Varchar	String	A variable-length non-Unicode string containing up to 8,000 characters.

The most common data types you will use in your program are **Char** and **Varchar**, which will hold string values. The primary difference between the two is that the **Char** data type reserves a fixed amount of space for the data, while the **Varchar** data type uses only the space it requires.

The next most common data types are **Int** and **Smallint**, which correspond to the Visual Basic **Long** and **Integer** data types. These are useful for storing numeric information. The **Datetime** data type should be used over the **Smalldatetime** data type since the former doesn't lose accuracy when you assign it a value from a Visual Basic **Date** data type.

Caution

> If you care about the accuracy of your data, avoid the **Float** and **Real** data types. Floating point numbers should never be used for calculations involving money. You should use the **Money** data type instead.

SQL Server Utilities

SQL Server includes a number of utility programs to help you manage your database. Two of the most powerful tools are the Enterprise Manager and the Query Analyzer. Though there are other tools available, you will be able to effectively manage your database once you learn these two.

Enterprise Manager

The Enterprise Manager is a tool that allows you to manage multiple SQL Server databases from a single computer. It uses the Microsoft Management Console facility to present information and perform functions. Some of its more interesting features allow you to:

- Manage the collection of logins
- Create and delete databases
- Create, delete, and change tables, indexes, and views
- Manage database users
- Back-up and recover databases
- View database event logs

The Management Console displays a tree containing the object hierarchy in the left pane of the window, while the objects inside the selected node appear in the right pane (see Figure 1-1). You can perform various

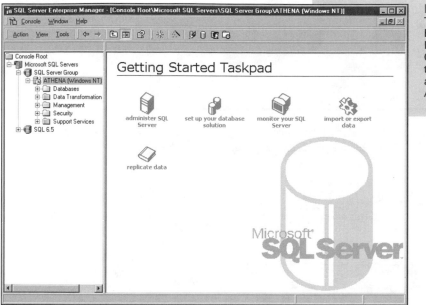

Figure 1-1
The SQL Server
Enterprise
Manager
Console shows
the functions
available on
Athena.

functions by right-clicking on an object and selecting an option from the pop-up menu, or you can double-click on an object to further expand the tree or to display the object's properties.

Query Analyzer

The Query Analyzer is a utility primarily used to execute SQL statements and view the results. However, it will also describe how the query was executed and perform index analysis, which helps you improve the performance of your query statement (see Figure 1-2).

SQL Server Architecture

SQL Server is a type of database known as a *relational database*. A relational database appears to the user simply as a collection of tables, where each table consists of a series of columns or fields across the top and a series of rows or records down the side. The underlying data structure used to hold the data is totally invisible to the user.

Figure 1-2
The Query Analyzer retrieves rows from Addresses.

Most relational databases are created and accessed using a language called Structured Query Language (SQL). This language has been defined as the ANSI standard known as ANSI SQL-92. While a few other relational databases use different languages to manipulate their data, they aren't terribly popular.

Note Most database vendors have added their own proprietary extensions to the ANSI SQL-92 standard. This allows them to offer better performance, more flexibility, or special features that database programmers may find desirable. This also means that every database system is a little (or a lot) different, which at least partially defeats the purpose of a standard.

Database Server

While not specifically part of a database, the database server is the program responsible for processing all database requests. A request may be as simple as retrieving a single piece of data from a table or as complex as recovering a database from a database backup and a set of transaction log files.

A database server is usually a stand-alone program that receives a request from an application program and returns the result to that same program (see Figure 1-3). Ordinarily the database server will run on a different machine than the application program, but that isn't necessary. In some database systems, instead of there being two distinct programs, the database server runs inside the application program—but even then the database server remains separate from the application.

I use one computer (Athena) as my database server and another computer (Mycroft) as my database client on which I write and test my programs. They are connected over a standard 10-BaseT network. Since SQL Server allows a database server to be managed from any machine attached to the network (assuming use of a proper password), I generally do everything from Mycroft and never bother to touch Athena.

Databases

A database is simply a container that allows you to manage your collection of tables. It also contains such objects as indexes, views, stored procedures, and other database objects. Since SQL Server has the ability to handle multiple databases, you can create one database for testing purposes and an identical database for production purposes. In a

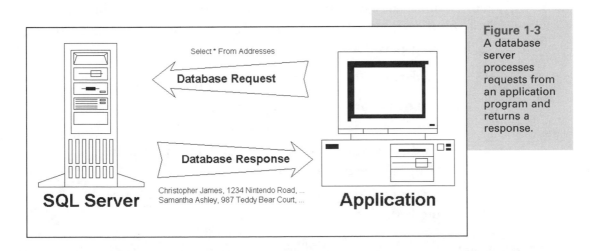

Figure 1-3
A database server processes requests from an application program and returns a response.

Select * From Addresses

Database Request

Database Response

Christopher James, 1234 Nintendo Road, ...
Samantha Ashley, 987 Teddy Bear Court, ...

SQL Server

Application

team environment, you may want to assign each programmer a database so that one programmer doesn't destroy another programmer's test data. You can also use databases to isolate one application's data from another's. This makes it easier when you have to back up or recover a database, and it also makes it easier to define security.

The database is kept in two basic types of normal Windows disk files: database files, where your data is kept, and transaction log files, which hold all the changes made to the database. The information in the transaction log is critical for two reasons. First, this information is used to undo any transaction that doesn't work properly or ends with a **Rollback** statement. The second reason is that, in the event of a database crash, the transaction logs are used to recover transactions made after the last database backup.

The following SQL statement creates a database called Wayne:

`Create Database` Wayne

A database can be deleted from the database server by using the following SQL statement:

`Drop Database` Wayne

Both of these statements rely on default values and options, which you can specify. However, I find it easier to use the Enterprise Manager's Create Database Wizard to create a database. It lets you review the defaults and change them as necessary. Note that the SQL Server System Administrator or someone assigned to the Server Administrator Role must enter the SQL statements or use the Enterprise Manager to create your database.

To create a database from the Enterprise Manager:

1. Start the Enterprise Manager by clicking on Start, Programs, Microsoft SQL Server 7.0, Enterprise Manager.

2. Select the database server in which you want to create the database (see Figure 1-4, database server).

3. Select the tools drop-down menu and select Wizards (see Figure 1-4).

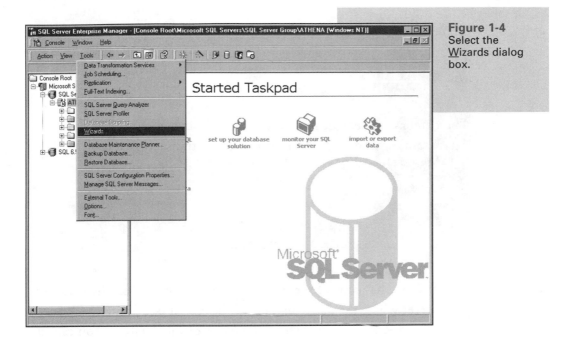

Figure 1-4
Select the Wizards dialog box.

4. Expand the Database node to see all the database-related wizards. Then double-click on the Create Database Wizard to start the wizard (see Figure 1-5).

5. Read the Create Database Wizard overview information (see Figure 1-6).

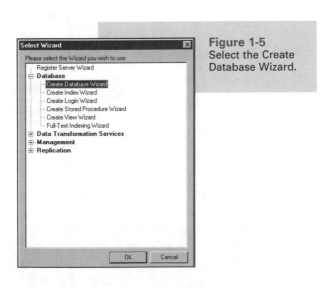

Figure 1-5
Select the Create Database Wizard.

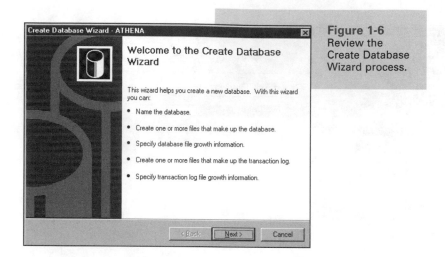

Figure 1-6
Review the
Create Database
Wizard process.

6. Specify the name of the database and the location on the database server where the database files will be stored (see Figure 1-7). In this case, I used my name as the name of the database. You can use your own name as the database throughout the rest of this chapter.

7. Specify the name of each database file you wish to use, along with each file's initial size (see Figure 1-8). Since this is a simple database, I put everything in a single file. However, in a more complex environment you may want to use multiple files, perhaps putting each table in a separate file. This allows you to

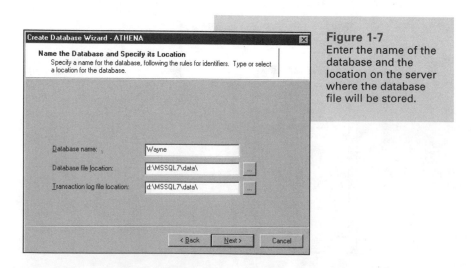

Figure 1-7
Enter the name of the database and the location on the server where the database file will be stored.

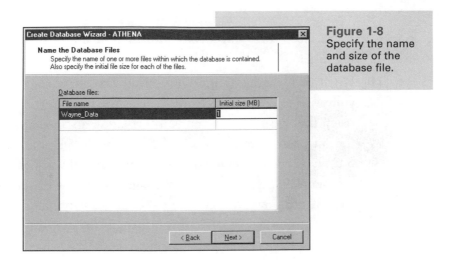

Figure 1-8
Specify the name and size of the database file.

spread your database activity over several disk drives, which will help to improve performance.

8. Decide if you want SQL Server to automatically grow your database file and how it should grow. If you choose to let SQL Server manage database file growth, it will automatically grow the database file by a fixed size or by a percentage of the current each time the database files run out of space. You also have the option of putting an upper limit on the size of the database file (see Figure 1-9).

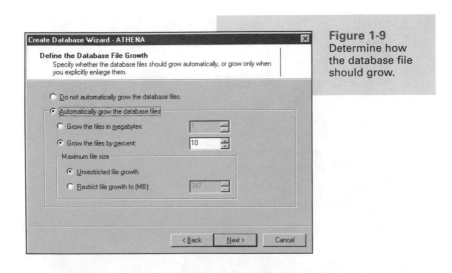

Figure 1-9
Determine how the database file should grow.

9. The next two steps in the wizard are similar to the preceding two steps, except that you specify information about the transaction log files.

10. Finally, review the options you selected to create the database. If you want to change any, simply press the Back button until you reach the screen that contains information about that particular option (see Figure 1-10). For the time being, just press the Finish button to create the database. The system will work for a few moments and then display a message box. Clear this message box. The wizard now prompts you to set up a maintenance plan. Press No for now—you'll cover this information later in the book.

Logins

You need a login in order to access SQL Server. A login is an identifier that allows you access to the database server. You can create a login that uses Windows NT authentication or SQL Server authentication. Under Windows NT authentication, the user's NT domain account for gaining access to the network is used directly by SQL Server without requiring the user to supply a password a second time. The SQL Server authentication approach requires a user to specify a login name and a password when connecting to the database.

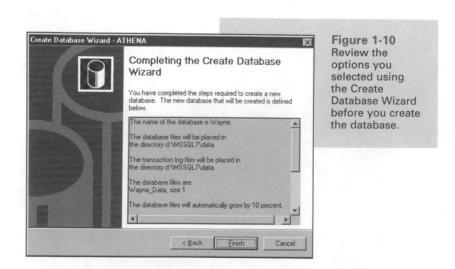

Figure 1-10
Review the options you selected using the Create Database Wizard before you create the database.

Tip Windows NT authentication works only with the users of an NT Domain. SQL Server authentication works for all users who will access the database, whether they are part of the same NT domain as the database server or not. In general, I prefer to use NT authentication for those functions running on the server and SQL Server authentication for everyone else. This means any outside users must supply login information in order to access the database and that you don't have to worry about passwords for any functions running on the database server.

Security Roles are used to categorize users into groups where each group has a common set of security permissions. Thus you don't have to specify permissions for each individual user. SQL Server includes standard roles for the following:

- System Administrators
- Security Administrators
- Server Administrators
- Setup Administrators
- Process Administrators
- Disk Administrators
- Database Creators

After you create a database, the next step in the process is to create a login ID. You will use this ID to manage the database. Note that there are other ways to perform this process, but you should use the wizard until you feel comfortable with all the options and choices you need to specify.

To create a new login ID:

1. Start the Enterprise Manager, choose the database server you want to access, and select the Create Login Wizard (see Figure 1-11).
2. Choose the Authentication Mode you wish to use (see Figure 1-12). Since this user will be external to the system, I've selected SQL Server authentication.

Figure 1-11
Display the
Create Login
Wizard overview
information.

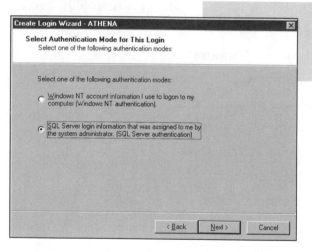

Figure 1-12
Choose
Authentication
Mode.

3. Enter the Login ID you wish to create and the Password associated with it (see Figure 1-13). Since I'm creating the database, I'm going to use Wayne. Enter your own name here.

4. Choose the roles you want assigned to your login (see Figure 1-14). I'm assuming the Database Creator role.

5. Designate which databases your login will be allowed to access (see Figure 1-15). Be sure to include access to the database you just created.

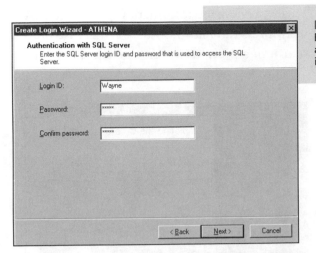

Figure 1-13
Enter a Login ID and Password information.

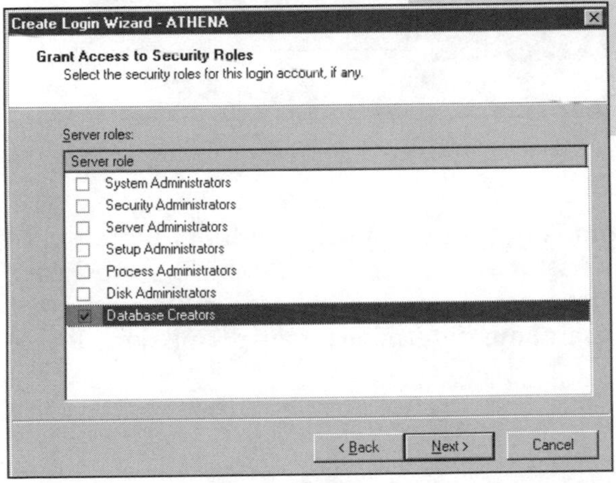

Figure 1-14
Choose the roles for the login.

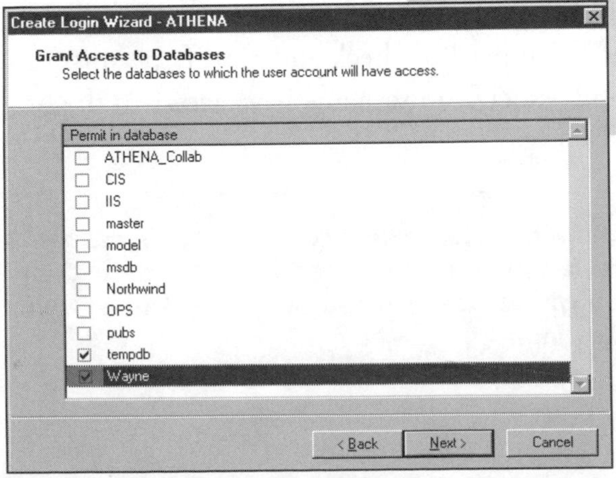

Figure 1-15
Designate the databases this login may access.

6. Finally, review the information you've entered. If everything's okay, press the Finish button. Otherwise press the <u>B</u>ack button to return to a previous screen to change options (see Figure 1-16).

Figure 1-16
Review the options for the new login account.

A login is not a username. Your login merely gives you access to the database server. The database server maps the login to a username in each database you're permitted to access. The username determines your permissions inside a database.

Users

Creating a login doesn't finish the process of allowing a user to access a database. You need to check and modify permissions to ensure that the login and associated username have access to the proper resources.

Tip

When you give users access to resources, give them only as much access as they need in order to do their jobs. Once you give a user a resource, you will find it hard to take back later.

Since the login ID Wayne is going to use the Wayne database, I'll set the default database for Wayne to Wayne. To set the default database for a user:

1. Start the Enterprise Manager. Select the database server, then select Security, Logins. The list of logins for the database server will be displayed on the right-hand side of the window (see Figure 1-17).

2. Double-click on the login ID you wish to change. Then change the default database property (see Figure 1-18) and click on OK.

3. Select the Database Access table and the database you just created. Then select all of the database roles (except for those beginning with db_deny for your login) and click on OK (see Figure 1-19). This will give your new login complete freedom for your new database. Also note that the Login ID Wayne is mapped to the user Wayne for the Wayne database. If I choose, I could easily enter a new user, but I find it convenient to use the same value for the login ID and user whenever possible.

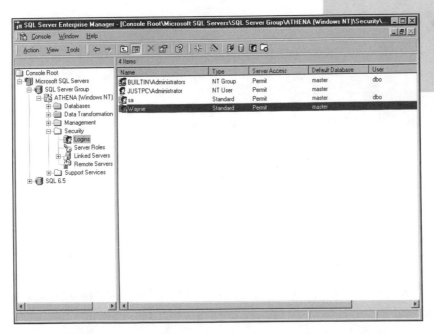

Figure 1-17
Select a login from the Enterprise Manager.

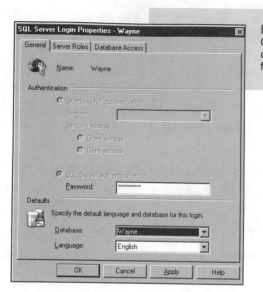

Figure 1-18
Change the default database property for a login ID.

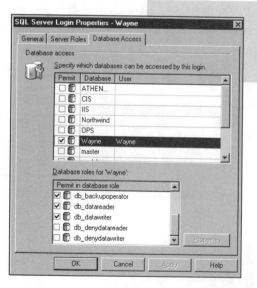

Figure 1-19
Give yourself all of the database roles for your database.

Tables

The table is the key object in a database. A table consists of a series of *columns* and *rows*, as shown in Figure 1-20. Each row in the table corresponds to a record that might be stored in a file. The rows in a table are not stored in any particular order, and the order may change each time you view the table.

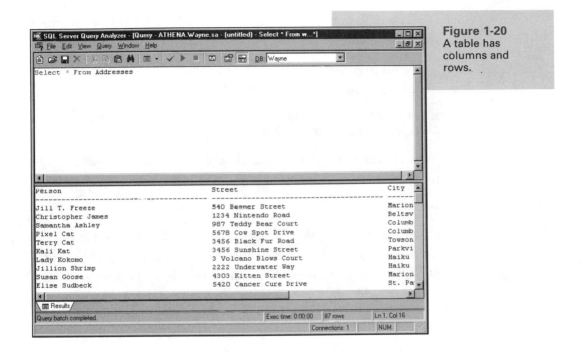

Figure 1-20
A table has
columns and
rows.

Each column in a table corresponds to a particular field in a record. A column is assigned a particular data type, such as **Int** or **Char**. The data type determines the amount of storage used for each column and the kind of data it can hold. Data types can hold numbers, character strings, date and time values, and binary data.

The **Char** data type is used to hold character data. Defining a column as **Char**(10) means that the column can hold up to 10 characters. If you don't specify the length, a default length of 1 character will be assumed.

If a column in a particular row doesn't contain a value, it is defined to have a value of **Null**. **Null** means that no value was assigned and should not be misconstrued as meaning the same thing as an empty string or a binary zero value.

You can prevent a column from accepting a value of **Null** by specifying the clause **Not Null** after the data type. Any attempt to change the value of that column to **Null** will trigger an error. You can also specify a default value for a column by using the **Default** clause. This comes in handy when you are inserting a new row into the table and don't specify all the column values. This clause can be used with or without the **Not Null** clause.

The following SQL statement creates a simple address list and ensures that a **Null** value can't be entered into the Name column:

```
Create Table Addresses(Person Char(40) Not Null, Street Char(40),
City Char(30), State Char(2), Zip Char(10))
```

To delete an existing table in the database, use the following SQL statement:

```
Drop Table Addresses
```

While you can also use the Enterprise Manager to create tables, I'm going to use the Query Analyzer for this exercise. This forces me to enter the raw SQL statements to create a table. You'll learn how to use Visual Basic to create tables in the next chapter.

To create the Addresses table using the Query Analyzer:

1. Start the Query Analyzer by clicking on Start, Programs, Microsoft SQL Server 7.0, Query Analyzer.

2. Specify the name of the database server you wish to use, enter your Login Name and Password, and press OK (see Figure 1-21).

Caution

You might log on to the wrong database when using the Query Analyzer. You should verify that you have logged in to the proper database by checking the DB drop-down box in the toolbar. To switch databases, choose the new database from the drop-down list. The Query Analyzer will automatically log you into your default database, so you should be fine with the login you just created. However, this may not be true for all the logins you create. Unless you check, you could easily create your table in the Master database and may not be able to find it the next time you log in.

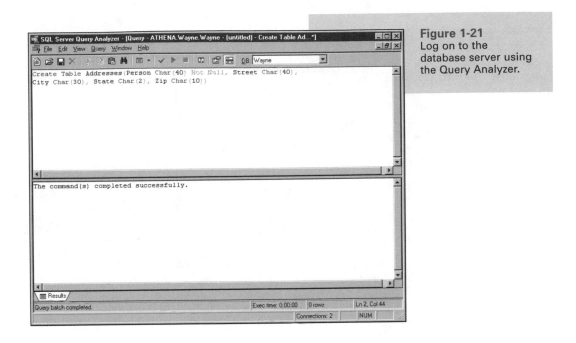

Figure 1-21
Log on to the database server using the Query Analyzer.

3. Enter the **Create Table** statement as specified above (see Figure 1-22) and press the Execute Query button.

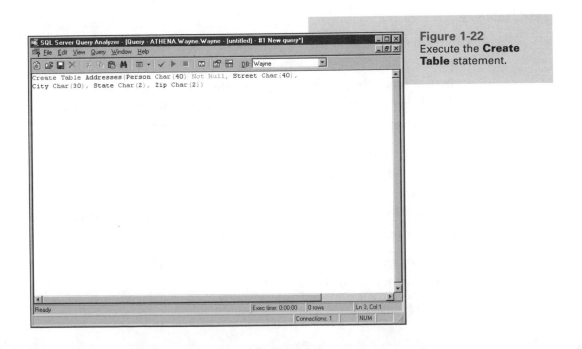

Figure 1-22
Execute the **Create Table** statement.

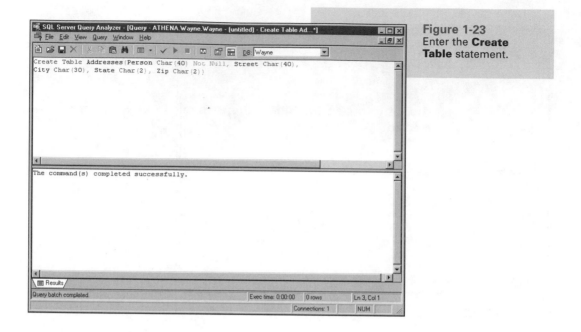

Figure 1-23
Enter the **Create Table** statement.

4. Enter the **Create Table** statement (see Figure 1-23) and press the Execute Query button.

Indexes

One of the problems with storing data in a table is that this makes it difficult to retrieve a single row quickly and efficiently. Since a table has no structure other than its list of rows—and you can't guarantee that the order of those rows will be the same each time you access the table—it is difficult to retrieve a single row. Indexes solve this problem.

An index is a special database structure that maintains a set of column values, sorted in a way that minimizes the search time, with pointers to specific rows in a table. This allows the database server to quickly find all the rows with a specific column value. The index is automatically updated whenever a row is inserted, updated, or deleted.

The following SQL statement creates an index called PersonIndex on the Person column of the Addresses table:

```
Create Index PersonIndex on Addresses(Person)
```

Tip

In a relational database, indexes can be created whenever you want because they are independent objects. If the table already contains data, the index will be created with pointers for all the rows in the table. If the table is empty, the index will be updated as new records are added to the index. If you choose to delete the index, the data in the table will not be affected.

You can use an index to ensure that a particular column value will be unique within the table. The next SQL statement creates a unique index on the Person column. Run the next statement using the Query Analyzer to generate the result shown in Figure 1-24.

Create Unique Index PersonIndex **on** Addresses(Person)

You can also use the index to force the database server to store the table in a specific order by requesting a clustered index. The following SQL statement creates a clustered index on the Person column of the Addresses table:

Create Clustered Index PersonIndex **on** Addresses(Person)

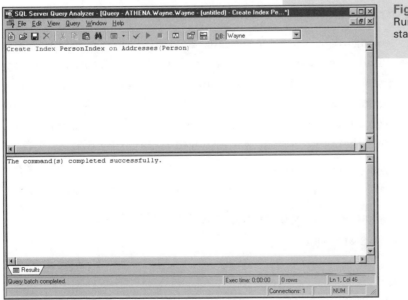

Figure 1-24
Run the **Create Index** statement.

To delete the PersonIndex, use the SQL statement below. Note that you must specify the table name since an index name must be unique for a table, though it needn't necessarily be unique within the database.

Drop Index Addresses.PersonIndex

Views

A view represents a dynamically created table based on data values that already exist or can be derived from other tables. From the perspective of an application program, there is no difference between a view and a table. The data used in a view is created with the **Select** statement.

There are two types of views: updateable and not updateable. An updateable view can be updated using the **Insert**, **Update**, and **Delete** statements just as if it were a real table. Updateability is possible when there is a one-to-one correspondence between the rows in the view and the rows in a table and when any missing columns have a default value or accept a value of **Null**. The following view is an updateable view since it forms a one-to-one correspondence between each row in the MDView and in the Addresses table. Only addresses where State = 'MD' are visible in this view.

Create View MDView **As**
Select *From Addresses **Where State** = 'MD'

The following SQL statement creates a virtual table containing the number of address entries made for each state. It also returns a column called Persons that is really the total number of Person rows found in each value of State (see Figure 1-25). Note that this view can't be updated since it contains a value that was derived from a series of data values rather than a value that was retrieved from a single row.

Create View StateCount **As**
Select State, **Count**(Person) Persons **From** Addresses **Group By** State

You can delete a view by using the following SQL statement:

Delete View StateCount

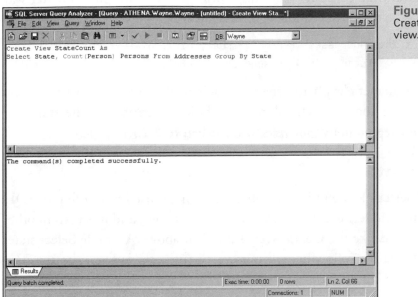

Figure 1-25
Create the StateCount view.

Accessing a Database

SQL grammar has four main statements for accessing data inside a table. They are **Insert**, **Delete**, **Update**, and **Select**. The first three statements can add, remove, and change the contents of one or more rows in a table, while the last statement allows you to retrieve some or all of the records in a table.

Insert

Use the **Insert** statement to add new rows to a table. The following SQL statement inserts the values into the Addresses table:

```
Insert Into Addresses Values
('Jill T. Freeze', '944 Porsche Lane', 'Beltsville', 'MD', '20705')
```

Note that this statement assumes that the values are entered in the same order that the columns are specified in the database. This is probably not a good idea since it is possible that someone might add a column like Street2 somewhere in the middle of the table. In that case, the data would be one column off starting with the value for City. A better way would be to use the following statement:

Insert Into Addresses (Person, Street, City, State, Zip) **Values**
('Jill T. Freeze', '944 Porsche Lane', 'Beltsville', 'MD', '20705')

This statement explicitly specifies each of the columns so there is no confusion about which column will hold which value. The results of executing this statement are shown in Figure 1-26.

Select

The **Select** statement is probably the statement used most often in SQL. It is used to retrieve data from one or more tables, and it is used in other statements like the **Create View** statement above. A simple **Select** statement like the following will retrieve all the records from the specified table (see Figure 1-27).

Select * From Addresses

Other useful variants of the **Select** statement use the **Where** clause, which is also part of the **Update** and **Delete** statements. In the following

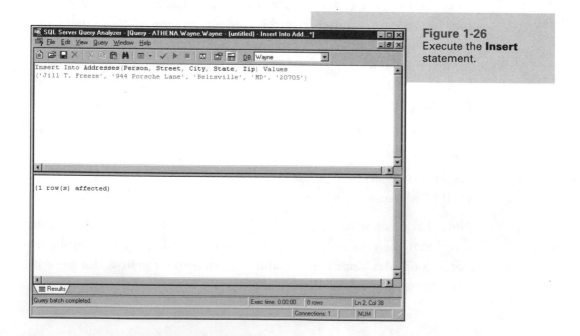

Figure 1-26
Execute the **Insert** statement.

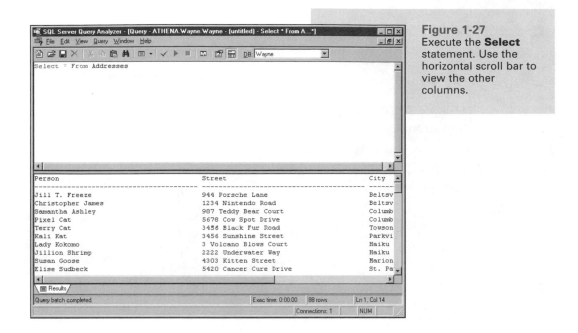

Figure 1-27
Execute the **Select**
statement. Use the
horizontal scroll bar to
view the other
columns.

statement, the **Where** clause is used to retrieve only the records from a single state:

```
Select * From Addresses Where State = 'MD'
```

This next **Select** statement uses the **Like** operator to retrieve rows where the string of letters 'Jill' is found somewhere in the Person column (see Figure 1-28):

```
Select * From Addresses Where Person Like '%Jill%'
```

The **Order By** clause specifies that the records be returned in order of the specified column:

```
Select * From Addresses Order By Person
```

Delete

The **Delete** statement is used to remove rows from a table. Unless you specify a **Where** clause, the **Delete** statement will delete every record in your table, as in the following statement:

```
Delete From Addresses
```

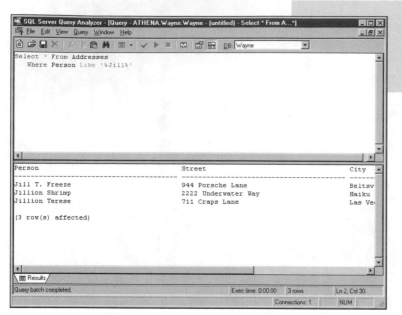

Figure 1-28
Retrieve from the
Person column only
those rows containing
the text string 'Jill'.

The next **Delete** statement, being more specific, is a little more practical. It takes advantage of the unique index on the Person column, which ensures that each Person value is unique. This means that you will only delete one record with the following statement (see Figure 1-29):

```
Delete From Addresses Where Person = 'Jill T. Freeze'
```

Update

The **Update** statement is used to replace the values in one or more columns with other specified values for each selected record. As with the **Delete** statement, you can use the **Where** clause to limit the scope of the **Update** statement to a single record (see Figure 1-30):

```
Update Addresses Set Street = '540 Beamer Street',
City = 'Marion', State = 'SD', Zip = '57043'
Where Person = 'Jill T. Freeze'
```

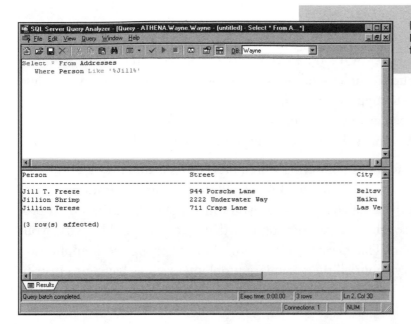

Figure 1-29
Delete one record
from Addresses.

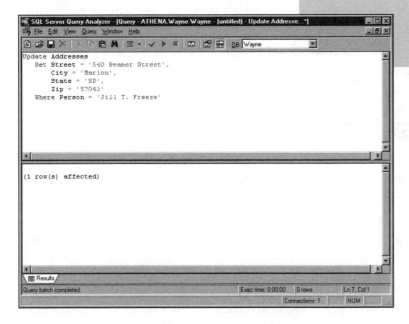

Figure 1-30
Update one record in
the Addresses table.

Stored Procedures

Stored procedures are small database programs written in a language called Transact-SQL. Transact-SQL is a superset of the ANSI SQL language and includes additional statements—such as **If, Case,** and **While**—to support control flow and the ability to define procedures that contain parameters and local variables. Thus you can write fairly complete subroutines that you can call from your Visual Basic application.

Another advantage of having stored procedures is that they are stored in the database and maintained separately from your application. Consequently, if the database changes, you can simply adjust the stored procedure so that it returns results that are compatible with your application. This means that you don't have to change your application and worry about all the secondary problems, such as having to distribute a new version and ensuring that the users don't run the old version after the database has been changed.

Since stored procedures are kept in the database as just another database object, you can control a user's access to them. The stored procedures run based on your database permissions, not the user's. Thus you can create a stored procedure that lets a user access a particular table without the user having permission to access that table.

Wrapping Up

SQL Server is a modern relational database management system with all the bells and whistles that are common in today's database marketplace. It is designed to be scalable. The same code runs on your workstation, a departmental workgroup server, and the corporate enterprise database server. This means that the same application can be run without change on all three types of computers.

SQL Server is based on a standard database language called Structured Query Language (SQL). SQL defines a number of statements that can be used to create database objects, such as the **Create Database, Create Table, Create View,** and **Create Index** statements. It also includes statements for identifying and changing records in the database, such as the

Select, Insert, Delete, and **Update** statements. You can execute these statements either directly through the Query Analyzer program, or indirectly as part of your Visual Basic program.

Another utility program, the Enterprise Manager, allows you to maintain the database structures on multiple database servers through an easy-to-use tree-structured form. It also includes many wizards that simplify some of the more complex tasks, such as creating new logins.

The stored procedure is an important concept. It enables you to create and compile SQL queries and store them in the database, much like you can create and compile Visual Basic programs. This allows you to build reusable queries that you can call from your application. These queries will run faster than the time it takes to perform the equivalent statements from your program, and they can be used as an additional level of security.

If you haven't worked through the examples in this chapter, it's worth taking a few minutes and trying them. The best way to learn about SQL is by writing SQL statements. While I only inserted one row's worth of data, you should insert at least five or ten. Then when you try the various clauses of the **Select** statement, you can retrieve a meaningful amount of data.

CHAPTER 2

Fundamentals of Database Programming Using Visual Basic

Microsoft has gone to great lengths to ensure that SQL Server 7 is the best database system to use with Visual Basic. They've included a number of special tools in Visual Basic 6 to make developing database applications easier and faster than ever before. The tools fall into three basic groupings. The Visual Database Tools are a set of well-integrated tools that allow you to create and change the structure of tables as well as view and change their contents. They also help you establish the connection between your program and the database.

The second major group of tools is the latest generation of Visual Basic and ActiveX controls. Most of the controls can be bound to a data source such as a table or a SQL **Select** statement. This is useful since all the interaction with the database is managed by data source and the

> **Note** While the Database Designer is a separate component, don't go looking for it. It is tightly integrated into Visual Basic.

bound controls. This means that you can build simple database programs quickly and easily and without a lot of code.

The last major group of tools is the set of ActiveX Data Objects, also known as ADO. This is a collection of objects that allow the Visual Basic programmer to access OLE-DB using a new universal data access model. This means that with the proper tools you can access data from many different types of databases using an ActiveX interface.

Database Programming Overview

To access a database server, an application program must first establish a connection to the server. You need to supply information such as the

---

ADO vs. RDO and DAO

Visual Basic can access databases using Data Access Objects (DAO), Remote Data Objects (RDO), and ActiveX Data Objects (ADO). DAO was first used to allow Visual Basic to access Microsoft Jet (Access) databases. You could also use DAO to access SQL Server databases by defining the SQL Server database inside the Jet database. This proved to be easy to use but somewhat slow, so RDO was introduced. RDO allows Visual Basic to access a SQL Server directly using Open Database Connectivity (ODBC).

Microsoft combined the best of both DAO and RDO in creating ADO. ADO is a low overhead method to use OLE-DB, which is a replacement for ODBC. ADO fully exploits SQL Server's new OLE-DB interface, which offers faster database access than RDO and DAO.

name of the database server, your login and password, and the database name, plus the name of the driver that your application will use to talk to the database server. Once the connection is opened, you gain access to all the resources inside the database that your user is permitted to access.

You never access an entire database from an application program at one time. Instead, you access a subset of the database called a recordset (see Figure 2-1). A recordset is simply a collection of records retrieved from a database. In its simplest form, a recordset can be a table. Each row of the table corresponds to a record in the recordset. A more complex recordset can be built dynamically by using a **Select** statement to specify the records retrieved.

Associated with the recordset is a cursor, which points to the current record. You can move the cursor forward to the next record and backward to the previous record. You can also jump to either the first or the last record. You can even bookmark a location and return at a later point in time. Additionally, you can insert, delete, or update the records in the **Recordset** object if it permits these operations.

Person	Street	City	State	Zip
Bucky Heyer	3423 Gaming Court	Deadwood	SD	57732
Christopher James	1234 Nintendo Road	Beltsville	MD	20705
Samantha Ashley	987 Teddy Bear Court	Columbia	MD	21045
Pixel Cat	5678 Cow Spot Drive	Columbia	MD	21045
Terry Cat	3456 Black Fur Road	Towson	MD	21204
Kali Kat	3456 Sunshine Street	Parkville	MD	21234
Lady Kokomo	3 Volcano Blows Court	Haiku	HI	98742
Jillion Shrimp	2222 Underwater Way	Haiku	HI	98742
Susan Goose	4303 Kitten Street	Marion	SD	57043
Elise Sudbeck	5420 Cancer Cure Drive	St. Paul	MN	55165
Tracy Tonner	2893 Kindergarten Lane	Duluth	MN	55815
Bryce Dau	1243 Schoolhouse Road	Annapolis	MD	21404
Linda Brigham	4546 Lostmy Way	Parkton	MD	89135
Big Starr	33 Blockbuster Street	Hollywood	CA	90078
Jeff Gordon	24 Speed Way	Daytona Beach	FL	32114
Little Starr	444B Picture Lane	Hollywood	MD	20636
Joan Williams	4595 Childcraft Court	Dallas	TX	75216
Lorrie Tiger	3421 Lion Way	Atlanta	GA	30311
Darrel Waltrip	35 Raceway Lane	Briston	TN	37621
B. Boy	1 Beach Road	Haiku	HI	96708
M. Love	409 Shore Line Way	Lahaini	HI	96767
Lilly Munster	1313 Mockingbird Court	Salem	SD	57058
Herman Munster	1313 Mockingbird Lane	Salem	MA	01971
Lurch Munster	1313 Mockingbird Street	Salem	OR	97311
Kyle Petty	44 Hot Wheels Way	Taladega	AL	35161
Rosie Girl	3423 Flower Court	Richmond	VA	23173
Timothy Jockey	4502 Horsetrack Lane	Charleston	WV	25365
Barbie B. Blubber	9993 Topoworld Road	Juneau	AK	99850
Terry Labonte	5 Racing Court	Daytona Beach	FL	32114
Bobby Labonte	18 Pontiac Drive	Briston	TN	37621
Chuckie Yeager	51 Mustang Road	Dayton	OH	45410

Figure 2-1
A recordset contains a collection of records from a database.

Each record in the **Recordset** contains a series of one or more fields. These fields correspond to the columns in a table or a view. For each field, you can determine its database name, its size and time, its current value, and its original value (as retrieved from the database).

The Database Designer

The Database Designer is not an independent tool that you use outside of Visual Basic, but rather a tool that is tightly integrated into the Visual Basic development environment. It allows you easy access to the database to manage database connections, tables, and other structures.

The Data Environment

To use the Database Designer you must first create a **DataEnvironment** object. This object is used at design time to help you design the objects you will use to access your database at run time.

Creating a Data Environment

Start Visual Basic and create a new Standard EXE project. To add the Data Environment Designer to Visual Basic, select Project, More ActiveX Designers, Data Environment from the Visual Basic menu. This will display the window shown in Figure 2-2.

Note

> You may have to add the Data Environment Designer to your Visual Basic development environment. Choose Project, Components, from the main menu and select the Designers tab. Then you should check Data Environment. While you're at it, you may want to check Data Report, DHTML Page, and WebClass. You'll be using all of these things before the end of this book.

A **DataEnvironment** object contains a collection of **Connections** and **Commands**. A **Connection** object describes a link to a database server with such information as the name of the database server, your login ID

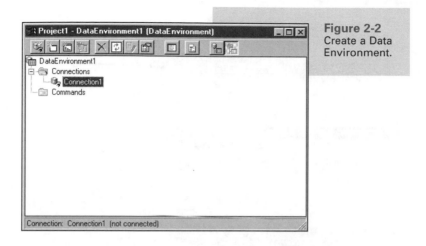

Figure 2-2
Create a Data
Environment.

and password, and the name of the database that you wish to access. A **Command** object contains information about the data to be retrieved from the database. This object can contain a reference to a database object like a table or a view, or it can contain a SQL statement. The **Command** object is considered to be recordset returning if it contains a reference to a table or a view or to a SQL Select statement. If a recordset is not returned, it is considered non-recordset returning.

Creating a Connection

The default Data Environment is created with a single **Connection** object called Connection1. However, before you can use this object you must configure it. To start the process, right-click on Connection1 and select Properties. This will display the Data Link dialog box, as shown in Figure 2-3.

Caution

> Don't confuse the **UserConnection** object with the **Connection** object. The **UserConnection** object is designed for use with Remote Data Objects, not ActiveX Data Objects.

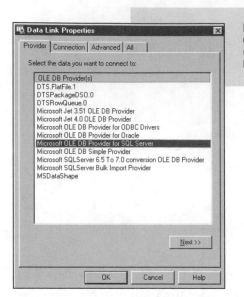

Figure 2-3
Configure Connection1 using the Data Link Properties dialog box.

This dialog box works much as a wizard does. From the Provider tab, select the Microsoft OLE-DB Provider for SQL Server and press Next. While you could use the Microsoft OLE-DB Provider for ODBC Drivers, the SQL Server provider offers better performance and supports all the features available in ADO.

Pressing Next takes you to the Connection tab, where you need to fill in the name of the database server, your login ID and password, and the name of the database you wish to access (see Figure 2-4). Pressing the Test Connection button will allow you to verify that all the information you entered was correct. If you were able to access the database properly, a message box will be displayed saying Test Connection Succeeded. Otherwise you will see a message box containing a description of the error encountered. After you've successfully tested the connection, press the OK button to save this information.

The Data View Window

Once you have created a Data Environment, you can open the Data View window (choose View, Data View Window from the main menu)

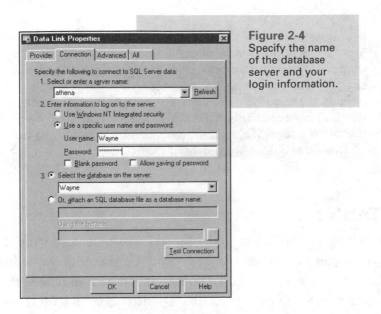

Figure 2-4
Specify the name of the database server and your login information.

to see information about the objects available via the Data Environment Connection you just created. Clicking on the Connection1 node displays the objects available from the database. There are four basic types of objects: Database Diagrams, Tables, Views, and Stored Procedures (see Figure 2-5).

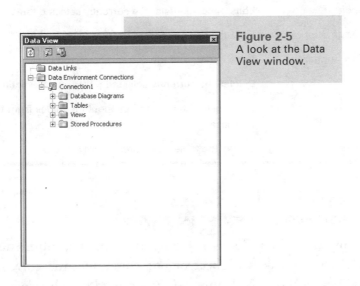

Figure 2-5
A look at the Data View window.

Tip

If you right-click on the Database Diagrams, Tables, Views, or Stored Procedures node directly, you can choose Filter by Owner to limit the amount of data displayed. When you specify your username (or another user's name), only the objects that you own (or that are owned by the other user) will be displayed. This makes it easier to find your own (or the other user's) objects without having to search in between all the accessible system-owned objects.

Tables

Clicking on the Tables node displays all the tables in the database to which you have access. Right-clicking on the Addresses table you created in Chapter 1 displays a pop-up menu with functions that you can perform (see Figure 2-6). Table 2-1 lists these functions with a short description of what they do.

Table 2-1 Functions Available for a Table in the Data View Window

Function	Description
New Table	Creates a new database table.
Open	Edits the contents of the currently selected table.
Design	Edits the design of the currently selected table.
New Trigger	Adds a trigger to the currently selected table.
Delete	Deletes the currently selected table from the database.
Refresh	Gets the latest information about the tables from the database.
Properties	Shows the table name and table's creator.

CREATING A NEW TABLE OR EDITING AN EXISTING TABLE

Selecting either <u>N</u>ew Table or <u>D</u>esign from the pop-up menu will display either a blank worksheet or one containing the current column properties, as shown in Figure 2-7. You can add or change any of these

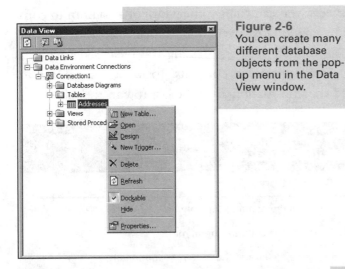

Figure 2-6
You can create many different database objects from the pop-up menu in the Data View window.

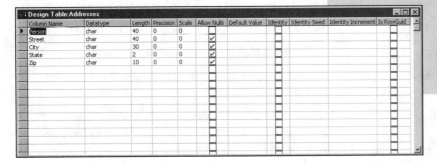

Figure 2-7
You can design a table by filling in the cells in the Design Table window.

properties directly. After you make your changes, simply close the window and Visual Basic will ask if you want to save your changes. Press Yes if you want to save your changes, No if you don't want to save them, or Cancel if you want to continue editing the table definition.

Each column defined in the database has a number of different properties, as shown in Table 2-2. Only the Column Name and the Datatype properties are required for all columns in the table. Depending on the data type chosen, Length, Precision, and Scale may also be required.

The row you are editing is identified by an arrow on the row header. The individual cell that you are editing is highlighted with inverse video. To change a value, either type the name for a text cell, press the down arrow to make your selection from the drop-down list of items, or click in the cell to add or remove a check mark.

As with most worksheets, you can change the width of a column to control the amount of information displayed. You can select a row or column by clicking on the appropriate header. Pressing the Delete key while a row or column is selected will erase its contents. To add a new column to the table, simply add the information after the last row in the table.

Table 2-2 Properties of a Column in the Table Design Window	
Property	**Description**
Column Name	Contains the name of the column
Datatype	Specifies the column's datatype
Length	Contains the size of the data type (optional)
Precision	Specifies the number of digits of accuracy for numeric values
Scale	Defines the relative scale of the numeric value
Allow Nulls	Specifies that **Null** values are permitted in the column
Default Value	Specifies the default value for the column if not otherwise assigned
Identity	Instructs SQL Server to automatically assign a value to this column based on Identity Seed and Identity Increment whenever the row is inserted into the table
Identity Seed	Contains the initial value for Identity
Identity Increment	Specifies the value to be added to get the new value for the column
IsRowGuid	Contains **True** if the column contains a globally unique identifier

OPENING A TABLE

Sometimes it is useful to see or change the actual data in a table. You can do this by right-clicking on the table and selecting Open from the pop-up menu. This will display a worksheetlike grid, as shown in Figure 2-8.

Editing this information is as easy as using a worksheet. An arrow on the row label identifies the row that you are editing, while across the top is a list of column names. The individual cell that you are editing is displayed

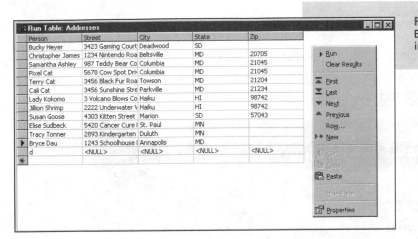

Figure 2-8
Edit the rows
in a table.

in reverse video. Simply type the new value into the cell to change it and the arrow in the row label becomes a pencil to indicate that the row hasn't been updated yet. When you move the cursor to a different row, the changes will automatically be made to the database. If you want to abandon your changes and not update the table, simply press Esc. This will restore the original values that were retrieved from the database.

You can insert a new row by moving the cursor to the last row in the table, which has an asterisk in the row header. Simply type the values you want to insert and move the cursor to another line. Note that the asterisk changes to an arrow when you move to the new row. Typing a value changes the arrow to a pencil and adds a new blank row at the end of the grid with an asterisk in the row label.

Right-clicking anywhere in the table dialog box displays the pop-up menu shown next to the grid in Figure 2-8. You can choose from a number of different options. You can rerun the query or move the cursor to the first, last, next, or previous row. You can also move the cursor to a particular row number or insert a new row. The Properties menu item allows you to make slight changes to the query.

Tip

If you want to add this capability to your own program, simply use the **DataGrid** control, covered later in this chapter.

Views

The Views node stores all the views you have access to in the database. Right-clicking on a view displays a menu similar to the one in the Tables node (see Figure 2-9), except that you can't add a new trigger since you cannot add triggers to views.

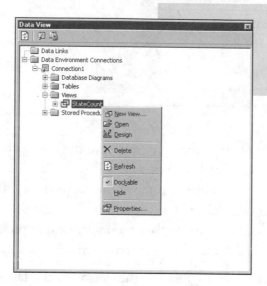

Figure 2-9
The View pop-up menu is similar to the Table pop-up menu.

Note

Opening a view doesn't necessarily mean that you can update any of the rows even though the grid will let you change the values. The moment you change a value in a row, you may get an error saying that the view can't be updated for one reason or another. Only when a view has a one-to-one correspondence with its base table can you update the contents of a view (assuming, of course, that you have update permission on the underlying table).

Stored Procedures

Visual Basic includes the ability to create and debug stored procedures from within Visual Basic. Since using stored procedures can improve your application's performance, this feature comes in handy. And you don't have to switch to a different application simply to write your stored procedure. See Table 2-3 for a list of the functions available for stored procedures. These functions are just a right-click away after choosing a stored procedure in the Data View window (see Figure 2-10).

Table 2-3 You can perform a number of different functions on stored procedures directly from Visual Basic.

Function	Description
New Stored Procedure	Creates a new stored procedure.
Design	Edits the currently selected stored procedure.
Save As Text	Saves the currently selected stored procedure as a text file.
Debug	Runs the T-SQL Debugger using the currently selected stored procedure.
Delete	Deletes the currently selected stored procedure from the database.
Rename	Changes the name of the currently selected stored procedure.
Refresh	Gets the latest information about the stored procedures from the database.
Properties	Shows the name, the creator, and other information for the current stored procedure.

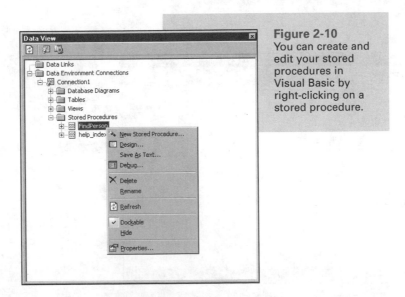

Figure 2-10
You can create and edit your stored procedures in Visual Basic by right-clicking on a stored procedure.

DESIGNING A STORED PROCEDURE

Selecting <u>D</u>esign or <u>N</u>ew Stored Procedure from the Stored Procedure pop-up menu will start the Stored Procedure Designer (see Figure 2-11). The Stored Procedure Designer allows you to edit a stored procedure. All the keywords, operators, and constants are highlighted to make it easier to edit your code.

While in the Stored Procedure Designer, you can create new stored procedures, open a text file that contains a stored procedure, or save a stored procedure to the database or a text file. However, only code stored in the database can be executed or debugged. You can send a copy of your code to the printer or use the typical find, cut, copy, and paste editing commands. Pressing the Debug button will run your stored procedure using the T-SQL Debugger.

THE T-SQL DEBUGGER

The T-SQL Debugger (shown in Figure 2-12) is one of the most important new features in Visual Basic 6. It enables you to debug your stored procedures directly on the database server. It includes features that allow you to:

- Display the stored procedure
- Set breakpoints

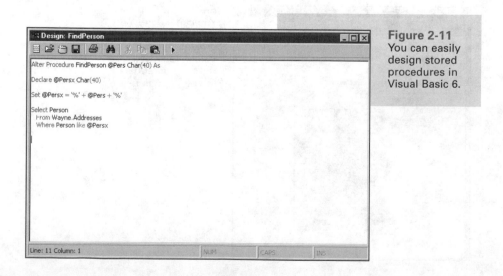

Figure 2-11
You can easily design stored procedures in Visual Basic 6.

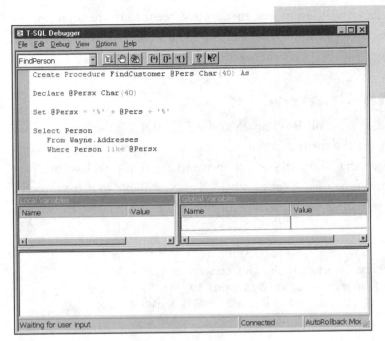

Figure 2-12
The T-SQL Debugger can be used to execute stored procedures.

- Execute statements
- Display and set local variables and parameters
- Display global variables
- Display the call stack

Data-Bound Controls

The easiest way to access a database using Visual Basic is by using data-bound controls. Data-bound controls are controls that can be connected to a data control, such as the ADO data control. The data control is connected to the database and accesses a single table, view, or query. It maintains a cursor to the database, which points to the current record. Each field in the current record is passed to the appropriate control for display or another action.

Each time the current record is changed, the contents of the data-bound controls will be updated with the new values. If the user changes the contents of any of the controls, the modified values will be saved to the database when the user moves to another record. If the user moves beyond the last row, a new record is created and added to the database when the user moves to another record.

The ADO Data Control

The ADO data control, also known as the ADODC, is the link between the controls on the form and the database (see Figure 2-13). This control has arrows that allow the user to move to the first row, last row, previous row, and next row. A caption field is also available to display useful information, such as the current record number or a relative key value.

Tip If you prefer, you can make this control invisible (**Visible = False**) and provide your own buttons to move around the database, which will make it easier for the user to use.

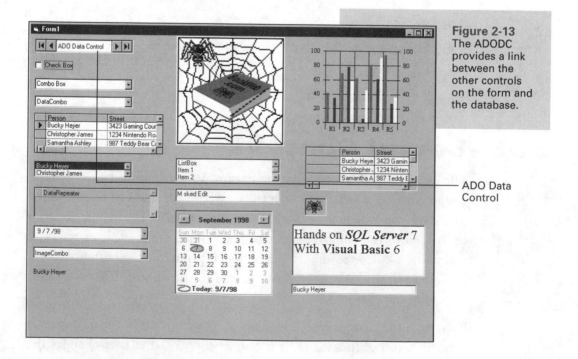

Figure 2-13
The ADODC provides a link between the other controls on the form and the database.

ADO Data Control

Properties of the ADO Data Control

The ADO data control contains a number of unique properties (see Table 2-4) that are necessary to access the database. You can find them by viewing the Properties Window (press F4 or choose View, Properties Window from the main menu to display this window). The

Table 2-4 Selected Properties of the ADO Data Control	
Property	**Description**
BOFAction	Moves to the first record or stays at the beginning of file (BOF) when the user encounters the BOF
CacheSize	Indicates the number of records cached locally, default value is 1
CommandType	Describes the type of **Command** object specified in **RecordSource** that will be used to retrieve data from the database
ConnectionString	Describes the information necessary to connect to the database
ConnectionTimeout	Equals the number of seconds to wait before returning an error when making a connection to the database server
CursorType	Designates the use of local or remote (default) cursors
EOFAction	Moves to the first record, stays at the end of file (EOF), or adds a new record when the user encounters the EOF
LockType	Specifies the type of lock to be used
MaxRecords	Limits the number of records retrieved from a query
Mode	Specifies how the connection will be opened
Orientation	Specifies if the control is aligned horizontally or vertically
Password	Contains the password associated with the login ID in **UserName**
Recordset	Returns an object reference to the recordset containing the results of the query
RecordSource	Specifies the query, table name, or stored procedure that will be used to query the database
UserName	Contains the login ID used to gain access to the database server

ConnectionString property contains the information needed to connect to the database server. You can enter the information directly or specify the name of a file containing the information. This information can be generated with the Data Link Wizard or by manually specifying the values. The **UserName** and the **Password** properties are used with the **ConnectionString** to access the database server. The **RecordSource** property and **CommandType** property describe the data to be retrieved from the database.

> **Tip**
>
> Set the **CommandType** value that corresponds to the information you entered in **RecordSource** rather than leaving the default value of adCmdUnknown. This speeds up processing in the database server since it doesn't have to try to analyze the value in **RecordSource** to determine how it needs to be processed.

The **Recordset** property contains an object reference to the underlying **Recordset** object containing the data from the database. All the Recordset's properties and methods are available. You'll learn about the **Recordset** object in more detail later in this chapter.

The **BOFAction** and **EOFAction** properties dictate what happens when the user scrolls past the beginning of file (BOF) marker or the end of file (EOF) marker. You can specify that the cursor remains before or after the file, in which case you will not have a current row to display in the bound controls. You can specify that when the BOF or the EOF is reached the cursor will remain on the first or last row of the query, respectively. Finally, on the **EOFAction** only, you can specify that a new row is created when the EOF is reached.

> **Tip**
>
> When you use the ADO data control, you should leave **BOFAction** set to adDoMoveFirst so that the user never moves beyond the first record. However, you should change the **EOFAction** to adDoAddNew. This will allow the user to insert a new record simply by scrolling past the end of the query. It feels natural to the user to add new records at the end of the query and simplifies your program.

Events in the ADO Data Control

The ADO data control comes with a bunch of events that allow you to take action before and after changes are made to the database (see Table 2-5). Changes to the fields in the current row trigger the **WillChange-Field** and **FieldChangeComplete** events. An array of the **Field** objects that will be changed are passed to the events, so in the **WillChangeField**

Table 2-5	Selected Events of the ADO Data Control
Event	**Description**
EndOfRecordset	Gets triggered when either the BOF or the EOF is encountered.
Error	Gets triggered when a database error occurs while no Visual Basic code is being executed.
FieldChangeComplete	Occurs after the field value has been changed.
MoveComplete	Occurs after the current row has been changed.
RecordChangeComplete	Occurs after the record has been updated.
RecordsetChangeComplete	Occurs after the recordset has been changed.
WillChangeField	Gets triggered before the value property of any field is changed.
WillChangeRecord	Gets triggered before changing a record using any of these methods: **Recordset.CancelBatch**, **Recordset.CancelUpdate**, **Recordset.Delete**, **Recordset.UpdateBatch**, and **Recordset.Update**.
WillChangeRecordset	Gets triggered before changing to a new recordset using any of these methods: **Recordset.Close**, **Recordset.Filter**, **Recordset.Open**, **Recordset.Requery**, and **Recordset.Resync**.
WillMove	Gets triggered before moving to a new row using any of these methods: **Recordset.AddNew**, **Recordset.Delete**, **Recordset.Bookmark**, **Recordset.Move**, **Recordset.MoveFirst**, **Recordset.MoveLast**, **Recordset.MoveNext**, **Recordset.MovePrevious**, **Recordset.Open**, **Recordset.Requery**, and **Recordset.Resync**.

event you can check the values and optionally cancel the change. In the **FieldChangeComplete** event you can check the same status flag (adStatus) to determine if the change was successfully applied to the database.

The **WillChangeRecord** and **RecordChangeComplete** events are fired before a row is changed in the database and after the row is changed, respectively. Like the **WillChangeField** and **FieldChangeComplete** events, you can cancel the change and make sure that the change was made successfully. The **WillMove** and **MoveComplete** events also work the same way.

It is also possible to bind controls to data sources other than a data control. You can use an ADO **Recordset** object, a **DataEnvironment** object, or even your own ActiveX control. This can give you additional flexibility when you don't want to use the ADO data control or when you need to access data that isn't stored in a database.

The Data-Bound Controls

For the most part, the data-bound controls are the controls you have already been using to write your Visual Basic programs, like **TextBox**, **ComboBox**, and **CheckBox**. Other controls such as **DataCombo**, **DataGrid**, and **DataList** are specifically designed to take advantage of the data control.

Binding to the Data Control

Controls are bound to a data control by using a group of properties (see Table 2-6). The primary display property (usually either **Caption**, **Text**, or **Value**) will display the data associated with the database field specified by **DataField**.

The source of the data is specified using the **DataSource** property. This property usually contains an object reference to an **ADO Data Control** or an ADO **Recordset**. However, it can be a reference to any object that can act as a data source. If you specify a **DataEnvironment** as the value for **DataSource**, you must also fill in the **DataMember** property with

Table 2-6 Properties That Allow You to Bind to a Data Source Such as the ADO Data Control	
Property	**Description**
DataBindings	Returns a collection of **DataBinding** objects that allow you to bind other properties of a control to a field in the database
DataChanged	Means, when **True,** that the contents of the control were updated by something other than the database
DataField	Specifies the name of the database column that will be bound to the control
DataFormat	Specifies how the data will be formatted when displayed by the control
DataMember	Specifies the **Command** object used when the data source is a DataEnvironment
DataSource	Contains an object reference to a data control or other object that can be used as a data source

the value of the command that will be used to generate the data.

The **DataFormat** property is a powerful tool that allows you to describe the format of the data that is extracted from the database. This is very important when you want to display an image directly from a binary field or when you have a numeric value that needs to be converted to a string of characters.

The **DataChanged** property is set to **True** whenever something other than the database changes the value of the control. This allows you to determine if you need to test the new value to make sure it is valid or perform other special processing.

Validating Your Data

All the data-bound controls also contain a property called **CausesValidation** and an event called **Validate**. They work together to prevent you from shifting focus from one control to another if the control contains invalid data. Using the **Validate** event is more efficient than using the **LostFocus** event, since the **Validate** event occurs before the focus is shifted rather than after the focus has shifted with the **LostFocus** event.

When the **CausesValidation** property on a control is **True**, before the focus is shifted to this control, the **Validate** event on the control that currently has the focus is fired. If in the **Validate** event the program chooses to cancel the request to shift focus, the focus remains with the current control. Assuming that the **CausesValidation** property on a control is **False**, then the focus will be shifted normally without triggering the **Validate** event.

For example, consider a form with two text boxes labeled A and B. Also assume that there are two buttons, OK and Cancel. Both text boxes have a **Validate** event, and all controls except for the Cancel button have their **CausesValidation** property set to **True**. When the user tries to move the focus from A to B, the **Validate** event in A will be fired and the focus will be shifted to B only if the **Validate** event permits it. The same thing will happen if the user tries to shift the focus from A to the OK button, since the OK button also has the **CausesValidation** property set to **True**. However, if the user tries to shift the focus from A to the Cancel button, the Cancel button will always receive the focus.

Introducing the Data-Bound Controls

This section covers each of the controls that can be bound to the ADO data control or other data source. Each of these controls, unless otherwise specified, supports the **DataChanged**, **DataField**, **DataFormat**, **DataMember**, and **DataSource** properties, the **CausesValidation** property, and the **Validate** event.

THE CHECKBOX CONTROL

The **CheckBox** control is an intrinsic control that displays a box with a caption that is either checked or not checked (see Figure 2-14). This control works best when displaying Boolean values.

☐ Check Box

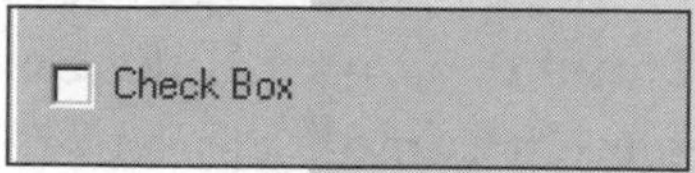

Figure 2-14
The **CheckBox** is great for displaying Boolean values.

THE COMBOBOX CONTROL

The **ComboBox** control is an intrinsic control that combines a list box with a text box (see Figure 2-15). You can populate the list at run time by using the **AddItem** method. Then the user can select a value from the list by pressing the down arrow on the right side of the text box. The selected value will be displayed in the text box; it is also the value that will be stored in the database. See the **DataCombo** control for more power control that can retrieve the list from the database as well as display database information in the text box area.

THE DATACOMBO CONTROL

This is an ActiveX control that is essentially the same as the **ComboBox** control, but the information displayed in the list box is retrieved from the database (see Figure 2-16). The list box information is loaded into the control by using the **ListField** and **RowSource** properties. The **ListField** property corresponds to the **DataField** property and the database column containing the values to be displayed in the list. The **RowSource** property corresponds to the **DataSource** property and contains a reference to an ADO data control or another ADO data source that contains the data to be displayed.

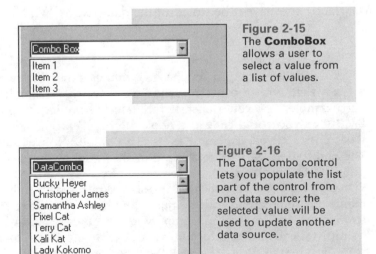

Figure 2-15
The **ComboBox** allows a user to select a value from a list of values.

Figure 2-16
The DataCombo control lets you populate the list part of the control from one data source; the selected value will be used to update another data source.

Caution

> The DataCombo control has been optimized to work with ADO data sources, such as the ADO data control and ADO **Recordsets**. The DBCombo control is nearly identical to the DataCombo but is optimized for use with DAO and RDO database access. Since you should be using ADO to access SQL Server 7, you shouldn't use the DBCombo control.

Caution

> Don't use the **DataFormat** property with the DataCombo control, since only the top item will be formatted. The rest of the items in the drop-down box will not be formatted. The two different formatting schemes will often confuse the user, especially when the value selected from the drop-down box is reformatted for display.

In the simplest case the value selected by the user in the drop-down box is moved into the database field specified by **DataField** and **DataSource**. Setting the **BoundColumn** property to the same value you used for the **ListField** property is all that is necessary. However, you can choose any column from the data returned by the data object in the **RowSource** property. This is useful when you want the user to select a value like "Maryland" and have it be stored in the database as "MD".

Tip

> Often when designing a database, it makes sense to translate a large field with a constant value into a much smaller field. For example, you could encode the value "Maryland" as "MD," or you could code the book title "Leveraging Visual Basic with ActiveX Controls" as its ISBN value, "0761509011". The codified value uses less space in the database and also prevents the problem where someone else may have entered "Leveraging VB with ActiveX Controls". While both book titles mean the same thing to a human, they mean different things to a computer. In some programming languages, it can be a painful task to codify information, but with the **DataCombo** control in Visual Basic, the task becomes almost trivial.

THE DATAGRID CONTROL

This is an ActiveX control that allows you to view and update a database table or query using a worksheetlike grid (see Figure 2-17). You saw this facility earlier as the Open item on the Table and View pop-up menu in the Data View window. Each row in the grid corresponds to a row from the query and each column in the grid corresponds to a column from the query. Assuming that you can update the results of the query, simply changing the value in a cell and moving to a different row is all that it takes to make a change to the table. You can also insert a new row by moving beyond the last row of the table and just typing in the new values. This is a quick and easy tool you can add to your program to let you view the data at run-time.

Caution

The **DataGrid** control has been optimized to work with ADO data sources, such as the ADO data control and ADO **Recordsets**. While the **DBGrid** control is nearly identical to the **DataGrid**, it is optimized for use with DAO and RDO database access. Since you should be using ADO to access SQL Server 7, you shouldn't use the **DBGrid** control.

Tip

Sometimes it is useful to have a tool that will let you view the raw contents of the database buried deep in your program. The easiest way to do this is to use the **DataGrid** control to display the information. Just create a new form and add the **DataGrid**, a text box to hold a new query, and a command button that will refresh the contents of the grid. At run time, simply enter your query and press the Refresh button to see the raw data that your application is using.

	Person	Street	
▶	Bucky Heyer	3423 Gaming Cour	
	Christopher James	1234 Nintendo Ro.	
	Samantha Ashley	987 Teddy Bear Co	

Figure 2-17
The DataGrid control allows you to access the contents of a table using a worksheetlike grid.

THE DATALIST CONTROL

This is an ActiveX control that is similar to the **DataCombo** control in that it lets you display the list information from one database query while updating a second database query with the value selected by the user (see Figure 2-18).

>
> **Caution**
>
> The **DataList** control is optimized to work with ADO data sources, such as the **ADO Data Control** and ADO **Recordsets**. While the **DBList** control is nearly identical to the **DataList**, it is optimized for use with DAO and RDO database access. Since you should be using ADO to access SQL Server 7, you shouldn't use the **DBList** control.

THE DATAREPEATER CONTROL

The **DataRepeater** control is an ActiveX control that provides a container for another data-bound control. The contained control will be repeated for each row from the data source (see Figure 2-19).

> **Tip**
>
> The **DataRepeater** control allows you to build forms such as an order entry form where you have a lot of header information (like name and address) at the top of the form. Then on the bottom part of the form you have a variable number of lines for detail information like order item, quantity, price, etc.

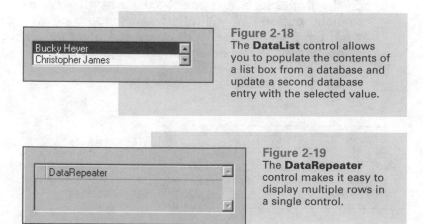

Figure 2-18
The **DataList** control allows you to populate the contents of a list box from a database and update a second database entry with the selected value.

Figure 2-19
The **DataRepeater** control makes it easy to display multiple rows in a single control.

THE DATAREPORTER OBJECT

The **DataReporter** object is not a true control but an object similar to a form that allows you to create complex reports that can be previewed on the screen or sent to the printer (see Figure 2-20). While this object can use an ADO **Recordset** as the **DataSource**, it can't use an ADO data control. You would use the Data Report Designer to create the actual report.

THE DATETIMEPICKER CONTROL

The **DateTimePicker** control is an ActiveX control that you can use to specify date and time values (see Figure 2-21). This control has two modes. The first mode displays a drop-down calendar, from which you can choose a date value. The second mode displays a formatted date and time value, where the user can individually choose values for each field.

Figure 2-20
The DataReporter object allows you to build complex reports quickly.

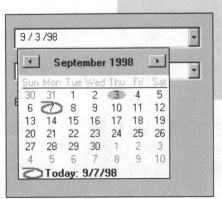

Figure 2-21
The **DateTimePicker** control allows you to select a date value from a drop-down calendar.

THE IMAGE CONTROL

The **Image** control is an intrinsic control that will display a graphic image (see Figure 2-22). It can display BMP, JPEG, and GIF-formatted images in addition to icons and metafiles.

> You should set the **DataFormat** property to Picture to properly display an image from the database.

THE IMAGECOMBO CONTROL

The **ImageCombo** control is an ActiveX control that provides a function similar to the **ComboBox** control. It can display a graphic image next to each item in the drop-down box (see Figure 2-23). You can access database information just like the **ComboBox** control, but the items are managed as a collection rather than the array used by the **ComboBox** control.

Figure 2-22
The Image control is used to display a graphic image stored in a database field.

ImageCombo ▾

Figure 2-23
The **ImageCombo** control works like a **ComboBox** control, except it displays an image next to each item in the drop-down box.

THE LABEL CONTROL

The **Label** control is an intrinsic control that displays information in a read-only text box (see Figure 2-24). Since the user can't modify the data displayed in a label, the **CauseValidation** property and the **Validate** event are not included with the control. The control is designed to blend in with the rest of the form, so you will not see any distinct boundaries for the control.

THE LISTBOX CONTROL

The **ListBox** control is an intrinsic control that displays a list of items and from which the user may select one or more items (see Figure 2-25). Only the selected item can be changed using the **DataSource** and **DataField** properties. The rest of the items are added using the same **AddItem** method used in the **ComboBox** control. If you want to load the list of items from the database, you should use the **DataList** control.

THE MASKEDEDIT CONTROL

The **MaskedEdit** control is an ActiveX control that forces the user to enter a value that matches a predefined format string (see Figure 2-26). This is useful when you have a complex piece of information (such as a social security number or a telephone number) to enter into the field.

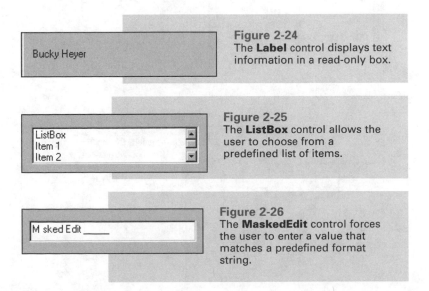

Figure 2-24
The **Label** control displays text information in a read-only box.

Figure 2-25
The **ListBox** control allows the user to choose from a predefined list of items.

Figure 2-26
The **MaskedEdit** control forces the user to enter a value that matches a predefined format string.

THE MONTHVIEW CONTROL

The **MonthView** control is an ActiveX control that allows a user to choose a date or range of dates (see Figure 2-27). This is similar to the **DateTimePicker** control, except that the calendar is always displayed rather than being displayed on demand.

THE MSCHART CONTROL

The **MSChart** control is an ActiveX control that can create charts similar to those created by Excel (see Figure 2-28). You need to define a database query using either the ADO data control or an ADO **Recordset** that retrieves the values you want to chart and assign it to the **DataSource** property. The **MSChart** control does the rest.

> Unlike many of the controls discussed here, the **MSChart** control only works with an ADO **Recordset** or ADO **Data Control**. It will not work with RDO or DAO.

Figure 2-27
The **MonthView** control displays a calendar.

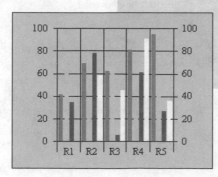

Figure 2-28
The **MSChart** control displays a chart based on the results of a query.

THE MSHFLEXGRID CONTROL

The **MSHFlexGrid** control is an ActiveX control that can display the results of a hierarchical query in a PivotTable-like format (see Figure 2-29). While the information presented is read-only, it can be sorted, merged, and formatted to meet your requirements. Unlike the **Data-Grid** control, the **MSHFlexGrid** control isn't something you're likely to use unless you are implementing your own version of a PivotTable.

THE PICTUREBOX CONTROL

The **PictureBox** control is an intrinsic control that can display a graphic image (see Figure 2-30). This is similar to the **Image** control but features additional capabilities that you may want to exploit, such as the ability to draw on top of the image and the ability to automatically resize the control based on the contents of the image.

THE RICHTEXTBOX CONTROL

The **RichTextBox** control is an ActiveX control that displays a rich text formatted document (see Figure 2-31). The document can include multiple character fonts, colors, embedded images, etc.

Tip

You can use the **RichTextBox** to display text information that is too large to be displayed in a normal **TextBox**.

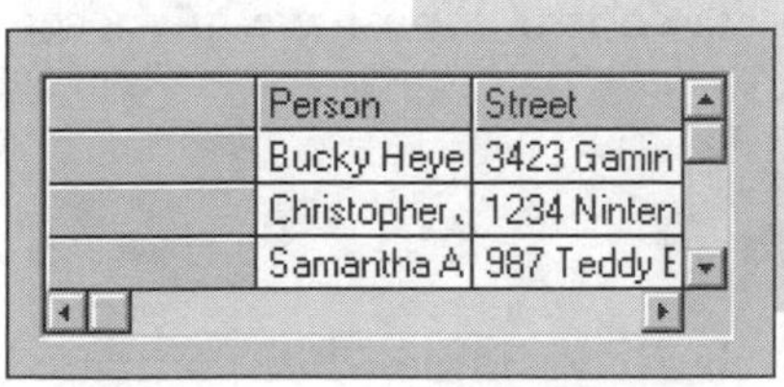

Person	Street
Bucky Heye	3423 Gamin
Christopher	1234 Ninten
Samantha A	987 Teddy E

Figure 2-29
The **MSHFlexGrid** control assists your user in performing data analysis of tabular data.

Figure 2-30
The **PictureBox** control can display graphic images from your database.

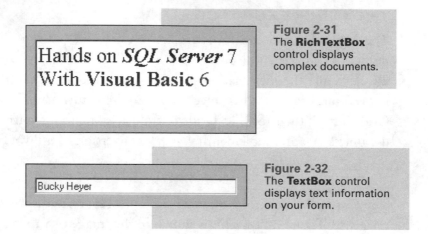

Figure 2-31
The **RichTextBox** control displays complex documents.

Figure 2-32
The **TextBox** control displays text information on your form.

THE TEXTBOX CONTROL

The **TextBox** control is an intrinsic control that is used to display text information on a form (see Figure 2-32). This is the most commonly used control to display database information. By using the **DataFormat** property, you can even display numeric data using this control.

Accessing Databases with ActiveX Data Objects

It isn't necessary to use the ADO data control or ActiveX Data Objects in order to access the database. You can also access the ADO object model directly in Visual Basic. This means that you are not limited to the facilities in the ADO data control. You have full access to all OLE-DB facilities.

The ADO Object Model

The ADO object model is relatively simple when compared to the DAO object model. However, don't let its simplicity fool you, as it's very robust and designed for high performance.

There are three main objects in the ADO object model: the **Connection** object, the **Command** object, and the **Recordset** object. There are four lower-level collections and objects used in ADO: the **Properties** collection with the **Property** object, the **Errors** collection with the **Error** object, the **Parameters** collection with the **Parameter** object, and the **Fields** collection with the **Field** object (see Figure 2-33).

The Connection Object

The **Connection** object contains the information about a session with a database server. Table 2-7 contains a list of properties associated with the object. The **ConnectionString** contains information necessary to connect to the database server. The **Errors** property contains an object reference to the **Errors** collection, which contains the set of errors

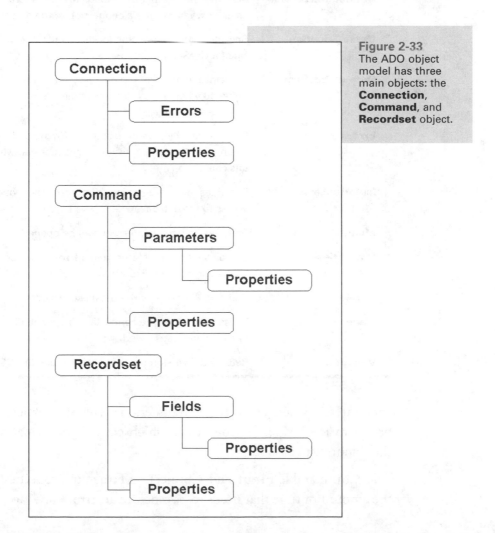

Figure 2-33
The ADO object model has three main objects: the **Connection**, **Command**, and **Recordset** object.

Table 2-7 Properties of the ADO Connection Object

Property	Description
Attributes	Specifies whether executing **CommitTrans** automatically starts a new transaction and executing **RollBackTrans** automatically starts a new transaction
CommandTimeout	Specifies the number of seconds to wait before returning an error while running a command
ConnectionString	Describes the information necessary to connect to the database
ConnectionTimeout	Specifies the number of seconds to wait before returning an error when making a connection to the database server
CursorLocation	Specifies either client side (adUseClient) cursors or server side (adUseServer) cursors
DefaultDatabase	Contains the name of the database that should be assumed when a table or view name is specified without a database name
Errors	Contains an object reference to the **Errors** collection containing information about errors encountered while using this connection
IsolationLevel	Describes the degree of isolation from other concurrent access to the database
Mode	Specifies how the connection will be opened
Properties	Contains an object reference to a **Properties** collection containing additional information about the connection
Provider	Contains the name of the database provider
State	Indicates whether the connection is open (adStateOpen) or closed (adStateClosed)
Version	Returns the version number associated with ADO

encountered when executing a transaction. The **Properties** property points to the **Properties** collection, which contains information about the remote database server.

The **CommandTimeout** and **ConnectionTimeout** properties contain the amount of time that needs to pass before an error condition is raised when executing a command or connecting to the server. The **Default-Database** contains the name of the database that should be assumed when you access an unqualified table or view.

Associated with the **Connection** object is a set of methods that allow you to perform various database tasks (see Table 2-8). The **Open** method establishes the link to the database and the **Close** method stops the connection. While the connection is open, you can use the **Begin-Trans**, **CommitTrans**, and **RollbackTrans** methods to mark the beginning and end of transactions. Inside a transaction, you can use the **Execute** method to run a query or a stored procedure or to open a table or a view. The **OpenSchema** method is used to request specific pieces of information from the database.

> **Note**
>
> **When you look at some of the facilities in ADO like the OpenSchema method and wonder why they're there, remember that tools like Visual Basic need to ask the database for information about itself. Visual Basic doesn't know what type of database it is talking to, so it can't merely query the appropriate table for the information.**

Table 2-8   Methods of the ADO Connection Object

Method	Description
BeginTrans	Marks the beginning of a transaction
Close	Closes the connection and any open **Recordset** objects that were associated with the connection
CommitTrans	Closes the current transaction and saves the changes to the database
Execute	Runs the specified SQL statement or stored procedure or opens the specified table or view
Open	Opens a connection to the database
OpenSchema	Returns structural information about the database and database objects
RollbackTrans	Aborts the current transaction without making changes to the database

The **Errors** collection and the **Error** object are referenced as part of the **Connection** object. This contains all the errors encountered during a single ADO operation. This can be an operation performed directly from the **Connection** object or any other objects that reference the **Connection** object, such as the **Command** and **Recordset** objects.

The **Errors** collection has the **Item** method and **Count** properties like most collections, but since **Error** objects are created by ADO, the only other method available is the **Clear** method. The **Clear** method simply erases all the **Error** objects in the collection. Note that each new operation will clear the **Errors** collection, so you don't have to worry about clearing the collection each time you perform an operation.

Table 2-9 lists the properties of the **Error** object. The **Number** property contains the actual error code, while **Description** contains a human- (or at least a database administrator-) readable description of the error. The **HelpContext** and the **HelpFile** properties work together to identify a reference in a Windows help file that may contain additional information about the error. **NativeError** contains the raw error code as generated by the database server, while **SQLState** returns the ANSI standard five-character code describing the error condition. **Source** contains the name of the object that raised the error condition.

Table 2-9   Properties of the ADO Error Object

Property	Description
Description	Contains a text description of the error
HelpContext	Contains a reference for a description of the error in a Windows help file
HelpFile	Identifies the name of the help file containing the description of the error pointed to by **HelpContext**
NativeError	Contains the native error code from the database server
Number	Contains the numeric value of the error code
Source	Contains the object that raised the error condition
SQLState	Contains the five-character ANSI error code for the error

It is not unusual for a single error to generate many error messages. The trick is to identify the original cause of the error and ignore the rest of the error messages. Some methods, such as the **UpdateBatch** error, may generate lots of errors but not actually trigger an error condition in your program.

> The **Err** object is used by Visual Basic to describe an error condition in your program. The **Error** object is used by ADO to describe an error encountered while performing a database operation. Sometimes a database error that will generate a new **Error** object will also set the **Err** object, which can abort your program. When checking for error conditions, make sure you are checking the right error object for the right type of error.

The Command Object

The **Command** object describes how the data should be retrieved from the database. The **Command** object also has a **Parameters** collection containing **Parameter** objects. Each **Parameter** object also contains information that will be used when the command is executed using the **Connection** object's **Execute** method.

Table 2-10 lists the properties associated with the **Command** object. The **Name** property contains the name of the **Command** object. The **ActiveConnection** property must be set before attempting to execute the command. The **CommandText** property contains the name of the stored procedure, the table, the view, or the SQL statement to be executed. The type of information stored in the **CommandText** should be reflected in **CommandType** for optimal performance. The parameters and their values for a stored procedure or parameterized query are stored in the **Parameters** collection. The parameters can be retrieved from the database automatically or manually entered in the program by using the **CreateParameter** method.

Table 2-10   Properties of the ADO Command Object

Property	Description
ActiveConnection	Returns an object reference to an open **Connection**
CommandText	Contains a SQL statement or the name of a stored procedure, table, or view
CommandTimeout	Specifies the number of seconds to wait before returning an error while running a command
CommandType	Specifies the type of information stored in **CommandText**
Name	Contains the name associated with the **Command** object
Parameters	An object reference to the **Parameters** collection that contains values that will be substituted into the stored procedure or parameterized query
Prepared	When **True**, the database should compile and save the query for use later in the session; when **False**, the database should recompile the query each time it is run
Properties	Contains information about the **Command** object
State	Indicates whether the command is open (adStateOpen) or closed (adStateClosed)

The **Prepared** property lets the database server know whether to keep a compiled copy of the query around for later use in the session. The **State** property tracks the open or closed state of the **Command** object.

The **Execute** method is used to run the **Command** object on the remote database server (see Table 2-11). A **Recordset** object will be returned if the query returns any rows. The **CreateParameter** method is used to add a new parameter to the **Command** object.

Table 2-11   Methods of the ADO Command Object

Method	Description
CreateParameter	Dynamically creates a parameter that will be passed to the database server when the stored procedure or parameterized query is executed
Execute	Runs the command on the database server

The Parameter Object

In order to pass information parameters to a stored procedure, the **Parameters** collection is used. The **Parameters** collection is a typical collection containing the methods to **Append**, **Delete**, and **Refresh** data. The total number of parameters is held in the **Count** property.

You access information using the **Item** method, which has a number of properties and methods listed in Tables 2-12 and 2-13. The **Name** property contains the name of the parameter. The **Type** property describes the parameter's type, while the **Value** property contains the value of the parameter. When dealing with long values, you can use the **Append-Chunk** method to add information to the end of the value. This is useful when you are dealing with very large values, such as a sizable image file that you are reading in multiple chunks from disk.

Caution

> Before using the **AppendChunk** method, you must assign something to the **Value** property; otherwise, an error will occur.

The **Size** property contains the size of the parameter's value, while **NumericScale** and **Precision** describe a numeric parameter. The **Attributes** property describes whether the parameter can contain **Null** values and other information. The **Direction** property indicates whether the parameter is used as input to the stored procedure, output from the stored procedure, or both. It also can indicate that the parameter contains the return value.

Table 2-12 Properties of the ADO Parameter Object

Property	Description
Attributes	Describes whether the parameter can contain **Null** values, signed values, or long binary values
Direction	Describes whether the parameter is passed to the stored procedure, is returned by the stored procedure, is passed and returned by the stored procedure, or contains the return value from the procedure ➡

Table 2-12	Properties of the ADO Parameter Object
(continued)	
Property	**Description**
Name	Contains the name of the parameter
NumericScale	Contains the number of digits to the right of the decimal point
Precision	Contains the total number of digits in a number
Properties	Contains a collection of properties associated with the parameter
Size	Returns the total size in bytes or characters of a parameter's value
Type	Contains the type of data stored in the parameter
Value	Contains the value of the parameter

Table 2-13	Methods of the ADO Parameter Object
Method	**Description**
AppendChunk	Appends data to the end of the **Value** property for long parameters

The Recordset Object

The **Recordset** object contains the results from the database after running the **Command** object. The **Recordset** object also has a **Fields** collection containing **Field** objects. Each **Field** object has its own **Properties** collection that describe the information contained in each field.

Table 2-14 contains a list of properties and Table 2-15 contains the list of methods available in a **Recordset** object. The **Source** property describes how the recordset was created. The **ActiveConnection** property provides a link to the connection object that should be used to communicate with the database server. Both properties must be set before you can Open the recordset. When you are finished, you must Close the recordset to release the resources it was using. You can also Clone the recordset, thereby creating a second recordset that is identical to the first. Any updates made to one are immediately reflected in the other. The Clone method is useful when you want to have two current record pointers.

Note

Using the Clone method results in a second recordset whose objects can be interchanged with the first. On the other hand, creating a second recordset using the same Source but with the Open method instead results in the same values being retrieved from the database though the objects between the two recordsets are not interchangeable.

Table 2-14   Properties of the ADO Recordset Object

Property	Description
AbsolutePage	Returns the page number containing the current record
AbsolutePosition	Returns the relative row number in the current recordset
ActiveConnection	Returns an object reference to an open Connection
BOF	Returns True when the current record is before the first row of the current recordset
Bookmark	Contains a unique value that can be used to reposition the current record pointer to this row
CacheSize	Contains the number of rows that will be held locally in memory
CursorLocation	Specifies whether the recordset should be opened with a client-side cursor or a server-side cursor
CursorType	Specifies the type of cursor used
EditMode	Indicates whether the current record is in the process of being updated or a new record has been added
EOF	Returns True when that the current record is beyond the end of the current recordset
Fields	Returns a collection of Field objects, with each object containing information about a single field in the current row
Filter	Further restricts the rows already returned in the recordset ➡

Table 2-14 Properties of the ADO Recordset Object
(continued)

Property	Description
LockType	Describes the type of locks that will be used when accessing the data for the recordset
MarshalOptions	Indicates, when using a client-side recordset, that only modified records should be returned to the server when updating the recordset
MaxRecords	Contains the maximum number of records that will be returned by the recordset
Properties	Contains a collection of properties associated with the recordset
PageCount	Contains the number of logical pages in the recordset
PageSize	Contains the number of rows in a logical page
RecordCount	Contains the number of rows in the recordset
Source	Describes how the data for the recordset is generated; the source can be a Command object, a SQL query, or the name of a table, view name, or stored procedure
State	Indicates whether the recordset is open (adStateOpen) or closed (adStateClosed)
Status	Contains the status of the current record when performing batch updates

Table 2-15 Methods of the ADO Recordset Object

Method	Description
AddNew	Adds a blank row to the current recordset
CancelBatch	Cancels a pending batch update; this is used with the **UpdateBatch** method
CancelUpdate	Cancels an update to the current record. This is used with the **Update** method
Clone	Duplicates a recordset
Close	Closes a recordset

➡

Table 2-15   Methods of the ADO Recordset Object
(continued)

Method	Description
Delete	Removes the current record or a set of rows specified by the **Filter** property from the database
GetRows	Retrieves multiple rows of the recordset into a two-dimensional array
Move	Moves the specified number of rows from the current record, first record, or last record in the recordset
MoveFirst	Moves the current record pointer to the first row in the recordset
MoveLast	Moves the current record pointer to the last row in the recordset
MoveNext	Moves the current record pointer to the next row in the recordset
MovePrevious	Moves the current record pointer to the previous row in the recordset
NextRecordset	Returns the next recordset for those queries that return multiple recordsets
Open	Opens a recordset
Requery	Runs the same query again; this is the same as performing a **Close** followed by an **Open**
Resync	Refreshes the data in the current recordset from the database; can refresh one row, the rows affected by the **Filter** property, or all rows
Supports	Determines which features are supported for this recordset
Update	Writes the changes made to the current record to the database
UpdateBatch	Writes all pending batch updates to the database

Once the recordset has been opened, you are positioned at the first row of the recordset. The recordset only contains one row from the database at any point in time. This row is called the current record. You can use the **MoveFirst**, **MoveLast**, **MoveNext**, and **MovePrevious** methods to scroll through the recordset looking at one row at a time. The **Move** method allows you to skip over multiple rows in one statement. You can use the **Bookmark** property to remember the location of a row and to return to it later.

You can access the **Field** objects for this row by using the **Fields** collection. The **Fields** collection contains a set of **Field** objects, each of which corresponds to a single column in the current record. You can access the values through the object to display or change them. Once you change the value, you should use the **Update** method to write the changes to the database.

You can delete the current record by using the **Delete** method. After the row has been deleted, it still remains the current record, although you can't access any of the information in the **Fields** collection. Once you move to another row, the deleted row becomes unavailable.

Using the **AddNew** method creates a new row with default values. Then you can change these values by accessing the **Fields** collection. The row is saved to the database by using the **Update** method.

If you decide not to save your changes to the current record to the database, you can use the **CancelUpdate** method to restore the values in the **Fields** collection. Also, you can check the **Status** property to determine whether the previous method was successful or whether the record has updates that are pending.

A useful feature of the **Recordset** object is the concept of pages. A page is a fixed number of records whose size is determined by the **PageSize** property. The number of pages in a recordset is stored in **PageCount**. You can use the **AbsolutePage** property to return the page number of the current record or move to the first row in that particular page. These three properties make it easy to build a program that scrolls through a query a fixed number of rows at a time.

If you anticipate making a lot of changes, you can set the **LockType** to adLockBatchOptimistic to enable batch mode updates. This allows you to make changes to a number of rows locally and save the changes all at one time using the **UpdateBatch** method. You can abort the changes by using the **CancelBatch** method.

Caution

> The **UpdateBatch** method may not update all the rows properly. This can happen if another user is accessing the database and changing rows at the same time. Check the **Errors** collection in the **Connection** object to determine what rows, if any, weren't properly updated.

The Field Object

The **Fields** collection is a pretty standard collection with an **Item** method that returns a **Field** object, a **Refresh** method to get the most current information, and the **Count** property containing the number of **Field** objects in the collection.

Table 2-16 contains a list of properties associated with the **Field** object. Obviously the **Name** property holds the name of the field, while the **Value** property holds the current value of the column. The **Original-Value** property holds the value that was originally retrieved from the database. The **UnderlyingValue** property holds the current value from the database. While you might expect the **OriginalValue** and **Underlying-Value** to be the same, it is possible that someone else has updated the value in the database since the recordset was created. Then knowing the **UnderlyingValue** as well as the **OriginalValue** can help you resolve problems where you are doing optimistic batch updates.

Table 2-16	Properties of the ADO Field Object
Property	**Description**
ActualSize	Contains the actual size of the field
Attributes	Contains information about whether the field can be updated, can accept a **Null** value, or contains a long binary value or a unique identifier
DefinedSize	Contains the maximum possible size of the field
Name	Contains the name of the field
NumericScale	Contains the number of digits to the right of the decimal point
OriginalValue	Contains the value of the field before any changes were made to it

➡

Table 2-16	Properties of the ADO Field Object *(continued)*
Property	**Description**
Precision	Contains the total number of digits in a number
Properties	Contains a collection of properties associated with the field
Type	Contains the type of data stored in the field
UnderlyingValue	Retrieves the current value of the field from the database
Value	Contains the current value of the field

The **DefinedSize** and **ActualSize** describe the maximum size and actual size of the column. For **Int** or **Char(32)** values these properties will be equal. But in the case of a **Varchar(32)** it's possible that the column will hold only a single character. Thus the **DefinedSize** would be 32, but the **ActualSize** would be 1.

The **Field** object has two methods that help you manage long values (see Table 2-17). The **AppendChunk** method allows you to add a chunk of data to the end of the **Value** property. Note that you must assign the first chunk of data to the **Value** before using the **AppendChunk** method or an error will occur.

The **GetChunk** property works in the opposite direction. The first call to **GetChunk** returns the specified amount of data. Each subsequent call returns the next chunk of data. You will reset the chunk pointer to the beginning of the **Value** if you read or write a value into any other field in the current record of this **Recordset**. Accessing a field's **Value** in another recordset will not affect the position of the chunk pointer.

Table 2-17	Methods of the ADO Field Object
Method	**Description**
AppendChunk	Appends data to the end of the **Value** property for long parameters
GetChunk	Retrieves in pieces the specified number of characters or bytes of data from the **Value** property

The Property Object

The **Properties** collection and the **Property** object are used to communicate information from the OLE-DB provider to the application program. The **Properties** collection is a standard collection with an **Item** method (which returns a **Property** object), a **Refresh** method (to get the most current information), and the **Count** property (containing the number of **Property** objects in the collection).

Table 2-18 lists the available properties for the **Property** object. **Name**, **Type**, and **Value** are basically the same as in the **Field** object. The **Attributes** property contains information about the **Property** object, such as if it is required or optional and if you can view or change the property.

Table 2-18	Properties of the ADO Property Object
Property	**Description**
Attributes	Indicates if the provider supports the property, if the property is required or optional, and if you can view or change the property
Name	Appends data to the end of the **Value** property for long parameters
Type	Contains the type of data stored in the field
Value	Contains the value of the property

> **Tip**
>
> The **Property** object contains a lot of information about the database and the provider. While I won't say that most of this information is useless, I would suggest that you don't worry about trying to access it unless you're really curious about it.

Wrapping Up

In this chapter, you covered a lot of information about using SQL Server 7 with Visual Basic 6. Most of it you'll see again as you start building your own database applications. The rest of the material provided a framework to help you understand how it all fits together.

You learned how to create a **DataEnvironment** from which you can perform many SQL Server functions from within Visual Basic. This includes creating your own tables and views interactively and building and debugging your own stored procedures. You also covered how to use the ADO data control and bound controls to create database programs quickly and easily. Finally, you studied in detail the ADO object model and how it fits in between Visual Basic and SQL Server.

You should spend a few minutes in Visual Basic and build a simple EXE program that uses a **DataEnvironment** to access your database you created in Chapter 1. Access the data you loaded into your Addresses table.

Next, add the controls covered here to your Visual Basic program. (If you forget how to add a new control to your Visual Basic toolbox, try Project, Components). Look at their properties using the Properties Window and use the Object Browser (View, Object Browser) to see the properties, methods, and events available in the controls and ADO data objects.

HANDS ON PROJECT 1

THE CUSTOMER INFORMATION SUBSYSTEM

- Determine application requirements
- Develop Entity/Relationship models
- Access databases with the **ADO Data Control**
- Design forms with bound controls
- Insert, delete, and update database records
- Import data using Data Transformation Services
- Perform database backups and recoveries

Project Overview

The Customer Information Subsystem builds on your current knowledge of Visual Basic while introducing you to the world of database programming. When you've finished with the project, you'll have experienced how to hold a brainstorming session to design a database and how to build a simple Visual Basic program that allows a user to view, modify, and enter data into the database.

Along with the programming, you will learn about some common SQL Server 7 administration functions such as creating databases and setting up maintenance schedules. You will also learn how to use database utility programs to perform functions that previously required custom database programs.

CHAPTER 3

What Is the Customer Information Subsystem?

Now that you understand some of the basic concepts used by SQL Server and Visual Basic, it's time to start building a real application. Creating an application requires that you follow these four steps:

- **Gather information** for the application
- **Design** the application
- **Build** the application
- **Test** the application

Each of these steps will be discussed in the next four chapters. However, since the idea behind this application is to teach you about SQL Server and Visual Basic, you'll use many different tools and techniques throughout the development process. For the purposes of this book, it's important that you be exposed to as many features and tools as possible. By the end of this phase of the project you will have learned the following:

- How to determine data elements by brainstorming
- Basic relational database concepts
- The fundamentals of Entity/Relationship modeling
- How to use Enterprise Manager to create databases and tables
- How to use the ADO Data Control and bound controls in a Visual Basic program
- How to export a file using the Data Transformation Services
- How to automatically back up a database

Even though the application is called WebBooks.com and your ultimate goal will be to let customers place their orders over the Web, the focus in this phase of the project will be on building traditional SQL Server/Visual Basic client/server applications. You'll learn the basics of database programming without having to cover all the issues related to Web programming as well.

The first phase of the WebBooks.com project is to create a set of database tables that will contain information about a customer and implement the programs that will access those tables. Also, you need to understand the levels of security associated with both the information and the functions that are performed against the information.

Database Elements

Everything related to a customer is managed by this subsystem. Most of this information will be developed in Chapter 4, but at a minimum, the application needs to track the following information pertaining to the customer:

- Name
- Address
- E-mail address

- Credit card information
- History of previous orders

Application Functions

Simply storing data is not enough. You need to perform operations against this data. Usually these operations are done using traditional application programs, although you can often use standard utility programs to perform these functions. The Customer Information Subsystem will need to be able to:

- Update customer information
- Search customer information
- Export a list of customers
- Back-up and recover customer information

This subsystem has several goals, but the most important is to show you the basics of designing and building a relatively simple application.

The Data Elements

The first step in building a database application is to understand what elements are needed. My favorite way to do this is to make a list of every possible piece of information that may be related to a customer. Look for information that is atomic, meaning that it can't be broken into smaller pieces.

Next, focus on building relationships between the data elements in your database. Separate items in terms of their relationship to other objects. Elements that have a one-to-one relationship will usually be grouped together in a table. Elements having a one-to-many relationship will be located in two tables with the elements grouped together as a key.

After building the database, the next step is to build a program to access it. In this case, you'll use the ADO DataControl and a set of data controls to access the database. This simplifies the amount of code required to build the program.

The Browse and Update Information function displays information about a single customer on a form. It includes the ability to scroll through the list of customers, find a customer in the database, and then update the information.

The Export a List of Customers function creates a file containing the information from the Customer Information Subsystem. This file will be formatted as a comma separated value (CSV) file that can be imported into a spreadsheet like Microsoft Excel.

Not all functions in a database application require writing a program. Sometimes you can just use standard database utilities. For the Backup and Recovery subsystem, you'll learn how to automatically back-up your database to protect yourself from data losses resulting from hardware errors and application problems. You'll also learn the process of restoring a database using a backup.

Wrapping Up

In this chapter, you began to brainstorm with the Customer Information Subsystem. In the next phase of the project, you will build a relatively simple database to hold information about WebBooks.com's customers. You should begin to get comfortable using the database tools and the database tools in Visual Basic. You should also take time to review some of the Visual Basic tools and facilities that you have used before.

Before continuing with this project, spend a little time at some of the commercial Web sites selling books. The biggest Web site is **www.amazon.com**, but you may find some interesting ideas from **www.clbooks.com** and **www.barnesandnoble.com** as well.

CHAPTER 4

Gathering Information for the Customer Information Subsystem

Now that you've taken on the job of building this system, you need to determine the customer's requirements for phase one, the Customer Information Subsystem. Begin by working with the customer to determine the data elements needed for the database. Then work with the customer to determine the relationships between the data elements, while at the same time refining exactly what these elements mean. Finally, work with the customer to determine the operations that need to be performed against these data elements.

Determining the Data Elements Needed

Brainstorming is merely the process of listing all the ideas you can come up with about a particular topic, even if the ideas are bad. Once you cannot come up with any other ideas, review the list to eliminate the duplicate elements. Also during this process you will assign each data element a general data type from the list below:

- Boolean
- Currency
- Date
- Floating point
- Integer
- String

At the time you are reviewing the data elements and assigning them data types, you need to begin thinking about how to verify that the data entered into a field is correct. In some cases you can verify information, such as checking for a valid state or a numeric zip code. But in most cases you can't. For example, you can't verify that a person's name or e-mail address is spelled correctly. However, you can at least verify that a user entered a value by not allowing them to leave a field blank.

Once you have finished this process, you then use a technique called Entity/Relationship (E/R) modeling to help you understand the relationships between these elements. You'll cover this process in Chapter 5 when you begin to design the database.

Involving the customer in the brainstorming process is a good idea, since the customer will bring a different viewpoint to the application. The people who participate in the brainstorming session should be extremely knowledgeable about their business and how it operates in the real world. Also, it's desirable that they have no preconceived notions about how the application should be designed. Therefore, having non-technical people at the session is better because they will be more apt to focus on the data elements important in their business rather than trying to design the database themselves.

The Brainstorming Session

The actual brainstorming session should be held around a whiteboard where you can put ideas on the board as they are discussed. However, since you can't actively participate in this brainstorming session right now, the following lists some points to consider:

- Customer name
- Customer's first name
- Customer's last name
- Customer's middle initial
- Customer user ID
- Customer password
- Address
- Street
- City
- State
- ZIP code
- Telephone number
- Credit card number
- Sales history

- Company name
- Age
- Sex
- Education
- Tax-exempt status
- Date of last purchase
- Types of books the customer is interested in
- Billing address information
- Country
- Customer contact
- Preferred shipping method and vendor

Reviewing the Results

Looking through this list, you'll see that customer name is listed two ways: once as a single field and then as the individual pieces of the name. You'll also notice some elements (like sales history and types of books the customer is interested in) that won't easily translate well into a single database field. Other information (such as sex, age, and education) may be interesting, but the customer may feel that supplying that information is a violation of privacy.

Reviewing the information after the brainstorming session often provides new and better insight into the fields you really need. Part of the reviewing process is to ensure that each element is atomic, meaning that it can't be reduced further. This helps to ensure that each data element can be easily translated into a field in a database. While reviewing this information, revise the list of data elements needed and assign each field a data type and attempt to create some basic validation rules.

Sometimes you can't reduce a field into a single atomic data element. This typically happens when you have a collection of information where each piece of information shares a common structure with the other members of the collection. This concept is called a repeating group.

Repeating Groups, Repeating Groups, Repeating Groups

A repeating group is a collection of objects with the same data type, such as a collection of book titles or a collection of keywords. Another way to think of a repeating group is as an array where each element has the same data type and a similar meaning.

Customer Name

Choosing a format for customer name is an issue that has spawned many debates over the years, and those debates will probably continue for many years to come. However, it really boils down to an issue of personal preference. Both forms contain all the information needed to identify an individual. Using separate fields for the first and last names makes it easier to identify an individual by first name in correspondence and to find an individual by last name in the database. However, it confuses the issue about how to handle a person's title (Mr., Mrs., Miss, Dr., Ms., etc.) and a person's suffix (Junior, Senior, Ph.D., III, etc.).

Using a single field for the entire name solves these problems but makes it somewhat difficult to extract the first name for the reasons listed above. However, knowing the person's first name isn't all that critical for most applications. This field should be a string value and you shouldn't allow blank values.

Customer Address

The fields of the customer address include address, city, state, ZIP code, telephone number, company name, country, and customer contact. Addresses tend to fall into one of three different categories: consumer addresses, corporate addresses, and international addresses. Most of the fields in each of the categories are identical or at least very similar, and it's better to have one common address format than three different ones.

Corporate addresses require a company name in addition to all the regular stuff. However, the contact person field isn't really necessary, since the customer name field can be used to hold that information.

One problem that didn't show up during the brainstorming session is that sometimes two lines are needed to describe a street address. This often happens in corporate addresses where there is a department name in addition to the company name and street address. You could either make address a repeating group and allow as many address lines as needed or you could create two separate elements with similar but different names. Since I believe that two lines are sufficient, I'm going to do the latter.

International addresses closely parallel U.S. addresses, except that only U.S. addresses use states and ZIP codes. This type of information is still needed, only it is known by different names. In Canada, for example, states are called provinces and ZIP codes are called postal codes. My solution for this issue is to use the same fields for both states and provinces and for both ZIP codes and postal codes and to handle the contents of the fields based on the value of the country field.

All of these fields, even ZIP code, contain string values. Since the ZIP code field will also contain postal codes from countries outside the United States, I have to allow for nonnumeric characters that some countries (such as Canada) use. I can (and should) make the default country the United States, since most of the orders will be placed by customers in the United States.

User ID and Password

While processing a customer's order, you need to know that the person on the other end of the connection is really the person who established the account. For this reason, you want a user ID and password associated with each customer. There are several approaches to choosing a user ID, but they all require that only the user ID must be unique to the customer.

The first and simplest approach is to use the value of customer name as a user ID. However, this approach is easy to discard since there will be at least two people in the country called J. Smith, and then you'll have to worry about uniquely identifying the correct J. Smith.

A better option would be to let the customer pick the user ID and then store it as a separate field in the database. This has the advantage of being user-friendly, but it has the side effect of allowing two or more users to pick the same user ID. For instance, assume that Chris wants to be known as "booklover" and Samantha also wants to be known as "booklover". Samantha may end up choosing "booklover1" and will probably occasionally forget the "1" at the end and try to log on as "booklover" and then get frustrated when it doesn't work.

However, my favorite option introduces another field that was forgotten in the brainstorming session: e-mail address. Since you can assume that the e-mail address is unique to an individual, this makes the perfect user ID. The user is not likely to forget it, and you should have the person's e-mail address anyway for confirming orders and announcing new books.

One problem associated with user IDs is that people often forget their passwords. When this happens, the user will either apply for a new customer account or need to contact someone to get his or her password changed. This often requires someone to receive the request and process it. However, sometimes all the user needs is a hint to remember his or her password. This hint is often meaningless to someone other than the person who entered the password in the first place. For instance, I might use the hint "Somewhere Near Japan" when using the password "oursong" since that is the name of first song played at my wedding.

All of these fields contain string values, and while I can't really verify an e-mail address or a password, I can verify that the password hint is not the same as the password. Some customers may choose to repeat the password, which could allow someone to try to guess a password by entering the value for the password hint. Your job is to make accessing the system easy for someone who has the proper access and as difficult as possible for those who don't.

Real Security Threats

Contrary to popular belief, most security breaches come not from a person running a mysterious program on a computer that attempts to break into your computer, but from a person with inside knowledge about your organization and its computers. You would be amazed at how many people willingly give out their passwords over the telephone.

It's very easy for someone to pose as technical support personnel and call a user to ask about any recent problems. Then the imposter asks the user for user ID and password to verify that they are correct.

While 9 out of 10 users might be smart enough to ask for identification or more information about the caller, this means that as many as 10 percent of your users might be willing to give out that information. This could spell disaster for your company. Instruct your customers that they should keep their passwords secret and never ever give them out. You also need to give the same lecture to your staff, since they have access to information from all of your customers.

In an application like this, your customers have to trust you. You need to show them you are serious about protecting their personal information. When users have to select a password, explain why choosing a good password is important and then allow them to make their own decision.

Credit Card and Billing Information

This is important, since the user has the option to enter credit card information once and the database will be used to hold it. This allows the customer to place an order without having to enter the credit card number again. The customer can call WebBooks.com and give a credit card number over the phone where it can't be intercepted, or the customer can send it via a secure Hypertext Transfer Protocol (HTTP) link to the Web server. In either case, normal orders are more secure since the customer doesn't need to send the credit card number each time.

However, knowing the credit card number is not sufficient. I need to know the type of credit card (i.e., MasterCard, Visa, Discover, American Express, etc.). Also, most credit card companies need the person's name on the card and the expiration date before a transaction can be completed. The cardholder's name is important since it may be different than the name of the person actually placing the order.

One of the brainstorming fields is billing address. This recognizes the possibility that some customers may want to send the books to one address and send the bill to another address. However, the address information here is really the billing address information. While this address will be used as the default shipping address, you can still allow the customer to supply a different shipping address while placing an order.

Along with this information, a few other fields are probably needed, such as for an invalid credit card flag and a tax-exempt license. These fields are used while processing an order to request new credit card information and to calculate sales tax properly.

When you look at these fields, all of the files except for the invalid credit card flag and tax-exempt license (which are Boolean) should be strings. While this is obvious for the credit card name and credit card type, it isn't so obvious for credit card number and expiration date. While these values are basically numeric, the number of digits and the different formatting rules suggest that storing these values as strings will be simpler in the long run.

Sales History and Customer Profile

This section deals with the remaining data elements from the brainstorming session. Probably the broadest data element is the sales history. Sales history is a vague term applied to the cumulative information that allows WebBooks.com to understand the buying patterns of a customer.

While this is a good idea, the most detailed data will come from the list of books that a customer has purchased over time. This information is really produced from the Order Processing Subsystem.

However, there are some fields that are related to the customer, such as the date the account was created and the date of the last purchase. These two dates could be used to determine an inactive customer. If the last purchase is more than a year old, you may want to delete the customer as inactive and delete them from the database. Likewise, if the customer never made a purchase since the account was created you might want to delete it from the database. Of course you might instead want to send the customer an e-mail message saying that nothing had been ordered from WebBooks.com for a while and enclose a discount coupon worth five dollars off the next order.

Another idea would be to allow the customer to track a list of books and book topics that might be of interest. Then as new books are acquired, the application would send an e-mail note to the customer announcing the arrival of a new book. The one problem with this issue is that the element isn't atomic, since you would like the customer to specify more than one book or topic. However, each topic keyword is essentially the same, so what you really want is a collection of topic keywords representing the topics the customer is interested in. Each individual keyword is really an element in a string array.

You might also want to keep a running total of purchases that a customer makes. This information might be helpful when talking to a customer about a problem. While all customers should be treated fairly, a customer who has spent a lot of money with WebBooks.com might warrant a special exception or two. Since this value contains money, the currency data type should be used.

Preferred shipping method and vendor sounds complex, but it really isn't. You can easily store this information in a single field, with values like FedEx Priority Overnight, UPS Ground, and USPS Priority Mail. This field contains a set of characters, so you can store it as a string.

Information such as sex, age, and education might be useful to know when analyzing buying patterns of groups of customers. However, I'm not going include this information in the database now. You can always add it in a future version of the application.

Final Data Elements

The brainstorming session generated 25 ideas for data elements. Reviewing them with an eye for creating atomic data elements yielded 23. I changed or refined many of these elements during this process. After analyzing the original 25 elements, I identified several new elements and added them to the list.

Table 4.1   Data Element Rules for the Customer Information Subsystem

Data Element	Data Type	Nulls Allowed?	Default Value	Other Edits
Customer name	String	No	—	None
Company name	String	Yes	—	None
Address1	String	No	—	None
Address2	String	Yes	—	None
City	String	No	—	None
State/Province	String	No	—	Check state name if country = "United States"
ZIP code/Postal code	String	Yes	—	Check value if country = "United States"
Country	String	No	"United States"	Must match list of specified countries
Telephone number	String	Yes	—	None
E-mail address	String	No	—	None
Password	String	No	—	None
Password hint	String	No	—	Must have different value than password
Credit card type	String	Yes	—	Must match list of specified credit card vendors
Credit card number	String	Yes	—	Required if credit card type is specified

Table 4.1   Data Element Rules for the Customer Information Subsystem *(continued)*

Data Element	Data Type	Nulls Allowed?	Default Value	Other Edits
Credit card name	String	Yes	—	Required if credit card type is specified
Expiration date	String	Yes	—	Required if credit card type is specified
Invalid credit card	Boolean	No	False	None
Tax-exempt status	Boolean	No	False	None
List of keywords	String array	Yes	—	None
Date account was created	Date	No	Current date	None
Date of last order	Date	No	Current date	None
Total value of all orders	Currency	No	0	None
Preferred shipping method	String	No	—	Must match list of specified shipping methods

Determining the Functions Needed

The general types of functions that are needed for the Customer Information Subsystem include updating and searching for customer information, saving the customer information as a comma separated value (CSV) file, and creating utilities to back-up and recover the data in the Customer Information Subsystem.

Types of Users

Different users will need different levels of access to various components and data elements in this subsystem. This is done to protect the confidentiality of some data items and to ensure that only the appropriate individual performs the specific task. The six basic types of users for this subsystem are:

- The customer ordering the books
- The clerk assisting customers via the telephone
- The supervisor who assists the clerks
- The manager who directs and plans activities
- The computer operator who performs routine functions
- The database administrator

The customer is allowed to enter, review, and change most of their own personal information at any time. However, the customer is not permitted to access or change another customer's information.

The clerk provides assistance (over the phone) to customers who are having problems with their order. The clerk will need to be able to access all of the information in a customer's record. However, some information (such as credit card information) may not be viewable.

The supervisor assists clerks with solving customer problems. The supervisor is permitted to view credit card information, in addition to having the same level of access that a clerk has.

The manager plans activities and performs general administrative tasks, such as preparing e-mail messages to customers advertising new books and data analysis.

The computer operator needs sufficient access to back up the database but doesn't need the ability to write any data and shouldn't be permitted to perform any other operations against the database.

The database administrator has complete access to any data element. This means that the database administrator can read and write any value. Another responsibility is that of restoring a database when a problem occurs.

Of course this is not a complete application, so keep in mind that the application must be easy to change. You'll update this subsystem later in the book to integrate it with the other subsystems. While it would be better to design the application all at the same time, that rarely happens in the real world, so learning how to build an easily updatable application is very important.

The Update Customer Information function must allow a user to retrieve a customer's information from the database and to update it. It must also allow a user to insert new customers and delete existing customers. All three of these processes are subject to validation checks and any other business rules. All classes of users except for operators will use this function.

The Search for Customer Information function must provide an easy way for a clerk or supervisor to find a particular customer in the database when trying to resolve a problem with that customer over the telephone. This function should be integrated with the function to update customer information, so again everyone except for operators will use this function.

Often managers will want to analyze data and create pie charts. While I don't fully understand the attraction of creating pie charts, someone once told me that managers only understood information when it was broken into three to five pie slices. Anything more complex than this, and they were unable to share it with other managers. Since the easiest way to create pie charts is using Microsoft Excel, exporting this data is a natural way to share the information. This is strictly a management function. If you can export a list of customers into a .CSV file, you can give it to a manager. That will keep them happy summarizing it and creating tons of pie charts to show to their peers.

These functions rely on standard database utilities to create database backup copies that can be restored in case of a problem. Restoring a database is not done easily, since it is possible that some information may be lost. However, if your server had a disk failure, it is better to lose some of your data than all of it. Likewise, if your application has a bug that corrupts your database, having a backup can be a lifesaver. Both operators and database administrators need to be able to perform backups, while only database administrators need to be able to recover a database.

Wrapping Up

In this chapter, you covered the process to determine the data elements that should be in the database. You assigned them data types and learned some data validation rules that should be imposed on each element.

You also identified the requirements that the Customer Information Subsystem must meet. It must be capable of:

- Updating customer information
- Adding a new customer
- Deleting a customer
- Searching for customer information
- Exporting a list of customers
- Building backup and recovery tools

These functions are still relatively open as to how best to implement them. However, whenever possible, you want to take advantage of the tools and facilities available in SQL Server and Visual Basic.

Also, security is a concern, both in terms of the data that you want to keep and the functions that you want to provide. At this stage of the project, the best you can do is to identify the types of users that may access the data and functions. I'll address how to turn this information into security rules later in the project.

If you participated in the brainstorming session and came up with some additional data elements, hold onto them and add them to the database tables as you create them in the next chapter. If possible, try to involve some friends or co-workers to get the real feel of how one of these sessions actually works. The key to making a brainstorming session work is that no matter how stupid you may think the idea is, add it to the list. Sometimes, the best ideas arise from people who originally thought they were stupid.

CHAPTER 5

Designing the Customer Information Subsystem

In this chapter, you will design and build the database using the tools introduced in Chapter 2.

ON THE CD

The complete source code for these functions is included on the CD-ROM. Check the \HOSQLSrver7\Chapt05\cis directory for the SQL statements necessary to turn an empty database into the CIS database.

Designing the Database

Knowing which data elements you need to include in the database is half the battle. Organizing them is the other half.

Relational Database Concepts

A relational database is a database that appears to the user as simply a collection of tables, where each table consists of a series of columns or fields across the top and a series of rows or records down the side. The underlying data structure used to hold the data is totally invisible to the user.

Since a table is essentially a sequential set of rows, finding a particular row or rows means that you have to search the entire table for the value you want. An index is a structure that knows where to find specific values for a set of columns. The set of columns is known as a key. A primary key is defined in a way that uniquely identifies a row in the table. A secondary key is any other key in the table. It need not uniquely identify any rows. A foreign key is a key in a table that is also a primary key in another table. A key that contains more than one column is known as a composite key.

A field is defined to be atomic if it can't be broken into smaller pieces. For instance, a field called Name, which consists of three parts (Name.First, Name.Middle, and Name.Last), is not atomic because it can be broken into smaller pieces. A field that contains an unstructured name value would be atomic because there is no structure to the field.

A field contains a repeating group when there is more than one instance of the field. Thus any field that is an array or a collection is a repeating group.

A field is said to depend on another field when there is only one possible value of the second field for a specific value of the first field. Confused? Consider the following: you have a table with name and social security number. Since the social security number is unique for each individual and each individual has only one name, the name field is dependent on the social security number. Note that the reverse isn't true, since it is possible to have more than one social security number for a given name (two individuals might have the same name).

Normalization

Normalization is a way to classify a database structure. From a theoretical viewpoint, the more normalized your database is, the better. There are four basic types of database structures:

- **Unnormalized.** No rules are imposed on the database structure.

- **First normal form.** Each field must be atomic. Repeating groups and composite fields are not permitted.

- **Second normal form.** Every non-key field must depend on the entire primary key. A field must not depend on only part of a composite primary key. The database must also be in first normal form.

- **Third normal form.** A non-key field can't depend on another non-key field. The database must also be in second normal form.

Note	**Relational database theory also describes a fourth normal form, a fifth normal form, and a Boyce/Codd normal form.**

You can't build an unnormalized relational database, since repeating groups and composite fields are not permitted. (Of course there are ways around even these restrictions when you use SQL Server 7, as you'll see later in this chapter.) However, the most important thing to understand is that, as you move up the normalization ladder, the database's large tables become broken down into more and more small tables. This is done in the name of reducing data duplication.

For example, in a truly normalized database, you wouldn't store city and state information with someone's address, since you can get this information from the person's ZIP code. You would add another table to your database (containing city, state, and ZIP code) to keep this information.

So while database theory says this is good, practical experience has shown that the more normalized a database is, the slower it performs, because the database server has to access more tables to retrieve the data.

Entity/Relationship Modeling

E/R modeling in its simplest form is a way of describing the relationship between entities. An entity is a thing that can be uniquely identified, such as a customer, a book, an order, etc. Associated with the entity is a set of attributes, which help to describe the entity. Each customer has a name and an address. Each book has a title and an author. An order has

Database Performance

Believe it or not, having a faster CPU will not necessarily make your database server faster. A database server is very I/O intensive. Anything that allows the database to retrieve data faster from disk will help the server.

Adding memory to your server allows the database server to cache more data in memory. After all, retrieving data from memory is much faster than retrieving it from disk. This is the biggest change you can make to improve database performance, which is why Microsoft has released a modified version of Windows NT 4.0 Server, called the Enterprise Edition. It allows SQL Server to address 3GB of memory rather than the normal NT limit of 2GB.

After adding memory to your system, using SCSI disk drives is important. They not only allow you to manage up to 15 disk drives on a single card, but they also support concurrent operations on each drive. Thus you can have multiple disk drives performing seeks, while others are transferring data. SCSI-III can transfer data faster than SCSI-II or SCSI-I and should be used for best performance.

Finally, using faster disk drives themselves will also improve performance. Disks that spin at 7,200 revolutions per minute (rpm) will transfer data faster than those that spin at 5,400 rpm, although two 5,400-rpm disks will probably perform better than one 7,200-rpm disk (assuming that you can spread the activity evenly between the disks).

an order number and a date ordered. Relationships are formed between two entities, such as customers and orders, where a customer places an order or an order contains a list of books.

This is illustrated in Figure 5-1. The entities are drawn as rectangles. Each of the entity's attributes is drawn as an ellipse with a line linking the entity to the attribute. The relationships are diamonds with lines linking them to the related entities. Combining the names of the two entities forms the relationship's name. Obviously this is a relatively simple drawing, since each entity has only two attributes and there are only three entities.

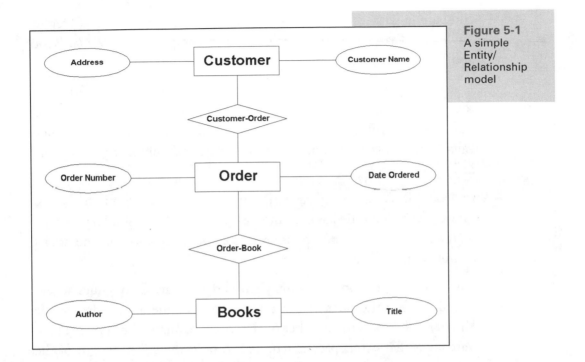

Figure 5-1
A simple
Entity/
Relationship
model

Designing the Customer Information Subsystem Database

Now use the relational database concepts and E/R modeling to design the Customer Information Subsystem database. The first step is to determine the entities that are needed. The second step is to review the data elements created in Chapter 4 and translate them into attributes that can be used with a SQL Server database. The third step is to construct the database using Visual Basic's Database Designer tools from Chapter 2. And the last step is to add some triggers and indexes to help you when it comes time to write the programs.

The Customer Information Subsystem Attributes

In Chapter 4, you assigned each data element a Visual Basic data type. However, SQL Server doesn't directly support Visual Basic data types. You have to choose the most appropriate SQL Server data type that is compatible with the Visual Basic data type you want to use (refer to Table 1-2, Features of SQL Server 7, for a comparison of Visual Basic and SQL Server data types).

I used four different data types—String, Boolean, Date, and Currency—when I compiled that list. Of the four, three are real easy to pick. Date becomes a **Datetime** value, Currency becomes a **Money** value, and Boolean becomes a **Bit**. The only real complications are the Strings.

In Visual Basic, a **String** can hold up to about two billion characters. However, that's a little large for most SQL Server databases. So you need to review each field and choose a reasonable size based on the actual contents of the data.

You also need to choose between **Char** and **Varchar**. **Char** values always contain a fixed number of characters, even if none are needed, while **Varchar** only stores the number of characters required. The downside to **Varchar** is that extra space is required to hold the actual length of the data. So for very small strings and strings that will always be the same length, **Char** is more efficient than **Varchar**. In this database, I'll use **Varchar** for the most part, since it is more efficient than using **Char**. In the few cases where **Char** might be more efficient, as for state and ZIP codes, I'll still use **Varchar,** since this will give me greater flexibility when dealing with foreign addresses.

Now you need to determine the maximum size value you should use. **Varchar** can hold up to 8,000 characters, but since the average name is smaller than that, you might want to determine a better value. You might wonder why this is important, since changing the maximum size from 80 to 8,000 doesn't really occupy any more space. The answer is that many tools, such as the Query Analyzer, will build their displays to hold the maximum size. I don't know about you, but scrolling through 7,985 blanks after the end of my name is not my idea of fun.

While a size of 40 characters is common for Name and Address fields, you should leave a little more room, so for most fields, you should allow 64 characters. You can make a few of the other fields a little smaller, but only if you're certain that they won't get that large.

In the Days of Old

Most databases in existence today allow 40 characters for a Name or an Address field. This is because most mailing labels are four inches wide. In the days before laser printers, most printers would print at 10 characters per inch, hence the 40 characters. Many organizations would even choose sizes for city, state, and ZIP code so that they could also be printed in a single 40-character line.

The Customer Information Subsystem Entities

Looking at Table 4-1 in the last chapter, you can see that I have identified 23 data elements, but only one entity, namely the customer. Since all the data elements are dependent on the customer entity, you need only a single table to hold all of this information.

However, this ignores the issue about keywords being a string array. This is really a repeating group. There are a couple different approaches to handling repeating groups. You can split the address field into two separate fields. However, this means that you have to allow space for each possible keyword, which wastes a lot of space.

A second option would be to store the keywords in a single string, with a separator between each keyword. This option probably makes the most sense from an efficiency point of view, but it causes problems when you're trying to link to other tables.

The classic solution is to create a separate keyword table using the primary key from the Customers table as one column and the keyword value as the second column. This has the advantage of storing lots of keywords. However, most users are probably not going to store that many keywords.

Of these three options, I'm going to implement the second option. While this is not as clean as using a separate keyword table, it will reduce the complexity of the database a little bit, which is probably a good idea, as you'll see in a moment.

I want to make a few changes in the fields for country, credit card type, and preferred shipping method. Each of these fields has a relatively small set of values, yet each has relatively long strings containing the information. What I will do with each of these fields is create a new field called CountryCode, CreditCardCode, and PreferredShippingCode and use a **Smallint** value. Then I'll create another table that I'll use to translate these values from the **Smallint** value to a **Varchar**(64) value. While this causes some extra work, it's actually not as bad as it seems.

I also want to introduce another entity that holds information about states and provinces. This entity is used primarily to verify that the information entered for the state value is valid. Since the value of state depends on the value of the country, I need to include the country code as well. Since the U.S. Postal Service prefers to use a two-character abbreviation for a state, I'll additionally include that information and also use it as part of the edit check.

Finally, I want to introduce another new data element. This is because there is a small problem resulting from my decision to use the e-mail address. Because it's the primary key for the customer entity, it's likely to be a foreign key in other tables. And since this field can reach up to 64 characters and e-mail addresses are rarely shorter than 15 to 20 characters, I'm going to add one more field, which I'll call customer ID. This field will be defined to have a type of **Identity**, which means that SQL Server will automatically increment this value when the row is inserted into the table.

The Final Database Design

All this work results in a total of five entities as shown in the E/R diagram in Figure 5-2. They are Customers (see Table 5-1), CountryCodes (see Table 5-2), CreditCardCodes (see Table 5-3), ShippingMethod-Codes (see Table 5-4), and StateCodes (see Table 5-5).

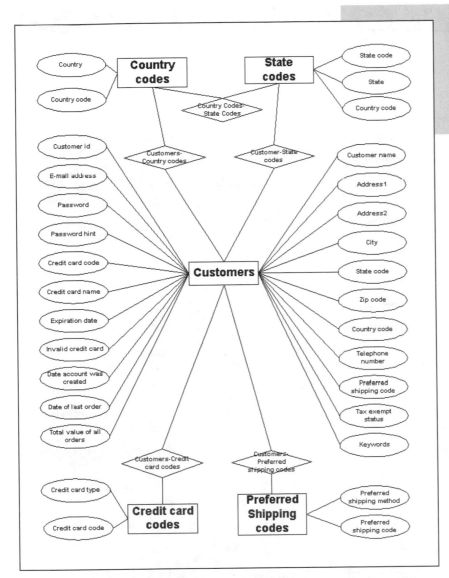

Figure 5-2
An Entity/
Relationship
diagram for
the Customer
Information
Subsystem
database

Table 5-1 Attributes of the Customers Entity

Data Element	Data Type	Nulls Allowed?	Default Value	Other Edits
Customer ID	**Int**	No	—	Starting value of 10,000 also primary key
Customer name	**Varchar**(64)	No	—	None

Table 5-1   Attributes of the Customers Entity *(continued)*

Data Element	Data Type	Nulls Allowed?	Default Value	Other Edits
Company name	**Varchar**(64)	Yes	—	None
Address1	**Varchar**(64)	No	—	None
Address2	**Varchar**(64)	Yes	—	None
City	**Varchar**(64)	No	—	None
State	**Varchar**(64)	No	—	Check value if country code = 1 ("United States")
ZIP code	**Varchar**(16)	Yes	—	Check value if country code = 1 ("United States")
Country code	**Smallint**	No	0	Link to countries
Telephone number	**Varchar**(24)	Yes	—	None
E-mail address	**Varchar**(64)	No	—	None
Password	**Varchar**(16)	No	—	None
Password hint	**Varchar**(64)	No	—	Must have different value than password
Credit card code	**Smallint**	Yes	—	Link to credit card codes
Credit card number	**Varchar**(24)	Yes	—	Required if credit card type is specified
Credit card name	**Varchar**(64)	Yes	—	Required if credit card type is specified
Expiration date	**Varchar**(12)	Yes	—	Required if credit card type is specified
Invalid credit card	**Bit**	No	False	None
Tax-exempt status	**Bit**	No	False	None
Keyword list	**Varchar**(256)	Yes	—	None
Date account was created	**Datetime**	No	Current date	None
Date of last order	**Datetime**	No	Current date	None
Total value of all orders	**Money**	No	0	None
Preferred shipping code	**Smallint**	No	0	Link to preferred shipping methods

Table 5-2 Attributes of the CountryCodes Entity

Data Element	Data Type	Nulls Allowed?	Default Value	Other Edits
Country code	**Smallint**	No	—	Primary key
Country	**Varchar**(64)	No	—	None

Table 5-3 Attributes of the CreditCardCodes Entity

Data Element	Data Type	Nulls Allowed?	Default Value	Other Edits
Credit card code	**Smallint**	No	—	Primary key
Credit card type	**Varchar**(64)	No	—	None

Table 5-4 Attributes of the PreferredShippingCodes Entity

Data Element	Data Type	Nulls Allowed?	Default Value	Other Edits
Preferred shipping code	**Smallint**	No	—	Primary key
Preferred shipping method	**Varchar**(64)	No	—	None

Table 5-5 Attributes of the StateCodes Entity

Data Element	Data Type	Nulls Allowed?	Default Value	Other Edits
Country code	**Smallint**	No	—	Primary key
State code	**Char**(2)	No	—	Primary key
State	**Varchar**(64)	No	—	None

Building the Database

Now it's time to build the actual database. To begin, you're going to use the SQL Server Enterprise Manager to create the database and set up the necessary permissions. However, I'm not going to bother using the Create Database Wizard, which I used in Chapter 1, though you should feel free to use the wizard if you want.

1. Select Start, Programs, Microsoft SQL Server 7.0, Enterprise Manager to run the SQL Server Enterprise Manager.

2. Double-click on the database server that you want to use.

3. Right-click on Databases and select New Database from the pop-up menu.

4. Fill in CIS for the name of the database and enter 10 megabytes as the initial size (see Figure 5-3).

5. Review the settings for Transaction Log. The default values are fine for this database.

6. Press OK to create the database.

Figure 5-3
Enter the information to create the Customer Information System database.

Creating the Tables

After creating the blank database, create the tables using the information from Tables 5-1 through 5-5. Starting with the Customer table, do the following:

1. Double-click on Databases to show the list of databases available on the server.

2. Expand the CIS node by double-clicking on it (see Figure 5.4) to see the list of objects stored in the CIS database.

3. Right-click on Tables and select New Table from the pop-up menu.

Tip

Once you've created at least part of the table, you can go back and edit your table values by right-clicking on Tables and selecting Design Table from the pop-up menu. The only difference between both functions is that when you create a new table, you have to specify the table name before the table window is shown.

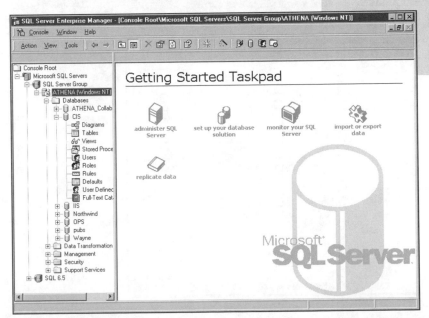

Figure 5-4
Expand the CIS node by double-clicking on it.

4. Enter "Customers" as the table name and press OK.

Some of the entities I've listed above contain spaces. While SQL Server allows you to use spaces in the name of database objects, I prefer to squeeze them out and capitalize the first letter of each word. If you choose to leave them in, you'll need to refer to them by surrounding the objects with square brackets when you write SQL queries, such as **Select * From [CountryCodes]** instead of **Select * From** CountryCodes. I also do the same thing with hyphenated fields.

5. Fill in the form with the appropriate information from Table 5-1 (see Figure 5-5).

If you want a column's default value to be the current date and time, specify the value **getdate()** as Default.

Column Name	Datatype	Length	Precision	Scale	Allow Nulls	Default Value	Identity	Identity Seed	Identity Increment	Is RowGuid
CustomerId	int	4	10	0			✓	10000	1	
CustomerName	varchar	64	0	0						
CompanyName	varchar	64	0	0	✓					
Address1	varchar	64	0	0						
Address2	varchar	64	0	0	✓					
City	varchar	64	0	0						
State	varchar	64	0	0						
ZipCode	varchar	16	0	0	✓					
CountryCode	smallint	2	5	0		(0)				
TelephoneNumber	varchar	24	0	0	✓					
EmailAddress	varchar	64	0	0						
Password	varchar	16	0	0						
PasswordHint	varchar	64	0	0						
CreditCardCode	smallint	2	5	0		(0)				
CreditCardNumber	varchar	24	0	0	✓					
CreditCardName	varchar	64	0	0	✓					
ExpirationDate	varchar	12	0	0	✓					
InvalidCreditCard	bit	1	0	0		(0)				
TaxExemptStatus	bit	1	0	0		(0)				
DateAccountCreated	datetime	8	0	0		(getdate())				
DateLastOrder	datetime	8	0	0		(getdate())				
TotalOrderValue	money	8	19	4		(0)				
PreferredShippingCod	smallint	2	5	0		(0)				
KeywordList	varchar	256	0	0	✓					

SQL Server Enterprise Manager - [2:Design Table 'Customers']
Console Window Help

Figure 5-5
Enter the information for the new table.

6. To set the primary key for the Customers table, right-click on CustomerId and choose Set Primary Key from the pop-up menu. You can set the primary key for the other tables the same way.

> **Note**
>
> **You can't use CountryCode or StateCode in the StateCodes table because neither value is guaranteed to be unique. However, together they are unique and can be used as the primary key.**

7. Press the Save toolbar button to create the table and close the window. After creating the Customers table, you need to create the CountryCodes, CreditCardCodes, PreferredShippingCodes and StateCodes using the same instructions.

Building the Triggers

I want to make sure that the value of State is valid. Normally I would use a foreign key; however, the name of the state depends also on the value of CountryCode. So to do this, I will build a trigger that will check the State and StateCode columns of the StateCodes table only if the value of CountryCode is zero.

The SQL statement in Listing 5-1 is used to ensure that the value of only valid state information can be inserted or updated in the Customers table.

Listing 5-1

```
Create Trigger StateCodeTrigger
    On dbo.Customers
    For Insert, Update

As

Declare @CountryCode as Smallint
Select @CountryCode = Inserted.CountryCode From Inserted

If @CountryCode = 1
    Begin
```

```
If Not Exists( Select *
    From StateCodes, Inserted
    Where StateCodes.StateCode = Inserted.State
        Or StateCodes.State = Inserted.State)
RaiseError('Invalid value for State, when Country = "United
➥States".',16,1)
    End
```

Note that I use a table called Inserted. This is a special table that is used in a trigger to hold the values that are about to be inserted or updated in a table. You can only use a **Select** statement to access it. There is a corresponding table called Deleted that holds the rows that will be deleted from a table. I also use the **RaiseError** statement to let the user know when an error has occurred.

To create a trigger, follow these steps:

1. Right-click on the Customers table and choose All Tasks, Manage Triggers (see Figure 5-6). This will display the Trigger Properties window with a skeleton trigger already listed.

2. Type in the trigger statement shown in Listing 5-1.

3. Press Check Syntax to verify that the statement is correct.

4. Press Apply to create the trigger.

5. Press OK to leave the Trigger Properties window.

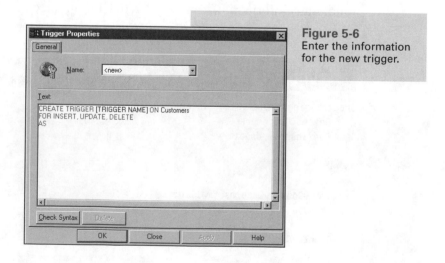

Figure 5-6
Enter the information for the new trigger.

Creating Check Constraints

In keeping with the philosophy of letting the database handle as much of the data verification as possible, I want to check to see if the values in the remaining fields requiring edits are legal. This is done by using check constraints. There are two types of check constraints: those that apply to a single column and those that apply to the entire table.

In the Customers table, I want to make sure that the value in Password and PasswordHint are different. This is a very easy expression and is shown in Listing 5-2. I also need to verify that, if a credit card type is specified, the rest of the credit card information is supplied. This expression is a little bit more complex and is shown in Listing 5-3.

Listing 5-2

```
([Password] <> [PasswordHint])
```

Listing 5-3

```
([CreditCardCode] = 0 Or ((not([CreditCardNumber] Is Null))) And
((Not(((Not([ExpirationDate] Is Null))))))
```

To create a check constraint, follow these steps:

1. From the Enterprise Manager's list of tables in the CIS database, right-click on the Customers table and select Design Table.

2. Once in the Design Table window, right-click anywhere on the table and choose Properties. Then select the Tables tab.

3. Press the New button in the CHECK Constraints for Table and Columns frame (see Figure 5-7).

4. Enter the check condition (as shown in Listing 5-2) into the Constraint Expression text box.

5. Type in a unique name for the constraint in Constraint Name.

6. Repeat this process to enter the constraint shown in Listing 5-3.

7. Close the window to return to the Design Table window. Press the Save button to make the changes to the database.

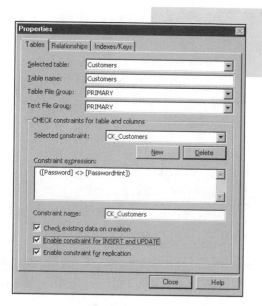

Figure 5-7
Enter the information
for the new trigger.

Creating Indexes

In a relational database, indexes are used to improve performance. They allow the database server to quickly identify a subset of a table without reading every record in the table. However, indexes come with a price. Every time you add a new row into a table, you have to update all the indexes associated with the table. Whenever you update a column that is used in an index, you have to update the index. So while it might seem reasonable to index every field in a table, you'll find that the cost of updating those indexes will become impractical.

Tip

Though the above discussion about indexes is true, there is an underlying assumption that may not be true. While nearly all databases are updated continually, some databases are not. These databases usually hold "frozen" data, like historical data or a translation code table that doesn't change on a daily basis. In these cases having lots of indexes may significantly improve the database's performance.

In the Customer Information Subsystem, I need to provide an index to the EmailAddress in the Customers table, since the customer will be using his or her e-mail address as user ID. This index should also ensure that the field will be unique, since only one customer in the table can have a particular value for EmailAddress. I also should provide an index on the State field of the StateCodes table to help process the trigger I created earlier. This means that an index for both State and StateCode would be very useful.

To create an index for EmailAddress, follow these steps:

1. From the Enterprise Manager's list of tables in the CIS database, right-click on the Customers table and select Design Table.

2. Once in the Design Table window, right-click anywhere on the table and choose Properties. Then select the Indexes/Keys tab.

3. Press the New button to create a new index (see Figure 5-8).

Note   **Specifying a primary key automatically creates an index on the field or fields that make up the primary key.**

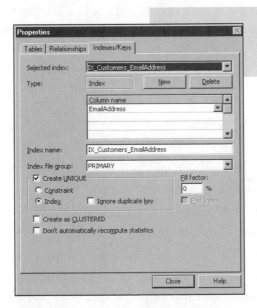

Figure 5-8
Enter the information
for the new index.

4. Select the column name or names that you want to include in the index. In this case select EmailAddress.

5. Type in a unique name for the index name.

6. Since you want the EmailAddress field to contain unique data, select the Create UNIQUE check box and check the Index option.

7. You would repeat this process to create any other indexes that are required for this table. In this case you do not need any more.

8. Close the window to return to the Design Table window. Press the Save button to make the changes to the database. Now follow these steps to create an index on the State field of the StateCodes table.

Tip   You don't have to specify all the indexes at design time. You can use SQL Server's Index Tuning Wizard to help you review your current indexes and recommend changes.

Create the Database Diagram

After creating all the database objects, it is useful to see the overall picture. To do this, use the Database Diagram facility. To create a diagram of this database, follow these steps:

1. From the Enterprise Manager's list of databases, select the CIS database, right-click on the Database Diagrams, and select New Database Diagram. This will start the Create Diagram Wizard.

2. Press Next to begin the process.

3. Select all the available tables in the database (see Figure 5-9) and press Next.

4. Review the tables you selected and press Finish. The wizard will perform a few tasks and return the diagram shown in Figure 5-10.

5. Review and rearrange the information if you want. Then press the Save button to save the diagram to the database or close the Diagram window. You will be prompted for a name of the diagram.

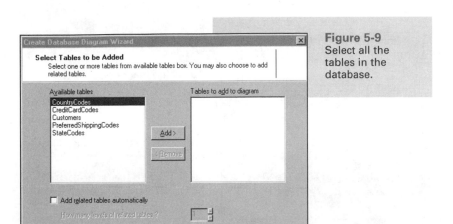

Figure 5-9
Select all the
tables in the
database.

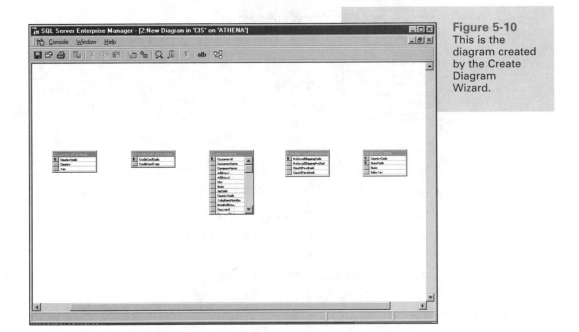

Figure 5-10
This is the
diagram created
by the Create
Diagram
Wizard.

Add Foreign Keys

Now that you have a database diagram, you need to add the foreign key
information to the Customers table to link it to the CountryCodes,
CreditCardCodes, and PreferredShippingCodes tables. Create links
between the tables on the database diagram you just completed.

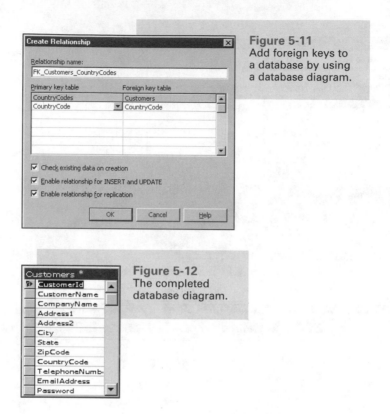

Figure 5-11
Add foreign keys to a database by using a database diagram.

Figure 5-12
The completed database diagram.

1. Choose the primary key value in the linked table and drag the cursor to the corresponding column in the Customers table.

2. The dialog box shown in Figure 5-11 will be shown. Verify that the information is correct and press OK. Repeat this process for all three linked tables. When you're finished, the database diagram will look like the one shown in Figure 5-12.

Save the Database Structure

The Enterprise Manager provides many tools and wizards that create database objects. You can also use the Query Analyzer to create the same objects using SQL statements. The Enterprise Manager will even create the SQL statements you would use to create the database using the Query Analyzer. It's a good practice to keep a backup copy of these statements just in case you need to recreate the database from scratch.

ON THE

CD

You don't need to save the SQL statements that you used to build the database because you can find the file on the CD-ROM as **\HOSQLSrver7\Chapt05\cis\cis.sql**. However, it's good practice for you to always keep a copy of the SQL statements used to build the database. As you design a database, it's easy to accidentally delete several hours' worth of work. Doing a backup will make it easy to recover your database structures.

To create SQL statements for the objects in the database, follow these steps:

1. From the Enterprise Manager's list of databases, right-click on the CIS database node and select All Tasks, Generate SQL Scripts. This displays the Generate SQL Scripts dialog box (see Figure 5-13).

2. On the General tab of the Generate SQL Scripts dialog box, choose Script All Objects. Checking this box will automatically select all the other objects on the form.

3. On the Formatting tab, select the Generate the CREATE <object> command for each object and the Generate the DROP <object> command for each object. While you don't really need to check the Generate Scripts for All Dependent Objects check

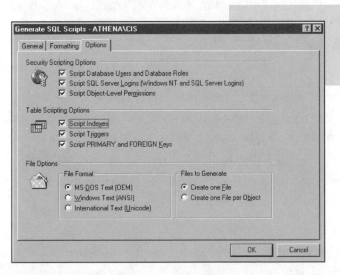

Figure 5-13
Choose options in the Generate SQL Scripts dialog box.

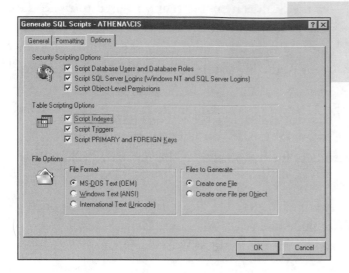

Figure 5-14
Choose more options in
the Generate SQL
Scripts dialog box.

box for this particular database, it's a good idea to check it, just
to make sure that any other objects will also be captured.

4. On the Options tab, check all the boxes under Security Scripting
Options and Table Scripting Options. Also select MS-<u>D</u>OS Text
(OEM) as the File Format (see Figure 5-14).

Tip

**Usually when a Windows application gives you the choice of
saving a file in either Windows Text (ANSI) or MS-DOS Text
(OEM), you should select MS-DOS. This guarantees that you
will be able to read your file using any editor you choose.**

5. After selecting all the options, press OK to create the script. A
Save <u>A</u>s dialog box appears. Choose the file name and directory
where the SQL statements should be stored and press <u>S</u>ave.

6. A progress bar appears. This tracks the progress of the SQL
statement generator. A message box appears when all the SQL
script has been finished.

To create the database again, follow these steps:

1. Use the SQL Enterprise Manager to delete and re-create the
database (as discussed above). If you choose, you can skip this

step and everything will probably be okay, but the only way to guarantee that everything has been reset is to delete the database. That way, you can be sure that no other objects remain that could possibly cause you problems later.

Caution

> **Rerunning this SQL script will delete all of your data, even if you don't delete the database. If you need to restore your data after running the script, you need to save it before you start. A simple backup of your data won't be useful, since the database structures are also restored. You should use the Data Transformation Services (DTS) utility (Chapter 6).**

2. Select Start, Programs, Microsoft SQL Server 7.0, Query Analyzer to run the Query Analyzer utility.

3. Specify the name of the database server, your login ID, and your password to connect to the database server.

4. Select File, Open, and choose the file with your script.

5. Select Query, Execute Query to run the script (see Figure 5-15).

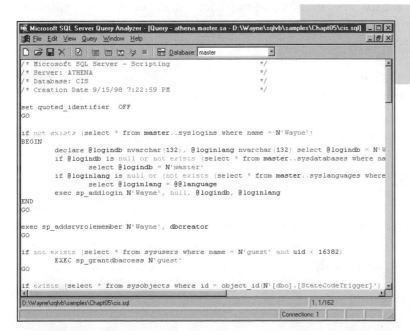

Figure 5-15
Watch the Query Analyzer rebuild your database.

Designing the Functions Needed

Now you need to create functions to enter information into the tables. In addition, there needs to be a general-purpose customer utility that allows someone to view customer information as well as to add new customers and update existing customers.

The Customer Information Form

After looking at the functional requirements, I decided that the following functions should be implemented in a single program:

- Adding a new customer
- Deleting an existing customer
- Updating an existing customer
- Searching for customer information

Any form that I use to add a new customer, to update an existing customer, or to search for a customer will be nearly identical. All the fields described in Table 5.1 need to be displayed. Also, the search is needed for both the update function and the delete function. After all, you have to find the customer before you can update or delete them.

Since this tool is designed for use by clerks, supervisors, and others at WebBooks.com, I focused on function rather than style. A clerk would rather have all the necessary information on a single form than have a fancy format that spreads information over several different forms. So with that in mind, I designed the form shown in Figure 5-16.

Customer Export Function

Often it is necessary to save the contents of a database table into a file. SQL Server makes this task easy using the Data Transformation Services tool. This tool allows you to move data from one format to another, quickly and easily, with little or no programming required. It is also available as an object that can be referenced from a Visual Basic program, so you can build your own user interface that even a manager can use.

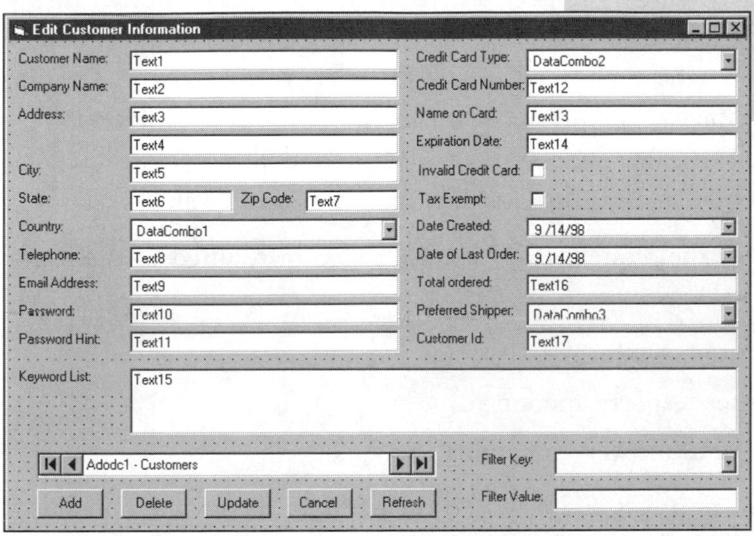

Figure 5-16
This is my customer information form.

Backup and Recovery Functions

It's important to back up your database on a regular basis. SQL Server supplies standard utilities to perform this function. You can back up your database to any media. Ideally, you should back up the database to some sort of tape drive so the backup can be safely stored and won't get destroyed if your server crashes. However, for function, I'm just going to back up the database to a file on the server and assume that the backup files are copied to tape by the server's normal backup process. This allows me to take advantage of SQL Server's facility (SQL Server Agent) that will let me schedule the execution of this function at any time for unattended operation.

Wrapping Up

Entity/Relationship modeling is a complex science with lots of people spending time researching new ways to make your life easier. E/R modeling begins by identifying the entities associated with your application and then determining their relationships. Finally you use this information to build an E/R model, which in turn is used to design your database.

Using E/R modeling, I designed a database to hold the Customer Information Subsystem. It contains five tables. The primary table is the Customers table, where all the customer's information is stored. Four additional tables—CountryCodes, CreditCardCodes, PreferredShippingCodes, and StateCodes—hold information that can be used to translate coded values in the Customers table into text values.

An analysis of the requirements of the subsystem resulted in the functions listed below:

- The customer information form
- Customers export function
- Backup and recovery functions

The first function will be implemented in Visual Basic. The remaining functions will use facilities built into SQL Server: the Data Transformation Services and the Backup and Recovery Services. I'll use the SQL Server Agent to launch the Backup process periodically to ensure that I can recover my data.

One thing that I didn't do in this design was to take advantage of ZIP code data available from the U.S. Postal Service (http://www.usps.gov). You can get a file containing all the zip codes in the country, with the city name and two-character state abbreviation. This means that, in a program where you have to enter lots of addresses, you only need to type in a five-digit zip code for each—the computer then searches a table using the ZIP code to get the values for city and state. The Postal Service also makes available the complete nine-digit zip code data, which will help you save money on postage if you do a lot of bulk mailing.

If you determined some additional data elements in the previous chapter, feel free to add them to the current tables. Just remember to allow **Null** values for each field, since the rest of the programs in this book don't know that they exist.

CHAPTER 6

Building the Customer Information Subsystem

Now that the database has been designed and the necessary functions are identified, it's time to begin building the programs for the Customer Information Subsystem. There are three functions to create for this subsystem:

- The customer information form
- Customer's export function
- Backup and recovery functions

ON THE CD

The complete source code for these functions is included on the CD-ROM. Check the \HOSQLSrver7\Chapt06 directory.

- **Custinf** contains the Customer Information program.
- **Export** contains an Excel worksheet containing data extracted from the database.

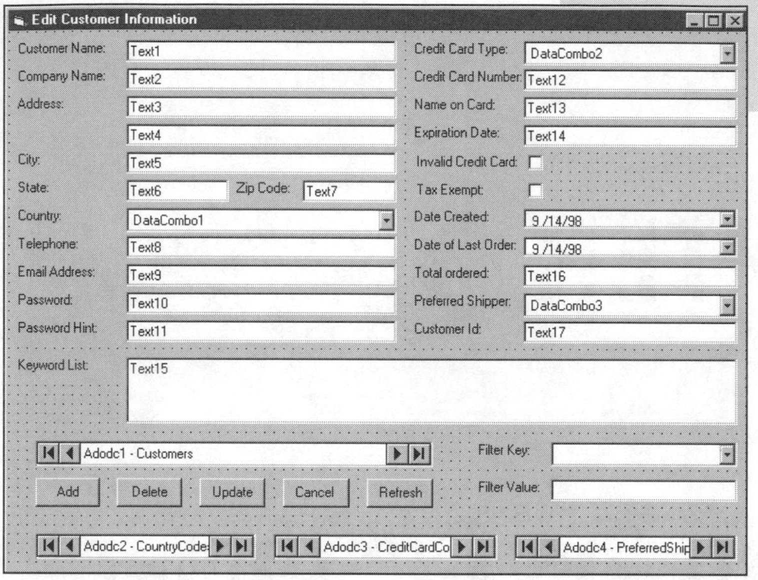

Figure 6-1
Build the Customer
Information Form.

The Customer Information Form

The Customer Information Form is a complex form that displays all the information about a customer, using text box, data combo, and date time picker controls. There are four ADO data controls that provide the link between the database and the fields. Five command buttons, a combo box, and a normal text box are used at the bottom of the form to provide functions that are not native to the ADO data controls (see Figure 6-1).

Rather than focus on the details of laying out a form like this, focus on how to build the program. Configure the ADO data control to talk to the database, bind the other controls to the ADO data controls, and add some code to perform a few functions that aren't included in the ADO data control.

Adding the Tools to the Toolbox

After starting a new Visual Basic Standard EXE program, I added some standard controls to this program. Select the Components dialog box (from the menu, choose Project, Components) and add the following controls:

- Microsoft ADO Data Control 6.0 (OLEDB)
- Microsoft DataGrid Control 6.0 (OLEDB)
- Microsoft DataList Controls 6.0 (OLEDB)
- Microsoft DataRepeater Control 6.0 (OLEDB)
- Microsoft Windows Common Controls—6.0
- Microsoft Windows Common Controls—2 6.0
- Microsoft Windows Common Controls—3 6.0

The DBList and DBCombo controls are called Microsoft Data Bound List Controls in the Components window, while the DataList and the DataCombo control can be found as the Microsoft DataList Controls. Make sure that you select Microsoft DataList Controls in order to get the ADO version of these controls.

I didn't use all of these controls in this program, but it's a good idea to include them in all of your database programs. Visual Basic 6 is smart enough not to include references to unused controls, so you don't have

I Haven't Written a COBOL Program in Years

Before I started writing full-time, I was responsible for one of those dinosaurs called a mainframe, which supported more than a thousand users logged in at one time. On that machine the language of choice was COBOL, but building a COBOL program from scratch was always time-consuming. Dumb little problems often took hours to find and fix. So, I got in the habit of taking the last COBOL program I wrote and modifying it to do what I wanted. This idea easily translates to Visual Basic. Therefore, if you're going to write multiple database programs, you should build one with everything you need and simply make a copy of it the next time you need to write a program.

to worry about extra overhead. And you just might find them convenient to have around if you modify any of your programs later.

Configuring the ADO Data Control

The key component of this program is the **ADO Data Control**. This control connects the program to the database server using an OLE-DB interface. The key to using this control is to set the properties properly. So by right-clicking on the **ADODC1** control and selecting ADODC Properties from the pop-up menu, you will display the control's Property Pages (see Figure 6-2).

There are two basic sets of properties that are important for the ADO data control. The first is the Source of Connection found on the General tab of the ADO data control's Property Pages. This contains information that will grant you access to the database server. The other is the RecordSource information located on the RecordSource tab. This information is used to specify which data should be retrieved from the database server.

Creating a Data Link File

On the General tab, you specify whether you want to use a data link file, an ODBC data source, or a connection string to connect to the database server. Forget about using the ODBC data source, since you want to use an OLE-DB data source, which is not the same thing. While you can use a connection string, it's not really advisable, since the connection information (including login ID and password) is hard-coded in your

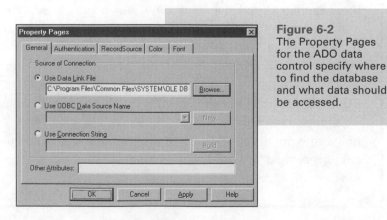

Figure 6-2
The Property Pages for the ADO data control specify where to find the database and what data should be accessed.

program and isn't easily changed. This leaves data link files as the only viable option.

Basically, the only difference between a data link file and a connection string is that the contents of the connection string are included in the object code of your program while the contents of the data link file are stored outside your program as a disk file. The same information is included in both.

To create a data link file, follow these steps:

1. Select Use Data Link File on the General tab of the ADO data control's Property Pages and press Browse. This displays the Select Data Link File dialog box (see Figure 6-3).

2. If you don't have an existing file that meets your needs, you should right-click inside the file list area and select New, Microsoft Data Link from the pop-up menu. Then change the name to something more meaningful, such as "AthenaCIS" (the CIS database on the Athena database server). This creates an empty data link file.

3. Right-click on the file you want to use and select Properties from the pop-up menu. This displays the Properties dialog box for the file.

4. On the Provider tab, select the Microsoft OLE-DB Provider for

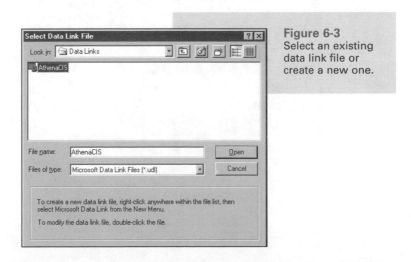

Figure 6-3
Select an existing data link file or create a new one.

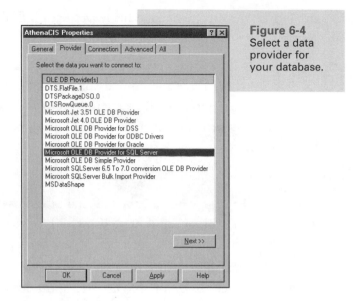

Figure 6-4
Select a data
provider for
your database.

SQL Server (see Figure 6-4). Then press the <u>N</u>ext button or select
the Connection tab.

5. On the Connection tab, specify the name of your database server
(in my case "Athena"), as well as the login ID and password you
want to use (in my case "sa"), and select the CIS database (see
Figure 6-5).

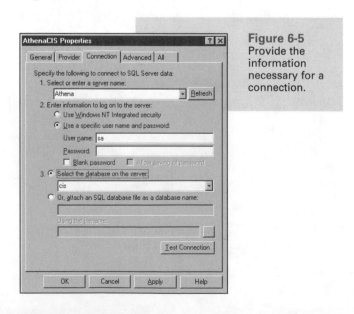

Figure 6-5
Provide the
information
necessary for a
connection.

6. Press the Test Connection button to verify that the information you entered was correct. If a message box appears saying that the test connection succeeded, press the OK button to accept the information. Then choose the file from the Select Data Link File dialog box (refer to Figure 6-2) and press Open to finish the process.

Defining Your RecordSource

A RecordSource defines how the collection of rows will be created for the **ADO Data Control**. The properties related to it are found on the RecordSource tab of the ADO data control's Property Pages. While there are only two properties associated with the control, there are three fields that can be specified on the page (see Figure 6-6). The Command Type field updates the **CommandType** property, while the other two fields update the **RecordSource** property.

The first field on the page specifies the Command Type, which is a value that will be assigned to the **CommandType** property. This property can take on four different values:

- Table (adCmdTable)
- Query (adCmdText)
- Stored Procedure (adCmdStoredProc)
- Unknown (adCmdUnknown)

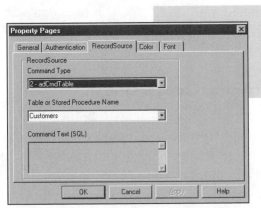

Figure 6-6
Specify the information needed to retrieve records from the database.

If you want to use a stored procedure or table, choose the appropriate value from the drop-down field labeled Table or Stored Procedure Name. If you want to use a query, you need to enter the query into the Command Text (SQL) field.

> **Tip**
>
> Don't let the system default to using Unknown for **CommandType**. This forces the provider to try to determine what type of value you should have specified for **RecordSource**. It checks with the database server to see if **RecordSource** contains a valid table name or stored procedure name. Then it tries to determine if the value is a legal query. All this extra work can be avoided if you specify the proper value for **CommandType**.

Binding Controls to the ADO Data Control

There are two general types of controls that you can bind to a data control. I call them simple and complex. Simple controls are like the text box control or a check box control and contain only one value from the database. Complex controls, on the other hand, are like the data combo control, which needs access to another data control to work properly.

> **Tip**
>
> Before trying to bind any controls using the ADO Data Control, you should insure that the data control's properties are set that allow it to access database. Then when you bind another control to the data control by setting the **DataSource** property, you can choose the field you want to bind from the drop-down list in the **DataField** property.

Binding Simple Controls

To bind a simple control, you must set two properties. The first property is the **DataSource** property. This should contain a reference to the data control containing the data you want to display (e.g., **ADODC1**). Then set the **DataField** property to the column from the row you wish to display. You can optionally set the **DataFormat** property to format a numeric value such as a **Money** field.

> One advantage of using bound controls is that a bound
> control is smart enough to correctly format the data
> directly from the database without requiring extra code.
> If you aren't happy with the way the value is displayed,
> select one of the many different formats available in the
> **DataFormat** property. If you're still not happy, you can
> even build your own format.

Binding Complex Controls

Binding complex data controls like the data combo and data list controls is merely a matter of setting a couple other properties. You still bind the **DataSource** and **DataField** properties as before, but now you introduce three more properties: **RowSource**, **ListField**, and **Bound-Column**.

The **RowSource** and **ListField** properties correspond to the **DataSource** and **DataField** properties. However, they reference the data control and field that contain the values that will be displayed in the list part of the control. This means that you don't have to add the values a user can choose from in a combo box control; instead, the data combo control will extract them from the database. The **BoundColumn** property contains the field name from the data control specified by **RowSource** with the value that will be saved into the field specified by **DataField**.

Figure 6-7 shows you how the **DataCombo** control in this program is configured. The ADODC2 control points to the CountryCodes table, with the Country and CountryCode fields. The ADODC1 control points to the Customers table, which contains, among other fields, the CountryCode field.

There are really two selected items and drop-down lists in the **Data-Combo** control. The first one is visible to the user, while the second is hidden inside the control. The data from the **ADODC2** control is used to populate both drop-down lists. The visible list is populated with the data from the **ListField** column, which in this case is the Country column. The **BoundColumn** field populates the hidden drop-down list with values from CountryCode.

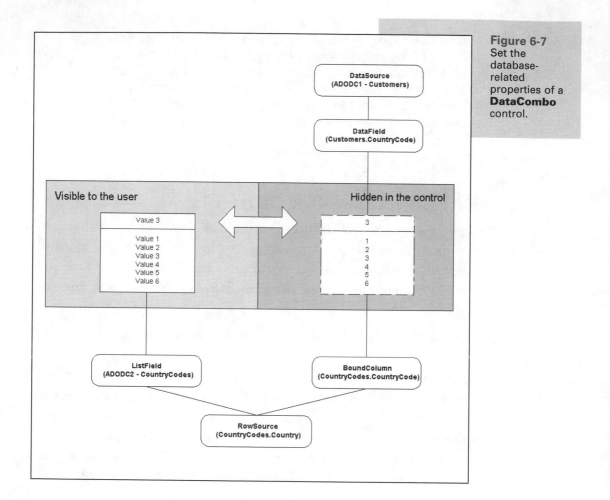

Figure 6-7
Set the database-related properties of a **DataCombo** control.

The **DataSource** property points to the ADODC1 control, which references the Customers table in the database. The **DataField** property references the Customers.CountryCode field. As the user scrolls through the visible list of values from CountryCodes.Country, the hidden list is also scrolled using the list of values from CountryCodes.CountryCode. The row containing the selected value for the visible drop-down list is also the row containing the selected value for the hidden drop-down list. The hidden selected value from CountryCodes.CountryCode is then used to update the value in the Customers.CountryCode field.

Note

Try thinking about it this way. The CountryCodes table really contains a list of values that allow you to translate a given CountryCode value to a Country value and back again. Thus the **DataCombo** control allows me to automatically translate the CountryCode value found in the Customers table using the CountryCodes table and makes it easier for users by allowing them to select the more meaningful value contained in Country rather than entering the CountryCode value directly.

Caution

When using code tables, you must be careful when changing the value associated with a particular code or you could completely change its meaning. For example, look at CountryCode 1 in the CountryCodes table. Changing Country to "USA" from "United States" doesn't change its meaning. However, changing it to "Mexico" means that you moved everyone in your Customers table from the United States to Mexico.

Adding Other Functions to the Program

Believe it or not, if all you did was properly bind all the controls on the form and press run, you would have a working program that would properly scroll through all the data in your database. (Assuming, of course, that you already had data in your database.) However, it wouldn't let you add or delete any data. Also, searching would be difficult, since you'd have to scroll through each record in the database to find the one you were looking for.

To make this program useful, add a few functions, such as add a customer, delete a customer, and find a customer. While you're at it, add a few other routines to display the current record number and to display error messages.

Adding a Customer

The first function is to add a new customer to the Customers table. (After all, it's a little hard to delete a row before you put it there.) To do this, use the **AddNew** method of the underlying **Recordset** object associated with the ADO data control. Executing this method will immediately add a blank row at the end of the table. Moving to a different row or using the **Update** method will commit these changes to the database. Using the **CancelUpdate** method will delete the new row and make the last row in the table the current row.

However, before you can use the **AddNew** method, make sure that someone hasn't already pressed the Add button or changed a value in a field without saving it. To check this, look at the **EditMode** property of the **Recordset** object (see Listing 6.1). Any value other than adEditNone means that either the record is being edited or added and you should commit the changes to the database using the **Update** method.

Add a new customer to the Customers table:

Listing 6-1

```
Private Sub Command1_Click()

'   Add a new record to the end of the database

On Error Resume Next

If Adodc1.Recordset.EditMode <> adEditNone Then
    Err.Clear
    Adodc1.Recordset.Update
    If Err.Number > 0 Then
        MsgBox Err.Description
        Exit Sub

    End If

End If

Adodc1.Recordset.AddNew

Adodc1.Recordset.Fields("CountryCode").Value = 1
Adodc1.Recordset.Fields("CreditCardCode").Value = 0
Adodc1.Recordset.Fields("PreferredShippingCode").Value = 0
Adodc1.Recordset.Fields("DateAccountCreated").Value = Date
Adodc1.Recordset.Fields("DateLastOrder").Value = Date
Adodc1.Recordset.Fields("TotalOrderValue").Value = 0

End Sub
```

While there is an **Error** event in the ADO data control, that event only traps errors while the control is processing data. Thus you have to handle any errors that may arise while performing other functions, even though they may use the resources that are owned by the ADO data control, such as the **Recordset** object.

You can handle errors that may arise in Visual Basic by using the **On Error Resume Next** statement. This statement allows your program to continue running with the next statement after an error is encountered. You need to explicitly check for errors after each statement that could cause an error. In this case, see if the **Update** method completed successfully by checking the **Err** object. If the **Err.Number** property contains a value of zero, then no errors were encountered.

Caution

> One side effect of the **On Error Resume Next** statement is that you must be certain that the Err object doesn't already contain an error before you execute the statement you want to check. If no error is encountered, the Err object will not be cleared. So you should clear the Err object before using it.

Finally, take the time to ensure that the appropriate default values are displayed to the user. While the database would normally assign the default values for these fields, they wouldn't appear until after the user has updated the database.

Deleting a Customer

Deleting a customer is even easier than adding one (see Listing 6-2). Calling the **Recordset.Delete** method will delete the current row. Before deleting the customer, display a message box asking the user to confirm that the customer really should be deleted. If the user says yes, clear the **Err** object and delete the row.

Delete an existing customer from the Customers table:

Listing 6-2

```
Private Sub Command2_Click()

'   Delete the current row

On Error Resume Next

If MsgBox("Are you sure that you want to delete " & Text1.Text & "?", _
        vbYesNo) = vbYes Then

    Err.Clear
    Adodc1.Recordset.Delete adAffectCurrent
    If Err.Number = 0 Then
        Adodc1.Recordset.MovePrevious
    Else
        MsgBox Err.Description
    End If

End If


End Sub
```

Since deleting a row leaves the cursor on the blank record, I move the cursor to the previous row if the delete was successful and display the error message if it wasn't. This ensures that the user will always see valid data rather than a record that isn't really there.

Updating and Not Updating a Row

The Update button fires the Command3_Click event to save the contents of the current row into the database. This is done using the **Update** method (see Listing 6-3). This uses logic similar to the add and delete customer routines already discussed.

Update the current row:

Listing 6-3

```
Private Sub Command3_Click()

'   Update the current row
```

```
On Error Resume Next

If Adodc1.Recordset.EditMode <> adEditNone Then
    Err.Clear
    Adodc1.Recordset.Update
    If Err.Number > 0 Then
        MsgBox Err.Description
    End If

End If

End Sub
```

Canceling an active update is even easier than updating a row, since all
you need to do is issue the **CancelUpdate** method if you have a row that
has been added or changed since it was displayed. Then use the **Move**
method to redisplay the original information from the database (see
Listing 6-4).

Cancel an update to the current row:

Listing 6-4

```
Private Sub Command4_Click()

'   Cancel the new row or updated data

If Adodc1.Recordset.EditMode <> adEditNone Then
    Adodc1.Recordset.Move 0
    Adodc1.Recordset.CancelUpdate
End If

End Sub
```

Finding Customers

One of the harder pieces of code to write in this program is for finding
a customer. I decided to use the **Filter** property of the **Recordset** object
to help me search for a customer. This property allows me to specify a
condition where only selected rows from the current recordset are to be
displayed. To do this, I included a combo box with all the fields in the
recordset and a blank text box on the form. The user would then enter

the search value in the blank text box and choose the corresponding field from the combo box. Then only the values matching the filter criteria would be displayed.

Initializing the combo box is very straightforward. Set the first item on the combo box to be "<everything>". I'll use this later to reset the filter. I also make it the default value when the form is loaded. Then I loop through the collection of field objects in the recordset and load them into the combo box (see Listing 6-5).

Initialize the combo box with the names of each field in the Customers table:

Listing 6-5

```
Private Sub Form_Load()

'   Initialize the filter information

On Error Resume Next

Dim f As ADODB.Field

Combo1.AddItem "<everything>"
Combo1.Text = "<everything>"

For Each f In Adodc1.Recordset.Fields
    Combo1.AddItem f.Name

Next f

End Sub
```

The real work in this routine is done in the Click event for the combo box. I handle three different conditions. If the user selects "<everything>", I set the **Filter** property to an empty string to disable it and clear the text box to tell the user that this function has been reset (see Listing 6-6).

Change filter fields:

Listing 6-6

```
Private Sub Combo1_Click()

'  Process filter

If Combo1.Text = "<everything>" Then
    Adodc1.Recordset.Filter = ""
Text18.Text = ""

ElseIf Len(Text18.Text) = 0 Then
    MsgBox "Must specify filter criteria before selecting field."
    Combo1.Text = "<everything>"

Else
    Adodc1.Recordset.Filter = "( " & Combo1.Text & " like '" & _
        Trim(Text18.Text) & "' )"

End If

End Sub
```

If the user selected a specific field name, I check to see if the user specified a corresponding value to look for. If not, I issue an error message and reset the combo box back to "<everything>".

Finally, if the user specified a field name and a search value, I build an expression similar to this one:

```
( CustomerName like 'jil*' )
```

This will restrict the records displayed to those values that begin with 'jil', such as 'Jill', 'Jillion', 'Jill T. Freeze', etc. You can also specify those rows that contain the characters 'jil' anywhere in the field by specifying '*jil*'. This will reduce the number of rows to just a handful, which anyone could easily scroll through.

Displaying Where You Are

Sometimes it's useful to display where you are in the recordset relative to the total number of rows retrieved. This is especially true in situations where you are filtering the data to find a particular customer. If you retrieve too many rows, you can always create a more complex filter value.

Displaying the value is very easy. Nearly all methods will fire the **Move-Complete** event for the ADO data control. Then it becomes a simple matter to display the **AbsolutePosition** property to get the current row number and the **RecordCount** property to show the total number of rows that have been retrieved (see Listing 6-7).

Update the current row counter:

Listing 6-7

```
Private Sub Adodc1_MoveComplete(ByVal adReason As ADODB.EventReasonEnum, _
    ByVal pError As ADODB.Error, adStatus As ADODB.EventStatusEnum, _
    ByVal pRecordset As ADODB.Recordset20)

'   Display current record number

On Error Resume Next

Adodc1.Caption = FormatNumber(Adodc1.Recordset.AbsolutePosition, 0) & _
    " of " & FormatNumber(Adodc1.Recordset.RecordCount, 0)

End Sub
```

Refreshing the Recordset

Occasionally it might be desirable to get a fresh copy of the data from the database. You can do this by using the **Requery** method. This method simply executes the same query that generated the current recordset over again. This means that it will pick up any new rows and ensure that deleted rows are not included. I also use this opportunity to reset the filter criteria back to the default values to make it a little easier for the user to use (see Listing 6-8).

Refresh the recordset:

Listing 6-8

```
Private Sub Command5_Click()

'   Get a new copy of the data

Combo1.Text = "<everything>"
Text18.Text = ""
Adodc1.Recordset.Filter = ""
Adodc1.Recordset.Requery

End Sub
```

Trapping Error Messages

Here's a very simple routine that is triggered whenever the ADO data control generates an error condition (see Listing 6-9). All it does is display the error message in a message box.

This routine displays any error messages it receives:

Listing 6-9

```
Private Sub Adodc1_Error(ByVal ErrorNumber As Long, _
    Description As String, ByVal Scode As Long, _
    ByVal Source As String, ByVal HelpFile As String, _
    ByVal HelpContext As Long, fCancelDisplay As Boolean)

MsgBox Description

End Sub
```

Exporting Customer Data to Excel

SQL Server 7 provides a general-purpose utility designed to move data from one place to another. It's called Data Transformation Services (DTS), and it exploits OLE-DB's ability to talk to many different data sources, plus it includes support for ODBC data sources and flat files. This means you can move data between any of these sources:

- Microsoft SQL Server 7 database
- Microsoft SQL Server 6.5 and earlier databases

- Microsoft Access databases
- Microsoft Excel worksheets
- Microsoft FoxPro databases
- IBM DB2 databases
- Oracle databases
- dBase databases
- Paradox databases
- Flat files like comma separated value files and fixed field length files

Building the DTS Package

To build a DTS package to move the data from the Customers table to an Excel worksheet, follow these instructions:

1. From the Enterprise Manager's list of tables in the CIS database, right-click on the table and select All Tasks, Export Data. This starts the DTS Export Wizard (see Figure 6-8).

2. Press <u>N</u>ext from the initial screen to move to the Choose a Data Source screen. You need to fill in the information to access the database, including the name of the server, your login ID and password, and the name of the database. You also should use the

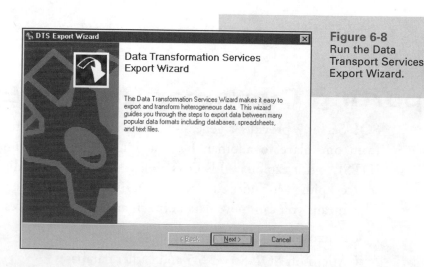

Figure 6-8
Run the Data Transport Services Export Wizard.

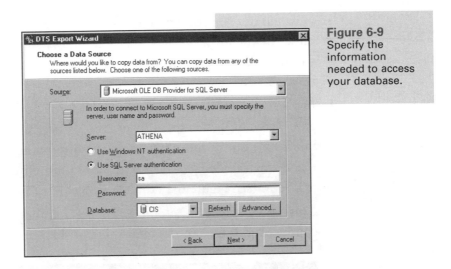

Figure 6-9
Specify the information needed to access your database.

OLE-DB provider for SQL Server 7 to access the database (see Figure 6-9).

3. In the following window, the wizard shows you the Choose a Destination form (see Figure 6.10). Since you're creating an Excel worksheet, you need to provide the name of the file. Note that you would need to designate username and password if you wanted to build the file on a machine where you don't have automatic permission to access its disk drives.

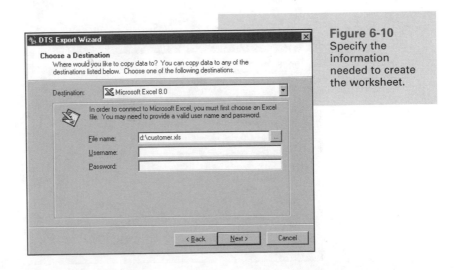

Figure 6-10
Specify the information needed to create the worksheet.

4. Next tell the wizard that you want to copy the results of a query rather than copy a simple table. This allows you to translate the CountryCode value into its text equivalent. Press Next when finished.

5. In the SQL statement window you have the option to directly type in the SQL statement or use the Query Builder to help build your query. Since the query is a little more complex than the Query Builder supports, you should just enter it directly in this form (see Figure 6-11 and Listing 6-10).

   This query creates a summary of the number of customers by country and state and the total value of their orders:

Listing 6-10

```
Select CountryCodes.Country, Customers.State,
    Sum(Customers.TotalOrderValue) TotalValue,
    Count(Customers.TotalOrderValue) TotalOrders
From CountryCodes,Customers
Where CountryCodes.CountryCode=Customers.CountryCode
Group By Country, State
Order By CountryCodes.Country, Customers.State
```

6. Select the name of the worksheet where the results of the query will be saved in the next window by modifying the destination table name. This is useful if you have a workbook with charts and

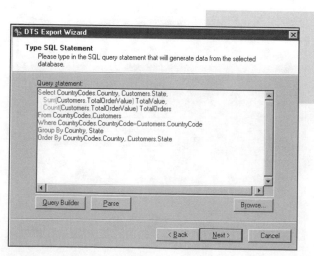

Figure 6-11
Select the columns you wish to return in your query.

Tip

The Query Builder is rather limited in its capabilities, and you are limited to checking the syntax of the statement while in the SQL statement window. You should develop and test your query using the Query Analyzer tool. Then you can copy and paste the working query into the SQL statement window.

other information already developed. Then the values from the extracted data will automatically update the other worksheets when the workbook is opened. Also, this window allows you to transform the data that is created before it is written to the worksheet (see Figure 6-12).

7. You can choose to run your export immediately or save it so you can run it later in the next window. If you choose to save your package, press Next to continue. The Save DTS Package form will be shown (see Figure 6-13). It allows you to use the SQL Server Agent to schedule the package for execution. This can be very useful if you need to update your workbook on a periodic basis. I gave this package a name of Customer01 and described it as "Extract info about customers by country and state." If you choose not to save your package, the wizard will jump to the next step.

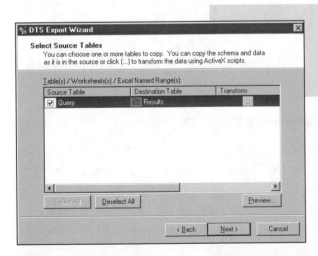

Figure 6-12
Verify the name of the worksheet in the workbook you want to use.

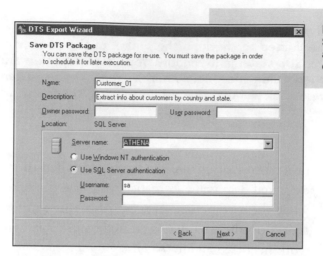

Figure 6-13
Specify the name
and description
of the package.

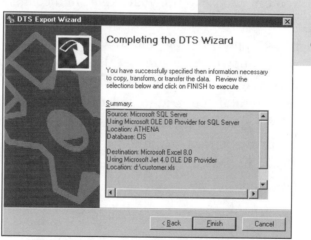

Figure 6-14
Review your
choices.

8. The last form in the wizard allows you to review your information before saving or running your package (see Figure 6-14).

Running Your DTS Package

There are two basic ways to run your DTS package. You can use SQL Server Enterprise Manager to execute the package from the list of available packages. To do this, select the Data Transformation folder and the Local Packages icon under your database server. Then simply right-click on the package name, in this case Customer01, and select Execute

Package (see Figure 6-15). It then displays a window that tracks execution and lets you know when it's finished (see Figure 6-16). You can also run the package without using the Enterprise Manager. Instead, use the program DTSRun, supplied by Microsoft. You can enter the command shown below in the Start, Run window. This will run the "Customer01" package on the server "athena" using the login ID "sa" with the password

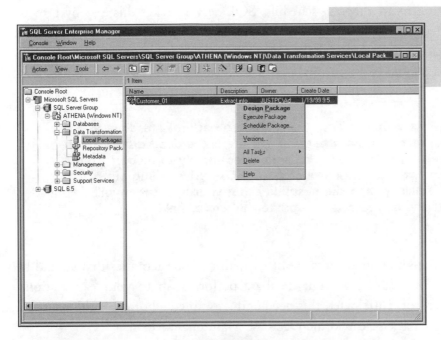

Figure 6-15
Run the Customer01 DTS package.

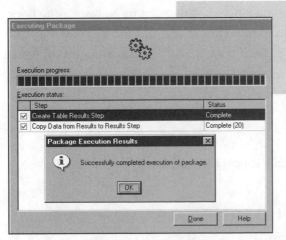

Figure 6-16
The Customer01 package completed successfully.

"Kokomo". This will start a short DOS session to run the command. When the DOS window disappears, the data transport process is finished.

```
DTSRun /S "athena" /U "sa" /P "Kokomo" /N "Customer01"
```

Backing Up Your Data

An important part of managing your database is to properly back it up according to a regular schedule. SQL Server makes this easy by providing a backup facility that can be scheduled to run unattended. Besides backing up your database, there are some other maintenance activities that should be performed.

Most people believe that database backups are done in order to recover from a hardware failure like a dead disk drive. In reality, database backups are used mostly to recover from software failures. The odds of a disk drive failing are much less likely than the possibility that your application will delete the wrong records or update the wrong field.

At the same time, there are other maintenance activities that should be run to ensure that your database performs up to your expectations. Microsoft anticipated this need and combined all of these things into a single package called the Database Maintenance Plan.

Before you create a maintenance plan, you'll need to go over some background material so you can better understand the choices you will have to make. The following sections provide information on the different types of backups available, an overview of the databases found on your server, and notes on optimizing your database for best performance.

Types of Backups

SQL Server Backup Wizard supports three basic types of backups:

- Full database backups
- Differential database backups
- Transaction log backups

Each of these backups has a different purpose. The full database backup makes a complete copy of your database. (Microsoft usually refers to this type of backup as just a database backup, while I prefer the term full backup.) This type of backup is important, since it gives you a base from which to begin recovering your database. The entire database is saved. Everything you need to restore the database is present, and when you restore the database, it will be complete as of the time the backup was made.

A differential database backup backs up only the new rows inserted into the tables and any changed or deleted rows. The primary advantage of the differential backup is that it will take a lot less time to run. This is very important on large databases, when backups may run for quite a while. (This is especially true if you are backing up your database to

Too Much Is Just Right

You should always keep around as many backup copies of your database as possible. You never know when you could have a database problem that might not show up for several days. Then having a backup copy from before the time that the problem occurred would be invaluable.

I suggest that you back up your transaction logs each night, when the load on your server is lightest. Then you should keep these for at least a week. Keeping your backups even longer, perhaps for a month or a full business cycle, is even better, though you will rarely have to recover data from that far back.

Some auditors will suggest that you keep your backups even longer, especially if you deal with financial information. If that's the case, you might want to keep your nightly backups for a month. Then keep the first backup of each month for a year. This not only keeps the auditors happy (which is always a good idea), but it also lets you recover data from a long time ago in the event of a real disaster.

tape.) In order to recover a database, you still need a full database backup. Then you apply the differential database backups to the newly restored database backup to make your database current as of when the last differential backup was made.

Transaction logs store every change that is made to the database. Normally the logs are used to allow users to perform rollbacks while processing transactions. However, the information in the logs can also be used to recover your database. When combined with full database backups and differential database backups, you can restore your database to almost any point in time before the database failed.

Databases on Your Server

As you have noticed by now, there are a lot of other databases in the database server. There are two basic classes of databases: system and user. System databases are used by SQL Server to perform various tasks. The following are system databases:

- **Master.** This database contains information about the other database and logins, as well as other information critical to the operation of SQL Server.

- **Model.** This database contains a skeleton database that is replicated each time you create a new database.

- **msdb.** This database contains information used by the SQL Server Agent tool to schedule and run various functions in the database, such as those created by the Database Maintenance Plan Wizard described below.

- **tempdb.** This database contains temporary information created by user queries and contains such things as temporary tables and stored procedures. It is re-created each time SQL Server is started.

User databases, on the other hand, hold your data. Microsoft supplies two databases:

- **Northwind.** This database contains the data for the Northwind Traders sample application, which imports and exports specialty foods from around the world.

- **Pubs.** This database contains data for Microsoft's sample publishing company. It is often used in the examples in SQL Server documentation.

Optimizing Your Database

A database is a complex organism that needs periodic attention in order to maintain optimum performance. As changes occur to the data in the database, statistics that are used by the Query Optimizer will change. Also, the data stored in the tables will become less ordered and the amount of space required by the database will grow. Both of these factors mean that more resources are needed to process each query.

Reorganize Data and Index Pages

If your database has a lot of insert and delete activity, you might want to repack the index data pages every now and again. As the updates are made, the index pages will become full and new pages will be added. This results in an increase in the time required to search the index.

The same thing can also happen to tables themselves, as rows are inserted and deleted. The tables will tend to grow over time, causing queries that read the table from beginning to end to run longer. Also, the location of related data will change with time, forcing even indexed reads to take longer.

Update Statistics

The **Update Statistics** SQL statement is used to scan through the database and compute various statistics about the actual data in your database. The Query Optimizer inside SQL Server uses this information to determine the best way to solve a query. To understand why this is necessary, consider the following example. Assume that you have a table called Books, which contains a list of books. This table has, among other fields, a field called Publisher, which contains the name of the company that published each book. Also, assume that there is an index on this field.

Consider the following query:

```
Select * From Books Where Publisher = 'Prima Publishing'
```

This query will search the table to find all the books published by Prima Publishing. The Query Optimizer has two options to solve the query. It can read through the entire Books table and check the Publisher field to see if it wants the record. Or it could use the Publisher index to determine which rows it should retrieve.

Common sense tells us that the second is most likely, but if your knowledge of the Books table is flawed, that might not be the best approach. For instance, assume that 50 percent of the books in the table are from Prima Publishing. Also assume that the cost to read a row found by an index entry is about five times higher than that of reading a row sequentially.

This means that it would be faster to read through the entire table if you are going to retrieve more than 20 percent of the rows. Since you know that Prima Publishing has 50 percent of the books in the table, it would make more sense to just read through the entire table rather than to use the index. So without the information created by the **Update Statistics** command, the Query Optimizer doesn't really know what would be the best way to solve the query.

Using the Database Maintenance Plan Wizard

To back up your database, follow these steps:

1. From the Enterprise Manager's list of servers, right-click on the server that contains your database and select Tools, Wizards. This displays the list of available wizards. Double-click on Management to display the list of management wizards (see Figure 6-17).

2. Double-click on the Database Maintenance Plan Wizard to start the wizard (see Figure 6-18). Press Next to continue to the next step.

3. Press Next to display all the databases on the server and choose which ones you want to back up. You should always back up master and msdb databases. Backing up the model database is also a good idea. And of course you want to back up the databases that hold your own data. In fact, backing up all of your databases is probably the safest approach of all.

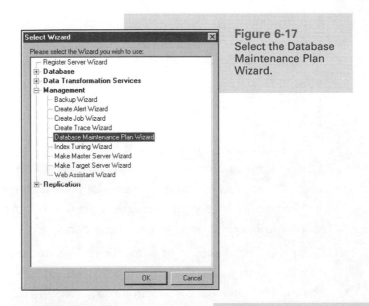

Figure 6-17
Select the Database Maintenance Plan Wizard.

Figure 6-18
Welcome to the Database Maintenance Plan Wizard.

Tip

If you don't need the sample databases around, delete them. Then you can back up all of your databases with the knowledge that you aren't backing up anything unnecessary. If you wish, you can always re-create the samples later by following the instructions in Microsoft's documentation.

4. The next step in the wizard allows you to perform three different tasks that will help to improve your database's performance.

I suggest that you select the Reorganize Data and Index Pages task (with the original free space option) and the Update Statistics task. Scheduling maintenance once a week is fine, unless your database has a lot of insert and delete operations. In that case, you might want do this more frequently depending on how long it runs.

5. The wizard gives you the option to run a Database Integrity Check every so often. Unless your server is very busy, this is also a good idea. You additionally have the option to run these tests before you back up your database. This is another good idea, since you may not want to back up a corrupted database.

6. Next the wizard shows the form for the Database Backup Plan. On this form you can select to back up the database as part of the maintenance plan. You can also specify where you want the backup to be stored (disk or tape) and when it should be run (see Figure 6-19).

7. If the default schedule is not desirable, you can change it by clicking on the Change button. You can choose to run the backup from one of four basic scheduling options: when the SQL Server Agent starts, when the CPU is idle, once at a specific date and time, or on a recurring schedule. By default, the backup runs at two o'clock on Sunday morning; however, this schedule is very

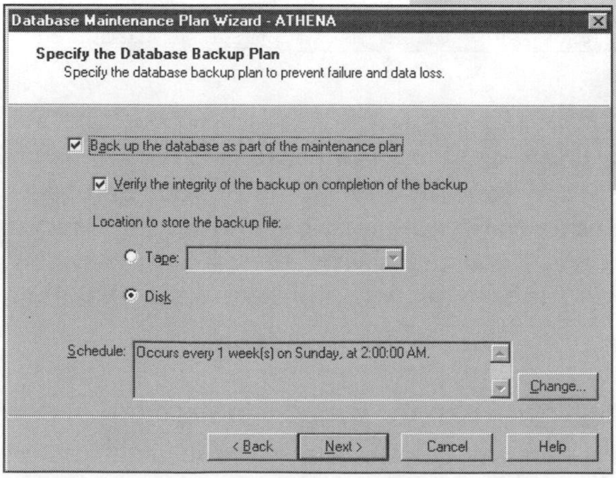

Figure 6-19
Choose the
Database Backup
Plan that benefits
your application
the most.

easy to change. (Note: This dialog box along with the next are the same ones used by other activities in the schedule, such as Reorganizing Data and Index Pages and the Database Integrity Check.) You can schedule a recurring job to run daily, weekly, or monthly (see Figure 6.20). A daily job can be run once each day at a specific time or periodically throughout the day. A weekly job can be scheduled to run every week on the specified set of days. Then on those days, the job will be run according to the daily schedule. A monthly job can be run on the same day of each month or the same relative day of each month. Note that you can also specify a date range during which the schedule will be run.

8. If you choose to back up your database to disk, on the next screen you need to specify the location on disk where the backups will be saved. You can optionally choose to remove backups older than a specified date.

9. The next step allows you to automatically back up the transaction log. By default, this is done on the days when the full backup is not done.

Tip

The transaction log files hold updates since the last database backup. Therefore, you must keep all the log files from the most recent database backup in order to recover your database correctly. However, after that you can keep logs as you want, as long as you save the corresponding database backup.

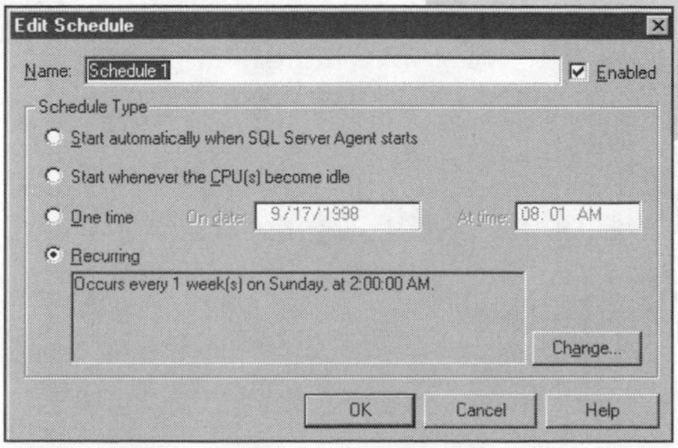

Figure 6-20
Change the schedule to suit your needs.

Edit Schedule

Name: Schedule 1   ☑ Enabled

Schedule Type

○ Start automatically when SQL Server Agent starts

○ Start whenever the CPU(s) become idle

○ One time   On date: 9/17/1998   At time: 08:01 AM

● Recurring

Occurs every 1 week(s) on Sunday, at 2:00:00 AM.

Change...

OK   Cancel   Help

10. As with the database backup task, you can choose where to store your files and how long to keep them.

11. Having all the database backups is nice, but it is also important to keep track of the information associated with them. The Database Maintenance Plan Wizard allows you to automatically generate this information in either text or HTML format.

12. In the next step, you can choose to save the maintenance history information in your local database server or to a remote server.

13. The last form in the wizard allows you to review the information and to go back and change anything that isn't right before you save your schedule. (see Figure 6.21). Press Finish to save your maintenance schedule.

You can review the maintenance plan at any time by selecting the Database Maintenance Plan icon under the selected database server and clicking on the name of the plan (see Figure 6-22). This will display the

Tip

After you define your maintenance plan, verify that the SQL Server Agent is running by using the SQL Server Enterprise Manager on the server directly. If the agent isn't running, your maintenance schedule will not run.

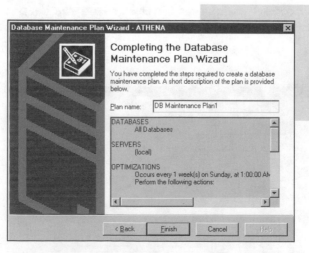

Figure 6-21
You can review your choices before finishing the Database Maintenance Plan Wizard.

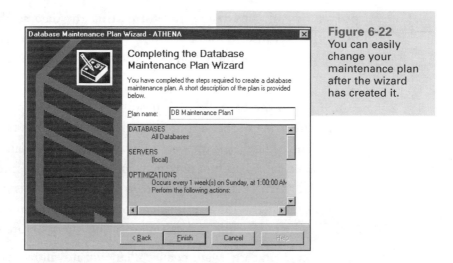

Figure 6-22
You can easily change your maintenance plan after the wizard has created it.

maintenance plan's properties window and allow you to update or change any of the values you entered with the wizard.

Wrapping Up

In this chapter, you built a simple program to demonstrate the power of using data bound controls. You also used the Data Transformation Services Wizard to build a utility to export some summary data into an Excel worksheet. Finally, you used the Database Maintenance Plan Wizard to create a batch job that would automatically back up the database, as well as perform a few other routine tasks.

The Edit Customer Information program is a relatively simple program built out of simple tools in Visual Basic, yet it was possible to build a fairly powerful program with only a minimal amount of effort. The only reason this program is somewhat complicated is the number of tables that it accesses.

Bound controls are a powerful programming tool. Using them simplifies a large number of issues that you would have to worry about under other circumstances. Imagine if you had to move data into and out of each of the display controls on your form each time you moved to a different record in the database. Having to worry about performing the proper type of conversions and formatting the data so that it displays properly has caused a lot of grief for Visual Basic programmers over the years. Whenever possible you should take advantage of bound controls in your own programs.

When I used the DTS Wizard to build the transport package, I had to specify the name of the output file and the name of the table that would be exported. DTS also supports a COM interface, which would let you create a Visual Basic program that could collect this information and build and execute a transport package on the fly. This is probably a better solution in the long run, since you have the option to specify the name of the output file and can modify the query before running it.

Using the Database Maintenance Plan wizard allows you to quickly define a schedule that performs most of the regular tasks that a database server like SQL Server requires. If you have used Microsoft Access or the Microsoft Jet database engine, you never really had to worry about backing up your database. You just copied the .mdb file to a different file. You never had to worry about transaction logs and all those other little details that drove database administrators crazy. The Database Maintenance Plan wizard may be one of the less exciting tools in SQL Server 7, but without it, your job would be a lot more difficult.

7
CHAPTER

Testing the Customer Information Subsystem

With an application ready to test, you'll need some data to store in the database. First you'll use the Data Transformation Services (DTS) Import Wizard to show you how to load data into your own database. Then with some test data, you'll test the Edit Customer Information program and export customer data into Excel. Next you'll review the results of the Database Maintenance Plan job to verify that everything ran properly. Finally, you'll recover a database from a backup file.

Loading the Sample Data

There are several files on the CD-ROM that contain the data for the Customer Information Subsystem's support tables. The easiest way to load them is by using the SQL Server Enterprise Manager's DTS Import Wizard. This is a very powerful tool that lets you load data in many different ways.

The test data for this subsystem is found on the CD-ROM in the **\HOSQLSrver7\Chapt07** directory. You will need to load the data for the following files:

- CountryCodes.CSV
- CreditCardCodes.CSV
- PreferredShippingCodes.CSV
- StateCodes.CSV
- Customers.CSV

Each of these files is formatted as a comma separated value (CSV) file. A CSV file is a normal text file, where each line contains one row of data. The first line of each file contains the name of each column of data. Each line is formatted as a series of values separated by commas. Numeric values contain only digits and an optional decimal point. If the value contains any other characters, it is considered text. However, to prevent confusion, text values are usually enclosed in double quotes("). This prevents problems from occurring when the text contains commas.

Tip

> **Use a spreadsheet to view or edit the data in a CSV file. CSV files were originally designed to transport tabular data from one spreadsheet program to another, so your favorite spreadsheet program (such as Microsoft Excel) can easily read them.**

Because of its dependencies on the other tables, the Customers table should be loaded last. The other tables can be loaded in any order. So you can begin with CountryCodes and then load CreditCardCodes, PreferredShippingCodes, StateCodes, and Customers. Follow these steps for each of these files:

1. From the Enterprise Manager's list of tables in the CIS database, right-click on the table you want to load and select All Tasks, Import Data. This will start the DTS Import Wizard (see Figure 7-1).

2. Press <u>N</u>ext from the initial screen to open the Choose a Data Source window. In the Source drop-down box, choose Text File.

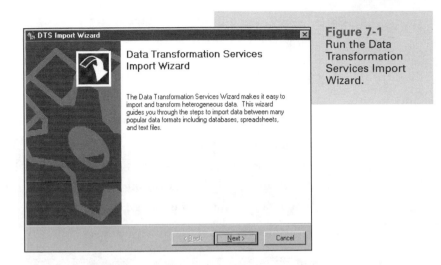

Figure 7-1
Run the Data
Transformation
Services Import
Wizard.

The form then changes to display the options appropriate for importing a text file, specifically the name of the file. Designate the name of the file you want to import and press Next.

3. The Select File Format form appears. This will show you the first four lines of the file you want to import. Since I created the data file on the CD-ROM as a simple MS-DOS-formatted text file, select File Type as ANSI, Row Delimiter as {CR}{LF}, and Text Qualifier as Double Quote. I also included the column headers in the data file, so you need to check the First Row Has Column Names box (see Figure 7-2). Press Next to continue.

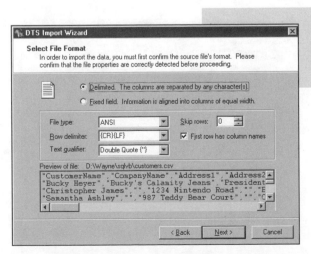

Figure 7-2
Choose the file
format of the
input file.

4. The Specify Column Delimiter window allows you to specify the character that is used to separate the fields. Since I created the data file using commas as separators, you should click on Comma. This will show a preview of the file and the data for each field. This is a good place to verify that the data is properly aligned before you load it into the database (see Figure 7-3).

5. The next step in the wizard allows you to choose the destination of the imported data. Since this is the Customer Information Subsystem's database, you should select an OLE DB connection to Athena and the CIS database (see Figure 7-4).

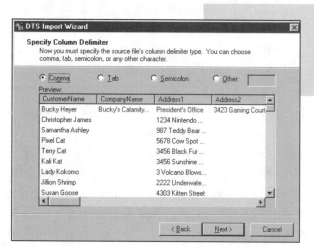

Figure 7-3
Verify that column breaks are in the right place.

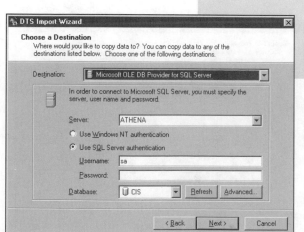

Figure 7-4
Choose the destination of the data.

6. Since the destination is a table, the wizard attempts to match your input file with a table of the same name in the Select Source Tables dialog box. It also gives you the ability to specify how the fields in the source table are transformed into the destination table. Since all of these tables have column names, the transformation isn't necessary for these files. But this is an interesting tool that may prove useful in other circumstances.

7. The Save, Schedule, and Replicate Package allows you to save this task for later execution or run it immediately. Since this is the only time you will run this function, select Run Immediately.

8. The last form in the wizard allows you to review the information and go back and change anything that isn't right before you run it (see Figure 7-5). Press Finish to start the load process.

9. The data transfer utility will load the data into the database and let you know when it's finished. If you receive an error message you should attempt to determine the error and rerun the job. In most cases you'll have to make sure that the table is empty before running it again.

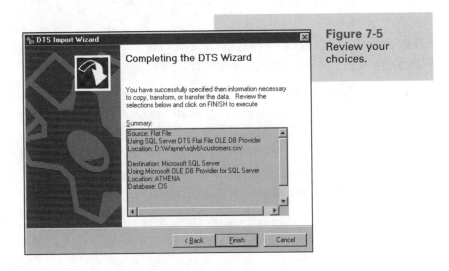

Figure 7-5
Review your choices.

Note

On the Select Source Tables form of the DTS Import Wizard is the Transform button. Pressing this button displays another dialog box that allows you to specify how the source fields are mapped to the destination fields. You can also write a small VBScript program that can perform a more complex transformation. One interesting feature is the ability to disable the Identity field in a table and insert data directly into that column without change. This is called Enable Identity Insert. While this isn't important for the current table, you may find it useful if you choose to export data from a table with an Identify field and load it back again.

Testing the Edit Customer Information Program

Testing the Edit Customer Information Program is merely a matter of trying each function to see if it works as designed. Randomly beat on the keyboard and the mouse, like a true user. After all, if the user always used your applications properly, you wouldn't have to include edit checks and other error-handling logic.

Running and Testing the Program for the First Time

After loading the data into the database and running your program, you should see a display similar to the one shown in Figure 7-6. Notice that all the fields have a value, except for InvalidCreditCard and TaxExemptStatus. Each of the values shown is appropriate for the fields. This means that the data was imported properly and that each of the controls was bound to the proper database field.

Next, go through each of the data combo controls and verify that the contents are properly loaded. These include Country, Credit Card Type, and Preferred Shipper. Again, this verifies the data load as well as the properties used to bind the control to the database.

Finally, scroll through some of the records to see if new customers are properly displayed. Be sure to scroll past the last row and to the row before

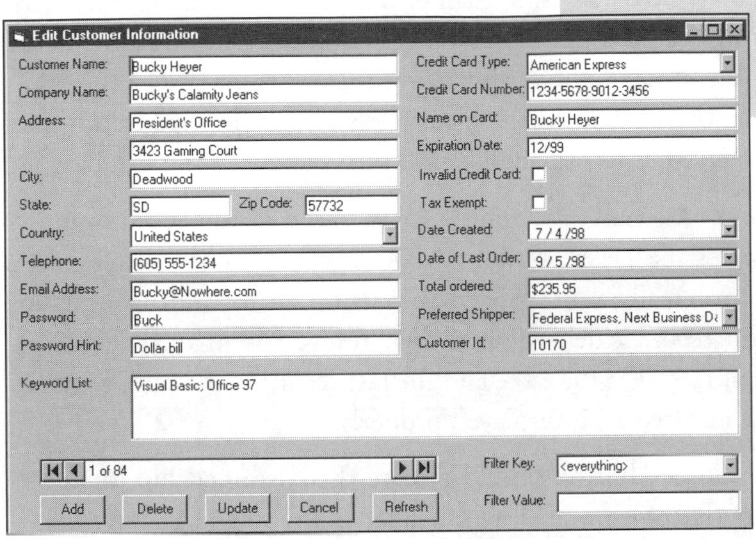

Figure 7-6
Run the Edit Customer
Information Program.

the first row. In both cases, the row displayed on the form shouldn't change.

The next step is to press the Add button and see what happens. If the add works properly, you should see the form shown in Figure 7-7. Notice that each of the fields where a default value was assigned shows that value, while the rest of the fields are blank.

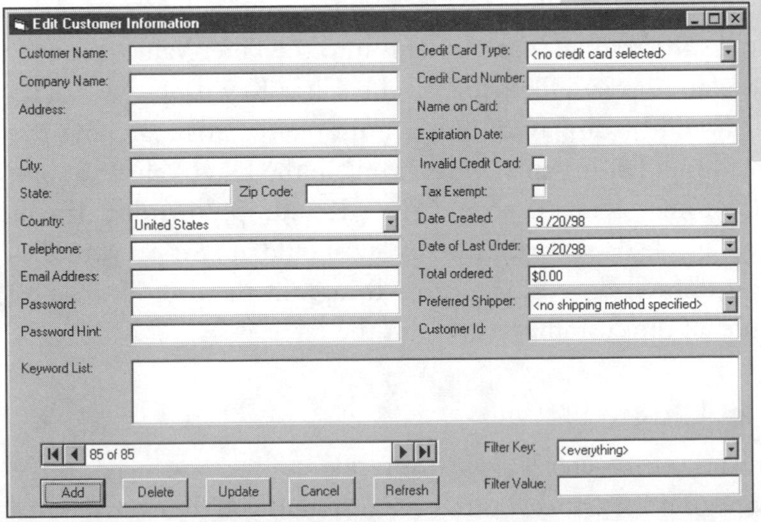

Figure 7-7
Adding a new
customer with the Edit
Customer Information
Program.

You should then enter values for each of the fields. Remember that there is a constraint that will prevent the Password and PasswordHint fields from being the same. Also, a valid state must be entered into the State field. Pressing the Update button or using any of the arrow buttons that will move to another record should save the changes to the database.

Deleting a record is very easy. Simply scroll to the customer you want to delete and press the Delete button. A message box will be displayed to confirm that you really want to delete the customer. Try both Yes and No. Verify that the record is deleted only when Yes is pressed. You should also delete the first record in the table and the last record in the table to make sure that the new record is displayed properly.

Pressing the Update button should update the customer's information. To make sure that this works, leave an error in the row (e.g., leave the e-mail address blank) and press the Update button. If the update works properly, the error should be detected and displayed in a message box.

Testing the Cancel button is easy. Simply add a new customer or change an existing customer and then press the Cancel button. The previous row will be displayed if you tried to add a customer or the original data for the customer will be restored if you tried to make changes.

The Refresh button retrieves a new copy of the data from the database. If this works properly, the first row should be redisplayed.

To make sure that the filter function is working, simply find a database value that looks interesting, type part of it into the Filter Value text box, and select the appropriate file name in the Filter Key drop-down box. The record should be displayed, unless multiple records matching the criteria were found. For instance, enter *sam* in the Filter Value text box and select Customer Name from the Filter Key drop-down list. If you are using my sample data, Samantha Ashley should appear on your display. Pressing Refresh or selecting <everything> in the drop-down box should restore all the customer records in the table.

Testing Like a User

This is the hard part—you have to think like a user. You need to try things like pressing the Cancel button even though you didn't make any changes. Press the Add button before you press the Update button or move to a new row. Enter values into various fields that don't make sense. Then check to see if the results are what you expect. If you don't find any bugs, you're not trying hard enough. I left at least one bug for you to find.

 Users often find ways to use your applications that you never intended. Then when your application breaks, they can't explain how they did it. It is important for you to test unlikely combinations of commands in your program before your users do.

Testing the Export Function

Finally, just to demonstrate that this process really works, Figure 7-8 shows the spreadsheet data I just exported with a simple pie chart created by Excel's Chart Wizard. You can verify the information in the spreadsheet, either by hand or by running the Query Analyzer.

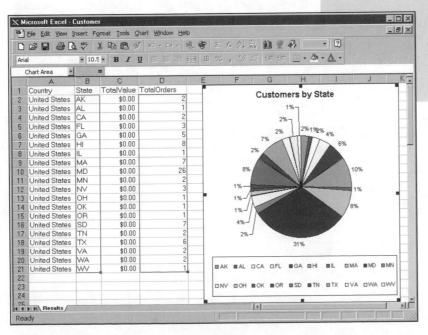

Figure 7-8
The data was properly exported to Excel.

Testing the Database Backup

There are only two ways to test a database backup job. The first way is to review the reports generated by the job and make sure that the backup worked. The second way is to actually restore the old database and verify that the old data is still there.

Reviewing the Reports

The first step in testing the database backup process is to verify that the backup process worked. When I defined the maintenance plan in the last chapter, I instructed the SQL Server Agent to produce reports showing the status of each job. Figure 7-9 shows a portion of the backup report.

Notice that it is more or less obvious that each of the database backups and backup verifications worked properly. The long column of successes is a pretty sure sign. However, if you are paranoid (a common trait of most good database administrators), you can also view this information in the database by using the SQL Server Enterprise Manager and

CIS	Backup database	9/20/98 2:00:05 AM	Success	Backup Destination: [d:\mssql7 \BACKUP\CIS_db_199809200200.BAK]
CIS	Verify Backup	9/20/98 2:00:06 AM	Success	
master	Backup database	9/20/98 2:00:10 AM	Success	Backup Destination: [d:\mssql7 \BACKUP\master_db_199809200200.BAK]
master	Verify Backup	9/20/98 2:00:12 AM	Success	
model	Backup database	9/20/98 2:00:13 AM	Success	Backup Destination: [d:\mssql7 \BACKUP\model_db_199809200200.BAK]
model	Verify Backup	9/20/98 2:00:13 AM	Success	
msdb	Backup database	9/20/98 2:00:17 AM	Success	Backup Destination: [d:\mssql7 \BACKUP\msdb_db_199809200200.BAK]
msdb	Verify Backup	9/20/98 2:00:19 AM	Success	
Northwind	Backup database	9/20/98 2:00:22 AM	Success	Backup Destination: [d:\mssql7 \BACKUP\Northwind_db_199809200200.BAK]
Northwind	Verify Backup	9/20/98 2:00:23 AM	Success	

Figure 7-9
Review the reports using Internet Explorer.

selecting the Jobs node under SQL Server Agent. This display lists all batch jobs managed by the SQL Server Agent and shows their status and next scheduled execution (see Figure 7-10).

Finally, there is one more way to check the status of the database maintenance jobs. Their results are stored in a table that you can see using Enterprise Manager. Simply select the Database Maintenance Plans node to display the available plans. Right-click on your maintenance plan and select History from the pop-up menu to display the Database Maintenance Plan History. You can choose to limit the data you are viewing by specifying filter criteria at the top of the dialog box. In this case I limited the data to just the CIS database to show you the information in Figure 7-11.

Reloading the Database

The biggest test of any backup is to successfully restore a database. Either it works or you get fired (well, maybe you'll just get stressed out for a while). It's always a good idea to test the reload function before you

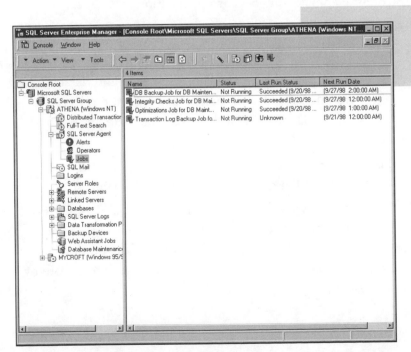

Figure 7-10
Verify that the batch jobs succeeded in Enterprise Manager.

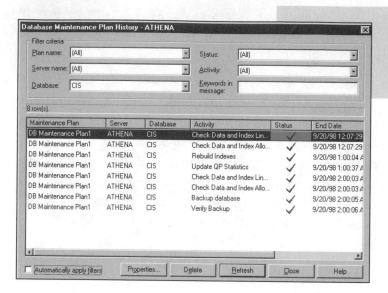

Figure 7-11
Examine the SQL Server Agent's database of results for the CIS database.

need it. I don't know how many times I've seen someone (even myself) ignore this advice only to realize later that it would have been advantageous to have tested the backup under more controlled circumstances, such as before the application goes into production.

Unlike some database systems, the SQL Server Restore Database process is very easy to use. Just follow these steps:

1. In Enterprise Manager, select the database server and database you wish to restore. Right-click on the database and select All Tasks, Restore Database. This will display the dialog box shown in Figure 7-12.

2. On this form, select the name of the database you want to restore. In this case I'm going to restore the CIS database.

3. Then on the same tab of the Restore Database dialog box, I need to select how I want to restore the database. I can restore the database backup, the filegroups or files, or the backup device. Since the Database Maintenance Plan makes it easy to restore by database backup, that's the option I'll use.

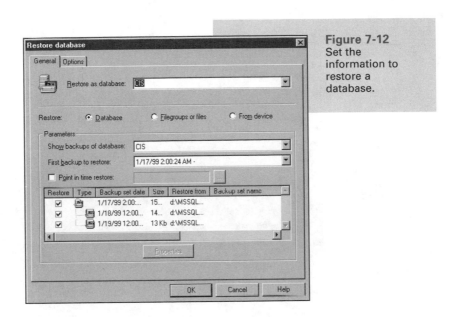

Figure 7-12
Set the information to restore a database.

4. Again on the same tab, you can choose the first backup you want to restore. Unless you have a reason to restore an old backup, you should select the most recent backup available. Next choose to restore everything to the most recent transaction log that was backed up or choose to restore to a point in time. For this example, I'll restore everything.

Tip

Recovering up to a certain point in time is very useful if you can identify when your program destroyed the database. (This usually happens when a program accidentally deletes some or all of the records in a database or changes everyone's name to Darth Vader or Captain Kirk.)

5. On the Options tab (see Figure 7-13), you can specify some additional parameters, such as restoring the database over the existing database (which I want to do in this situation) or prompting before restoring each backup. You can also choose to

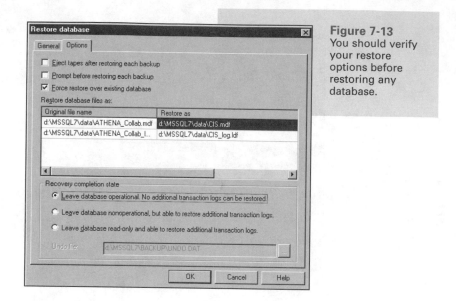

Figure 7-13
You should verify your restore options before restoring any database.

leave the database fully operational, totally nonoperational until additional transaction logs are applied, or in a read-only state where additional transaction logs may be applied. This last option may be useful when you need to allow users to access your database before you have restored all the transaction logs.

6. Once all the options have been set, press the OK button to perform the restore. A series of progress bars will be displayed indicating the restore's progress through each database backup and transaction backup. When the restore is finished, a message box will be displayed.

Wrapping Up

Testing your application is just as important as any other phase of the project. Without a properly working program, your users won't be very happy. Also, when you have to reload your database, it's better to know that it really works than to have to recover your database under pressure.

The sample data I supplied on the CD-ROM has at least one bug. While the bug isn't significant, it's up to you to find it. I'll give you a hint: Importing a blank line of data will try to insert Null values into every field in the table.

While I'm on the subject of bugs that you should be looking for, there's another bug that might prevent you from loading data into the database. It has to do with the CreditCardCode constraint. You should revise the constraint to fix the problem or at least disable it so that you can proceed. The trigger for StateCode also has an error. Can you find it? Consider what happens if someone in the US specifies a Canadian province. Also, I didn't verify any values for Canada. The changes aren't hard, but they will take you back to Chapter 5 for a few minutes.

The bug in the Edit Customer Information Program is subtle. To reproduce, add a new customer to the database, update the record, and then try to delete it. You get a message saying that "the specified row could not be located for updating: Some values may have been changed since it was last read." To correct this problem, you need to refresh the database before you delete a newly inserted record.

Bugs can also be easily disguised. For instance, entering an improper value in some of the fields might cause a nasty error. Can you find it? Try entering a non-numeric value where the database is expecting to see a numeric value. A hint: Bound controls prevent this problem from happening. Sometimes a bug isn't a bug, but a feature. Check the value of the record pointer when the filter returns no records. A little checking might prevent this bug from being visible.

An area that was ignored while you built the program was security. While the security was adequately defined for this subsystem, it was poorly implemented. The use of the ADO data control required that I either hard code a login ID and password into the application or supply that information in a nonencrypted file on the hard disk. This type of security is generally not acceptable. You should research other alternatives to see if they offer a better approach to security.

Project 1 Summary

At the end of this phase of the WebBooks.com project, you should have learned the following:

- How to determine the requirements for an application
- How to hold a brainstorming session to determine data elements
- How to use Entity/Relationship modeling to design a database
- How to access a database using the ADO Data Control
- How to use bound controls with the ADO Data Control
- How to import data into SQL Server using the Data Transformation Services
- How to back up and recover a SQL Server database

HANDS ON PROJECT 2

THE INVENTORY INFORMATION SUBSYSTEM

- ■ Design Databases with the Enterprise Manager
- ■ Create a **Data Environment** in Visual Basic
- ■ Use a **Data Environment** with bound controls
- ■ Access databases directly using **ActiveX Data Objects (ADO)**
- ■ Search for data using full-text indexes
- ■ Build IIS Applications

Project Overview

The Inventory Information Subsystem extends your knowledge of Visual Basic and SQL Server by introducing the Data Environment Designer that allows you to build more complex database applications. You'll also cover how to create and use full-text indexes, which allow you to perform complex boolean searches for information in your database.

Also, you will learn how to create Visual Basic IIS Applications, which allow you to build programmed responses for various Web requests. You will develop HTML forms to collect information that will be processed by the IIS Application, making it easy to build full-function, Web-based applications.

CHAPTER 8

What Is the Inventory Information Subsystem?

In the second stage of this project, you'll build on the knowledge gained in the first phase to implement a more complex part of the application, the Inventory Information Subsystem. As with the first phase, you'll progress through the following four steps:

- **Gather information** for the application
- **Design** the application
- **Build** the application
- **Test** the application

In this chapter, you'll cover the high-level requirements for the system and discuss how it will be used by the various customers and personnel within WebBooks.com.

Describing the Inventory Information Subsystem

The second phase of the WebBooks.com project is to design and build the database tables and programs necessary to manage WebBooks.com's inventory of books. Unlike the Customer Information System, some of the programs you will work with are going to come in two flavors: traditional client/server-based programs and Web server-based programs. While you're going to continue to use traditional client/server programs (because they are more efficient) to serve the needs of internal users, you may want to build some Web-based programs that will ultimately be used by the customer.

Database Elements

Everything that is related to a customer is managed by this subsystem. Most of this information will be developed in Chapter 9, but at a minimum, the application needs to track the following information:

- Title of the book
- Author
- Publisher
- Retail price
- Discount
- Quantity on hand

Application Functions

The Inventory Information Subsystem is designed to keep track of the books that are available for sale. It contains all the elements of a catalog, plus a few other elements that are necessary for sales support and inventory tracking. At a minimum, the Inventory Information Subsystem will need to perform these functions:

- Display information about a book
- Search for books

- Update inventory information
- Reorder books as needed from the publisher
- Notify customers as new books arrive
- Generate inventory reports

The Inventory Information Subsystem will have to communicate with the Customer Information Subsystem to perform some functions, such as getting customer keywords and e-mail addresses.

Types of Users

Different users will need different levels of access to various components and data elements in this subsystem. This is done to protect the confidentiality of some data items and to ensure that only the appropriate individual performs the specific task. The five basic types of users for this subsystem are:

- The customer who orders books
- The manager who directs and plans activities
- The purchasing agent who reorders books for the inventory
- The computer operator who performs routine functions
- The database administrator

Customers are allowed to view information about the books and search for books based on keywords. The manager plans activities and performs general administrative tasks, such as data analysis and preparing e-mail messages advertising new books to customers. The purchasing agent needs to know when the supply of a particular title is low and needs to order more copies from the publisher. The computer operator needs sufficient access to back up the database but doesn't need the ability to write any data and shouldn't be permitted to perform any other operations against the database. The database administrator has complete access to any data element and also has the responsibility of restoring a database when a problem occurs and will track the proper execution of the batch jobs.

Of course this is not a complete application, so one thing you should keep in mind is that the application must be easy to change. You'll update this subsystem later in the book to integrate it with the other subsystems. While it would be better to design the entire application at the same time, it rarely happens that way in the real world, so learning how to build an easily updateable application is very important.

Goals of the Inventory Information Subsystem

This subsystem has several goals, but the most important is to build more complex client/server applications and Web server-based applications.

Determining Data Element Needs and Structures

As you did in the Customer Information Subsystem, you'll brainstorm to identify the elements needed for the database. Then you'll refine them and use the information to build a database. While this is very similar to what you did in the Customer Information Subsystem, you'll also explore new areas like full-text indexes and storing images online.

Most books similar to this one use relatively small sample databases to demonstrate how to implement a database application. I did this with the Customer Information Subsystem, where the largest table held about 200 records and the primary table only held about 100 records. While such a sample database is relatively easy for the author to create, it doesn't give the reader a good feeling for what it's like to work with a real database. Therefore, I've arranged to use data for over 900 records. This means that you will have a database that uses over 10 megabytes (MB) of disk space. This makes tasks like loading and backing up your database a little more realistic. After all, in the real world, loading a big database can take hours or days, not the half-second that most sample databases require.

Building Programs to Access the Database

Now that you know how to use the **ADO data control**, use the ADO objects to directly access the database. This doesn't mean that you have to give up using bound controls though. You'll focus on the **WebClass** object and how it works under the Inventory Information Subsystem. While most of the Web pages are going to be plain (hey, this isn't a Web page design book—go read Prima Tech's *Create Your First Web Page In a Weekend, Revised Edition,* if you want to learn about Web page design), they're nevertheless going to include all the key elements that are required to make your application work.

The Browse and Update Information function is similar to the Edit Customer Information program developed for the Customer Information Subsystem. It basically presents the data in the database for someone to view and update. I'll also include the ability to search on various fields in the database.

Wrapping Up

The Inventory Information Subsystem is a little more complex than the Customer Information Subsystem. It will track all the book titles that are available for sale. Unlike the Customer Information Subsystem, this subsystem will have a large amount of data to give you the feel for operating a realistic database. In other words, your database won't load in two seconds and the Database Maintenance Plan that ran in less than two minutes for the Customer Information Subsystem will take a little longer.

Take a few moments and study some of the books you might have lying around. Look at how the ISBN is formatted on books from different publishers. See how many authors it took to write some of those 1,000-plus page books. Note that there's a biography of the author of the book tucked away somewhere inside.

Next, consider how you buy books. Do you go to the bookstore and browse through the table of contents? Do you read magazines and newsgroups to see what books other people find useful? If you buy books over the Web, what information do you find most useful? If you don't buy books online, what information would you need in order to change your mind? The answers to these questions will help you in the next chapter when you begin gathering information about the second phase of the application.

CHAPTER 9

Gathering Data for the Inventory Information Subsystem

By now you have some ideas about what the Inventory Information Subsystem should do. In this chapter, you'll brainstorm to determine the data elements needed and preview the various functions needed for this subsystem.

Determining the Data Elements Needed

Sit down with a piece of paper and try to identify all the aspects that should be part of an inventory control system for a bookstore. Only information about books for sale will be included in this subsystem, so items that you may consider to be inventory (like desks and computers) will be left for the store's accounting system. (In other words, forget about everything but books.)

The Brainstorming Session

If you are not familiar with the publishing industry, take a look at a few Web sites out there, such as Computer Literacy (www.clbooks.com) and Amazon.com (www.amazon.com). Both are excellent sites, and by looking at the information they provide for a specific book, you may be able to find some ideas for data elements for this application. The following is the list I came up with during my brainstorming session:

- Title
- Author
- ISBN
- Front cover
- Publisher
- Date published
- Table of contents
- List price
- Discount
- Quantity on hand
- Page count
- Description
- Reviews
- Reorder point
- Category
- Keywords

Reviewing the Results

There aren't as many elements in this subsystem as there were in the Customer Information Subsystem. However, that doesn't mean that this subsystem is less complex. In fact, even with fewer elements, this subsystem is much more complex. For the first time, you have to deal with image data. Also, some items like table of contents and description are clearly more complex than such data elements as customer name.

Basic Book Information

Every book contains certain basic information no matter who published it. This includes fields for the book's title, author, publisher, publish date, and ISBN. This will not be true for some of the other fields that you'll cover in a few minutes.

A book's title is a pretty straightforward object. It just contains a string of characters. The date published field contains either the year or the month and year when the book was initially released.

The author data element is not as simple as it might seem. While I generally write books by myself, I have written a few books with my wife, Jill. We are listed together as the authors of the book. This means that the author field has the same basic problems as the keywords field in the previous subsystem. So I'm going to use the same solution, which is to just list all the authors in a single string.

ISBN, which stands for International Standard Book Number, appears to be a straightforward field since it merely represents a unique number that is assigned to every book published. A typical ISBN looks like this:

ISBN 0-7615-1385-X

The ISBN number has some rather complex formatting rules that describe where to place the dashes. They are used to separate the four different values that are included in the number. I won't go into the details here, but when I write the code to format the value, you'll learn more about it than you really would like. However, the last digit always contains a check digit that is used to verify that the ISBN is valid. Its value can range from 0 to 10. Since it's really hard to represent 10 as a single digit, an X is used. This complicates matters, since the ISBN can't be used as a strictly numeric value.

This leaves two options when choosing a data type for this field: one, you can store the entire ISBN as a string; or two, you can lop off the last digit and recalculate the check digit as needed. Of the two, I think I want to lop off the last digit and save it as a numeric value. I can write a little code to handle the formatting and validation issues.

The field for publisher contains the name of the book's publisher. Note that this isn't necessarily the same as the company that published the book. Some book publishing companies publish books under several imprints. For instance, Macmillan publishes many different imprints, such as Que and Sams. So rather than storing the publisher's company name, I'm just going to store the imprint name. In order to contact the publisher, I'm going to add some of the fields that I used in the Customer Information Subsystem, such as Address1, Address2, City, State, Zip Code, Country, Telephone Number, and E-mail Address.

But this raises another issue. If I'm going to reorder books, I'll need some more information, such as the publisher's address, the telephone number, and the name of the person at the company who can take the order.

Optional Book Information

While every book contains the same basic information, there is a lot of information that may or may not be available. This includes such information as the table of contents, description, reviews, page count, and front cover. While this information may be present for most books, it is possible that it may not be available for some books. Most of this information comes directly from the publisher and may or may not be compatible with its presentation here.

For the most part, each of these elements is pretty self-explanatory. The table of contents is merely a text document that lists the chapters in the book, though some publishers may choose to provide more detail than just the chapter name. The description of the book is another document containing some text that gives the potential buyer an idea of the material covered in the book. Reviews include commentary about the book from other people, both professionals and general readers. Page count contains the number of pages in the book, while front cover contains a graphic image of the front cover of the book.

While the page count is a relatively simple value and can be stored as a numeric field, choosing data types for the other values is much more interesting. The table of contents, description, and reviews are documents that could exceed the **Varchar** limit of 8,000 characters. Also, there is the issue of how to format this information. Obviously the user doesn't want to read a review formatted with fixed-size fonts. Users instead would prefer to read a properly formatted review with proportional characters in various sizes, using bold and italic characters as necessary.

This raises a different issue, and that is how these documents should be formatted. Should the documents be formatted using Word in either Word's native format or rich text format or should they be formatted using HTML tags? This issue raises still another issue. Should the documents be stored inside the database or refer to an HTML document stored outside the database?

The same issue also surrounds the field for book cover. Since the book cover is really an image file, should the image be stored as a GIF, BMP, or JPEG? And should the image be stored in the database or stored on a disk drive?

Storing the data in the database for both documents and images simplifies creating client/server programs, but it makes building Web pages more complicated. Using a Word or rich text format document also simplifies client/server programming, but such documents are nearly impossible to format correctly on a Web page.

While it is important to think about these issues now, it's best to leave them unresolved (though I'm leaning towards keeping everything inside the database and using HTML as the formatting language for the documents). For now, assume that images and documents have unspecified formats. This issue will be resolved in the next chapter when the database is designed.

Another element that didn't come up in the brainstorming session is the type of binding used by the book. Most customers are willing to pay a little more to get a hardcover book than a trade-paper (softcover) book. Other types of binding are mass-market paperback, library binding, spiral-bound, ring-bound, or textbook.

Classification Information

Today most bookstores try to group similar books together to make it easier for customers to find books on a given topic. WebBooks.com needs to do the same thing, only electronically. Therefore, it is important to be able to identify the category of the book. For example, a category for a computer book might be programming or Internet.

However, categories do not completely describe a book. Additional information is needed to further clarify the book's contents. For instance, this book should also have associated with it keywords like Visual Basic, SQL Server, and database. Furthermore, popular variations of these keywords (such as VB, VB6, Visual Basic 6, and SQL Server 7) should be associated with the book as well.

To allow for multiple categories of a book, I'm going to include a data element called keywords. This value is structured exactly as the keywords value was structured in the Customer Information Subsystem.

While I'm also on the subject of classification, many computer books are classified by the level of the intended users. Thus you might see a book with a user level of beginner, intermediate, or advanced, though it is quite common to see books classified as being for beginner to intermediate, intermediate to advanced, or all levels.

Support Information

The last group of information that I want to cover concerns the fields that really support the Inventory Information Subsystem itself. Aside from the ISBN, all the other fields exist primarily to help sell the book. However, fields for such elements as list price, discount, quantity on hand, and reorder point serve to help process the customer's purchase.

These fields aren't complicated. List price holds the recommended list price of the book. Discount holds the percentage discount off of the list price that the customer will actually pay. Quantity on hand holds the number of books on-site available for shipment to customers, while reorder point specifies when additional books should be ordered.

Final Data Elements

Table 9-1 summarizes the data elements covered, with their preliminary data types and other information. Note that this list includes the new data elements I found during the review process, while a few of the original elements from the brainstorming session were deleted.

Table 9-1 Data Element Rules for the Inventory Information Subsystem

Data Element	Data Type	Nulls Allowed?	Default Value	Other Edits
Title	String	No	—	None
Author	String	No	—	None
Publisher	String	No	—	None
Contact name	String	Yes	" "	None
Address1	String	No	" "	None
Address2	String	Yes	" "	None
City	String	No	" "	None
State/Province	String	No	" "	Check value if country = "United States"
Zip code/Postal code	String	Yes	" "	Check value if country = "United States"
Country	String	No	"United States"	Must match item in list of specified countries
Telephone number	String	Yes	" "	None
E-mail address	String	No	" "	None
ISBN	Numeric	No	—	None
Date published	Date	No	—	None
Table of contents	String	Yes	" "	None
Description	String	Yes	" "	None
Reviews	String	Yes	" "	None
Page count	Numeric	Yes	0	None
Front cover	Image	Yes	—	None
Binding	String	Yes	—	None
Keywords	String	No	—	None
User level	String	Yes	—	None
List price	Money	No	—	None
Discount	Numeric	No	—	None
Quantity on hand	Numeric	No	—	None
Reorder point	Numeric	No	—	None

Determining the Functions Needed

This subsystem is a little more complex than the Customer Information Subsystem, mostly because I will be developing both Web and traditional client/server programs. However, the programs themselves will be similar to those I developed for the Customer Information Subsystem.

The Update Inventory Information function allows a clerk to review and change the contents of the Inventory Information Subsystem. This program will be similar to the Update Customer Information program and will also be a client/server-based application.

The Display Book Information function is a Web-based function that displays the information about a particular book. Not all the data elements will be displayed, since this function is aimed at customers who want to review the information about a book before purchasing it.

The Search for Book Information function is also Web-based. It allows a customer to enter very general search criteria in order to return a list of books. Then the customer can select a book from the list and display information about it using the Display Book Information program described above.

Wrapping Up

In this chapter, you covered the process to determine the data elements that should be in the database. You assigned them data types and reviewed some data validation rules that should be imposed on each element.

You also identified the requirements that the Inventory Information Subsystem must meet. It must be capable of:

- Updating the information related to a book
- Displaying book information via the Web
- Searching for books via the Web

Some of these functions are supposed to be implemented using traditional client/server programs, while others will be strictly Web-based. The user who will be using the application determines which approach is used. Customers who need to search for books and display information about a book will be accessing the database only from the Web, while the in-house users from WebBooks.com will almost always use a client/server-based application.

As with any design session, I'm sure that you found things that you would have implemented differently. Often while designing an application, many people have different opinions of how things should be done. In this case, I chose the information that I felt would be useful in making a purchase decision. You may have some additional items you would like to see. Therefore you should add them to the list of data elements that will be used in the database design. Then in the next chapter, you can incorporate them into the tables you create as well.

CHAPTER 10

Designing the Inventory Information Subsystem

In Chapter 9, you saw the different data elements and functions that need to be included in the database design. In this chapter, as you continue to build the WebBooks.com application, you'll use some different approaches to building SQL Server and Visual Basic programs.

ON THE CD

The complete source code for these functions is included on the CD-ROM. Check the \HOSQLSrver7\Chapt10\iss directory for the SQL statements necessary to create tables and indexes in the IIS database.

The Inventory Information Subsystem Attributes

In this subsystem, you need some new data types to hold information about the book's cover and discount. While the need for a new type to hold the image of the cover may be obvious, the discount may not be. **Discount** contains the percentage discount from the list price that the consumer will receive on a book purchase. The maximum discount on a book is 100 (which means that WebBooks.com is giving the book away). So if you only wanted to specify values in the range of 0 to 100, you could use a **Tinyint** field to hold the discount to the nearest percentage point.

However, using any integer value makes it more difficult to calculate the price of the book. To compute the price of a book where the discount is stored as an integer, you would use the following formula:

```
Discounted price = List price * (1 - Discount) / 100
```

However, if you store the discount as a decimal value in the range of 0.00 to 1.00, you can compute the cost of the book as:

```
Discounted price = List price * (1 - Discount)
```

The second option is a lot more reasonable, but it means an Integer field can't be used to hold the value. The choices are to use a **Decimal** value or a **Real** value. Since a **Decimal** value is an exact number and a **Real** value is not, and since money is involved, use a **Decimal** field. (You wouldn't want to explain to your accountant that you're storing information used to calculate a cost value in a field that isn't exact.)

To store the cover image, there are two options for data types: **Varbinary** and **Image**. The primary difference is that **Image** can hold a larger image than **Varbinary**, since **Varbinary** is limited to a maximum of 8,000 bytes. **Image** can hold a single value of up to 2GB. It's appropriate to use the **Image** data type in this case.

Choosing data types for description, table of contents, and reviews presents a similar problem. A **Varchar** field can hold up to 8,000 characters. While this should be enough for the description and table of contents, it probably isn't large enough for all the reviews a book might get. That is assuming I stored all the reviews in a single variable. However, 8,000 characters should be sufficient for any single review.

The Inventory Information Subsystem Entities

The data elements listed in Table 9-1 tend to fall into two groups: information about a book and information about a publisher. So immediately you have your first two entities, Books and Publishers. Since each book has a publisher, there will be a foreign key link between the two tables. And rather than using the publisher's name as the common value between the two tables, create a PublisherCode value, similar to the CountryCode value used in the Customer Information Subsystem.

Tip

Any time you specify that a column or columns are a foreign key into a different table, you should make sure that the other table has an index on those columns to improve performance.

The Books Entity

Unlike the Customers table, the Books table doesn't really need an ID value that is small and unique for each row. It already has one: the ISBN. But the ISBN value has one slight problem: Since the last digit can range from 0 to X, where X is a single character that stands for 10, you can't easily represent this value as an integer. However, removing the check digit from the ISBN does not affect the uniqueness of the remaining digits. Thus the remaining digits can be represented by an integer value ranging from 0 to 999,999,999. This value conveniently fits into an **Int** value, which can hold values up to 2,147,483,647.

The Authors, Author Biographies, and Author Books Entities

Author is the classic case of a repeating group. Every book has at least one author, while some may have 10 or more. Unlike the Address field in the Customers table, you really don't want to put 10 author fields in the Books table. This wastes space if all you have is one author. It also causes problems when you have a book with 10 authors. So you really need to normalize the entity so that there is a table that contains authors and books in addition to the Books table. However, normalizing this information can be difficult.

Consider the case of CountryCodes. Each address entry in the Customers table has exactly one value for a country. This is called a one-to-many relationship. One customer has one country, while one country can be used for many customers.

The AuthorBooks relationship is more complicated, since one author can have many books and a book can have many authors. This is called a many-to-many relationship. The only way to correctly represent this relationship is to create a table called AuthorBooks that contains a list of ISBNs and authors. If there is only one author for the book, only one row would be added; if there are two authors, then two rows would be needed, and so forth.

Rather than storing the author's name as each entry, create another table called Authors, with an AuthorID field and an AuthorName field. I'm going to create still another table to hold a short biography about the author. I don't really need to store this information in a separate table, since the author to author biography is a one-to-one relationship (i.e., each author has only one biography). However, because of the size of the author biography (I'm going to allow up to 8,000 characters in a **Varchar** field), I prefer to isolate the biography information, since it is going to be very infrequently used. I'll also add an AuthorNumber field to make sure that the authors are stored in the AuthorBooks relationship in the proper order.

Tip

Optimize your database by minimizing physical I/O operations. One thing that helps is to move large, low-activity fields away from the main table to a different table. This allows you to keep more rows in each page, which in turn reduces how often you have to read a page from disk. You can also place the low-activity data on a different disk drive to minimize the impact on your main table.

The Reviews Entity

As far as how the data will be used, a review, a description, and a table of contents are all very similar. Each contains a block of text that can be displayed on a form or a Web page. You can save all of these rather large values in a separate table. Then you can normalize the table so that you have one large text field and a key to retrieve the data. At least part of the key needs to be the ISBN. Then all you need to do is add a field to make the key unique. I call this field the ReviewNumber field.

The Review Number field serves two purposes. First, when combined with the ISBN, it makes the primary key unique. Furthermore, it allows me to name (or more correctly, number) the individual reviews. I also can specify that the description for a book has a review number of 0 and a table of contents has a review number of -1. I am free to include other comments, such as comments by the publisher, comments by the author, and a review by WebBooks.com staff (see Table 10-1). A side benefit of normalizing this data is that it moves the data away from the main Books table, which can improve performance and make it easier to maintain. Since I have a separate table for this information, I decided to keep a few other pieces of information (such as the reviewer's name and e-mail address) as part of the review.

Table 10-1	Values of Review Number
Review Number	**Description**
0	The description of the book
1	The book's table of contents
2	A review by WebBooks.com
3	Comments by the publisher
4	Comments by the author
> 4	A review by the reader

The Binding Codes and Publisher Entities

The Binding Codes entity is similar to the Country Codes entity from Chapter 5. It merely contains translation codes for the different types of bindings. Some possible values for bindings are Mass Market Paperback, Trade Paper, and Hardcover.

Information about each publisher is stored in a table using many of the same fields found in the Customers table. The primary key is the Publisher code used in the Books table. Also, many of the fields in this table are the same as those in the Customers table. I deliberately used the same names, since the definition of each field is still the same. The only new field is Contact Name, which holds the name of the individual that the WebBooks.com purchasing agent calls at that publisher.

The Final Database Design

The final database design is shown in Figure 10-1. It consists of eight tables: Books (see Table 10-2), Authors (see Table 10-3), Author Biographies (see Table 10-4), Author Books (see Table 10-5), Reviews (see

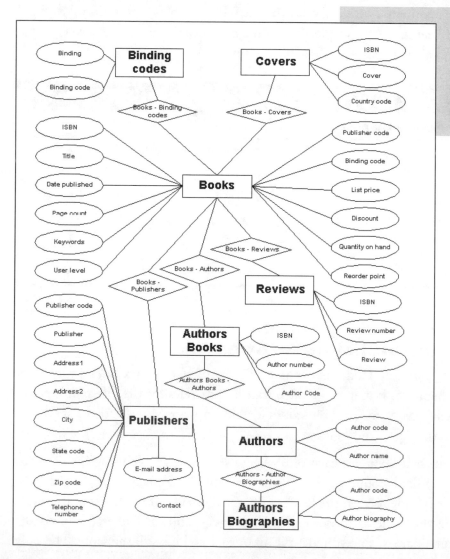

Figure 10-1
An Entity/ Relationship diagram for the Inventory Information Subsystem database.

Table 10-6), Covers (see Table 10-7), Binding Codes (see Table 10-8), and Publishers (see Table 10-9).

Table 10-2	Attributes of the Books Entity			
Data Element	**Data Type**	**Nulls Allowed?**	**Default Value**	**Other Edits**
Data Element	Data Type	Nulls Allowed?	Default Value	Other Edits
ISBN	**Int**	No	—	Primary key
Title	**Varchar**(64)	No	—	None
PublisherCode	**Smallint**	No	—	Link to publishers
DatePublished	**Datetime**	No	—	None
PageCount	**Int**	Yes	0	None
BindingCode	**Smallint**	Yes	—	Link to binding codes
Keywords	**Varchar**(255)	No	—	None
UserLevel	**Varchar(64)**	Yes	—	None
ListPrice	**Money**	No	—	None
Discount	**Decimal**(5,2)	No	—	None
QuantityOnHand	**Int**	No	—	None
ReorderPoint	**Int**	No	—	None

Table 10-3	Attributes of the Authors Entity			
Data Element	**Data Type**	**Nulls Allowed?**	**Default Value**	**Other Edits**
AuthorCode	**Int**	No	—	Primary key, identity field
AuthorName	**Varchar**(64)	No	—	None

Table 10-4	Attributes of the Author Biographies Entity			
Data Element	**Data Type**	**Nulls Allowed?**	**Default Value**	**Other Edits**
AuthorCode	**Int**	No	—	Primary key
AuthorBiography	**Varchar**(8000)	No	—	None

Table 10-5   Attributes of the Author Books Entity

Data Element	Data Type	Nulls Allowed?	Default Value	Other Edits
ISBN	Int	No	—	Primary key
AuthorCode	Int	No	—	Secondary key
AuthorNumber	Smallint	No	—	None

Table 10-6   Attributes of the Reviews Entity

Data Element	Data Type	Nulls Allowed?	Default Value	Other Edits
ISBN	Int	No	—	Primary key
ReviewNumber	Smallint	No	—	None
ReviewerName	Varchar(64)	Yes	—	None
E-mailAddress	Varchar(64)	Yes	—	None
Review	Varchar(8000)	No	—	None

Table 10-7   Attributes of the Covers Entity

Data Element	Data Type	Nulls Allowed?	Default Value	Other Edits
ISBN	Int	No	—	Primary key
Cover	Image	No	—	None

Table 10-8   Attributes of the Binding Codes Entity

Data Element	Data Type	Nulls Allowed?	Default Value	Other Edits
BindingCode	Smallint	No	—	Primary key
Binding	Varchar(64)	No	—	None

Table 10-9	Attributes of the Publishers Entity			
Data Element	Data Type	Nulls Allowed?	Default Value	Other Edits
PublisherCode	**Smallint**	No	—	Primary key
Publisher	**Varchar**(64)	No	—	None
ContactName	**Varchar**(64)	No	—	None
Address1	**Varchar**(64)	No	—	None
Address2	**Varchar**(64)	Yes	—	None
City	**Varchar**(64)	No	—	None
StateC	**Varchar**(64)	No	—	Check value if country code = 1 ("United States")
ZipCode	**Varchar**(16)	Yes	—	Check value if country code = 1 ("United States")
CountryCode	**Smallint**	No	1	Link to country
TelephoneNumber	**Varchar**(24)	No	—	None
E-mailAddress	**Varchar**(64)	No	—	None

Building the Database

In Chapter 5, you learned how to create your database one table at a time using a spreadsheet-like design tool you accessed by right-clicking on the Tables node inside your database in the SQL Server Enterprise Manager. This time you'll create your database using the Enterprise Manager that starts by creating a new database diagram.

The first step in building the Inventory Information Subsystem database is to create an empty database called IIS on the database server. Since you covered this in Chapter 5, it won't be repeated here. However, because of the volume of data, allocate a minimum of 20MB of space rather than the 10MB used in the previous subsystem.

Creating a Database Diagram

After creating the blank database, open it and right-click on the Diagrams node. Then select New Database Diagram from the pop-up menu. This will begin the process to create a new database diagram. Next a warning message will be displayed, which tells you that there are no tables to be added to the diagram but that you can create new ones within the designer. Pressing OK leaves you with a blank screen onto which you are going to paint your new tables (see Figure 10-2).

Adding a Table to the Diagram

Start building your database by creating the Books table. You may want to refer to Table 10-2 for details about the table.

> The Add Table button doesn't create a table in the database. It merely adds to the diagram a table that already exists in the database. (Remember that you can use the Database Designer to draw a picture of your current database also.) To create a table, you must press the New Table button.

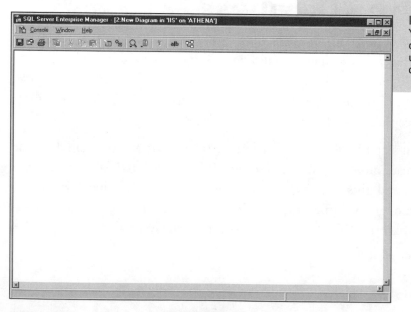

Figure 10-2
You can design your database graphically using the database diagram utility.

1. Press the New Table button (refer to Figure 10-2) to add a new table to the diagram. A dialog box will appear asking the name of the new table (see Figure 10-3). Enter "Books" and press OK.

2. After the dialog box disappears, a grid (similar to the one used in Chapter 5) will appear prompting you for the information needed to create a table. Enter the information for the Books table as specified in Table 10-2 (see Figure 10-4).

3. Place the cursor on the ISBN column and press the Set Primary Key button to make this column the primary key.

4. You can right-click anywhere on the table you just created to display the pop-up menu. Choose Keys from the menu to reduce the size of the display by showing just the Column Names, the table's Keys, or the table's Name Only. This is a good display since this makes the view of the table much smaller but leaves the keys visible for linking to other tables (see Figure 10-5).

5. Right-click one more time on the table and choose Save Selection to save the table structure to the database. Repeat this process for the remaining tables.

Choose Name ☒

Enter a name for the table:

Books

OK

Cancel

Help

Figure 10-3
Enter the name
of the new table.

Books

Column Name	Datatype	Length	Precision	Scale	Allow Nulls	D
ISBN	int	4	10	0		
Title	varchar	64	0	0		
PublisherCode	smallint	2	5	0		
DatePublished	datetime	8	0	0		
PageCount	int	4	10	0	✓	
BindingCode	smallint	2	5	0		
Keywords	varchar	255	0	0		
UserLevel	varchar	64	0	0	✓	
ListPrice	money	8	19	4		
Discount	decimal	5	5	2		
QuantityOnHand	int	4	10	0		
ReorderPoint	int	4	10	0		

Figure 10-4
Enter the
information for the
Books table.

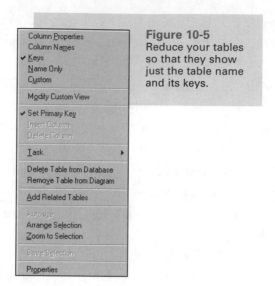

Figure 10-5
Reduce your tables so that they show just the table name and its keys.

Linking Tables Together

After you have entered the information for all your tables, you need to show the relationships between them, so follow these steps to define the foreign keys in the database:

1. Make sure that the columns you want to link are visible. You may have to right-click on the table to expose the columns, if they aren't already recognized as a key.

2. Press the left mouse button on the primary key field in the Primary Key Table and drag the dotted line to the column in the Foreign Key Table.

3. A dialog box will be displayed when you release the left button (see Figure 10-6). You should review this information and make sure that it is correct.

4. Repeat this process for the rest of the foreign keys. Then press the Arrange Tables button to see the display shown in Figure 10-7.

5. Save the diagram.

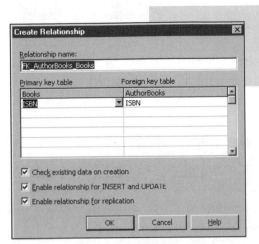

Figure 10-6
Review the columns selected for the primary and foreign keys.

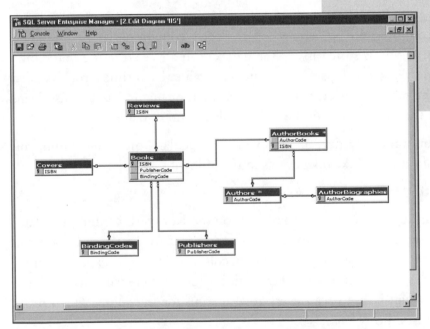

Figure 10-7
The completed database diagram shows the relationship between the tables.

Note

The links in the database diagram go from table to table, not from column to column. As long as the links go between the correct tables, you can check the properties dialog box to ensure that the correct fields are included in each link.

Building Full-Text Indexes

One of the new features in SQL Server 7 is the ability to create a full-text index in a table. This means that you can search large columns (such as the Review or Keywords columns) for a particular word much faster than you can search for a particular value using the **Like** operator.

How a Full-Text Index Works

Before using a full-text index, it is important to understand how it works and how it compares to a regular index. A full-text index allows you to find a row in a table that contains a single word or phrase. This is useful in situations like WebBooks.com where a user wants to find a book by searching for selected keywords.

A regular index keeps a copy of every unique value for indexed column or columns and pointers to all the rows containing that value. This information is stored inside the database in a tree structure that allows the server to quickly search for an exact value. Each time a row is added to the table (or deleted or updated), the index is updated. This means that the information in the index is always up to date.

If you want to retrieve all rows with a particular word in a column, you would use the **Like** operator as in the following sample:

```
Select * From Books Where Keywords Like '*Basic*'
```

Assuming that a regular index exists on the Keywords column, the database server would have to scan through every entry in the index looking for the word 'Basic' anywhere in the column. This is an expensive operation, since it has to read every index value. If there isn't an index, the server will have to scan every row looking for the value, which really increases the expense.

A full-text index is stored outside the database as a series of independent files that are managed by the database server. But unlike the case of a regular index, you are only permitted one full-text index per table. This isn't a big limitation, however, since you include multiple columns in the index and specify the column you want to search. The full-text index stores each unique word and a pointer to the row where it can be found.

When you have a full-text index, you would write your **Select** statement this way:

```
Select * From Books Where Contains (Keywords, 'Basic')
```

Note that you don't need the asterisks to denote that you can match any number of characters before and after the word 'Basic'. The **Contains** operator specifies that the word 'Basic' must appear somewhere in the Keywords field.

The biggest drawback to using a full-text index is that the index isn't updated as rows are added or changed in the table. This means that you won't find newly added rows in the table. However, you can run a batch job to perform the update as part of the database maintenance process. This can cause problems for many applications, but in this case, while new books and reviews are constantly added, it is not absolutely critical that the index be updated in real time.

You can exclude certain words from the index. These words are found in the FTData\SQLServer\Config\Noise file that is appropriate for your language. If you want to exclude a word from the index, simply add it to the file. Of course you will need to rebuild the indexes whenever you do this for the change to take effect.

Creating a Full-Text Index

To create a full-text index to the Books table, follow these steps:

1. Using the Enterprise Manager, display the pop-up menu by right-clicking on the Books table. Then choose Full-Text Index Table, Define Full-Text Indexing on a Table. This will display the Full-Text Indexing Wizard as shown in Figure 10-8. Press <u>N</u>ext to continue.

2. The next panel asks you to specify the name of a unique index. This value will be associated with the words stored in the index and used to retrieve the row from the table.

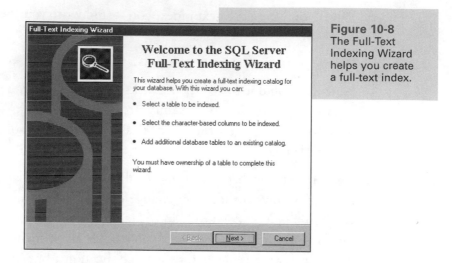

Figure 10-8
The Full-Text Indexing Wizard helps you create a full-text index.

3. Pressing <u>N</u>ext takes you to the panel where you select the columns that should be indexed (see Figure 10-9). Only character-based columns are listed, since only character-based columns can be indexed.

4. The next window tells the database where you want to put the index. If there is already an index in the database, you can choose to use it or you can specify the name of the file where the index will be stored.

5. You can optionally create a batch job managed by the SQL Server

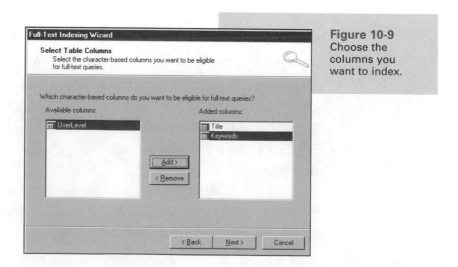

Figure 10-9
Choose the columns you want to index.

Agent to rebuild or update the index. Press the New Schedule button to create a new schedule.

6. You can either re-create your full-text index from scratch or apply the changes made since the last time the scheduled update was executed. I suggest doing both. Figure 10-10 shows the schedule I used for the weekly full update. Figure 10-11 shows both schedules in the Batch Job dialog box.

7. The last window allows you to review all your settings and go back and change them before completing the wizard. Pressing Finish will display a dialog box that shows the execution of the wizard. When it's finished, it will display the dialog box shown in Figure 10-12, which instructs you to use the Start Population menu option to initially populate the index.

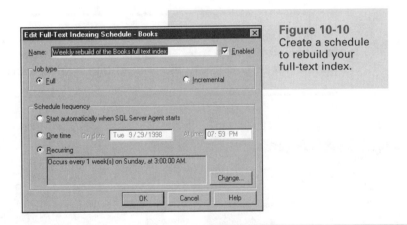

Figure 10-10
Create a schedule to rebuild your full-text index.

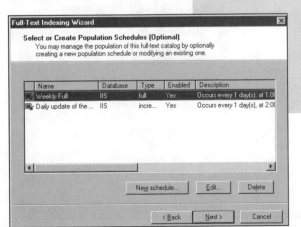

Figure 10-11
The schedules for the full rebuild and the incremental update for the full-text index for Books

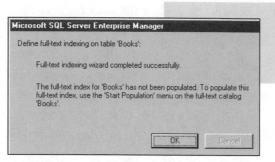

Figure 10-12
You should review your changes before pressing the Finish button.

8. Select the IIS database and the Full-Text Catalogs node to display the list of full-text indexes in the Enterprise Manager. Right-click on the Books index and select <u>S</u>tart Population, <u>F</u>ull Population to create the initial index (see Figure 10-13).

Caution ▶

> While a table has a full-text index, you can't make any changes to its structure. Of course you can always drop the index, make your changes, and rebuild it afterwards.

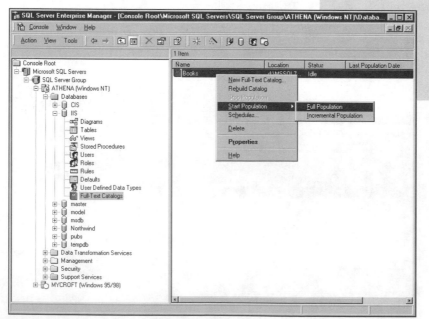

Figure 10-13
Use the <u>S</u>tart Population menu option to initialize the index.

Creating Triggers

While you can't establish a foreign key relation on a table in a different database, you can use triggers across database boundaries. In Listing 10-1 I've created my own foreign key clause for the Publishers table where I verify that the user can only enter valid CountryCode values. I took the trigger I built for the Customer Information Subsystem to ensure that only valid values for State were entered and added the CIS database prefix for the StateCodes table. The result in Listing 10-2 is not very different from that which was used in Chapter 5.

This trigger is used to duplicate the function of a foreign key clause:

Listing 10-1

```
Create Trigger CountryCodeTrigger
    On dbo.Publishers
    For Insert, Update

As

If not Exists( Select *
        From cis.dbo.CountryCodes, Inserted
        Where cis.dbo.CountryCodes.CountryCode = Inserted.CountryCode)
    Raiserror('Invalid value for Country',16,1)
```

The SQL statement in Listing 10-2 ensures that only valid state information can be inserted or updated in the Customers table:

Listing 10-2

```
Create Trigger StateCodeTrigger
    On dbo.Publishers
    For Insert, Update

As

Declare @CountryCode as Smallint
Select @CountryCode = Inserted.CountryCode From Inserted

If @Countrycode = 1
    Begin
    If Not Exists( Select *
        From cis.dbo.StateCodes, Inserted
```

```
        Where (cis.dbo.StateCodes.State = Inserted.State
            Or cis.dbo.StateCodes.State = Inserted.State))
            And CountryCode = 1
        Raiserror('Invalid value for State, when Country = "United
➡States".',16,1)
        End
```

Finishing Up the Database

After building your database, there are a few cleanup details that you should attend to. The first is to save the SQL statements that are used to build the database to disk. This will help you rebuild your database much faster, since you can open the file in the Query Analyzer tool and run the script. Then presto—your database structures are back again. Take the time to verify that the database is being properly backed up. You earlier learned how to use the Database Maintenance Plan Wizard to back up your database.

Wrapping Up

Creating a database by drawing a database diagram is a more natural experience to many than entering the information into a table. However, the end result is still the same: a collection of tables and other database objects that are ready for your application program to use.

The full-text index is a powerful tool that can help you do keyword searches against the data in your database. It's important to remember that the full-text index is not updated every time a row is updated, but only when you schedule the activity. This limits its usefulness to some degree, but if you run a daily update, being a day out of sync on a low volume table is probably not all that bad.

Did you know that you can access both the Design Table window and the Database Diagram window through Visual Basic? Take a few minutes and look at the Visual Basic help files to find out how. To get you started, take a look at the Data View window under your active connection to the database.

CHAPTER 11

Building the Inventory Information Subsystem

After designing the database, it's time to drag out Visual Basic and start writing some code. In this chapter, you'll do the following:

- Update the information related to a book
- Display book information via the Web
- Search for books via the Web

Unlike the previous phase of the WebBooks.com application, you'll use the Data Environment designer to create more complicated database access facilities insteading of using the **ADO Data Control**. Also, you'll learn about a feature introduced in Visual Basic 6 called the IIS Application. This allows you to build Web server-based applications using Visual Basic quicker than in PERL and more efficiently than in Visual InterDev.

ON THE

CD

The complete source code for these functions is included on the CD-ROM. Check the \HOSQLSrver7\Chapt11 directory.

- **BookInfo** contains the ActiveX EXE program with some of the business logic.
- **WebBooks** contains the IIS Application program that runs on the Web server.

Using Data Environments in Visual Basic

Bound controls are a powerful concept; however, using them with the ADO data control forces you to open the database immediately. This means that you have to save the login ID and passwords in an unprotected file on each person's system. This isn't really a good idea. However, by using the ADO components directly, it's possible to avoid this problem and still use bound controls. To do this, you must first add a Data Environment to your application.

Adding a Data Environment to Your Program

To create a Data Environment, follow these steps:

1. Start Visual Basic and create a new Standard EXE program.
2. Select Project, Data Environment. If you don't see Data Environment on the menu, look under More ActiveX Designers. (Only the first four designers show up directly under the Project menu item.) The form displayed in Figure 11-1 will be shown.

Adding a Connection Object to the Data Environment

Once you have a Data Environment object, you need to define how to access your database. A **Connection** object, which contains the information about how to access your data, is created by following these steps:

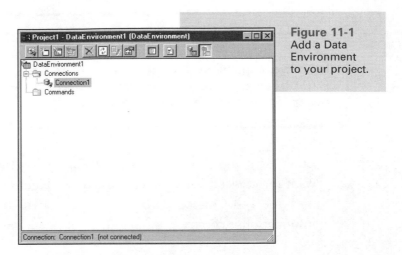

Figure 11-1
Add a Data
Environment
to your project.

1. Using the Data Environment you created above, right-click on Connection1 and select Properties from the pop-up menu. The Data Link dialog box will be displayed (see Figure 11-2).

2. Select Microsoft OLE DB Provider for SQL Server from the list of OLE DB Providers and press Next to continue to the next form.

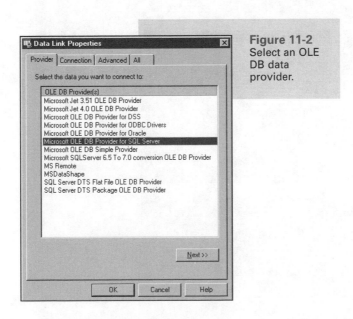

Figure 11-2
Select an OLE
DB data
provider.

Caution

> By default the Microsoft OLE DB Provider for ODBC Drivers is selected on the list of providers. While this provider works, it has fewer capabilities than the Microsoft OLE DB Provider for SQL Server. Since you are using SQL Server, there is no reason not to use the more advanced provider.

3. Enter the name of the database server and select the database you want to access on the Connection tab (see Figure 11-3). You can press the Test Connection button to verify that all of your information is correct.

Note

> If you don't specify your login ID and password on the Connection tab, the provider will ask you for it when you connect to the database. This means that your login ID and password are not buried in your program or on your hard disk. This helps to make your application more secure.

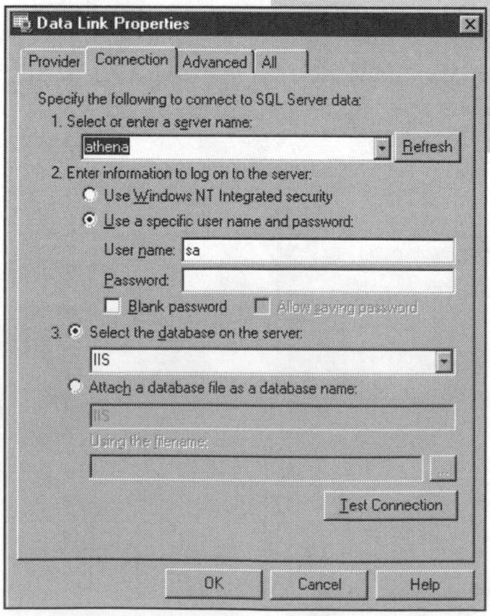

Figure 11-3
Enter database access information.

4. You don't need to enter any other information into this form. Press OK to accept these values.

Adding a Command Object to the Data Environment

Now that you have a way to access the database, you need to create a **Command** object that will contain the information necessary to access the data. You can create a **Command** object by following these steps:

1. In the Data Environment window, right-click on **DataEnvironment1** and select Add Command from the pop-up menu. This will create a new **Command** object in the **Commands** collection (see Figure 11-4).

2. Right-click on the new **Command** object and select Rename. Change the name to Books.

3. Right-click again on Books and select Properties to display the Properties window.

4. On the General tab, select Connection1 for the _C_onnection field, select Table as the _D_atabase Object, and select dbo.books. In the _O_bject Name field, select the Books table (see Figure 11-5). Press OK when finished.

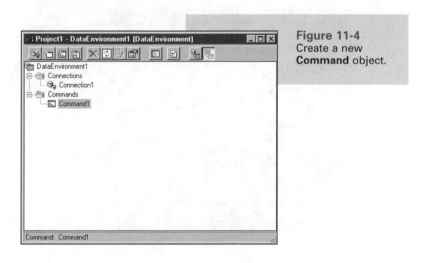

Figure 11-4
Create a new
Command object.

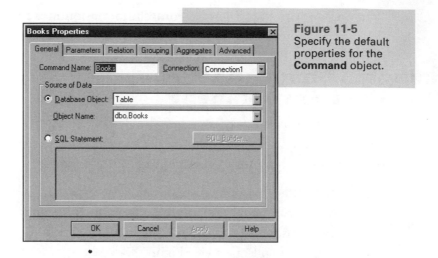

Figure 11-5
Specify the default properties for the **Command** object.

Tuning the Command Object's Cursor, Locking, and Cache

On the Advanced tab of the **Command** object's properties dialog box (see Figure 11-6), you will notice some properties that control the **Recordset** associated with the **Command** object. This includes properties such as **CursorType**, **CursorLocation**, **LockType**, and **CacheSize**.

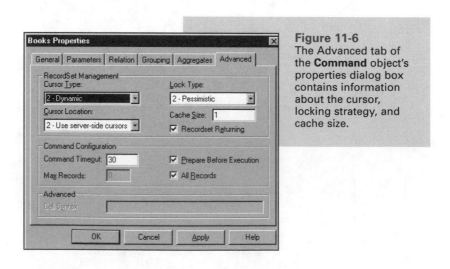

Figure 11-6
The Advanced tab of the **Command** object's properties dialog box contains information about the cursor, locking strategy, and cache size.

The type of cursor used in a **Recordset** determines many of its characteristics. This information is kept in the **CursorType** property. ADO supports these four different types of cursors:

- A static cursor points to a collection of rows that will not change until the **Recordset** is closed. Any rows that have been added, deleted, or updated by any other user are not seen in this **Recordset**.

- A dynamic cursor points to a collection of rows that change as other users make changes to the database. Any changes that have been made by other users can be seen in this **Recordset**.

- A keyset cursor points to a collection of rows that see all changes (including deletions) to the database except for new records.

- A forward-only cursor points to a collection of rows that can only be accessed in a forward direction. Moving backwards isn't permitted.

The cursor can also be resident in either the client's computer or on the server. This is set in the **CursorLocation** property. If you want the cursor to be kept on the client, then you must use a static cursor to access the data.

The **LockType** property determines how you and other users can access the data in the database.

- A read-only lock means that you can't alter any of the data in the **Recordset**.

- A pessimistic lock means that the row is locked immediately when the editing process begins. The lock will be released when the **Update** or **Cancel** method is used.

- An optimistic lock means that the data is locked just before the **Update** method is used to update a single row. If someone updated the data between the time that the editing began and the **Update** method was used, an error will be returned.

- A batch optimistic lock means that the data is locked just before the **UpdateBatch** method is used to update multiple rows at the same time. Any errors will be returned in the **Error** object associated with the **Connection** used by the **Recordset**.

> You should lock the least amount of data possible in order to make it easy to share data. If you don't need to update any of the data, you should use a read-only lock. For most other functions, you probably should use a pessimistic lock to prevent others from updating the data you are editing. You should use a batch optimistic lock when you plan to add or update many rows of data in your database; however, you should be prepared to detect and handle cases where someone changed the data after you retrieved it but before you updated it. Otherwise, you may lose some or all of your changes.

The **CacheSize** property determines how many rows are buffered in the client machine. Increasing this size allows the database server to operate more efficiently when returning data to the client system. It will also improve the performance of the client system since it will retrieve data from memory. However, information in your cache will not reflect the changes that other users may have made in the database. The more you keep in cache, the more likely that you'll have a problem. If you are using pessimistic locking, you probably should set **CacheSize** to 1 to prevent invalid records from sitting in your cache. For the Books command, I'm going to specify a static cursor with pessimistic locking and set the cache size to 1.

Building a Login Form

The first block of code you want to write takes a user's login ID and password and opens the **Connection** object. So add a few controls on Form1 to collect this information and then put a command button to run the login process (see Figure 11-7).

Pressing the command button executes the code found in Listing 11-1. This routine begins by using the **On Error Resume Next** statement to

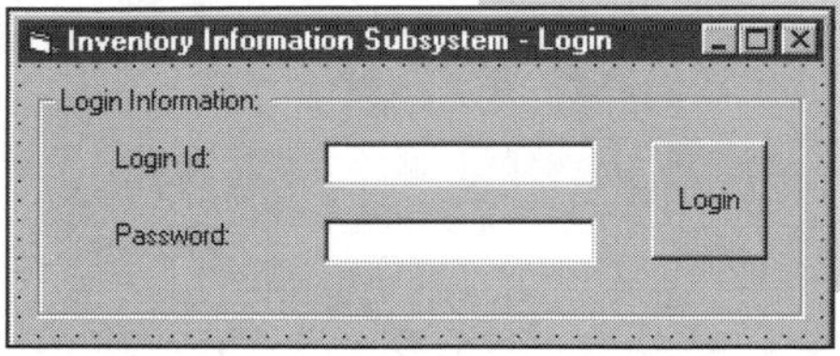

Figure 11-7
The Inventory Information Subsystem Login form collects the information needed to log into the server.

prevent run-time errors in this routine from killing the program. Then it checks to see if Connection1 is closed before attempting to open a connection. This is because you don't want to log on again if the connection is already open.

The **Command1_Click** event opens a connection to the database:

Listing 11-1

```
Private Sub Command1_Click()

On Error Resume Next

If DataEnvironment1.Connection1.State = adStateClosed Then
   Err.Clear
   DataEnvironment1.Connection1.Open , Text1.Text, Text2.Text
   If Err.Number = 0 Then
      BookInfo.Show 0
      Unload Me
   Else
      MsgBox "Invalid login information, please try again."
   End If

End If

End Sub
```

After making sure that no previous errors have set the **Err** object, use the connection's **Open** method to open a connection to the database. Send the values from the text1 and text2 text boxes, which contain the login ID and password, respectively, to the **Open** method. Note that I do not supply a value for the connection string, since I let that value default to the one supplied in the Data Environment's property dialog box.

If the login is successful, I show the BookInfo form (you'll create this in a moment), which allows the user to see information about the books in

Handling Errors in Visual Basic Programs

My favorite way to trap run-time errors in Visual Basic is to use the **On Error Resume Next** statement. If an error occurs while executing a statement, the entire statement is flushed and control is transferred to the next statement in the program.

This allows you to use the **Err** object to determine if an error occurred. You need to be careful, since any statement that fails will set the **Err** object. However, statements that run correctly don't clear the **Err** object. This means you should always use the **Err.Clear** method before the statement you want to check. Otherwise an error from a prior statement could set the **Err** object, and you wouldn't know it until you checked for an error condition.

the inventory. Close this form, since you don't need it anymore. If there is an error during the login process, issue an error message and let the user try again.

Closing the Database Connection

Since I went to the trouble of logging on to the database, I felt that I should also include a log-off procedure that would close the connection and end the program. This is included as the Logout button and is shown in Figure 11-8.

Pressing the Logout command button executes the code found in Listing 11-2. The first thing you do is to verify that the user really wants to end the program. You use the MsgBox function to display a message box to the user with Yes and No buttons. If the user presses the Yes button, then log the user out; otherwise, leave things alone and let the user continue to work.

The Command5_Click event closes the connection to the database.

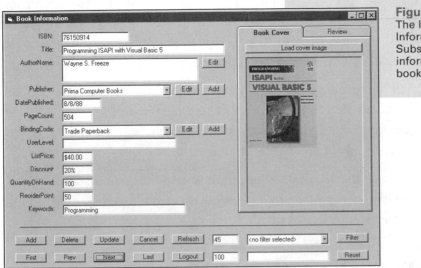

Figure 11-8
The Inventory Information Subsystem displays information about a book.

The Command5_Click event closes the connection to the database:

Listing 11-2

```
Private Sub Command5_Click()

Dim f As Form

On Error Resume Next

If MsgBox("Are you sure you want to logout?", vbYesNo) = vbYes Then
    For Each f In Forms
        If f.Name <> Me.Name Then
            Unload f
        End If
    Next f

    Err.Clear
    DataEnvironment1.Connection1.Close
    If Err.Number = 0 Then
        Unload Me
    Else
        MsgBox "Error logging off."
    End If

End If

End Sub
```

After the user presses Yes, close all the forms in this program except for this form. Use the **Forms** collection, which recognizes that a form is really just another object in Visual Basic. Use the **For Each** statement to loop the collection and use the **Unload** statement to close each form.

Once all the forms are closed, close the connection to the database. You want to allow each form to complete any database processing before it is closed. You will need to include some code in each **Unload** event that will clean up any open database transactions.

If you close the database connection successfully, unload this form, which will end the program. If you encounter any errors, issue a message and leave this form loaded.

Programming with the Data Environment Designer

Now that you have a way to access the database that doesn't involve the ADO data control, it's time to move on and build a program. Since this chapter focuses on the Inventory Information Subsystem, start by building a form for the Books table and then continue to the other tables in the database.

Adding Columns to Your Form the Easy Way

Data Environments not only work at run time, but they are also used at design time. Double-clicking on the Books command will display the login screen as shown in Figure 11-9. This happens because the Data Environment Designer requires an open connection to the database to get information about the various objects you will want to access.

Tip

The OLE DB Login window will also appear any time you try to open a recordset without a valid login ID and password. If you wish, you can use this window in place of the one you just built, though the user won't see it until after trying to access a particular function.

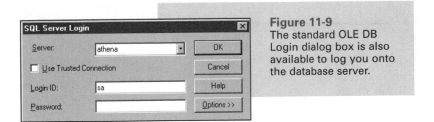

Figure 11-9
The standard OLE DB Login dialog box is also available to log you onto the database server.

After logging on, you can see the individual components that make up the Books command object (see Figure 11-10). In this case you can see that the Books **Command** object contains all the columns from the Books table. Now you can create the BookInfo form by following these steps:

1. Select Project, Add Form and select Form from the New tab of the Forms dialog box.

2. Change the caption of the form to read "Book Information". Also change the name of the form to "BookInfo".

3. Click and drag ISBN from the DataEnvironment1 window to the new Book Information form (see Figure 11-11).

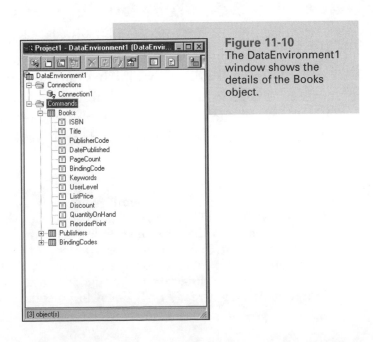

Figure 11-10
The DataEnvironment1 window shows the details of the Books object.

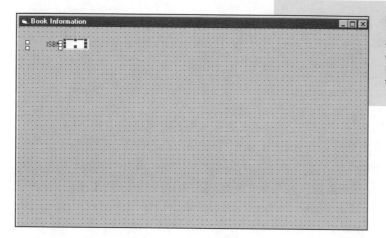

Figure 11-11
Dragging ISBN from
the DataEnvironment1
window to the Book
Information form adds
the field to the form.

4. Repeat the drag-and-drop operation for the other fields in Books.

5. Rearrange the controls on the form so they look right.

This process not only makes it easy to place the labels and controls on your form, but it handles all the binding issues, so if you were to run the program as it exists, you would see the first row of the Books table.

Navigating the Books Table Manually

Now that you can access the data from the Books table, you want to be able to move around and see the books, add and delete rows, and even search for a particular title or keyword. In short, these are the same basic functions included in the Customer Information Subsystem with the ADODC control. However, since I'm not using the control, I have to supply my own buttons and write the code to move the current record.

Note

Why bother with all this extra work, when you could just use the ADO data control? Part of the problem with using the ADO data control is that you have to live with the control's style. If you like it, fine, but I prefer the look of regular command buttons. This lets me arrange the form so that it looks better. The code to duplicate these functions isn't very complicated either. So it really boils down to personal preference.

When you look at a **Recordset** object, you're really looking at an object that has access to any one row out of a series of rows. This row is known as the current record pointer or the current row pointer. These rows are delimited at the beginning and at the end by a BOF (beginning of file) marker and EOF (end of file) marker (see Figure 11-12).

One problem with using Data Environment is that you have a **Command** object that returns a **Recordset**. An rs is automatically inserted in front of the **Command** object's name to create the name of the **Recordset** object. Thus the **Books Command** object will create the **rsBooks Recordset** object when the **Command** object is opened.

Knowing the current record is really important, since most of the operations are applied against the current record. You use the **Fields** property to look at and change the values of the columns in the current record. You use methods such as **Update** to make the changes permanent and the **Delete** method to remove a row from the table. You can move around in the table using a number of different move methods.

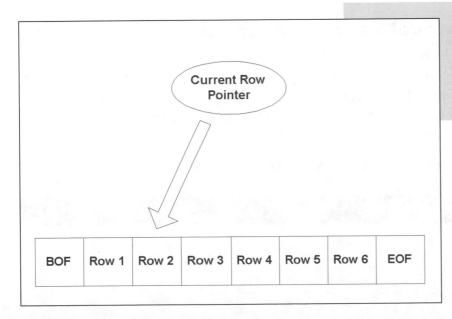

Figure 11-12
A Recordset which begins with a BOF marker and ends with an EOF marker.

> **Note**
>
> By now you may have noticed that I use the terms **record** and **row** interchangeably. If you were to think of a table as a flat file, then a row would obviously be a record. The basic concepts are the same. So while I should be using the term **row**, I sometimes slip and use the term **record**. However, in my defense, I'll point out that a lot of other people have this problem, including some at Microsoft. Otherwise, the **Recordset** object would be known as the **Rowset** object.

It is possible to have an empty **Recordset**. This may happen when your **Select** statement doesn't find any rows or when your database table is empty. Since there are no records in the **Recordset**, both the **BOF** and **EOF** properties are set and there isn't a current record. Accessing any of the properties and methods that depend on a valid current record, such as the **Fields** property and the **Delete** method, will cause a run-time error.

Now that you understand the basic structure of a **Recordset**, dig in and go through the methods that you'll use to move around the recordset. If some of these methods seem familiar, remember the buttons on the **ADO Data Control**. Pressing a button on the **ADO Data Control** merely calls the appropriate method.

MoveFirst and MoveLast

The **MoveFirst** and **MoveLast** methods are used to position the current record pointer to either the first row or the last row of the **Recordset**. Listing 11-3 contains the code to move the current record pointer to the first record in the Books table. I'll leave the detailed analysis of the code to you.

The Command2_Click event moves the row pointer to the first record:

Listing 11-3

```
Private Sub Command2_Click()

With DataEnvironment1.rsBooks
    .MoveFirst
```

```
End With


End Sub
```

MovePrevious and MoveNext

The **MoveFirst** and **MoveLast** methods are pretty straightforward, but the **MoveNext** and **MovePrevious** methods are a little more complicated. In a **Recordset** object, you will normally move to the next or previous record. Thus if row 2 is the current record, row 3 will become the current record after a **MoveNext** method. However, if you are at the last row in the **Recordset**, performing a **MoveNext** will move you to the EOF marker. This sets the **EOF** property **True,** and since the current record isn't a real record, you can't access any of the information about the record. Using the **Fields** property or the **Delete** method will trigger a run-time error.

The same discussion also to applies the **MovePrevious** and the BOF marker. So letting the current record pointer sit on either the BOF or EOF marker isn't a good idea. However, there is an easy fix. Since you can detect the BOF or EOF condition after performing a **MoveNext** or **MovePrevious,** you can then move the current record pointer back to the beginning or end of the **Recordset** by using the **MoveLast** or **Move-First** method (see Listing 11-4).

The Command4_Click event moves the row pointer to the next record:

Listing 11-4

```
Private Sub Command4_Click()

With DataEnvironment1.rsBooks
     .MoveNext

   If .EOF Then
      .MoveLast

   End If

End With

End Sub
```

Move Anywhere

Another interesting method is the **Move** method. This method allows you to move the specified number of rows forward or backward in the **Recordset**. A positive value means the movement will be toward the end of the **Recordset**. A negative value means the movement will be toward the front of the **Recordset**. A value of zero means the current record remains current. However, all the functions and events that would be triggered with a move will also be triggered (more about this in a few moments). If you are at the BOF marker and attempt to move backward, a run-time error will occur. The same is true if you are at the EOF marker and attempt to move forward.

Bookmarks

The **Bookmark** property provides a way to save and restore the location of a particular row in a **Recordset**. You can save this value into a **Variant** variable to remember the location of the current record. Then later you can assign this value to the **Bookmark** property, and the old record will become the current record.

WillMove and MoveComplete

After you issue any methods that will move to a new row, the **WillMove** and **MoveComplete** events will be fired. These events allow you to perform tasks before or after the move actually takes place.

In the **WillMove** event, you can set the adStatus parameter to adStatus-Cancel if you want to cancel the move. If adStatus is set to adStatus-CantCancel, you can't issue the cancel request. You may want to use this event to verify that the data in the current record is fine before you move to another record.

One of my favorite uses of these events is to use the **MoveComplete** event to display the number of records and the position of the current record in the **Recordset** (see Listing 11-5). I verify that I have at least one row in the **Recordset** and then display the numbers on the appropriate place on the form. Note that I have to qualify where the information should be displayed, since the **MoveComplete** event is found in the **DataEnvironment1** object and not the form where the move methods were used.

The **MoveComplete** event can be used to display information about the current record:

Listing 11-5

```
Private Sub rsBooks_MoveComplete(ByVal adReason As ADODB.EventReasonEnum,
  _
  ByVal pError As ADODB.Error, adStatus As ADODB.EventStatusEnum,_
  ByVal pRecordset As ADODB.Recordset)

With DataEnvironment1
    If Not (.rsBooks.BOF And .rsBooks.EOF) Then
        BookInfo.Text2.Text = FormatNumber(.rsBooks.AbsolutePosition, 0)
        BookInfo.Text3.Text = FormatNumber(.rsBooks.RecordCount, 0)

    End If

End With


End Sub
```

A more complicated example of this event is shown in Listing 11-6. Not only does the routine display the total rows in the table and the relative position of the current record, but it also goes out and opens recordsets that will contain the list of authors, reviews, and book cover associated with the current book.

The **MoveComplete** event can also retrieve rows in other related tables:

Listing 11-6

```
Private Sub rsBooks_MoveComplete(ByVal adReason As ADODB.EventReasonEnum,
    ByVal pError As ADODB.Error, adStatus As ADODB.EventStatusEnum,
    ByVal pRecordset As ADODB.Recordset)

With DataEnvironment1
    If Not (.rsBooks.BOF Or .rsBooks.EOF) Then
        BookInfo.Text2.Text = FormatNumber(.rsBooks.AbsolutePosition, 0)
        BookInfo.Text3.Text = FormatNumber(.rsBooks.RecordCount, 0)

        If .rsBooks.EditMode = adEditAdd Then
            CurrentISBN = 0
```

```
    ElseIf CurrentISBN <> .rsBooks.Fields!isbn Then
        CurrentISBN = .rsBooks.Fields!isbn

        If Authors.State = adStateClosed Then
            Set Authors.ActiveConnection = .Connection1
            Authors.LockType = adLockPessimistic
            Authors.CursorLocation = adUseServer
            Authors.CursorType = adOpenStatic
            Authors.Source = "Select a.AuthorCode, a.AuthorName, " & _
                "ab.isbn, ab.AuthorNumber " & _
                "From AuthorBooks ab, Authors a " & _
                "Where a.AuthorCode = ab.AuthorCode and " & _
                "ISBN = " & FormatNumber(CurrentISBN, 0, , , vbFalse) & _
                " Order by AuthorNumber"
            Authors.Open

Else

    Authors.Close
    Authors.Source = "Select a.AuthorCode, a.AuthorName, " & _
        "ab.isbn, ab.AuthorNumber " & _
        "From AuthorBooks ab, Authors a " & _
        "Where a.AuthorCode = ab.AuthorCode and " & _
        "ISBN = " & FormatNumber(CurrentISBN, 0, , , vbFalse) & _
        " Order by AuthorNumber"
    Authors.Open
End If

If Covers.State = adStateClosed Then
    Set Covers.ActiveConnection = .Connection1
        Covers.LockType = adLockPessimistic
        Covers.CursorLocation = adUseServer
        Covers.CursorType = adOpenStatic
        Covers.Source = "Select * From Covers " & _
            "Where ISBN = " & _
            FormatNumber(CurrentISBN, 0, , , vbFalse)
        Covers.Open

    Else
        Covers.Close
        Covers.Source = "Select * From Covers " & _
            "Where ISBN = " & _
            FormatNumber(CurrentISBN, 0, , , vbFalse)
        Covers.Open
    End If

    If Reviews.State = adStateClosed Then
        Set Reviews.ActiveConnection = .Connection1
        Reviews.LockType = adLockPessimistic
```

```
            Reviews.CursorLocation = adUseServer
            Reviews.CursorType = adOpenStatic
            Reviews.Source = "Select * From Reviews " & _
                "Where ISBN = " & _
                FormatNumber(CurrentISBN, 0, , , vbFalse) & _
                " Order by ReviewNumber"
            Reviews.Open

        Else
            Reviews.Close
            Reviews.Source = "Select * From Reviews " & _
                "Where ISBN = " & _
                FormatNumber(CurrentISBN, 0, , , vbFalse) & _
                " Order by ReviewNumber"
            Reviews.Open
        End If

        On Error Resume Next
        Set BookInfo.DataList1.RowSource = Authors
        Set BookInfo.Text9.DataSource = Reviews
        Set BookInfo.Text10.DataSource = Reviews
        Err.Clear
        Set BookInfo.Picture1.DataSource = Covers
        If Err.Number <> 0 Then
            BookInfo.Picture1.Picture = LoadPicture()
        End If
        End If

    End If

  End If

End With

End Sub
```

After displaying this position information, this routine checks to see if I'm adding a new book to the Books table. If I am adding a new record, I set the CurrentISBN number to zero. Otherwise, I check to see if the ISBN of the current row is the same value as in CurrentISBN. If they are the same, then I'll do nothing, since I've already retrieved this information. If they are different, then I'll retrieve the related information from the Authors, Covers, and Reviews tables and save the new ISBN in CurrentISBN.

Shaping Your Data with the *Shape* Command

Another way to retrieve data from multiple tables is to create child commands that are related to a parent command, much like multiple tables can be linked together in a **Shape** statement. The **Shape** statement works with the **Select** statement to create a hierarchical **Recordset**.

Usually you would use the Data Environment Designer to create the main **Command** object. Then you would create various child commands and link them back to the main **Command**. The Data Environment Designer will automatically build a single **Shape** statement, which will be used when the **Command** is used.

You can also build your own **Shape** statement and use it in the **Recordset.Source** property when you open the **Recordset**. This merely involves coding the **Shape** statement with all the various options.

When using the Data Environment Designer, you can bind various fields on your form to the child commands, just like you can with the parent command, and each time you move to a new row in the **Recordset,** the child commands will be updated automatically.

The primary drawback to this approach is that you can't update any of the data in the child commands. In a way, this is very disappointing since there are many situations where you would like to update these values. However, it is possible to design your database with this feature in mind. You would use secondary tables to hold static information or information that would be updated from a different process.

This facility was designed with the **MSHFlexGrid** control in mind. The **MSHFlexGrid** allows you to sort, merge, and format your data into tables containing both strings and pictures. These two tools provide a quick and easy way for your user to examine the data.

I repeat the same logic for each of the three tables, so I'll just go through it once. I begin by seeing if the Authors table is closed. If it is, then I know that this is the first time through the loop and I need to initialize all the information in the recordset. I set the **ActiveConnection** property to **DataEnvironment.Connection1**, which I use for all **Recordsets**.

Next I assign values for the cursor and locks. Being a negative sort of person, I use pessimistic locks. This ensures that the data is updated properly the first time and I don't have to worry about what to do if the data was changed before I updated it. I also choose to use a static cursor on the server. While using the static cursor allows me to capture position information, the main reason I'm using it here is to be consistent with the Books table. Then I build a SQL **Select** statement to retrieve only the rows associated with the current book and open the **Recordset**. If the **Recordset** is already open, I simply **Close** the **Recordset**, build the new query, and **Open** it again.

Armed with the new values in the **Recordsets**, I need to refresh the values in the various controls that are bound to these **Recordsets**. To do this, I simply use the **Set** statement to reassign the **Recordset** to the **DataSource** property of each bound control. If the **Recordset** is empty, an error will occur. However, I can safely ignore the error since the information in the **TextBox** controls will be cleared. The **PictureBox** control doesn't work this way. In order to clear the picture, I need to use the **LoadPicture** function without any parameters.

Refreshing Your Recordset

When using data-bound controls, you have to live with their limitations. One of the biggest is that they will automatically open the associated **Command** object when the form is loaded. This means that you can't easily change the query you are using to display the data or even refresh the information from the server.

One of the limitations of a static cursor is that you don't see the latest information from the database. Other users could have added or deleted information in the database and you wouldn't know it. However, it is possible to refresh the contents of a Data Environment object if you understand how the Data Environment objects are organized.

In Listing 11-7 you can see the code I use to refresh the rsBooks **Recordset** object. All I do is **Close** the **Recordset** and then **Open** it again. This forces the query to be reexecuted , therefore retrieving a fresh copy of the Books table. Then all I have to do is to refresh the contents of each bound control by setting the **DataSource** property to DataEnvironment1.

Use the RefreshBooks subroutine any time you need to refresh the contents of the rsBooks **Recordset**:

Listing 11-7

```
Private Sub RefreshBooks()

DataEnvironment1.rsBooks.Close
DataEnvironment1.rsBooks.Open
Set txtISBN.DataSource = DataEnvironment1
Set txtTitle.DataSource = DataEnvironment1
Set DataCombo2.DataSource = DataEnvironment1
Set txtDatePublished.DataSource = DataEnvironment1
Set txtPageCount.DataSource = DataEnvironment1
Set DataCombo1.DataSource = DataEnvironment1
Set txtUserLevel.DataSource = DataEnvironment1
Set txtListPrice.DataSource = DataEnvironment1
Set txtDiscount.DataSource = DataEnvironment1
Set txtQuantityOnHand.DataSource = DataEnvironment1
Set txtReorderPoint.DataSource = DataEnvironment1
Set txtKeywords.DataSource = DataEnvironment1

End Sub
```

Tip

Closing a **Recordset** object that is bound to a control leaves the control in a state of limbo. The last data displayed in the control remains, even if you **Open** the **Recordset** again. The easiest way around this problem is to use the **Set** statement to assign the same value to the **DataSource** property. This will force the bound control to rebind to the specified data source, and the control will work properly again.

Filtering for Results

One problem with grabbing a table full of information is that there is too much information to scroll through one record at a time. The sample database included with this application is relatively small compared to the millions of books that can be found by the big bookstores like Amazon.com and Computer Literacy. So I added the ability to narrow the books displayed by using the **Filter** property.

> You can use the **Filter** method to restrict the rows in a **Recordset** rather than closing the **Recordset** and reopening it. You can also use a filter to specify a range of rows you want to delete. Just specify adAffectGroup after the **Delete** method.

The **Filter** property works with the Data Environment objects just as well as it did with the ADO data control used in Chapter 6. You can use this feature instead of closing a **Recordset**, specifying a new value for **Source**, and opening the **Recordset** again.

In this program, I made it easier for the user to use this function than that which I implemented in Chapter 6 by providing two buttons to control the process. One button applies the filter while the other resets it. I preserve the values in the combo box containing the search fields and the text box containing the search value. Thus all the user has to do is select the search field, enter the search value, and press filter. If the user isn't happy with the results, changing the value and pressing **Filter** again will help with the search.

You should note that the **AbsolutePosition** and the **RecordCount** properties change after the filter has been applied. These values reflect the filtered rows rather than the entire **Recordset**. This is useful information for the user when trying to find a particular book and using the **Filter** property to reduce the number of rows to be examined.

In Listing 11-8, you see how easy it is to filter your **Recordset**. Simply build an expression that you would normally use as part of a **Where** clause and assign it to the **Filter** property. In this case I'm using the **Like** operator to make it easy to match patterns. For example, the following expression would be typical of the value I would assign to the **Filter** property:

```
(Title Like 'Programming*')
```

This value would restrict the **Recordset** to titles like *Programming ISAPI with Visual Basic 5* and *Programming Web Server Applications* (see Figure 11-13).

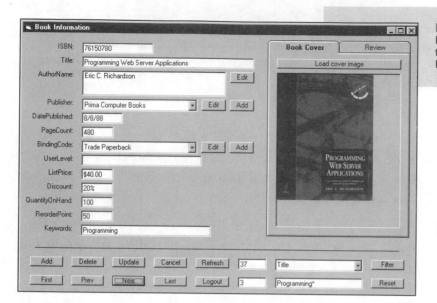

Figure 11-13
Filter for titles
that begin with
Programming.

Use the RefreshBooks subroutine any time you need to refresh the contents of the rsBooks **Recordset**:

Listing 11-8

```
Private Sub Command11_Click()

With DataEnvironment1.rsBooks
    .Filter = "( " & Combo1.Text & " like '" & _
        Trim(Text1.Text) & "' )"

End With

End Sub
```

Adding a Book to the IIS Database

Adding a book to the IIS database involves a more complex procedure than you might think. Simply adding a book to the Books table is a relatively easy job, but you also need to populate the Covers table, the Reviews table, the AuthorBooks table, and possibly the Authors table.

Adding a Book to the Books Table

This is a relatively straightforward process, as shown in Listing 11-9. I look at the **EditMode** property to determine if I'm already adding or updating another record. If I am, then I use the **Update** method to save the information to the database and check for errors that may result from performing the update.

Adding a book to the Books table is similar to what I've done in the CIS phase:

Listing 11-9

```
Private Sub Command6_Click()

Dim e As ADODB.Error

On Error Resume Next

With DataEnvironment1.rsBooks
    If .EditMode <> adEditNone Then
        Err.Clear
        .Update
        If Err.Number <> 0 Then
            For Each e In DataEnvironment1.Connection1.Errors
                MsgBox e.Description
            Next e
            Exit Sub
        End If
    End If

.AddNew
    .Fields("ISBN").Value = 0
    .Fields("Title").Value = ""
    .Fields("PublisherCode").Value = 1
    .Fields("DatePublished").Value = Date
    .Fields("PageCount").Value = 0
    .Fields("BindingCode").Value = 1
    .Fields("UserLevel").Value = ""
    .Fields("ListPrice").Value = 0
    .Fields("Discount").Value = 0
    .Fields("QuantityOnHand").Value = 0
    .Fields("ReorderPoint").Value = 0
    .Fields("Keywords").Value = ""
    Set DataList1.RowSource = Nothing
    Picture1.Picture = LoadPicture()
    Text9.Text = ""
```

```
        Text10.Text = ""

    End With

End Sub
```

After updating the previous record if needed, I simply invoke the **AddNew** method to create a blank row. Then I assign default values for each of the fields in the row. I know that the database server will assign default values for these fields, but I prefer to include them here just to make things clear. Note that I also initialize the **Picture** control that displays the cover, the **DataList** control that displays the authors, and the text boxes associated with the reviews. These fields wouldn't be initialized by the **AddNew** method since they aren't part of the Books table.

Adding Authors to the AuthorBooks Table

Adding a book is easy compared to adding an author. This is because all the author information is stored in other tables. First the author must exist in the Authors table. Then the AuthorCode from the Authors table must be inserted into the AuthorBooks table, along with the ISBN from the Books table and a sequence number that keeps the authors in sequence.

To change the list of authors for a book, the user will press the Edit button next to the AuthorNames field. This will display a form like that shown in Figure 11-14. This form is relatively straightforward to use. You can select any author in the database from the right side of the form and add it to the window on the left side.

The general approach I'm going to use with this form is to use the same Authors **Recordset** that I used in the BookInfo form, plus a new **Recordset** called AllAuthors, containing a list of all the authors in the database. The Authors **Recordset** will populate a DataList control on the left side of the form, while the AllAuthors **Recordset** will populate the right.

Preparing to Add Authors

Listing 11-10 contains the code that happens when the form is loaded. It saves the book title and the ISBN on two text fields at the top of the

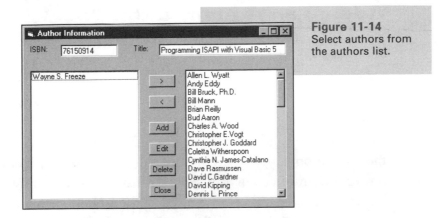

Figure 11-14
Select authors from
the authors list.

form. Then it builds the AllAuthors **Recordset** by creating a new
instance of a **Recordset** object, setting the cursor, locking, and connection information, and specifying a query that retrieves the entire
Authors table sorted by author name. Then it opens the table and
refreshes both **DataList** controls.

The Form_Load event in AuthorInfo initializes the AllAuthors
Recordset:

Listing 11-10

```
Private Sub Form_Load()

Text1.Text = BookInfo.txtISBN.Text
Text2.Text = BookInfo.txtTitle.Text

With DataEnvironment1
    Set AllAuthors = New ADODB.Recordset
    Set AllAuthors.ActiveConnection = .Connection1
    AllAuthors.LockType = adLockPessimistic
    AllAuthors.CursorLocation = adUseServer
    AllAuthors.CursorType = adOpenStatic
    AllAuthors.Source = "Select * from Authors Order by AuthorName"
    AllAuthors.Open
    Set DataList2.RowSource = AllAuthors
    Set DataList1.RowSource = Authors

End With

End Sub
```

Adding an Author to the Book

When the user selects an author from the list of all authors and presses the "<" button, the author will be added to the end of the list of authors for the current book. Since the list of all authors is kept in a **DataList** control, when the user selects an entry, the **DataList**'s **SelectedItem** property contains a bookmark to the record in the bound **Recordset** containing the value. However, since it is possible for the user to press the "<" button without selecting an author, the first step in the code to process this information is to verify that the **DataList** control is returning a valid bookmark. I do this by using the **IsNull** function to see if the **SelectedItem** property is **Null** (see Listing 11-11).

If the property isn't **Null**, I'll assume I have a valid bookmark. So I use the bookmark to find the selected row in the AllAuthors **Recordset**. I then open a temporary **Recordset** using the AuthorBooks table and insert a new row containing the AuthorCode from the selected row in AllAuthors and the ISBN from the current book. I compute a value for AuthorNumber by counting the number of rows in Authors **Recordset** and adding 1. Then I use the **Update** method to save the new row, close the **Recordset,** and release the resources held by the **Recordset** object by setting it to **Nothing**. Finally, I **Requery** the Authors **Recordset** to refresh its contents, and the new author will appear on the form.

Add an author to the end of the list of authors for the current book:

Listing 11-11

```
Private Sub Command2_Click()

Dim a As ADODB.Recordset

If Not IsNull(DataList2.SelectedItem) Then
    AllAuthors.Bookmark = DataList2.SelectedItem
    Set a = New ADODB.Recordset
    a.ActiveConnection = DataEnvironment1.Connection1
    a.Source = "iis.dbo.AuthorBooks"
    a.LockType = adLockPessimistic
    a.CursorLocation = adUseServer
    a.CursorType = adOpenDynamic
    a.Open
    a.AddNew
```

```
          a.Fields!AuthorCode = AllAuthors.Fields!AuthorCode
          a.Fields!AuthorNumber = CInt(Authors.RecordCount) + 1
          a.Fields!isbn = CLng(Text1.Text)
          a.Update
          a.Close
          Set a = Nothing
          Authors.Requery
      End If

  End Sub
```

Removing an Author from the Book

To delete an author, I use the same basic approach that I used for adding an author (see Listing 11-12). I check to see if the user selected a row from the **DataList** control. Then I create a temporary table that will hold the record I want to delete. If the table isn't empty (and it shouldn't be empty), I'll delete the record. Then I'll close the temporary **Recordset** and refresh the Authors table to make the changes visible to the user.

Remove an author from the list of authors for the current book:

Listing 11-12

```
Private Sub Command1_Click()

Dim a As ADODB.Recordset

If Not IsNull(DataList1.SelectedItem) Then
    Authors.Bookmark = DataList1.SelectedItem
    Set a = New ADODB.Recordset
    a.ActiveConnection = DataEnvironment1.Connection1
    a.Source = "Select * From AuthorBooks Where AuthorCode = " & _
        FormatNumber(Authors.Fields!AuthorCode, 0, , , vbTrue)
    a.LockType = adLockPessimistic
    a.CursorLocation = adUseServer
    a.CursorType = adOpenDynamic
    a.Open
    If Not (a.EOF And a.BOF) Then
        a.Delete
    End If
    a.Close
    Set a = Nothing
    Authors.Requery
End If

End Sub
```

Adding a New Author

What happens if the author you want to add isn't in the database? The user would press the Add button and see the InputBox shown in Figure 11-15. Since a row in the Authors table consists of only two fields (AuthorName and AuthorCode) and the AuthorCode is automatically generated when a new row is added, this is probably the simplest routine in the program to add a complete row.

The AllAuthors **Recordset** is opened with an update cursor so that I can directly update the table. All I have to do is use the **AddNew** method and assign a value to the AuthorName field by using the **InputBox** function. Then an **Update**, a **Requery**, and a **ReFill** are all that's required to complete the process (see Listing 11-13).

Add a new author to the Authors table:

Listing 11-13

```
Private Sub Command5_Click()

AllAuthors.AddNew
AllAuthors.Fields!AuthorName = InputBox("Enter Author Name:", _
   "Author Information")
AllAuthors.Update
AllAuthors.Requery
DataList2.ReFill

End Sub
```

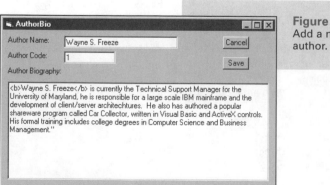

Figure 11-15
Add a new author.

Deleting an Author

Deleting an author is more complicated than adding an author, because I have to delete entries in both the Authors and AuthorBiographies tables (see Listing 11-14). So after verifying that the user really wants to delete the author (see Figure 11-16), I then create a temporary **Recordset** that holds the author's information from the AuthorBiographies table and delete the record if present. Then I can delete the record from the AllAuthors recordset and refresh the information displayed in the list of all authors.

Note When deleting rows from multiple tables, it is important to understand the relationship between them. If the two tables are not related to each other, then the order doesn't matter. But if one table contains a foreign key into another table, then you need to delete the rows in the table with the foreign key first and delete the rows in the primary table. Since you added the row to the primary table first in order to add the foreign key table, you delete them in the opposite direction.

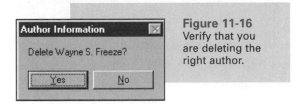

Figure 11-16
Verify that you are deleting the right author.

Delete an author from the Authors table:

Listing 11-14

```
Private Sub Command6_Click()

Dim a As ADODB.Recordset

If Not IsNull(DataList2.SelectedItem) Then
    AllAuthors.Bookmark = DataList2.SelectedItem
    If MsgBox("Delete " & AllAuthors.Fields!AuthorName & "?", _
        vbYesNo, "Author Information") = vbYes Then
        Set a = New ADODB.Recordset
```

```
        a.ActiveConnection = DataEnvironment1.Connection1
        a.Source = "Select * From AuthorBiographies Where AuthorCode = " & _
            FormatNumber(AllAuthors.Fields!AuthorCode, 0, , , vbTrue)
        a.LockType = adLockPessimistic
        a.CursorLocation = adUseServer
        a.CursorType = adOpenDynamic
        a.Open
        If Not (a.EOF And a.BOF) Then
            a.Delete
        End If
        a.Close
        Set a = Nothing
        AllAuthors.Delete
        AllAuthors.Requery
        DataList2.ReFill
    End If
End If

End Sub
```

Editing an Author's Information

While it only takes an author's name to create an entry in the Authors table, you probably want to enter or edit the author's biographical information as well. I do this by using the Author Biography form shown in Figure 11-17.

When the form loads, the code in Listing 11-15 is run to initialize the form and create a **Recordset** object that contains the author's biography. I use the same basic methods I've used before to create a new **Recordset**

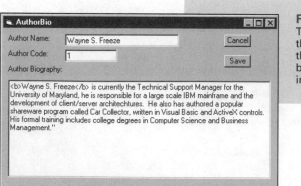

Figure 11-17
This form allows the user to edit the author's biographical information.

object. The only real difference is that I recognize when the **Recordset** is empty and automatically add a new row. This means that all I have to do when the user is finished with the biography is to **Update** the recordset. Adding a new record is treated the same as editing an existing record.

Access the database for the author's biography information:

Listing 11-15

```
Private Sub Form_Load()

With DataEnvironment1
    Set ThisAuthorBio = New ADODB.Recordset
    Set ThisAuthorBio.ActiveConnection = .Connection1
    ThisAuthorBio.LockType = adLockPessimistic
    ThisAuthorBio.CursorLocation = adUseServer
    ThisAuthorBio.CursorType = adOpenDynamic

    ThisAuthorBio.Source = "Select AuthorCode, AuthorBiography " & _
        "From AuthorBiographies " & _
        "Where AuthorCode = " & AuthorInfo.AllAuthors.Fields!AuthorCode

    ThisAuthorBio.Open


    If ThisAuthorBio.BOF And ThisAuthorBio.EOF Then
        ThisAuthorBio.AddNew
        ThisAuthorBio.Fields!AuthorCode = _
            AuthorInfo.AllAuthors.Fields!AuthorCode
    End If

End With

Set Text1.DataSource = AuthorInfo.AllAuthors
Set Text2.DataSource = ThisAuthorBio
Set Text3.DataSource = ThisAuthorBio

End Sub
```

The code in Listing 11-16 is used to commit the changes to the database once the user has finished editing the changes. It tests to see if a change to the database was made and then uses the **Update** method to save the changes. Then it closes the **Recordset** and unloads the form.

Save the user's changes to the database:

Save the user's changes to the database:

Listing 11-16

```
Private Sub Command2_Click()

If ThisAuthorBio.EditMode <> adEditNone Then
    ThisAuthorBio.Update
End If

ThisAuthorBio.Close

Unload Me

End Sub
```

The code that executes when the user presses the Cancel button is nearly identical to the code shown in Listing 11-16, except that the **Update** method is replaced with the **Cancel** method.

Editing Binding Codes

Updating a binding code on a book is very simple for the user. All they have to do is to select the description from the drop-down list. If the desired code isn't on the list, pressing the Add button next to the drop-down list allows you to change the code, while pressing the Edit button allows the user to change the translation text (see Figure 11-18).

In the Book Information form, pressing the Edit button will trigger the code in Listing 11-17. This code uses the **Filter** property of the rsPublishers **Recordset** to isolate the record I'm interested in changing. Then I show the BindingInfo form and allow the user to update the description. The user can close the Binding Information form by closing it, which will execute the **Cancel** method or update the information in the database using the **Update** method.

Figure 11-18
Change the binding information.

Binding Information		_ □ X
Binding:	Trade Paperback	
BindingCode:	1	
Close	Update	

Display the information about the current BindingCode:

Listing 11-17

```
Private Sub Command16_Click()

With DataEnvironment1
    .rsBindingCodes.Filter = "BindingCode=" & _
        FormatNumber(.rsBooks.Fields!bindingcode, 0, , , vbFalse)
    BindingInfo.Show 1
    .rsBindingCodes.Filter = ""
    Set DataCombo1.RowSource = DataEnvironment1
    Set DataCombo1.DataSource = DataEnvironment1

End With

End Sub
```

Changing Publishers

The process to change publishers is very similar to that of changing binding codes. A form is displayed containing information about a publisher (see Figure 11-19), and the user is free to change any of the values.

When the user has finished, pressing the Update button runs the code in Listing 11-18. Basically all it does is perform an update to the database and display any errors it may encounter.

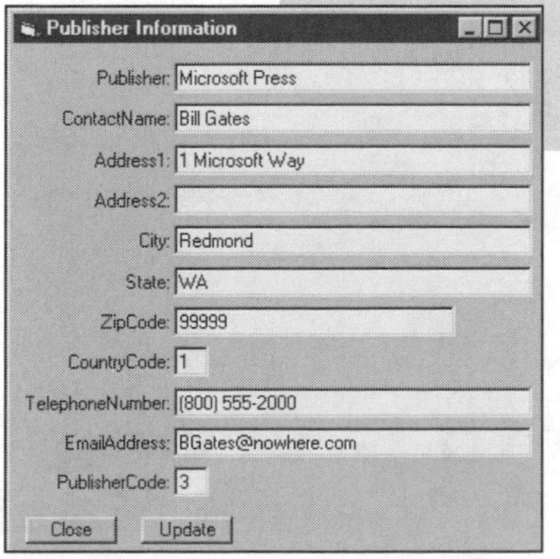

Figure 11-19
Update information about a publisher.

Save the user's changes to the database:

Listing 11-18

```
Private Sub Command2_Click()

On Error Resume Next

With DataEnvironment1.rsPublishers
    .Update
    If Err.Number <> 0 Then
        MsgBox Err.Description
    End If

End With

End Sub
```

After updating the database, the user presses the Close button to return to the Book Information form by using the **Unload** statement. Then the code in the **Unload** event (see Listing 11-19) verifies that the **Recordset** has been changed since the last update. If it was updated, it uses the **Cancel** method to abort the changes and then allows the user to return to the main program.

Abort any outstanding edits before closing the form:

Listing 11-19

```
Private Sub Form_Unload(Cancel As Integer)

With DataEnvironment1.rsPublishers
    If .EditMode <> adEditNone Then
        .Cancel
    End If
End With

End Sub
```

An Introduction to Creating IIS Applications with Visual Basic

One of the new features in Visual Basic 6 is the ability to create IIS Applications. An IIS Application is really an ActiveX DLL that gives a Visual

Basic programmer a high-level way to use the facilities in Internet Information Server (IIS). This results in a high-performance Visual Basic program that can generate Web pages and respond to Web page requests.

This contrasts with Active Server Pages, which are Visual Basic script files that must be interpreted when run. IIS Applications are much more efficient, since IIS Applications contain compiled and optimized code. Unlike DHTML Applications, which rely on extensions to the HTML that are not supported in all Web browsers, IIS Applications can generate any sequence of HTML tags and can communicate with all Web browsers.

Note To build an IIS Application, you should have a good understanding of HTML tags and document structure, since much of the code in an IIS Application will be devoted to writing out strings of HTML. Unfortunately, Visual Basic doesn't provide a graphical way to build HTML documents.

Tip If you're not sure how to write HTML, here's the lazy programmer's way: use a tool like FrontPage that allows you to create a Web page graphically. Then look at the HTML code generated. It's an easy step to copy and paste the statement or two you need into your IIS Application.

Accessing the IIS Application

The IIS Application appears to the user as an Active Server Page (ASP) file. Unlike ASP files generated by Visual InterDev, which contain Visual Basic script code, the IIS Application ASP file points to the ActiveX DLL file containing the application code. A typical URL to access the application is:

```
http://www.justpc.com/WebBooks.ASP?WCI=Search
```

The WebBooks.asp references the ASP file that will launch the IIS Application, and the ?WCI=Search is used to specify the **WebItem** object inside the IIS Application that will respond to the request for information.

State Management

State Management is the process of holding information about the current state of the user's Web session. HTTP is designed as a stateless protocol, which means that each request is independent of all the others. However, users have come to expect that at least some information will be maintained from one request to the next. For example, a user will become extremely frustrated if required to log on to the server for each and every Web page that was transmitted.

When you build your IIS Application, you have a choice of how you maintain state information. You can choose to store the information in the object itself, in other objects on the server, in a database, or on the client's machine as part of a URL or in a cookie. Each of these approaches has its own set of trade-offs.

The first time someone references the ASP, the DLL file is loaded into memory. Then each time a request comes in, the IIS Application will respond with the requested information. However, since no state information is kept, each request must be serviced by itself and without any information from a previous state.

Keeping State Information in the Web Page

A very common practice is to keep any state information as part of the Web page. This can either be done by creating a hidden field as part of the form or by adding information to the URL as a parameter, such as in the sample below. In this case the & is used to separate the parameters WCI and ISBN. The values of the parameters are easily retrieved.

```
http://www.justpc.com/WebBooks.ASP?WCI=Search&ISBN=12345678
```

Using hidden fields that are part of a form can be a useful approach. You can set and get values from these fields just like any other field, but the user can't see it. The following HTML tag shows you how to hide a field:

```
<input size="20" name=hidden value="hide me" style="visibility:hidden">
```

Keeping State Information in the Session Object

By using the **Session** object, you can store data about a single user on the server. You can use this object to hold such information as the contents of the user's electronic shopping cart or the user's nickname. While the **Session** object uses a cookie to hold this information, the programming interface is very simple. You just read and write values like they were members of a property collection. For example, you use the following code to assign a value to the **Session** object:

```
Session("ValueName") = "Some value"
Or you can use this statement to check the value of an object:
If Session("ValueName") = "Some value" Then
     ' do something
End If
```

The **Application** object is similar to the **Session** object but is available to all users, not just the user associated with a particular session. This is useful when you want to keep a global page counter or set other global variables.

Keeping State Information in the Database

Another popular idea is to keep state information in a database table. WebBooks.com does this by storing some information such as credit card type and number in the database. The user doesn't have to reenter this information each time it is used, and it has the advantage of not being transmitted over the Internet, which helps to make the process of buying a book more secure.

Keeping State Information in the WebClass Itself

Keeping state information inside the **WebClass** object means that each user must have a separate copy of the object. This means you can store all of your information in variables local to the object and expect to get the same values each time the **WebClass** is called. The downside to this is the additional overhead of managing all the extra copies of the object.

> **Tip**
>
> **You aren't limited to any one of these state management approaches. In most cases you may want to use more than one. For instance, you may want to store the user's e-mail address (used for a user ID) as a cookie in the user's Web browser, the user's credit card and mailing information in the database, and the user's password as part of the Session object.**

IIS Application Object Model

The IIS Application is built around the **WebClass** object, which contains a set of **WebItems**. Each **WebItem** is an object that contains the information and code that can respond to a Web page request. The **WebClass** object also contains references to the six objects listed below, which contain information about the server's environment, the user's request, and the response to the request that you'll generate.

- The **Request** Object
- The **Response** Object
- The **Session** Object
- The **Application** Object
- The **Server** Object
- The **BrowserType** Object

The **Request** object contains information about the request from the Web browser. The **Response** object contains information about the program's response to the request. The **Session** object tracks information about the current session. The **Application** object stores information across multiple IIS Applications. The **Server** object contains information about the Web server. The **BrowserType** object identifies features available in the browser.

The WebClass Object

The **WebClass** object is the root object in an IIS Application. It contains a series of **WebItem** objects, which are used to respond to individual URL requests, and it contains object references to each of the objects listed above. The **WebClass** object also includes the properties listed in Table 11-1, methods in Table 11-2, and events in Table 11-3.

The **StateManagement** property is used to create a new instance of the **WebClass** object for each user, and the **ReleaseInstance** method will destroy the object after it is no longer needed. The **NameInURL** and **URLData** properties contain the information that is used by the **URLData** method to create a URL for the current **WebItem**. The **Error** object contains information about any errors that occur while processing a request. A serious error will trigger the **FatalError** event.

Table 11-1	Selected Properties of the **WebClass** Object
Property	**Description**
Error	Returns an object reference to an ASP **Error** object, which can be used in the **FatalError** event to determine the cause of the error.
NameInUrl	Contains the name of the ASP file that is in the URL to access the WebClass object.
NextItem	Contains an object reference to the next **WebItem** to be processed when the current **WebItem**'s event is completed.
StateManagement	Allows the programmer to specify that a new **WebClass** object will be created for the first HTTP request. Default is just to create a new instance of the object.
URLData	Contains information that is appended to the end of a URL in the **URLFor** method.

The **NextItem** property contains an object reference to another **WebItem** and is used to link multiple **WebItems** together to respond to a single request. When the first **WebItem** finishes, control is transferred to the **WebItem** specified by **NextItem**. This process is repeated until the last **WebItem** doesn't set a value for **NextItem**.

The **Trace** method is used to display debugging information. The specified string is written using the OutputDebugString API, and this information can be viewed by using a tool like DBMON. You may want to use this facility to record information.

Table 11-2 Methods of the WebClass Object

Method	Description
ReleaseInstance	Works with the **StateManagement** property to release a **WebClass** object that is no longer needed.
Trace	Sends debugging output using theWin32 OutputDebugString API.
URLFor	Returns a URL reference for a **WebItem** object.

The **Initialize** event occurs when the **WebClass** is first loaded. This is a good place to include any code that you only want to run once, such as initializing global variables and objects in the **Application** object. Likewise, the **Terminate** event is called just before the **WebClass** is unloaded. You should use it to do any cleanup work before the **WebClass** is unloaded.

The **BeginRequest** and **EndRequest** events can be used to perform any common processing before and after any of the processing that is done by the individual **WebItems**. These events could be used to begin building the response document by including a common header or footer for all documents. The **Start** event is triggered whenever the user specifies the **WebClass** ASP file without including a specific **WebItem**. The **FatalErrorResponse** event allows you to suppress the message that the system will

Table 11-3 Events of the WebClass Object

Event	Description
BeginRequest	Gets triggered before any other processing is done.
EndRequest	Gets triggered after all other processing is complete.
FatalErrorResponse	Occurs when a fatal error is encountered while processing a request.
Initialize	Occurs when the **WebClass** object is first loaded.
Start	Occurs when the user specifies the base URL without specifying a specific **WebItem**.
Terminate	Occurs when the **WebClass** object is unloaded.

automatically generate in case of a fatal error. This allows you to substitute your own error message or take any necessary recovery actions.

> You should always include code for the **Start** event since it allows your users to specify a much shorter URL than one that contains an address for a specific **WebItem.** You can either set the **NextItem** property to send the control to a specific **WebItem** or you can return a main menu for your application.

The WebItem Object

There are two forms of the **WebItem** object. The first form is called Custom **WebItem** while the second is called an HTML Template **WebItem**. The Custom **WebItem** object is used to respond to an HTTP request. The HTML Template **WebItem** is associated with an HTML template file that can be returned to the user. Table 11-4 lists the properties, Table 11-5 lists the method, and Table 11-6 lists the events of the **WebItem** object.

Table 11-4	Properties of the **WebItem** Object
Property	**Description**
Properties	A collection containing a set of user-defined properties
RescanReplacements	When **True,** the HTML document is repeatedly scanned looking for tag names beginning with the value in **TagPrefix** property. The scanning ends when no **TagPrefix** tags are found
TagPrefix	Contains a string of characters used to identify tag names that will be replaced in the **ProcessTag** event
URLData	Contains data that will be appended to the end of a URL generated in the **URLFor** method

Table 11-5	Method of the **WebItem** Object
Method	**Description**
WriteTemplate	Outputs the associated HTML to the **Response** object

Table 11-6   Events of the **WebItem** Object

Event	Description
ProcessTag	Occurs when a tag matching the value in **TagPrefix** is found
Respond	Triggers when the user specifies ?WCI=webitem as part of the URL request or activated as the next Web item specified in the **NextItem** property
UserEvent	Fires in response to a run-time defined event

Tip

If you need to build a table or list of information retrieved from the database and you don't know the exact number of rows that will be returned, simply build your table with one row of replacement tags. Then in the **ProcessTag** event when you replace the last field, append a new row of replacement tags that is identical to the first if you are not at the end of the recordset or table. With the **RescanReplacments** property set to **True**, the event will be triggered for each of the fields again in the next row.

The **WebItem_Respond** event is called in response to the user specifying ?WCI=WebItem at the end of the URL where *WebItem* is the name of a Custom **WebItem**. It can also be triggered when another routine finishes and sets the **NextItem** property. In general, you will use this event to build a Web page on the fly and return it to the user.

The **WriteTemplate** method will send the HTML Template **WebItem** to the user's browser. You can bury your own codes in an HTML template document that can be replaced on the fly when the template is sent to the user's Web browser. The **TagPrefix** property specifies the leading characters that mark the beginning of a tag that should be replaced. When the text is found, then the **ProcessTag** event will be fired, allowing you to replace the characters in the HTML document with a different value. This would be useful if you want to use the identifier as a placeholder for a database field. The **RescanReplacements** property is used to start another scan after the first one has finished. This process is repeated until no more special tags have been found.

The **Properties** collection is used to keep track of information that is specific to the **WebItem** object. The **URLData** property contains information that will be appended to the HTML document being output during the **WriteTemplate** process. This information, when used with the **URLFor** method, can be used to generate a URL address that can trigger either the normal **Respond** event or a custom event that will be handled in the **UserEvent** event. The **UserEvent** traps all custom events and passes the event name to the event handler. Within the handler, you should use a **Select** statement to determine which event actually occurred and then take the appropriate action.

The Request Object

The **Request** object contains information about the user's request to the Web server. Tables 11-7 and 11-8 contain the list of the properties and the lone method available for this object. Most of the properties contain information that has been extracted from the request and made easily available for access. This includes the information from the **ClientCertificate**, **Cookies**, **Form**, and **QueryString**. The **ServerVariables** collection contains additional information about the request, such as the raw header information and information about the server, including the server's name and port.

Table 11-7 Properties of the **Request** Object

Property	Description
ClientCertificate	Contains the fields from the client certificate.
Cookies	Contains the values of the cookies sent with the request.
Form	Contains the values from the form fields in the previous HTML document.
QueryString	Contains the parameters specified as part of the URL.
ServerVariables	Contains a set of variables with information about the server.
TotalBytes	Contains the total size of the request in bytes.

The **BinaryRead** method retrieves the specified number of bytes from the request. You should use a variable to pass this value, since the method will change the variable's value to the actual number of bytes returned. The maximum size is contained in the **TotalBytes** property.

Caution

You can either use the **BinaryRead** method to retrieve the information from the user's form variables or you can access the information from the **Form** collection. Once you access this information one of these ways, trying to access it the other way will cause an error.

Table 11-8 Method of the **Request** Object	
Method	**Description**
BinaryRead	Returns the raw information submitted to the server.

The Response Object

The **Response** object is used to generate a Web page and return it to the user. The properties and methods for this object are summarized in Tables 11-9 and 11-10. Most of the properties are associated with setting various HTTP header values, such as **CacheControl**, **Charset**, **ContentType**, **Expires**, **ExpiresAbsolute**, and **Pics**. The **Cookies** property makes it easy to set cookie values in the user's browser. The **Status** property can be used to return a standard HTTP status code to the user. For instance, you could return "401 Unauthorized" if the user isn't authorized to access a particular IIS Application function. You can add other headers to the return document by using the **AddHeader** method.

The **IsClientConnected** property allows you to determine if the user has disconnected to the server. If this occurs, you may want to log the user off from your application. This will make your application more secure.

Table 11-9	Properties of the **Response** Object
Property	**Description**
Buffer	Means, when **True,** that the page output is buffered.
CacheControl	Contains the HTTP cache-control header information.
Charset	Contains the name of the character set for the content-type header.
ContentType	Contains the HTTP content-type header information.
Cookies	Contains the values of the cookies sent with the response.
Expires	Specifies how much time before the page will expire in the user's cache.
ExpiresAbsolute	Specifies the absolute date and time when the page will expire in the user's cache.
IsClientConnected	Means, when **True,** that the user is connected to the server.
Pics	Sets the value of the PICS label field in the response header.
Status	Contains the three-digit HTTP status code.

You will get very familiar with the **Write** method after writing a short IIS Application. Basically this statement is the equivalent of the **Print** statement. Practically anything you wish to send to the user that is not incorporated into a template has to be sent using the **Write** method. There is also a **BinaryWrite** method that you would use to send binary data, such as an image or binary file, to the user's browser.

The **Buffer** property determines whether the Web page is sent to the user as you build it (**False**) or hold it locally until you finish it (**True**). The default is to send data to the user as it is created. If you buffer the data, you must use either the **End** or **Flush** method to send the page to the user or the **Clear** method to erase the buffer and send nothing.

Table 11-10	Methods of the Response Object
Method	**Description**
AddHeader	Sets the specified header to the specified value.
AppendToLog	Outputs the specified string to the Web server's log file.
BinaryWrite	Sends the output to the user's browser as a binary string.
Clear	Clears any buffered output.
End	Finishes the Web page.
Flush	Sends any buffered output to the user's browser.
Redirect	Attempts to redirect the user's browser to another URL.
Write	Sends the specified string to the user's browser.

You can use the **Redirect** method to automatically transfer a user to another Web page. Using the **AppendToLog** method, you can add information to the server's log file, such as when a user logs on to the system, and you can track which Web pages they visit.

The Session Object

The **Session** object holds information that is unique to a particular user's session (see Table 11-11). The **SessionId** property returns a unique identifier that is associated with this particular session. This object will also automatically abandon the session if the user hasn't talked to the server in the number of minutes, as specified in the **Timeout** parameter. You can also explicitly kill the session by using the **Abandon** method (see Table 11-12).

The **CodePage** and **LCID** properties describe the language and location of the user. You can store your own information in this object by using the **Contents** and **Value** properties. The **Contents** collection keeps a dictionary of the locally defined names and values. The **Value** property is an alternate way to retrieve the information from the **Contents** collection using a value for the name. The **StaticObjects** tracks information about all the objects used in the session that was defined by the Object HTML tag.

Table 11-11	Properties of the **Session** Object
Property	**Description**
CodePage	Sets or returns the code page that will be used when reading or writing information to the user's browser.
Contents	Contains the collection of the names of the user-defined values in the object.
LCID	Sets or returns the local information used when reading or writing information to the browser.
SessionID	Returns the session identifier for this user.
StaticObjects	Contains the collection of static objects defined in the session.
Timeout	Contains the number of minutes of inactivity before the session will be disconnected.
Value	Returns the user-defined value associated with the specified name.

Table 11-12	Methods of the **Session** Object
Method	**Description**
Abandon	Terminates the session and releases all the resources associated with the user.

The Application Object

The **Application** object holds information that is common to the entire IIS Application (see Tables 11-13 and 11-14). You can store your own information in this object by using the **Contents** collection. You can also reference this information using the **Value** property. The **StaticObjects** contains information about all the objects added to the application that were defined by the Object HTML tag.

Table 11-13	Properties of the **Application** Object
Property	**Description**
Contents	Contains the collection of the names of the user-defined values in the object.
StaticObjects	Contains the collection of static objects defined in the IIS Application.
Value	Returns the user-defined value associated with the specified name.

Table 11-14	Methods of the **Application** Object
Method	**Description**
Lock	Locks the **Application** object.
UnLock	Releases the lock on the **Application** object.

To ensure that only one copy of the application is updating the **Application** object at any time, you can use the **Lock** and **Unlock** methods to gain exclusive control of the **Application** object. Thus you might want to use the following code fragment to ensure that the value of "Counter" is properly maintained:

```
Application.Lock
Application.Contents("Counter") = Application.Contents("Counter") + 1
Application.Unlock
```

The Server Object

The **Server** object provides access to server variables (see Table 11-15) and utility functions (see Table 11-16). The **ScriptTimeout** property determines how long a single function can run before the server will kill it. The **CreateObject** method allows the programmer to dynamically add a new object to either the **Application** or **Session** object. This means that the associated code will be available for processing future requests in the **StaticObjects** collection.

Table 11-15	Properties of the **Server** Object
Property	**Description**
ScriptTimeout	Contains the amount of time the application can run before it is killed.

Table 11-16	Methods of the **Server** Object
Method	**Description**
CreateObject	Adds the object to the **Application** or **Session** object.
HTMLEncode	Encodes a string of characters into HTML.
MapPath	Converts a relative URL path to an absolute file path.
URLEncode	Encodes a string of characters as a URL.

The **HTMLEncode** method takes a string of characters and encodes it into HTML such that the string will be displayed exactly as it was passed to the method. This is useful when you have some characters that could be misinterpreted as an HTML tag. The **URLEncode** method does the same thing for URLs. The **MapPath** method is useful for converting a URL path that may include virtual directories to the physical disk location on the server. This makes it easy to open the physical file.

The BrowserType Object

Unlike the preceding objects, the **BrowserType** object's properties are not fixed. They are based on the values in the file called Browscap.ini. This file translates an HTTP user agent header (browser name) into a set of properties. Listing 11-20 contains a small subset of the file concerning the Internet Explorer 4.0 browser.

Look in from the Browscap.ini file for information about Information about the Internet Explorer 4.0 browser:

Listing 11-20

```
;;;;;;;;;;;;;;;;;;;;;;;;;;;;;;;;;;;;;;;;;;; IE 4.x
[IE 4.0]
browser=IE
Version=4.0
majorver=4
minorver=0
frames=TRUE
tables=TRUE
cookies=TRUE
backgroundsounds=TRUE
vbscript=TRUE
javascript=TRUE
javaapplets=TRUE
ActiveXControls=TRUE
Win16=False
beta=False
AK=False
SK=False
AOL=False
crawler=False
cdf=True

;;ie 4 final release
[Mozilla/4.0 (compatible; MSIE 4.0; Windows 95)]
parent=IE 4.0
platform=Win95
beta=False
```

This listing contains information about two browsers. Any line that begins with a semicolon (;) is treated as a comment. Any line that begins with an open bracket ([) contains the HTTP user agent header. Following the header information is a series of properties that describe the browser (i.e., **Frames** = TRUE, **Cookies** = TRUE). These are the properties that appear in the **BrowserType** object.

There is one special property known as **Parent**. This property doesn't appear in the first browser listing, but does in the second. It's used as a link to another browser description. In this case it links to the first browser entry. All the properties of the parent description are inherited in the child entry. However, if there is a duplicate property in both the parent and the child, the value of the child's property will override the value of the parent's property.

To use this object, you must define an object variable and set it equal to the **BrowserType** object. Then you can test for the properties you find in the Browscap.ini file. This is shown in the following code fragment:

```
Dim o as Object

Set o = BrowserType
If o.Browser = "IE" Then
    Response.Write "You're using Internet Explorer"
Else
    Response.Write "You aren't using Internet Explorer"
End If
```

Creating Your First IIS Application

Sometimes the best way to build an application using a new technology is to write a program that you plan to throw away. It's usually known as a Hello World program, though I prefer to call it the Hello Jill program (after the person who inspired me to become a writer). The following steps show you how to build your own Hello Jill program (or Hello Chris or Hello Sam or whatever you prefer):

1. Start Visual Basic and open a new IIS Application (see Figure 11-20).

Figure 11-20
Select a new IIS Application from the initial startup screen.

2. Go to the Project window and expand Designers to show WebClass1 (see Figure 11-21). Then double-click on WebClass1 to display the WebClass designer.

3. Right-click on the Custom WebItems folder and select Add Custom WebItem. Name the new WebItem Jill (see Figure 11-22).

4. Double-click on Jill to display the code window for WebClass1 (see Figure 11-23).

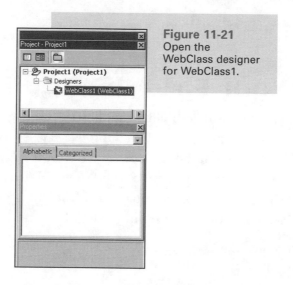

Figure 11-21
Open the WebClass designer for WebClass1.

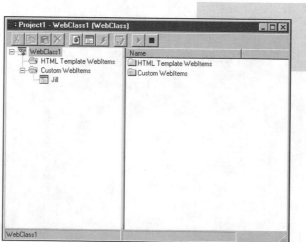

Figure 11-22
Create a WebItem object named Jill.

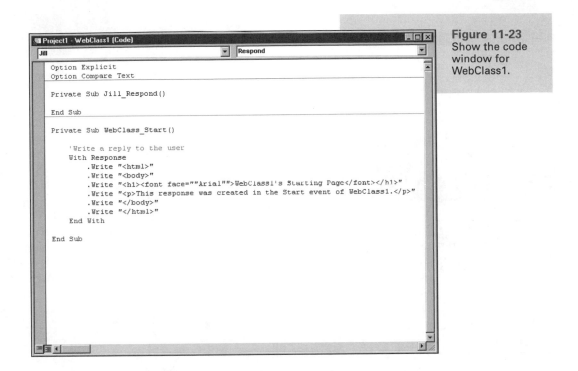

Figure 11-23
Show the code window for WebClass1.

5. Add the following code to the subroutine Jill_Respond (see Figure 11-24):

```
With Response
    .Write "<html>"
    .Write "<body>"
    .Write "Hello Jill!"
    .Write "</body>"
    .Write "</html>"
End With
```

6. Select Run and press OK on the Debugging dialog box, as shown in Figure 11-25.

7. As the program starts, so will your Web browser. It will display the default Web page, as shown in Figure 11-26. This page was generated automatically by the default IIS Application in the WebClass_Start event.

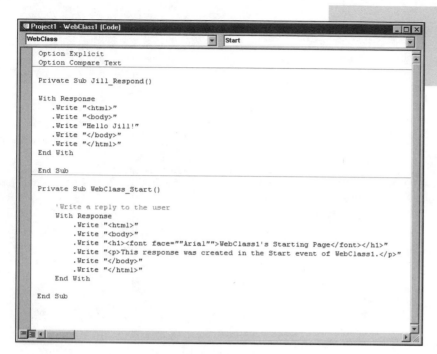

Figure 11-24
Add code to the
Jill_Respond
subroutine.

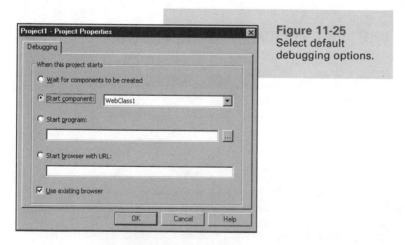

Figure 11-25
Select default
debugging options.

8. Add ?WCI=Jill to the end of the URL in your Web browser
   and press enter to display your first IIS Application (see
   Figure 11-27).

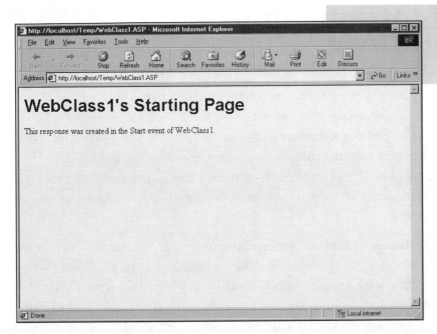

Figure 11-26
See the default Web page for WebClass1.

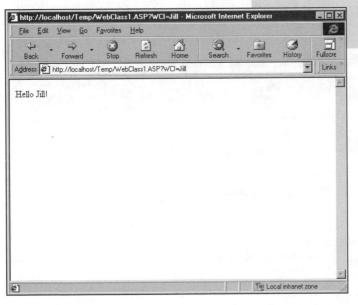

Figure 11-27
Say Hello Jill!

A Brief Introduction to HTML Tags

This isn't meant to be a complete introduction to HTML, but just enough for you to get by while working on this project. All the Web-Books.com Web pages follow the basic model shown in Figure 11-28. This is done to make the user comfortable with the site. No matter what page the user sees, the information is in the same relative location. This also helps me when I implement it, since I can isolate the code that creates that particular part of the Web page and use it across the entire application.

The Web page is broken into five main parts. In the top-left corner of the Web page is a simple graphic containing a book called Web-Books.com, with a spider below it sitting on a big spiderweb. This is the WebBooks.com big logo. In the top-right part of the page is the Web-Books.com name and its slogan. In the center-left section is a list of Web page links. The center-right section contains the main material being displayed. In this case it is the featured book. In other Web pages it will

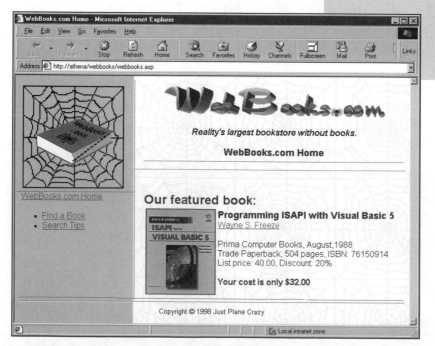

Figure 11-28
The parts of a WebBooks.com Web page

How Did You Do That?

Creating interesting text graphics is very easy if you know some dirty tricks. I created the WebBooks.com name using Word 97's Word Art feature, then copied and pasted it into Adobe Photoshop, where I pasted in the little spider in place of the period and then saved the entire image as a GIF 89 formatted image file with a transparent background.

The background was even easier. I found a spiderweb image I liked, cleaned it up a little bit in Photoshop, and saved it. Then I created a new image that was roughly 200 pixels high by 1,600 pixels wide. I drew a vertical line that was roughly 200 pixels from the left-hand edge of the image and colored it light blue. Then I lightened the spiderweb by playing around with the contrast and brightness controls and pasted it starting at the edge of the blue and continuing until I had no more room for another copy. Then I cropped the image to a full copy of the spiderweb. This left an image that was about 1,400 pixels wide—more than enough to support anyone's display without repeating the image horizontally.

It's important to remember that the background image must not distract anything that may be placed over the top of it. I suggest using light colors and washed-out images. This works well with black text. However, you can use dark colors and images if you use white text. Just be sure that there is sufficient contrast between the foreground and background colors and images.

The last image took the most time, and probably wasn't necessary, but I used Photoshop again, taking the original spiderweb graphic plus images of the spider and a book and stacked them on top of each other. Then after placing the WebBooks.com text on the image, I used the distort tool to adjust it so that it looked like the name was on the book. Finally, I crunched everything down to a single layer and saved it as a transparent GIF.

I am not a graphic artist. While I used Photoshop to build these images, you can use many different tools to achieve the same effect. Microsoft has Image Composer, which they bundle with FrontPage, and you may also want to look at a shareware program called Paint Shop Pro. All three programs are very good, and you really need at least one of them to generate nice graphics for your Web page. Just remember that if I can create interesting graphics with these tools, so can you.

be the book's information, a search form, an author biography, or whatever. The bottom of the page contains a simple copyright statement. You can easily expand this section to include other information, such as the date the page was last updated, additional legal terms and conditions, or whatever legalese your lawyers may want to see there. (I like to think of this part as the fine print that nobody reads anyway.)

The HTML Tag

An HTML document is built out of a series of commands called *tags*. Most tags have a *begin tag* and an *end tag*. Everything in between inherits those characteristics. For example, the first tag in an HTML document is the <HTML> tag, while the last tag is the </HTML>. The stuff in between these tags is an HTML document.

An HTML document is composed of two parts: the head and the body. The <HEAD> tag marks the beginning of the head section, which contains information that describes the document but that doesn't actually appear anywhere. The <BODY> tag marks the beginning of the body, which contains the information that will be displayed to the user. The following example shows a simple HTML document, containing the <HTML>, <HEAD>, <TITLE>, and <BODY> tags:

```
<HTML>
<HEAD>
<TITLE>
The Hello Jill Web Page
</TITLE>
</HEAD>
<BODY>
Hello Jill! Hello Chris! Hello Samantha!
</BODY>
</HTML>
```

The HEAD and TITLE Tags

In the head section, I usually only bother to include the <TITLE> tag. The text between the <TITLE> and the </TITLE> is considered the title of the Web page. This title is not the same title that may be displayed on the Web page. Rather it is the name by which the document is known. This is displayed in the title bar of the Web browser and is also used when you save the document into your collection of favorite Web pages.

The BODY Tag

In the body section, you see for the first time something other than a simple tag. Inside the <BODY> tag, there are two attributes: BGCOLOR and BACKGROUND. The BGCOLOR is used to set the background of a Web page to a specific color value. It's specified as a series of color values. In this case using BGCOLOR is redundant since BACKGROUND is also included. BACKGROUND specifies the name of an image that will be displayed as the background of the Web page. If the image is not large enough, it will be repeated horizontally and vertically to fill out the Web page.

In the following example, I set the background color to white (#FFFFFF) and the background image to the file backgrnd.gif. If the image can't be downloaded, the Web page will be displayed with a white background. The color is specified by a Red Green Blue (RGB) value where #000000 is black, #FF0000 is red, #00FF00 is green and #0000FF is blue. You can create any color value you want by choosing the correct values for each color. If the image can be downloaded, it will be tiled to fit the visible background of the Web page and the background color will not be used.

```
<BODY BGCOLOR="#FFFFFF" BACKGROUND="backgrnd.gif">
```

Since I'm using a GIF image that is nearly 1,400 pixels wide, I'm not likely to repeat the image horizontally. However, it will be repeated vertically as many times as needed.

While you may prefer to build your Web pages for Internet Explorer, remember that there are many different browsers on the market today. Some browsers do not display images at all. Some users turn off image display to let them load Web pages faster. Defining a background color using BGCOLOR is a cheap, easy way to accommodate these users without a lot of extra effort.

The TABLE Tag and Other Table Tags

One of the most powerful tags in HTML is <TABLE>. It allows you to structure your Web page (or even just part of your Web page) into a series of columns and rows. The <TR> tag marks the beginning and end of each row. Each cell within a row is delimited by the <TD> tag. You can use attributes inside the <TD> tag to specify the relative size of the cell or specify the alignment of data in the cell. In general I want to keep the size of the left column about the size of the blue area on the screen. I can do it by specifying either the size in pixels or the size as a relative percentage of the total width available. The following example shows a simple table with two rows and two columns:

```
<TABLE>
<TR>
<TD>
Row 1, Column 1
</TD>
<TD>
Row 1, Column 2
</TD>
</TR>
<TR>
<TD>
Row 2, Column 1
</TD>
<TD>
Row 2, Column 2
</TD>
</TR>
</TABLE>
```

Note

The <TABLE> tag has many more attributes and ways to use it than I'm describing here. Check the documentation that comes with your browser or read Prima Tech's **Learn HTML In a Weekend, Revised Edition,** by Steve Callihan, to learn about the full range of options available. Or you can be the lazy programmer and do what I usually do. I create a basic Web page using FrontPage and then copy the HTML tags into my program.

Tip

While you may think that you can only use one table at a time, you're wrong. You can put a table inside a table. I often do this when I want to display more than one image in a table's cell or arrange text around an image.

The IMAGE Tag

An image is displayed on a Web page by using the <IMAGE> tag. You can also use <IMG> as a shorter form of <IMAGE>. There are a number of attributes available for this tag. You can specify the name of the file to be displayed using the SRC attribute. You can also specify the name of the file by using the HREF attribute and specifying a hyperlink to the image. The ALT attribute allows you to specify a string of characters that would be displayed while the image is loading or displayed in place of the image in a Web browser that doesn't display images. You can also reserve space for the image by specifying values for the image's height and width. The following example shows how to display an image:

```
<IMG SRC="image1.jpg" ALT="This is an image">
```

The Paragraph, Break, and List Tags

When displaying text on the Web page, it is automatically formatted to fit the display. Extra spaces and blank lines are ignored. However, this causes a problem when you need a break for a paragraph. To solve this problem, you need to insert a paragraph tag, or <P>. This will end the current paragraph, display a blank line, and pick up with a new paragraph. The following example shows how to separate two paragraphs with a blank line:

```
Paragraph 1
<P>
Paragraph 2
```

While this is nice for most paragraphs, sometimes you may want to display a line immediately after the end of the previous line. To do this, you need to use the break tag, or <BR>. This will merely force the text to continue at the beginning of the line with the blank line that the paragraph tag produces. The following example shows how to display two lines without a blank line between them:

```
Line 1
<BR>
Line 2
```

It is very easy to create lists using HTML. You mark the beginning and end of the list using the <OL> (ordered list) or <UL> (unordered list) tag. Then inside the list, you identify each list item with the <LI> tag. This tag will be replaced with either a number (ordered list) or a bullet (unordered list) when the page is displayed. The following example shows a bulleted list:

```
<UL>
<LI>Item 1
<LI>Item 2
</UL>
```

The Font and Other Text Tags

The <FONT> tag allows you to change the name of the font and many other attributes such as face, size, and color. You can use the tag <BIG> to make all the characters larger until the </BIG> end tag. <SMALL> works in the same way. You can even use multiple <BIG> or <SMALL> tags to make the size change even greater. You can use the tag <STRONG> to make the characters bold and the <EM> (emphasize) to display the characters in italics. This example shows how to specify an alternate character font and then display the text "HELP ME!" in bold letters two sizes larger than normal:

```
<FONT FACE="ARIAL">
<STRONG><BIG><BIG>
HELP ME!
</BIG></BIG></STRONG>
```

Caution　　Use caution when specifying a value for font face. The browser tries to find the font on your local system. If it isn't there, the closest available font will be used, which will often defeat the purpose of specifying the font in the first place.

The Anchor Tag

The anchor, or <A>, tag is used to define a hyperlink. Everything between the <A> and </A> is considered the hyperlink. Clicking on any part of this text or any images that may appear will take you to the Web page(s) specified inside the <A> tag, using the HREF attribute. The following example shows how to include a hypertext link that will send me a piece of e-mail:

```
<A HREF="mailto:WFreeze@JustPC.com">Wayne S. Freeze</A>
```

The next example shows how to embed a hyperlink reference in the middle of a sentence:

```
Feel free to visit my Web site at
<A HREF="http://www.JustPC.com">
www.JustPC.com
</A>
any time you like.
```

The Form Tag

The <FORM> tag is used to define a form on an HTML document. A form can contain a number of fields where the user can enter data, plus buttons to take action on the user's data. There are two key attributes to the <FORM> tag. The first is the ACTION attribute that defines where to send the data. Usually this will be a URL that specifies the name of a program that will receive the data and return a response. The other key attribute is the METHOD, which describes how the data will be sent to the server. When writing IIS Applications, you should always use POST. The sample form below would be used to collect someone's e-mail address and send it to the server:

```
<FORM METHOD=POST ACTION="webbooks.ASP?ProcessForm">
<INPUT TYPE="TEXT" NAME="EmailAddress"SIZE=30>
<SELECT NAME="Notify">
   <OPTION VALUE="New Visual Basic books">
   <OPTION VALUE="New JAVA books">
   <OPTION VALUE="New C++ books">
   <OPTION SELECTED VALUE="Any new programming books"
</SELECT>
<TEXTAREA NAME="Comments" ROWS="5" COLUMNS="20">
Enter you comments here
</TEXTAREA>
```

```
<INPUT TYPE="SUBMIT" VALUE="Press to submit form">
<INPUT TYPE="RESET" VALUE="Press to clear form">
</FORM>
```

Note You can only use <INPUT>, <TEXTAREA>, and <SELECT> tags inside a <FORM> tag.

Tip You should include a NAME attribute with every field that contains data. Without this attribute, you will not be able to access the information in your application.

The Input Tag

The <INPUT> tag is used to define an input field on an HTML form. Input fields can be several different types. The text input field is a one-line box that holds a series of characters. The user can type any sequence of characters into this box. The user can continue typing characters even beyond what appears to be the end of the box, being able to scroll within the box. The hidden input field is also a one-line box that holds a string of characters. Unlike the text input field, these characters aren't visible when displayed. You can specify a default value for both fields by using the VALUE attribute.

You can display a button with the input tag as well. When TYPE is SUBMIT, pressing the button will submit the contents of the form to the server. When TYPE is CLEAR, pressing the button will reinitialize the form's contents to the default value. The VALUE attribute will display the associated text on the face of the button.

The Select Tag

The <SELECT> tag is used to define a drop-down list of a fixed set of choices. The choices are listed between the <SELECT> and </SELECT> tags, using the <OPTION> tag. You can choose the default value that will be displayed in the drop-down box by using the SELECTED attribute.

The Textarea Tag

The <TEXTAREA> tag specifies a multiline text box in which the user can enter multiple lines of text. The default value for this field is placed between the <TEXTAREA> and </TEXTAREA> tags. You need to specify the number of rows and number of columns that will be displayed, though like the <INPUT> tag, the displayed text will automatically scroll if the size exceeds the box's boundaries.

You can check the documentation on the MSDN CD-ROM that accompanies Visual Basic for more detailed information about these tags and many others.

Building an IIS Application for WebBooks.com

Now that you know how to build an IIS Application, it's time to build one for WebBooks.com. Figure 11-29 shows the WebBooks.com home

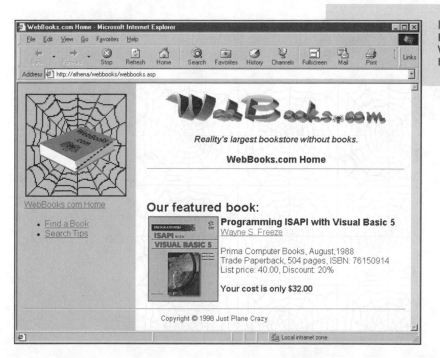

Figure 11-29
Here is the WebBooks.com home page.

page. Note that unlike the Hello Jill program, I've added a lot of graphics and special HTML formatting. This page is displayed whenever the WebBooks.asp file is referenced in a URL without any other information. Note that both the book and the author's name are hyperlinks to other places in this Web site. Clicking on the book will display the book information page, while clicking on the author will display a list of books written by that author.

Figure 11-30 shows the book information page for the same book. While much of the information displayed on the home page is also displayed here, this page includes additional information such as a description of the book, a WebBooks.com review, comments from the publisher and author, and a few reviews by readers.

Finally, the user can add a review to the list by using the form shown in Figure 11-31. This form is relatively simple. It allows the user to enter

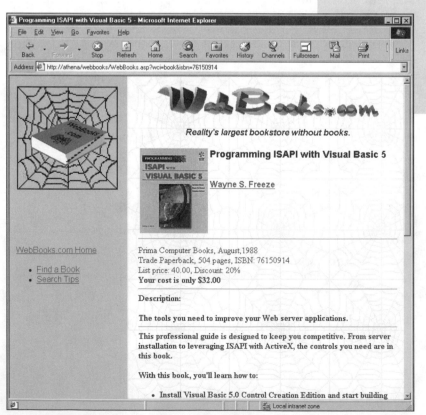

Figure 11-30
Here is the book information page about *Programming ISAPI with Visual Basic 5.*

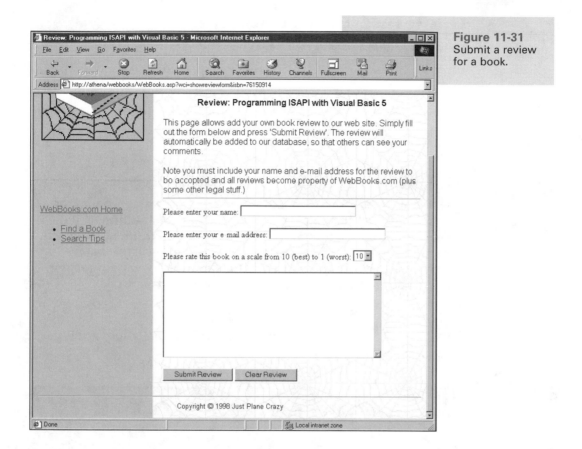

Figure 11-31
Submit a review
for a book.

his or her name, an e-mail address, a rating for the book, and a review of the book. After filling out the form, the user can press Submit Review to send it to the Web server for processing or Clear Review to erase the contents of the form and start over again.

Displaying the WebBooks.com Home Page

Writing IIS Applications means getting your hands dirty with HTML. It also means getting your hands dirty by using the ADO interface directly rather than using bound controls and other high-level approaches to get information from the database. So I want to begin by looking at the HTML generated by the IIS Application for the Web-Books.com home page and then go through the code that generated it.

The HTML Source for the WebBooks.com Home Page

While I plan to automate this as much as possible, Listing 11-21 contains the HTML source document for the WebBooks.com home page as previously shown in Figure 11-28. I begin this process by defining information for the head, which in this case merely contains the title of the Web page.

> **Note**
>
> Believe it or not, choosing a title for a Web page can be important. Most Web browsers will show as much of the title as possible, but usually they don't have enough space to show all of the title. So while a title can be any size, smaller is probably better—and if you can't make it smaller, at least try to put the most important information at the front of the title.

This is the HTML source document for the WebBooks.com home page, as shown in Figure 11-28:

Listing 11-21

```html
<html>
<head>
<title>WebBooks.com Home</title>
</head>
<body bgcolor="#ffffff" background="background.gif">
<table border="0" width="100%">
<tr>
<td width="32%" valign="top"><img src="logo.gif"
alt="WebBooks.com logo" align="top" WIDTH="200" HEIGHT="200">
</td>
<td width="68%" valign="top" align="middle">
<img src="webbooks.gif" alt="WebBooks.com" WIDTH="426" HEIGHT="60">
<p>
<font face="Arial">
<strong><em>
Reality's largest bookstore without books.
</em></Strong>
<div align="left">
<p>
<center><big><strong>WebBooks.com Home</strong></big></center>
<hr>
</TD>
```

```
</TR>
<tr>
<td width = "32%", valign="top">
<font face="Arial">
<a href="webbooks.asp">WebBooks.com Home</a>
<ul>
<li><a href="WebBooks.ASP?WCI=ShowSearchForm">Find a Book</a>
<li><a href="WebBooks.ASP?WCI=ShowTips&WCU">Search Tips</a>
</ul>
</td>
<td width = "68%", valign="top">
<font face="arial"><strong><big><big>
Our featured book:
</big></big></strong>
<br>
<table><tr><td width="20%" valign="top">
<a href="WebBooks.asp?wci=book&isbn=76150914">
<img src="webbooks.asp?wci=cover&isbn=76150914">
</td>
<td width="80%" valign="top"></a>
<p>
<strong><big>
Programming ISAPI with Visual Basic 5
</big></strong>
<br>
<a href="WebBooks.asp?wci=author&authorcode=1">
Wayne S. Freeze</a>
<p>Prima Computer Books, August, 1988
<br>Trade Paperback, 504 pages, ISBN: 76150914
<br>List price: 40.00, Discount: 20%
<p><Strong>Your cost is only $32.00</strong>
</td>
</tr>
</table>
<hr>
<center>
<font face="Arial">
<small>Copyright © 1998 Just Plane Crazy</small>
</font>
</center>
</html>
```

The body of the document occupies most of the code. You can see that I specify that the background should be white (#ffffff) if a background image isn't displayed and that the background image called Background.gif should be used. Since I don't specify any directory information, nor do I give it a complete address, the image must exist in the same directory as the IIS Application.

Note When you build a Web-based application, you will have a number of files such as the image files that need to be kept with the application. While some individuals tend to keep image files in their own directory, separate from the HTML files, I usually don't bother. By keeping everything in a single directory I have the advantage of needing to deal with only one directory when I move the application to another system or when I want to create a backup copy of the application.

Given the structure of the Web page that I've already discussed, the most natural way to implement it is to use a table that contains two rows and two columns followed by some full-width text. So I use the <TABLE> tag to mark the beginning of the table. I specify that the border should be set to 0. This means that you won't see any gridlines for the table. I always disable the border in cases like this where I'm using a table to organize my Web page rather than displaying tabular information.

Note You structure your Web site to use the frames rather than tables. Frames generally offer more flexibility and ease of use for the user but are often more complicated to implement and may not be compatible with all browsers. If you are familiar with frames, you may want to try to redesign this application using frames rather than tables to see what the real differences are.

After starting the table, I define the first row in the table with the <TR> tag and the first cell in the table with the <TD> tag. I choose to allocate 32 percent of the total browser's width to this column. I then display the image Logo.gif with an alternate title of "WebBooks.com Logo." After I close this cell, I open a new cell with a width of 68 percent of the display. In this cell I display the WebBooks.gif that contains a cute version of the WebBooks.com company name. Below that image I display the corporate slogan "Reality's largest bookstore without books" (this is part of the never-ending battle to make consumers believe that we're the leader in our market) and the title of the Web page.

Then I draw a horizontal line using the <HR> tag. I find this tag very useful—it serves to mark the end of the heading information without being disruptive. And since the <HR> tag expands to go from left to right, it's restricted to this single cell.

I display the links under the logo image as a header link to this page, followed by some other useful links displayed in an unordered list. Note that I display a link to this page even though it seems unnecessary. This is because I will generate this same set of links for every Web page.

After closing the cell and row with the </TD> and </TR> tags respectively, I begin a new row and column. In the first column I provide a list of links that the user should find convenient. The three links listed here aren't complete, but then again the application isn't really complete either.

The links specify references to the WebBooks.asp IIS Application and specify which **WebItem** should be called by using the WCI parameter. For instance, in the hyperlink information below, the **WebItem ShowSearchForm** will be called whenever the user clicks on the words "Find a Book":

```
<a href="WebBooks.ASP?WCI=ShowSearchForm">Find a Book</a>
```

In the next to last section of the Web page comes the most important material. I choose to display a featured book, including an image and some key information about the book. For the most part this is just formatted text; however, the author's name has a hyperlink to the author **WebItem** and passes along with it a parameter containing the author-code as shown below:

```
WebBooks.asp?wci=author&authorcode=1
```

This runs the WebBooks.asp program again but will trigger the **Author_Respond** event. This event will display a list of books by the author specified by the authorcode=1.

Finally, I end this Web page by closing the cell, row, and table. Then I display another horizontal line using the <HR> tag and display the legalese at the bottom of the page.

The Web page I just created is a traditional Web page. Many Web sites use this style of Web page. However, there is a new trend where the first Web page a user sees is crammed full of information. This new approach is known as a **portal Web page**. It works by using minimal graphics and as many hyperlinks as possible. This means that the Web page will load faster (downloading graphic images takes far more time than downloading text), and the user can easily reach many different places in the Web site.

Displaying an Image

Before I discuss how to build the WebBooks.com home page, I want to talk about a simpler problem: how to extract an image from the database. The main reason for this is that I want to focus on some of the database code without having the complications of generating an HTML page.

The Web page includes the following <IMG> tag:

```
<img src="webbooks.asp?wci=cover&isbn=76150914">
```

This tag specifies that the image can be found by running the Web-Books.asp file with the parameters WCI=cover and ISBN=76150914. The WCI parameter specifies the name of the **WebItem** cover, and specifying it as part of the WebBooks.asp file will trigger the **Cover_Respond** event. The ISBN=76150914 means that the cover associated with that ISBN should be displayed.

Listing 11-22 shows the global variables used by the **Cover_Respond** event. The db variable will be used to hold an ADO connection to the database, and the GetCover command will be used to hold a reference to a stored procedure that retrieves a cover image from the database.

The global variables used by the Cover_Respond event are used to hold database information:

Listing 11-22

```
Dim db As ADODB.Connection

Dim GetCover As ADODB.Command
```

I've included a small fragment of the **WebClass_Initialize** event in Listing 11-23 that shows you the parts of the code relevant to the **Cover_Respond** event. In the **Cover_Respond** event I'll open the connection to the database. I do this by creating a new instance of the **ADODB.Connection** object and then using the **Open** method to establish a connection to the database server called Athena.

The WebClass_Initialize event performs some processing in preparation for the Cover_Respond:

Listing 11-23

```
Set db = New ADODB.Connection

db.Open "provider=sqloledb;data source=Athena;" &
    "initial catalog=iis", "sa", ""

Set GetCover = New ADODB.Command
Set GetCover.ActiveConnection = db
GetCover.CommandText = "GetCover"
GetCover.CommandType = adCmdStoredProc
```

Then I'll create a new instance of the **ADODB.Command** object to hold a stored procedure. I set the **ActiveConnection** property to the **Connection** I just opened and set the **CommandText** and **CommandType** to point to the stored procedure **GetCover** (see Listing 11-24). This procedure will return the cover image stored in the database as a field stored in a recordset. All I have to do is open that recordset using the **GetCover** command and pass the appropriate ISBN value to retrieve the proper cover image.

The GetCover stored procedure returns a cover image from the database:

Listing 11-24

```
Create Procedure GetCover @i As
Select Cover
    From iis.dbo.covers
    Where iis.dbo.covers.isbn = @i
```

The **Cover_Respond** event shown in Listing 11-25 assumes that everything is ready to go. It begins by declaring a local **Recordset** object and uses the **Execute** method of the already defined command object to retrieve the information from the database. I pass the ISBN number that was included as part of the URL. This is easily found by looking in the **QueryString** property of the **Request** object.

The Cover_Respond event returns an image of a book cover from the database:

Listing 11-25

```
Private Sub Cover_Respond()

Dim rs As ADODB.Recordset

Set rs = GetCover.Execute(, CLng(Request.QueryString("isbn")))
If Not (rs.BOF And rs.EOF) Then
   With Response
      .ContentType = "image/JPEG"
      .BinaryWrite rs.Fields!Cover
      .End
   End With
End If

rs.Close

End Sub
```

I don't bother checking to see if the stored procedure worked or not. Rather I just check to see if both the **BOF** and **EOF** properties are **False**. **False** implies that no matching records were returned, while **True** implies that at least one cover was found. Since the database is designed such that only one cover image can exist per ISBN, I'm safe in assuming that there won't be more than one image.

So if a cover image was found, I set the content type of the response document to reflect a JPEG image and then perform a binary write of the Cover value. Then I use the **End** method to close and send the image back to the user. Finally, I close the recordset, since I'm done with it for now, and exit the event.

All in all, there is very little code needed for this routine. While the other routines in the IIS Application are more complex than this one, most of their complexity results from using multiple recordsets and multiple fields, not from a more complicated approach to processing the data.

Looking at the Global Declarations

The global declarations for this program can be seen in Listing 11-26. As you saw earlier, I created an object called db that contains the ADO **Connection** object and serves as the link between the program and the database. Following that is a set of declarations for ADO **Command** objects. These will be associated with stored procedures that will be used to retrieve or insert data into the database. Not all of these **Command** objects will be used to display the home page or the book information page. Many of them will be used in functions that support searching for information in the database, which I'll discuss later in this chapter.

WebBooks.com IIS Application uses a number of global variables to communicate with the database:

Listing 11-26

```
Option Explicit
Option Compare Text

Dim db As ADODB.Connection

Dim FindAuthorBooks As ADODB.Command
Dim FindAuthors As ADODB.Command
Dim GetAuthorBiography As ADODB.Command
Dim GetAuthors As ADODB.Command
Dim GetBook As ADODB.Command
Dim GetCover As ADODB.Command
Dim GetReviews As ADODB.Command
Dim InsertReview As ADODB.Command

Dim HomePageBook As Variant
```

Options Available

Note that two other statements are included at the beginning of the global declarations: **Option Explicit** and **Option Compare Text**.

I highly recommend **Option Explicit** since it forces you to declare variables before they are used. This helps to prevent errors, where you spell a variable one way in one part of the code and spell it another way somewhere else. With **Option Explicit** in your program, this will cause an error. Without **Option Explicit**, the second variable will be created automatically with a value of zero or an empty string or whatever is appropriate. This means that your program may run and may even run correctly. But sooner or later it will die. If you're lucky, you will get a run-time error and the program will crash right away. If you're not lucky, you could end up deleting all of your data in the database before it dies. Either way, it isn't a pretty sight.

Option Compare Text is also a good option to have enabled. It forces Visual Basic to compare your strings in a case-insensitive manner. This means you don't have to include the **UCase** or **LCase** functions any time you want to compare two strings. Of course there is a slight performance penalty when using this statement, but it is less than what you would see if you constantly used the **UCase** function.

When I originally wrote the code for the home page, it always displayed and asked why I didn't make it display a random page each time the home page was accessed. However, when my wife saw that, she teased me and asked why I didn't make it display a random page each time it was displayed. Well, I couldn't resist a challenge, so I decided to make the **WebClass_Start** event a little more complicated. Each time the **WebClass_Start** event was called, I would pick the next book in the Books table. To keep track of which book I processed, I kept a bookmark in a global variable, hence the last variable in the list HomePage-Book. However that left me with a problem obtaining the first bookmark. Since it's something I'm going to do only once, I'll use the **WebClass_Initialize** event.

Initializing the WebBooks.com IIS Application

Listing 11-27 contains the entire routine of the **WebClass_Initialize** event. I repeated the same set of actions for each of the stored procedures so that I'd have the objects I need to get the data from the database when I really needed it.

The WebClass_Initialize event is called only once, each time the Web-Class is loaded by the Web server:

Listing 11-27

```
Private Sub WebClass_Initialize()

Dim rs As ADODB.Recordset

Set db = New ADODB.Connection

db.Open "provider=sqloledb;data source=athena;" & _
    "initial catalog=iis", "sa", ""

Set FindAuthorBooks = New ADODB.Command
Set FindAuthorBooks.ActiveConnection = db
FindAuthorBooks.CommandText = "FindAuthorBooks"
FindAuthorBooks.CommandType = adCmdStoredProc

Set FindAuthors = New ADODB.Command
Set FindAuthors.ActiveConnection = db
FindAuthors.CommandText = "FindAuthors"
FindAuthors.CommandType = adCmdStoredProc

Set GetAuthorBiography = New ADODB.Command
Set GetAuthorBiography.ActiveConnection = db
GetAuthorBiography.CommandText = "GetAuthorBiography"
GetAuthorBiography.CommandType = adCmdStoredProc

Set GetAuthors = New ADODB.Command
Set GetAuthors.ActiveConnection = db
GetAuthors.CommandText = "GetAuthors"
GetAuthors.CommandType = adCmdStoredProc

Set GetBook = New ADODB.Command
Set GetBook.ActiveConnection = db
GetBook.CommandText = "GetBook"
GetBook.CommandType = adCmdStoredProc
```

```
Set GetCover = New ADODB.Command
Set GetCover.ActiveConnection = db
GetCover.CommandText = "GetCover"
GetCover.CommandType = adCmdStoredProc

Set GetReviews = New ADODB.Command
Set GetReviews.ActiveConnection = db
GetReviews.CommandText = "GetReviews"
GetReviews.CommandType = adCmdStoredProc

Set InsertReview = New ADODB.Command
Set InsertReview.ActiveConnection = db
InsertReview.CommandText = "InsertReview"
InsertReview.CommandType = adCmdStoredProc

Set rs = New ADODB.Recordset
Set rs.ActiveConnection = db
rs.Source = "Select * From iis.dbo.Books"
rs.CursorType = adOpenStatic
rs.LockType = adLockReadOnly
rs.Open
rs.MoveFirst
HomePageBook = rs.Bookmark
rs.Close

End Sub
```

However, near the bottom of the routine is a chunk of code with the sole purpose of initializing the global variable HomePageBook with the bookmark of the first book in the Books table. To do this, I create a new **Recordset** object and set the **ActiveConnection** property to the object variable db, which contains a valid ADO connection to the database.

Using this **Recordset** object, I specify a simple **Select** statement as the source of the data. I also specify a static cursor with a read-only lock before opening the query. Then I move to the first record and save its bookmark value into HomePageBook before closing the recordset. All this does is get me the bookmark of the first record in the table. (Note that this does assume that there is at least one record in the table, but I think that should be a safe assumption—at least once I load the data in Chapter 12.)

Building Templates

There's only one set of things left to do before I start building the code for the home page. I need to build a few template files. Using FrontPage, I created a rough version of the Web page, with the idea that I would use various parts of this page as templates in my larger program. That way, all I had to do was perform a **WriteTemplate** to copy the file into the response document.

Listing 11-28 shows the contents of one of the Footer.htm template files. I edited the HTML document I created using FrontPage and deleted all but the last few lines to create this file. Then I loaded the file into Visual Basic as an HTML Template WebItem.

The FooterForm template contains the HTML tags that will be displayed at the bottom of a Web page:

Listing 11-28

```
</tr>
</table>
<hr>
<center>
<font face="Arial">
<small>Copyright © 1998 Just Plane Crazy</small>
</font>
</center>
</html>
```

To load this document into Visual Basic, follow these steps:

1. Right-click on the HTML Template WebItem folder in the WebClass Designer and select Add HTML Template from the pop-up menu.

2. Select the file to use as a template using the Open dialog box.

3. After the file is opened, the WebItem will be given a default name of Template1 (or whatever the next available template number is). You can change it now if you want to (see Figure 11-32) or later by right-clicking on the WebItem and selecting Rename from the pop-up menu.

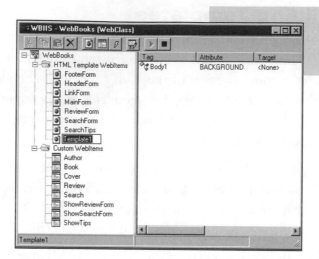

Figure 11-32
Give your template
a new name.

4. When you want to modify the template, right-click on the template WebItem and select Edit HTML Template. Then your HTML editor (usually Notepad) will pop up with your HTML file.

5. After you've finished editing your file, you will see a message saying that the template has changed and ask you if want to refresh it. If you respond with yes, the WebClass Designer will update its internal information about the template.

Caution

While using templates, I found that refreshing a template that contains only part of an HTML file will sometimes add extra HTML tags to make it a complete HTML document. You can edit the template again to check it. If it was changed, you can delete the changes, save the template, and refresh it again.

Generating the Home Page

You're now ready to begin generating the WebBooks.com home page (see Listing 11-29). The first thing you need to do is to get the ISBN of the book you want to display on the home page. Do this by opening a recordset just like the **WebClass_Initialize** event. Then set the current record pointer to the value saved in the bookmark. Move to the next row in the **Recordset**. This will be the book that you'll display. After saving the bookmark of the current row in HomePageBook, save the ISBN number in the variable isbn. Then close the recordset.

The WebClass_Start event is used to build the default Web page for an IIS Application:

Listing 11-29

```
Private Sub WebClass_Start()

Dim isbn As Long
Dim rs As ADODB.Recordset
Dim rs1 As ADODB.Recordset

Set rs = New ADODB.Recordset
Set rs.ActiveConnection = db
rs.Source = "Select * From iis.dbo.Books"
rs.CursorType = adOpenStatic
rs.LockType = adLockReadOnly
rs.Open
rs.Bookmark = HomePageBook
rs.MoveNext
If rs.EOF Then
    rs.MoveFirst
End If
HomePageBook = rs.Bookmark
isbn = rs.Fields!isbn
rs.Close

With Response
    Set rs = GetBook.Execute(, isbn)
    .Write Title("WebBooks.com Home")
    HeaderForm.WriteTemplate
    .Write "<p><center><big><strong>"
    .Write "WebBooks.com Home</strong></big></center>"
    LinkForm.WriteTemplate
    .Write "<font face=""arial""><strong><big><big>"
    .Write "Our featured book:</big></big></strong><br>"
    .Write "<table><tr><td width=""20%"" valign=""top"">"
    .Write "<a href=""WebBooks.asp?wci=book&isbn="
    .Write  rs.Fields!isbn & """>"
    .Write "<img src=""webbooks.asp?wci=cover&isbn="
    .Write rs.Fields!isbn & """>"
    .Write "</td><td width=""80%"" valign=""top""></a>"
```

```
.Write "<p><strong><big>" & rs.Fields!Title
.Write "</big></strong>"

Set rs1 = GetAuthors.Execute(, isbn)
Do While Not rs1.EOF
    .Write "<br><a href=""WebBooks.asp?wci=author&authorcode="
    .Write rs1.Fields!authorcode & """>"
    .Write rs1!authorname & "</a>"
    rs1.MoveNext
Loop
rs1.Close

.Write "<p>" & rs.Fields!publisher & ", "
.Write Format(rs.Fields!DatePublished, "mmmm,yyyy")
.Write "<br>" & rs.Fields!binding & ", "
.Write rs.Fields!PageCount & " pages, "
.Write "ISBN: " & rs.Fields!isbn
.Write "<br>List price: "
.Write FormatNumber(rs.Fields!listprice, 2)
.Write ", Discount: " & FormatPercent(rs.Fields!discount, 0)

.Write "<p><Strong>Your cost is only "
.Write FormatCurrency(rs.Fields!listprice * (1 - rs.Fields!discount))
.Write "</strong>"
FooterForm.WriteTemplate
.End
rs.Close

End With

End Sub
```

The next step in the process is to get the information about the book by using the GetBook stored procedure. Save this information into the **Recordset** variable rs. The GetBook stored procedure (see Listing 11-30) uses the Books, Publishers, and BindingCodes tables to gather all the information about a book. It does this by using the ISBN as a parameter (@i) into a **Select** statement. It also translates BindingCode into Binding and retrieves all the information about a publisher. Thus all the information about a book is available, except for the list of authors, which you retrieve using a different stored procedure.

You can use the GetBook stored procedure to retrieve information about a book:

Listing 11-30

```
CREATE Procedure GetBook  @i Int As
Select *
   From iis.dbo.Books, iis.dbo.publishers, iis.dbo.bindingcodes
   Where iis.dbo.books.isbn = @i
      and iis.dbo.books.publishercode = iis.dbo.publishers.publishercode
      and iis.dbo.bindingcodes.bindingcode = iis.dbo.books.bindingcode
```

After retrieving information about the book, call the routine Title to initialize the response document and set the <TITLE> tag to the value specified as a parameter. Then write the template from the HeaderForm template. This template contains nothing but some HTML tags. Use the **WriteTemplate** method to send it to the **Response** object.

The only somewhat tricky part is recognizing that more than one author can write a book. So at the appropriate location, use the GetAuthors stored procedure (see Listing 11-31) to get a **Recordset** containing the authors who wrote the book. As with GetBook, retrieve information based on the ISBN. However, this time make sure that the author names are listed in order by AuthorNumber, so that the authors are listed in the same order as they are on the book.

The GetAuthors stored procedure returns a recordset that contains a list of AuthorName values sorted by AuthorNumber:

Listing 11-31

```
CREATE Procedure GetAuthors @i Int As
Select a.AuthorName, a.AuthorCode
   From iis.dbo.Authors a, iis.dbo.authorbooks ab
   Where ab.isbn = @i
      and a.authorcode = ab.authorcode
   order by authornumber
```

When writing the code, assume that the stored procedure works and display all the authors sequentially. Note that if there are no authors, then nothing will be displayed.

This routine continues to output the HTML tags by using the **Write** and the **WriteTemplate** methods as needed. Display database fields where they should be displayed and remember to properly format the nontext values (such as dates and currency) using the appropriate **Format** statement.

Displaying the WebBooks.com Book Information Page

Displaying the WebBooks.com book information actually involves two Web pages. The first is the book information itself. The other is the page that allows a reader to review a book.

Displaying the Book Information Page

For the most part, the Book_Respond event (see Listing 11-32) is very similar to what I wrote for the WebBooks.com Home Page, except that it displays information on a specific book. As I begin this routine you see that I create two **Recordsets** using the same GetBook and GetAuthors stored procedures I used above. Then I check to see if I have a valid book and begin returning my Web page.

The Book_Respond event displays information about a book:

Listing 11-32

```
Private Sub Book_Respond()

Dim rs As ADODB.Recordset
Dim rs1 As ADODB.Recordset

Set rs = GetBook.Execute(, CLng(Request.QueryString("isbn")))
Set rs1 = GetAuthors.Execute(, CLng(Request.QueryString("isbn")))

If Not (rs.BOF And rs.EOF) Then
    With Response
        .Write Title(rs.Fields!Title)
        HeaderForm.WriteTemplate
        .Write "<p><table><tr><td>"
        .Write "<img src=""webbooks.asp?wci=cover&isbn="
        .Write Request.QueryString("isbn") & """></td>"
        .Write "<td valign=""top""><strong><big>"
        .Write rs.Fields!Title & "</big><p>"
```

```
Do While Not rs1.EOF
    .Write "<br><a href=""WebBooks.asp?wci=author&"
    .Write "authorcode=" & rs1.Fields!authorcode & """>"
    .Write rs1!authorname & "</a>"
    rs1.MoveNext
Loop
rs1.Close

.Write "</strong></td></tr></table>"

LinkForm.WriteTemplate

.Write rs.Fields!publisher & ", "
.Write Format(rs.Fields!DatePublished, "mmmm,yyyy")
.Write "<br>" & rs.Fields!binding & ", "
.Write rs.Fields!PageCount & " pages, "
.Write "ISBN: " & rs.Fields!isbn
.Write "<br>List price: "
.Write FormatNumber(rs.Fields!listprice, 2)
.Write ", Discount: "
.Write FormatPercent(rs.Fields!discount, 0)
.Write "<br><Strong>Your cost is only "
.Write FormatCurrency(rs.Fields!listprice * _
    (1 - rs.Fields!discount))

Set rs1 = GetReviews.Execute(, CLng(Request.QueryString("isbn")))

Do While Not rs1.EOF
    .Write "<hr>"
    Select Case rs1!reviewnumber
        Case 0
            .Write "<strong>Description:</strong>"

        Case 1
            .Write "<strong>Table of Contents:</strong>"

        Case 2
            .Write "<strong>A WebBooks.com review:</strong>"

        Case 3
            .Write "<strong>Comments from the publisher:</strong>"

        Case 4
            .Write "<strong>Comments from the author:</strong>"

        Case Else
            .Write "<strong>Reviewed by: " & rs1!reviewername
            .Write "</strong>"
```

```
        End Select

        .Write "<p>" & rs1!Review
        rs1.MoveNext

    Loop

    rs1.Close

    .Write "<hr><a href=""WebBooks.asp?wci=showreviewform&isbn="
    .Write rs.Fields!isbn & """>"
    .Write "<p>Click here to add your own review of this book.</a>"

    FooterForm.WriteTemplate
    .End

  End With

End If

rs.Close

End Sub
```

The first half of the routine is very similar to the code I used to build the home page. However, after I write out all the book information, I'm ready to handle the large blocks of text found in the Reviews table. Table 11-17 shows the meaning of the different values of ReviewNumber. Since the order of the values in ReviewNumber represents a logical way to present this information, I want to retrieve all the values from this table in that order. This is reflected in the stored procedure shown in Listing 11-33.

The GetReviews returns a recordset that contains a list of rows from the Reviews table for a particular ISBN sorted by the ReviewNumber:

Listing 11-33

```
CREATE Procedure GetReviews  @i Int As
Select *
   From iis.dbo.Reviews r
   Where r.isbn = @i
   Order by r.ReviewNumber
```

Table 11-17	Values of ReviewNumber
ReviewNumber	**Description**
0	The description of the book
1	The book's table of contents
2	A review by WebBooks.com
3	Comments from the publisher
4	Comments by the author
> 4	A review by the reader

The part of the code to process the stored procedure's output uses a loop to go through the resulting **Recordset**. I examine ReviewNumber to determine the type of information I'm going to display and output a header using a **Select Case** statement with each value of ReviewNumber of having its own **Case.** After I print all the reviews, I leave a hyperlink to the Book Review page, which will allow the reader to submit a review.

Generating the Form to Submit a Book Review

When the reader clicks on Click Here to Add Your Own Review of This Book, the IIS Application will generate and return an HTML form. The form uses the same layout as the other Web pages I've built so far. The key part of the HTML is shown in Listing 11-34.

The form is relatively simple, containing two input boxes (for the reviewer's name and e-mail address), a drop-down box allowing the reviewer to rate the book, and a text area for the actual review. Also included with this form are two buttons: one to submit the review and the other to clear the form. Note that the WebClass Designer added an attribute to each of the form tags called DESIGNTIMESP. This attribute allows the WebClass Designer to track changes in the form. It doesn't affect the operation of the HTML at all.

This form accepts a book review for *Programming ISAPI with VB5*:

Listing 11-34

```
<form action="WebBooks.asp?wci=review&isbn=76150914"
method="post" name="review">
Please enter your name:
<input size="30" name="Reviewer" designtimesp=986>
<p designtimesp=987>
Please enter your e-mail address:
<input size="30" name="Email" designtimesp=988>
<p designtimesp=989>
Please rate this book on a scale from 10 (best) to 1 (worst):
<select name="Rating" size="1" designtimesp=990>
    <option value="10" designtimesp=991>10</option>
    <option value="9" designtimesp=992>9</option>
    <option value="8" designtimesp=993>8</option>
    <option value="7" designtimesp=994>7</option>
    <option value="6" designtimesp=995>6</option>
    <option value="5" designtimesp=996>5</option>
    <option value="4" designtimesp=997>4</option>
    <option value="3" designtimesp=998>3</option>
    <option value="2" designtimesp=999>2</option>
    <option value="1" designtimesp=1000>1</option>
</select></font></p>
<p designtimesp=1001>
<textarea rows="10" cols="50" name="ReviewText" designtimesp=1002></textarea>
<p designtimesp=1003>
<input type="submit" name="Submit Button" value="Submit Review" design-
timesp=1004>
<input type="reset" name="Clear Button" value="Clear Review" design-
timesp=1005>
</form>
```

The code to generate this form is shown in Listing 11-35. The code is very similar to the code I've already discussed. It merely outputs HTML and HTML templates to the user's browser.

Create a form in the ShowReviewForm_Respond event:

Listing 11-35

```
Private Sub ShowReviewForm_Respond()

Dim rs As ADODB.Recordset

Set rs = GetBook.Execute(, CLng(Request.QueryString("isbn")))
```

```
With Response
    .Write Title("Review: " & rs.Fields!Title)
    HeaderForm.WriteTemplate
    .Write "<p><strong><center>Review: " & rs.Fields!Title
    .Write "</center></strong>"
    .Write "<p>"
    .Write "This page allows add your own book review "
    .Write "to our web site. Simply fill out the form below "
    .Write "and press 'Submit Review'. The review will "
    .Write "automatically be added to our database, so "
    .Write "that others can see your comments."
    .Write "<p>"
    .Write "Note you must include your name and e-mail "
    .Write "address for the review to be accepted and all "
    .Write "reviews become property of WebBooks.com "
    .Write "(plus some other legal stuff.)"
    LinkForm.WriteTemplate
    .Write "<form action=""WebBooks.asp?wci=review&isbn="
    .Write rs.Fields!isbn
    .Write """ method=""post"" name=""review"">"

    ReviewForm.WriteTemplate
    FooterForm.WriteTemplate
    .End

End With

rs.Close

End Sub
```

Processing the Book Review

Responding to the book review is a fairly straightforward task. The only complicating factor is that for the first time I have to update a database table rather than just read it. To solve this problem, I've created a slightly more complex stored procedure than you've seen yet (see Listing 11-36) for two reasons. First, it includes more than one parameter, which makes the Visual Basic program a little more complicated. Second, it has more than one statement in the procedure, which makes the procedure more complex in itself.

Consider what has to be done to add a review to the Reviews table. Since I don't know the highest ReviewNumber in the table, I have to find the highest ReviewNumber in the table so that I can add one to it to create the new value for ReviewNumber. Then I can insert the rest of the fields normally. This leaves me with two choices. First, I could call the database to determine what the value should be and then make a second call to insert the new review. Second, I could add a routine on the database server that combines both functions into a single database call.

Since there is a rather high cost associated with a database call, I choose to build that function into the stored procedure. Doing this is relatively simple. In the stored procedure editor, I declare the stored procedures' header including all the different parameters. Next I declare a temporary variable called @rn to hold the largest ReviewNumber in the table. I then check to see if there is already a review. If there isn't, I set @rn to 4, the number of the first review. Otherwise, I set it to one more than the highest value already in the database. Then I use the **Insert** statement to insert all the information into the Reviews table.

The InsertReview stored procedure adds a new review to the database:

Listing 11-36

```
CREATE  Procedure InsertReview
    @isbn Int,
    @reviewer VarChar(64),
    @email VarChar(64),
    @rating Smallint,
    @review VarChar(8000) As
Declare @rn Smallint
if not exists(select * from reviews where isbn = @isbn)
    set @rn=4
else
    select @rn=max(reviewnumber) from reviews where isbn = @isbn
set @rn = @rn +1
Insert into Reviews
    (ISBN, ReviewNumber, ReviewerName, EmailAddress, Review)
    Values (@isbn, @rn, @Reviewer, @email, @review)
```

Back in the IIS Application, I set up for the insert by declaring a **Variant** array that will contain the parameters for the insert (see Listing 11-37). This is required since the **Execute** method of the **Command** object takes a single parameter that will contain the parameters for the stored procedure. Since this stored procedure has five parameters, it accepts them in a single **Variant** array. So I enter the parameters into the array starting with element zero, in the order in which they were defined in the stored procedure. Then I execute the stored procedure.

Since the stored procedure doesn't return any values, I simply repeat what the user had entered for the review. To do this requires that I translate the ISBN into a title and other information, so I use my favorite stored procedure GetBook to grab the information I need and send it back to the user. After repeating the review information, I provide the user a hyperlink back to the book form to enable the user to see his or her new review.

Respond to the Book Review form:

Listing 11-37

```
Private Sub Review_Respond()

Dim rs As ADODB.Recordset
Dim parms(4) As Variant

Set rs = GetBook.Execute(, CLng(Request.QueryString("isbn")))

With Request
    parms(0) = CLng(.QueryString("isbn"))
    parms(1) = .Form("reviewer")
    parms(2) = .Form("email")
    parms(3) = .Form("rating")
    parms(4) = .Form("reviewtext")
    InsertReview.Execute , parms

End With

With Response

    .Write Title("Thanks for your review of " & rs.Fields!Title)
    HeaderForm.WriteTemplate
    .Write "<p><center><strong><big>"
    .Write "Thanks for your review of " & rs.Fields!Title
    .Write ".</big></strong></center>"

    LinkForm.WriteTemplate

    .Write "<strong>Reviewed by: <a href=""mailto:"
    .Write Request.Form("email") & """>"
    .Write Request.Form("reviewer") & "</a></strong>"
```

```
        .Write "<p>Rating: " & Request.Form("rating")
        .Write "<p>" & Request.Form("reviewtext")
        .Write "<hr>"

        .Write "Return to "
        .Write "<a href=""WebBooks.asp?wci=book&isbn="
        .Write rs.Fields!isbn & """>"
        .Write rs.Fields!Title & " "
        .Write "</a>."

        FooterForm.WriteTemplate
        .End

    End With

    rs.Close

End Sub
```

Adding Search Capabilities to WebBooks.com

There are two ways you can search for books on WebBooks.com. First, you can click on an author's name and display the author's biography and all the books written by that author (see Figure 11-33). You can also take advantage of the full-text indexes I created in Chapter 10 to search for any word or words in the Author, Title, Keyword, or ISBN fields (see Figure 11-34) and see the results (see Figure 11-35).

Displaying Books by a Particular Author

The **Author_Respond** event is used to display the author's biography and the list of books written by that author. Like most of the other routines in this WebClass, this one expects a parameter in the URL that will be used to drive the results. In this case, authorcode is used to identify the author I want to display information about.

Listing 11-38 contains the code used to display the author's books and biography. This is a relatively simple routine that begins by finding the author's name using the FindAuthors stored procedure. Then assuming that I find the author, I write the author's name in the title and at the top of the Web page.

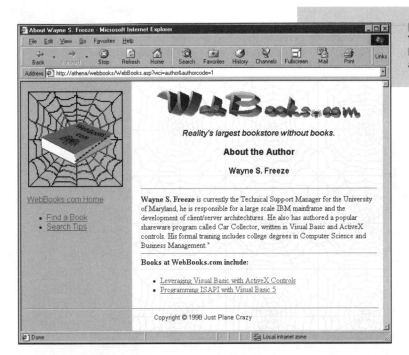

Figure 11-33
You can list all of the books for a particular author's name.

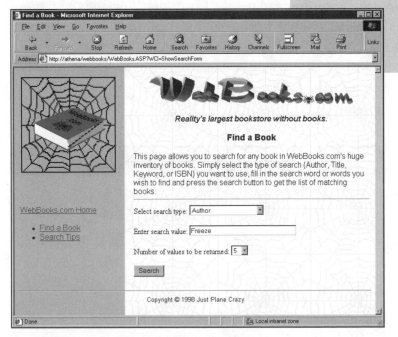

Figure 11-34
You can enter search information to find books in the database.

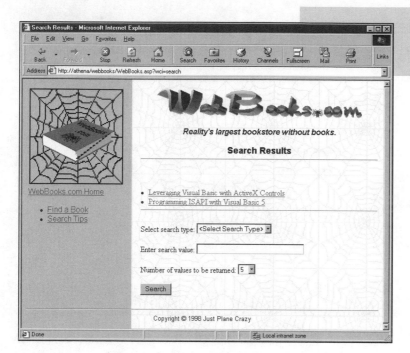

Figure 11-35
Display the search results.

Then I close the **Recordset** and use the GetAuthorBiography to retrieve the author's biography. After writing the biography, I close that **Recordset** and use the FindAuthorBooks stored procedure to retrieve the titles of the books written by this author. Finally, I write the footer information to close out the Web page and exit the routine.

List the author's biography and books written:

Listing 11-38

```
Private Sub Author_Respond()

Dim rs As ADODB.Recordset

With Response

   Set rs = FindAuthors.Execute(, _
      CLng(Request.QueryString("authorcode")))

   If Not (rs.BOF And rs.EOF) Then
      .Write Title("About " & rs.Fields!authorname)
```

```
HeaderForm.WriteTemplate
.Write "<p><center><strong><big>About the Author</big><p>"
.Write rs.Fields!authorname & "</strong></center><p>"

rs.Close

LinkForm.WriteTemplate

Set rs = GetAuthorBiography.Execute(, _
    CLng(Request.QueryString("authorcode")))

If Not (rs.BOF And rs.EOF) Then
    .Write rs.Fields!AuthorBiography
    .Write "<hr>"
End If

rs.Close

.Write "<strong>Books at WebBooks.com include:</strong><ul>"

Set rs = FindAuthorBooks.Execute(, _
    CLng(Request.QueryString("authorcode")))

Do While Not rs.EOF
    .Write "<li><a href=""WebBooks.asp?wci=book&isbn="
    .Write rs.Fields!isbn & """>"
    .Write rs!Title & "</a>"
    rs.MoveNext
Loop

rs.Close
.Write "</ul>"

FooterForm.WriteTemplate
.End

    End If

End With

End Sub
```

Entering Search Information

Searching for books on WebBooks.com is fairly easy—you simply click on Find a Book Link in Any Page, after which a form will be displayed asking for your search information. This form is very similar to the form I developed for submitting an author review, in that it takes advantage of drop-down lists, <INPUT> text fields, and an <INPUT> submit button (see Listing 11-39).

Collect search information using an HTML form:

Listing 11-39

```
<form action="WebBooks.asp?wci=search" method="post" name="search">
Select search type:
<select name="SearchKey" size="1">
    <option>&lt;Select Search Type&gt;</option>
    <option>Author</option>
    <option>Title</option>
    <option>Keyword</option>
    <option>ISBN</option>
</select>
<p>
Enter search value:
<input size="30" name="SearchValue">
<p>
Number of values to be returned:
<select name="ResultsReturned" size="1">
    <option selected value="5">5</option>
    <option value="10">10</option>
    <option value="20">20</option>
    <option value="25">25</option>
    <option value="50">50</option>
</select></font></p>
<p>
<input type="submit" name="Submit Button" value="Search">
</form>
```

The user can select from one of four different search keys: Author, Title, Keyword, or ISBN. Then the user can supply any valid search value. Typically this is a single word, though SQL Server supports a rich and complex search value. Finally, you can limit the number of entries the user is able to retrieve.

Running the Search

When the user sends search criteria to the Web server, **the Search_Respond** event will be triggered (see Listing 11-40). The first step in processing the request is to determine which field the user is searching on. Then I build a query that will return the ISBN and title of each book that is matched.

Searching for Books in Them Thar Hills

Searching for information in a database is a lot like digging for gold. You get the maximum return for the minimum investment if you know exactly what you are looking for. The full-text indexing supported by SQL Server includes a rich set of capabilities supplied by the **Contains** predicate in the **Where** clause.

You can search for any single word by simply specifying **Contains**(title, 'programming').

You can search for multiple words by enclosing them in double quotes, as in **Contains**(title, '"Visual Basic"').

You can search for the first part of the word by using double quotes and specifying an asterisk as a wildcard character, as in **Contains**(title, '"pro*"'). This would find matches on such words as programming, professional, project, professor, and procession.

You can create complex search expressions by enclosing each term in double quotes and using **And, Or,** and **Not,** like **Contains**(title, '"Visual Basic" **Or** "VB" **Or** "V B"'). Note you can't use an **Or Not** condition.

You can locate words that are close together by using **Near,** like this **Contains**(title, '"Visual" **Near** "Basic"'). This would find matches on Visual Basic, Visual Guide to Basic, etc.

You can search for different forms of a word by using the **Formsof** operator, as in **Contains**(title, '**Formsof(Inflectional**, 'program')'). This would match program, programs, programmed, programming, etc.

You can use the **Isabout** operator to provide multiple search conditions, each with its own relative weight. For example, **Contains**(title, '**Isabout**(Basic **Weight**(.8), C++ **Weight**(.6), Java **Weight**(.4))') returns books containing Basic, C++, and Java.

The **Containstable** predicate provides the same capabilities as the **Contains** predicate but also returns a rank saying how well the selected row matched the criteria. This can be very useful with the **Isabout** and **Near** operators.

> **Tip**
>
> Always use the **Top** clause to limit the number of rows retrieved while using a full-text index. You should see a significant improvement in performance, and you don't overwhelm the user with too much information.

> **Note**
>
> While you might think that you can use the **Contains** predicate in a stored procedure, you're half right. While you can use the predicate, you can't specify any parameters for the search information. So if you want to use full-text indexes in your databases, be prepared to give up using stored procedures whenever you need to access the index.

After building the query, I create a **Recordset** on the fly using it. If no matches are found, I report that. Otherwise, I display the results in an unordered list. As I write each book to the **Response** object, I create a hyperlink to the book information page with the ISBN number. That way the user can click on the title and see the information for that particular book.

Search_Respond creates a list of books matching the specified search value:

Listing 11-40

```
Private Sub Search_Respond()

Dim rs As New ADODB.Recordset
Dim sel As String

On Error Resume Next

Select Case Request.Form("SearchKey")
    Case "Author"
        sel = "Select Top " & _
            FormatNumber(Request.Form("ResultsReturned"), 0) & _
            " b.ISBN, b.Title " & _
            "From iis.dbo.Authors a, iis.dbo.Books b, " & _
            "iis.dbo.AuthorBooks ab " & _
```

```
                        "Where a.authorcode = ab.authorcode and " & _
                        "ab.isbn = b.isbn and " & _
                        "Contains(a.AuthorName, '" & _
                        Request.Form("SearchValue") & "')"

               Case "Title"
                   sel = "Select Top " & _
                       FormatNumber(Request.Form("ResultsReturned"), 0) & _
                       " b.ISBN, b.Title " & _
                       "From iis.dbo.Books b " & _
                       "Where Contains(b.title, '" & _
                       Request.Form("SearchValue") & "')"

               Case "Keyword"
                   sel = "Select Top " & _
                       FormatNumber(Request.Form("ResultsReturned"), 0) & _
                       " b.ISBN, b.Title " & _
                       "From iis.dbo.Books b " & _
                       "Where Contains(b.keywords, '" & _
                       Request.Form("SearchValue") & "')"

               Case "ISBN"
                   sel = "Select Top " & _
                       FormatNumber(Request.Form("ResultsReturned"), 0) & _
                       " b.ISBN, b.Title " & _
                       "From iis.dbo.Books b " & _
                       "Where b.ISBN = " & Trim(Request.Form("SearchValue"))

               Case Else
                   sel = "Select Top " & _
                       FormatNumber(Request.Form("ResultsReturned"), 0) & _
                       " b.ISBN, b.Title " & _
                       "From iis.dbo.Books b "
           End Select

       With Response
           .Write Title("Search Results")
           HeaderForm.WriteTemplate
           .Write "<p><center><big><strong>"
           .Write "Search Results"
           .Write "</center></big></strong>"
           LinkForm.WriteTemplate
           Err.Clear
           Set rs = db.Execute(sel, , adCmdText)
           If Err.Number <> 0 Then
               .Write "No matches were found."

           Else
               .Write "<bl>"
```

```
        Do While Not rs.EOF
            .Write "<li>"
            .Write "<a href=""WebBooks.asp?wci=book&isbn="
            .Write rs.Fields!isbn & """>"
            .Write rs.Fields!Title & " "
            .Write "</a>"
            .Write vbCrLf
            rs.MoveNext
        Loop
    End If
    .Write "</bl>"
    .End
    rs.Close
    .Write "<hr>"
    SearchForm.WriteTemplate
    FooterForm.WriteTemplate
    .End

End With

End Sub
```

Wrapping Up

The Inventory Information Subsystem is a rather large subsystem compared to the Customer Information Subsystem. It has many more tables and offers the ability to access information from a traditional client/server program and via the user's Web browser. The client/server program is far more secure than the previous program since I am able to prompt for a login ID and password, which I can use to establish database security.

The traditional client/server program was built using the Data Environment Designer. This facility offers many new features that help you build your database programs. While this facility has many advantages over the ADO data control, it isn't as powerful as using the native ADO database objects. Having used both facilities extensively in this chapter, I prefer the native object interface. The code is clearer and easier to understand without the strange quirks that are sometimes introduced by the Data Environment Designer.

When I display the book information in the IIS Application, I check to see if I have a valid book, but I don't return anything to the user if I don't find the book in the database. It would be a good idea to display an error message. In theory, any time I create a hyperlink to book information, it will be because the ISBN is already in the database. But there is a possibility that someone may create a bookmark for a book that may be removed from the database somewhere down the road. The database may also become corrupt and contain an invalid ISBN which could also cause the same error. You should work through this problem on your own and test your results by displaying an invalid ISBN.

After designing the IIS database, I found a couple of changes that I wanted to make. I allow the reviewer to enter a rating for a book, yet there isn't a field in the database for rating. To fix this problem, you have to add a field to the Reviews table and modify the Book_Respond event to display the review information.

The other change also affects the Reviews table. As the process stands now, anyone can say anything about a book in a review. This probably isn't fair to an author, because someone could anonymously submit an unfavorable or obscene review. While I don't believe in censorship, at a minimum someone should review the review to make sure that it isn't slanderous. Implementing this change is a little harder than the other one. You will need to add a field to the database to hold the status of the review. This value is either waiting on approval or approved. You will need to modify the Book_Respond event to display only the reviews that have been approved. The Review_Respond event will need to be modified to generate an e-mail message and send it to the book reviewer.

CHAPTER 12

Testing the Inventory Information Subsystem

Testing the Inventory Information Subsystem programs involves walking through all the features of the programs and making sure that they get the correct results. The best way to do this is by exercising the program against a set of known test data and comparing the results to what you expect. However, to test against sample data, you first have to load the sample data into the database.

ON THE

CD

The complete source code for the programs in this chapter are included on the CD-ROM, along with the sample data. Check the \HOSQLSrver7\Chapt12 directory.

- **Data** contains the sample data files used to populate the database. The .csv files contain information that should be loaded using DTS (these should be loaded first), while books.txt and the .jpg files are loaded with the program in the **Loader** directory.

- **Loader** contains the program that loads the data file into the books.txt and the jpg image files into the database.

Loading the Sample Data

The sample data for this chapter is stored in a different format than the data you loaded in Chapter 7. While I prefer to use comma separated value files, I choose to load the data for each book using a format common to the bookselling industry. This file can be found on your CD-ROM as \HOSQLServer7\Chapt12\Data\Books.txt. (A sample book from the file is shown in Listing 12-1 below.)

Of course there are a few CSV files that contain data for the other tables in this subsystem. These are found in \HOSQLServer7\Chapt12\Data. Each book's cover is stored as a separate JPG file in the same directory. So with a sample database of about 800 books, you get 700 different JPG files, a couple of CSV files, and one large text file.

Considerations for Loading the Sample Data

The data file shown in Listing 12-1 contains information that updates four different tables in the database: the Books, Authors, AuthorBooks, and Reviews tables. (Remember, the Reviews table holds a book's description besides reviews about the book.) No information is included in this file (at least not directly) for the Covers, Publishers, BindingCodes, and AuthorBiographies tables.

Here is a sample format for a book's information:

Listing 12-1

```
ISBN: 0761509143
FullTitle: Programming ISAPI with Visual Basic 5
Series:
Author: Freeze, Wayne S.
Edition: 0
Pages: 500
Publisher: Prima Publishing
Binding: TP
ListPrice: 40.00
PubDate: 970401
```

```
Description: Programming ISAPI with Visual Basic 5 teaches you how
to build your own ActiveX controls that are called from Microsoft's
Internet Information Server (IIS) using the Internet Server
Application Programming Interface (ISAPI). The key to this is a tool
called OLEISAPI2. This program translates the calls from IIS's ISAPI
to a standard ActiveX COM interface, which can be used by Visual
Basic programs. The book starts at the beginning by building a very
simple program that demonstrates how OLEISAPI2 works. Then it shows
you how to build several more programs increasing in complexity,
until you build your own intranet server program, called WebMaster.
WebMaster includes such functions as electronic chat groups,
calendaring facility, and a project tracking tool. The OLEISAPI2
program itself is examined to understand the ActiveX and ISAPI
interfaces from a C++ programming point of view.
END
```

Like the Customer Information Subsystem, some tables in this subsystem must be loaded before others. The Publishers and BindingCodes tables must be loaded before the Books table is loaded. This can be done easily by simply importing the two CSV files into their associated tables as was done earlier with the Customer Information Subsystem. The Books table must be loaded before the Reviews table and the Covers table are loaded. The Authors table must be loaded before the Author-Biographies table is loaded. Both the Books and the Authors tables must be loaded before the AuthorBooks table is loaded.

Another issue that seems rather minor at first but turns out to be rather important is that I need to enter an author's name into the database only once. That means that I need to translate the author's name into an AuthorCode value. The other values included in this data that are stored as coded values are much easier to obtain.

The Good, the Bad, and the Ugly

Prima was kind enough to supply the data file I'm loading into the database. However, this file contains only information about books from the various divisions of Prima Publishing. I decided that adding some books from other publishers would be a good idea. Since I already had the information for the books my wife Jill and I have written, I decided to use those.

As with most real-life data, there are errors. These errors range from missing values, incorrectly formatted values, and incorrect values. You can't do much about missing information besides marking it as missing. Incorrectly formatted values can wreak havoc with a program, so you will have to add a little more error detecting and correcting in the program. Information that is merely incorrect is impossible to correct or even detect, so this information must remain until someone outside the application development team recognizes that it is bad. Once this problem is recognized, it's easy to use the utility from Chapter 11 to make any necessary corrections to the data.

I had two choices. One choice would be to reformat the single file into multiple files with each file containing the data for a single table. However, this method can get a little messy when trying to keep values like AuthorCodes, which are generated by the database in sync with other values stored in the database.

The other choice would be to try to load the data file directly into the database. This means parsing the file on the fly and stuffing the data into the correct tables. While this has the advantage of being logically simpler, it also has its share of problems.

The Data File

Listing 12-1 contains a sample book from the data file. Each line of the file consists of a keyword followed by a colon and a space followed by a value. The end of the line is marked by the standard carriage return/line feed pair of characters. Even the row containing the Description keyword is a single line. (I wrapped the text to make it easier for you to see the entire line of information.) The line that marks the end of the book contains the keyword END. The information for the next book follows the END keyword.

The ISBN keyword contains the ISBN for the book. This value should not contain any formatting characters. An ISBN contains exactly 10 characters. Each character contains a value ranging from zero to nine, except for the last one, which can also contain an X. In WebBooks.com, we don't bother to save the last character since it can be derived from the others.

The FullTitle field contains the full title of the book. Note that the database field Title holds only 64 characters, which may cause some titles such as *Programming ISAPI with Visual Basic 5 for Windows 95 and Windows NT, First Edition with CD-ROM Containing Trial Copy of VB5* to be truncated. (While this title is a bit excessive, some publishers try to cram as much information as possible into a title hoping to catch the eye of the potential purchaser. It also works well when customers use a search engine looking for specific keywords in a title.)

The Series keyword specifies the name of the book's series. For instance, this book is part of the Hands On series from Prima. While it is obvious that this book is part of a series, other books may not be so obvious. They may have titles that have nothing to do with the series name. So some publishers need a separate field to describe this information. For purposes of the WebBooks.com application, this field is ignored. However, it would be a good exercise for you to add this field to the appropriate tables and modify both the Book Info program and the Loader program to accommodate this information.

The Author keyword specifies the list of authors who wrote the book. This field should always have a value. Author names are listed as last name first, followed by a comma, and then the first name. If more than one author is listed for the book, then a semicolon must be used to separate the names.

The Edition keyword specifies the edition number of the book. This is another piece of information that isn't stored in the IIS database. It is used primarily to identify books that have been revised while keeping the same title.

The Pages keyword specifies the number of pages in the book. This value corresponds to the PageCount field in the database.

The Publisher keyword specifies the name of the book's publisher. In order to use this value in the Books table, I need to convert it to a PublisherCode value first. This value is then used as a key into the Publishers table.

The Binding keyword specifies the binding code. This value is translated into BindingCode as shown in Table 12-1.

Table 12-1 Translating the Binding Value into BindingCode and Back Again

BindingCode	Binding Value	Description
1	TP	Trade Paperback
2	MM	Mass Market
3	HC	Hardcover
4	LB	Library Binding
5	AC	Audio Cassette
6	AD	Audio Compact Disc
7	VHS	VHS Videotape
8	CL	Calendar
9	SP	Spiral-Bound
10	RB	Ring-Bound
11	CD	CD-ROM
12	PT	Textbook
13	—	Other

The ListPrice keyword specifies the list price of the book. This value is formatted without a dollar sign but can contain a decimal point.

The PubDate keyword specifies the date the book was originally published. The date format is YYMMDD, where YY contains a two-digit year, MM contains the two-digit month, and DD contains a two-digit day. Obviously this field is not Year-2000 compatible.

The Description keyword contains a summary of the book. This value is stored in the Reviews table, with ReviewNumber set to zero. Note that this field may be very large, since all the information is stored on a single line. If the review contains 500 words and the average word length is six characters, then the total number of characters in this line would be 3,000 characters. A line this large may confuse some word processors and text editors, so edit this file with caution.

A Detailed Look at the Import Program

The IIS Data Load program is a relatively simple program containing a rather large subroutine that does all the work (see Figure 12-1). While it contains a few other subroutines, the Command1_Click event (see Listing 12-2) performs most of the work to load the database. In addition to the four tables—Authors, Books, AuthorBooks, and Reviews—I choose to load the Covers table at the same time. This routine is where most of the problems lie. The first thing you notice is that it's very long. In fact, it's too large and should be broken into smaller pieces. However, this routine didn't start out that way—it just evolved over time.

Tip

In general, if you can't see an entire subroutine on the screen at the same time, it's too large. The larger the routine you write, the harder it is to debug. It's also hard to add new functions. About the only time you should have a routine this large is when it consists of a single statement such as a **Select Case** or **If Then/ElseIf** type of statement that allows you to select one situation from many different cases. Then it's acceptable to have a large routine, since all you're really doing is selecting one option.

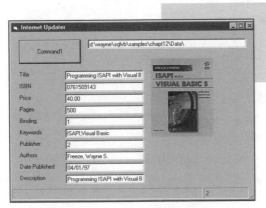

Figure 12-1
Run the initial data load for the IIS database.

The Command1_Click event loads the sample data into the database:

Listing 12-2

```
Private Sub Command1_Click()

Dim db As ADODB.Connection
Dim AuthorBooks As ADODB.Recordset
Dim Authors As ADODB.Recordset
Dim Books As ADODB.Recordset
Dim Covers As ADODB.Recordset
Dim Reviews As ADODB.Recordset
Dim cmd As ADODB.Command

Dim BookCount As Long
Dim i As Long
Dim BookInfo As TextStream
Dim w As String
Dim x() As String
Dim y() As String
Dim z() As Byte

BookCount = 0

Set BookInfo = fso.OpenTextFile(Text1.Text & "books.txt")

Set db = New ADODB.Connection
db.Open "provider=sqloledb;data source=athena;" & _
    "initial catalog=iis", "sa", ""

Set cmd = New ADODB.Command
Set cmd.ActiveConnection = db
cmd.CommandType = adCmdText

cmd.CommandText = "Delete From AuthorBooks"
cmd.Execute

cmd.CommandText = "Delete From Authors"
cmd.Execute

cmd.CommandText = "Delete From Covers"
cmd.Execute

cmd.CommandText = "Delete From Reviews"
cmd.Execute

cmd.CommandText = "Delete From Books"
cmd.Execute
```

```
Set cmd = Nothing

Set AuthorBooks = New ADODB.Recordset
Set AuthorBooks.ActiveConnection = db
AuthorBooks.Source = "Select * From iis.dbo.AuthorBooks"
AuthorBooks.CursorType = adOpenStatic
AuthorBooks.LockType = adLockOptimistic
AuthorBooks.Open

Set Authors = New ADODB.Recordset
Set Authors.ActiveConnection = db
Authors.Source = "Select * From iis.dbo.Authors"
Authors.CursorType = adOpenStatic
Authors.LockType = adLockOptimistic
Authors.Open

Set Books = New ADODB.Recordset
Set Books.ActiveConnection = db
Books.Source = "Select * From iis.dbo.Books"
Books.CursorType = adOpenStatic
Books.LockType = adLockOptimistic
Books.Open

Set Covers = New ADODB.Recordset
Set Covers.ActiveConnection = db
Covers.Source = "Select * From iis.dbo.Covers"
Covers.CursorType = adOpenStatic
Covers.LockType = adLockOptimistic
Covers.Open

Set Reviews = New ADODB.Recordset
Set Reviews.ActiveConnection = db
Reviews.Source = "Select * From iis.dbo.Reviews"
Reviews.CursorType = adOpenStatic
Reviews.LockType = adLockOptimistic
Reviews.Open

Do While Not BookInfo.AtEndOfStream
    x = Split(BookInfo.ReadLine, ": ", 2)
    If UBound(x) > -1 Then
        Select Case x(0)
            Case "ISBN"
                Text3.Text = x(1)

            Case "FullTitle"
                Text2.Text = x(1)
                Text7.Text = GetKeywords(x(1))

            Case "Author"
```

```
            If Len(x(1)) = 0 Then
               Text9.Text = "Information not available."
            Else
               Text9.Text = x(1)
            End If

    Case "Pages"
        Text5.Text = x(1)

    Case "Publisher"
        If x(1) = "Prima Publishing" Then
            Text8.Text = "2"
        ElseIf x(1) = "Microsoft Press" Then
            Text8.Text = "3"
        ElseIf x(1) = "Ventana" Then
            Text8.Text = "4"
        ElseIf x(1) = "Sams" Then
            Text8.Text = "5"
        ElseIf x(1) = "Que" Then
            Text8.Text = "6"
        ElseIf x(1) = "Sybex" Then
            Text8.Text = "7"
        ElseIf x(1) = "Carrol and Graf" Then
            Text8.Text = "8"
        Else
            Text8.Text = "1"
        End If

    Case "Binding"
        If x(1) = "TP" Then
            Text6.Text = 1
        ElseIf x(1) = "MM" Then
            Text6.Text = 2
        ElseIf x(1) = "HC" Then
            Text6.Text = 3
        ElseIf x(1) = "LB" Then
            Text6.Text = 4
        ElseIf x(1) = "AC" Then
            Text6.Text = 5
        ElseIf x(1) = "AD" Then
            Text6.Text = 6
        ElseIf x(1) = "VHS" Then
            Text6.Text = 7
        ElseIf x(1) = "CL" Then
            Text6.Text = 8
        ElseIf x(1) = "SP" Then
            Text6.Text = 9
        ElseIf x(1) = "RB" Then
            Text6.Text = 10
```

```
        ElseIf x(1) = "CD" Then
            Text6.Text = 11
        ElseIf x(1) = "PT" Then
            Text6.Text = 12
        Else
            Text6.Text = 13
        End If

    Case "ListPrice"
        If IsNumeric(x(1)) Then
            Text4.Text = x(1)
        Else
            Text4.Text = 0
        End If

    Case "PubDate"
        Text10.Text = Mid(x(1), 3, 2) & "/" & _
            Mid(x(1), 5, 2) & "/" & Mid(x(1), 1, 2)

    Case "Description"
        If Len(x(1)) = 0 Then
            Text11.Text = "Information not available."
        Else
            Text11.Text = x(1)
        End If

    Case "End"
        BookCount = BookCount + 1
        StatusBar1.Panels(2).Text = FormatNumber(BookCount, 0)

        Books.AddNew
        Books!ISBN = Left(Text3.Text, 9)
        Books!Title = Left(Text2.Text, 64)
        Books!publishercode = Text8.Text
        Books!datepublished = CDate(Text10.Text)
        Books!BindingCode = Text6.Text
        Books!PageCount = Text5.Text
        Books!keywords = Text7.Text
        Books!UserLevel = "All levels"
        Books!ListPrice = Text4.Text
        Books!Discount = 0.2
        Books!quantityonhand = Int(Rnd * 50) + 50
        Books!reorderpoint = Int(Rnd * 50)
        Books.Update

        Reviews.AddNew
        Reviews!ISBN = Left(Text3.Text, 9)
        Reviews!ReviewNumber = 0
        Reviews!ReviewerName = "Comments from the publisher"
```

```
          Reviews!EmailAddress = ""
          Reviews!Review = Text11.Text
          Reviews.Update

          w = Text1.Text & Mid(Text3.Text, 2, 8) & ".jpg"
          If Len(Dir(w)) > 0 Then
              ReDim z(FileLen(w) - 1)
              Open w For Binary Access Read As #1
              Get #1, , z()
              Close #1
              Covers.AddNew
              Covers!ISBN = Left(Text3.Text, 9)
              Covers("Cover").AppendChunk z
              Covers.Update
              Image1.Picture = LoadPicture(w)
          Else
              Image1.Picture = LoadPicture()
          End If

          y = Split(Text9.Text, ";")
          For i = LBound(y) To UBound(y)
              If Len(xTrim(y(i))) > 0 Then
                  Authors.Filter = "AuthorName = '" & _
                      Replace(xTrim(y(i)), "'", "''") & "'"
                  If Authors.BOF And Authors.EOF Then
                      Authors.AddNew
                      Authors!AuthorName = xTrim(y(i))
                      Authors.Update
                      Authors.MoveFirst
                  End If
                  AuthorBooks.AddNew
                  AuthorBooks!ISBN = Left(Text3.Text, 9)
                  AuthorBooks!authorcode = Authors!authorcode
                  AuthorBooks!AuthorNumber = i + 1
                  AuthorBooks.Update
              End If
          Next i

          DoEvents

      End Select
    End If
Loop

Reviews.Close
Covers.Close
Books.Close
Authors.Close
AuthorBooks.Close
```

```
db.Close
BookInfo.Close

MsgBox FormatNumber(BookCount, 0) & " books loaded!"

End Sub
```

This routine begins by declaring a bunch of recordsets, one for each database table I plan to access. I also declare an ADO **Connection** object that allows me to connect to the database and an ADO **Command** object that I'll use to issue SQL statements that don't return any records. I also declare a few regular variables that I'll use in various ways throughout the routine.

The BookCount variable keeps track of the number of books loaded. This program will run a rather long time, and knowing that it's making progress can be very useful. So the first thing I do is to set BookCount to zero. Then I open the data file. The Text1 text box contains the directory where the data file is kept.

After opening the data file, I open a connection to the database server. Then I create a command object with the following SQL statement:

```
Delete From AuthorBooks
```

This statement will delete all the rows from the AuthorBooks table. I use similar statements for the other tables I load in this section. Once I finish deleting the data, I set the **Command** object to **Nothing** to release its resources.

Next I open all the tables using a **Select** statement that retrieves all the rows. I use optimistic locking with a static cursor, since there isn't any usable data in these tables until after this routine finishes.

After opening the tables, I start a big loop that reads the data from the file one line at a time. The data I read from the input file is immediately passed to the **Split** function where the data is separated by a colon followed by a space. I also specify that the **Split** function should return a maximum of two strings. If two strings are returned, the first string contains the keyword, while the second contains the value. If only one string is returned, I'll ignore it, since there wasn't a keyword to process. Most likely the blank line found between books was responsible for the missing colon. After using the **Split** function, the value string will be stored in x(1), while the keyword string will be stored in x(0).

> By now you've heard about most of Visual Basic 6's features, but there are two you may not have heard about: the **FileSystemObject** and the **Split** function. The **FileSystemObject** makes it easy to access directories and sequential text files on your system through its object model, which is far less cumbersome to use than the older Visual Basic statements. The **Split** function is even more impressive. By specifying a value such as a colon or a string like **vbCrLf**, you can easily break one long string into an array of smaller strings. This is useful when you use the **ReadAll** method of the **TextStream** object and you want to access the individual lines.

Then I use a big **Select** statement to determine what action to take based on the keyword's value. For the most part, I just want to assign the value string to a text box to display it to the user and hold the value for later processing. However, in some cases I need to verify that there's valid data in the value string or I have to perform some additional processing to generate some additional data.

Consider the case of the Author keyword. Occasionally, in the file, I would come across an Author keyword with a blank value. This can cause problems when I try to insert this value into the database. So I'll change a blank value to one that says "Information is not available." Also, whenever I encounter the FullTitle keyword, I'll try to manufacture some information about the Keywords for this book. In the live database, this information would be entered by a clerk who has briefly reviewed the book or by the publisher who may supply this information in order to help customers find the book.

I also handle two special situations: Publishers and Binding. With the Binding keyword, I merely translate the Binding value to the Binding-Code value I use in the database. I do this with a bunch of **If Then/ElseIf** statements. Since there are only a limited number of codes available, this is an acceptable solution. I manually add the information in both the Publishers and Bindings tables before I run the program and am careful to preserve that data throughout the testing process.

A more efficient way to translate the Binding value into a BindingCode would be to do the following:

```
i = (InStr(1, Left(Trim(x(1)), 2), "TPMMHCLBACADVHCLSPRBCDPT" & _
   Left(Trim(x(1)), 2)) + 1) / 12
```

This statement is a little tricky, but basically it will return a value in the range of 1 to 13 corresponding to the position of the first two nonblank characters in the value string (x(1)) in the string "TPMMHCLBA-CADVHCLSPRBCDPT". To allow for the possibility that the data isn't in this string, I append the first two characters to the end of the string. This will always force the **InStr** function to return a match in the range of 1, 3, 5, ... 25. Adding one makes the range from 2, 4, 6, ... 26, and dividing by two makes the range from 1, 2, 3, ... 13.

If you're curious about why I didn't use this approach, I didn't think it was worth the effort. Creating this statement takes a bit of time to ensure that the values and subscripts are correct. It's much easier to simply code a bunch of **If** statements. When I was testing this part of the code, the program loaded the data so fast that I wasn't worried about speed.

I used a similar solution with the Publisher keyword. Though if this were a general-purpose program, I probably wouldn't. Since I know which publishers I will encounter during this load, I can easily add them to the database. Otherwise, I'd want to let the load program handle this automatically. However, this causes its own set of problems, as you'll see in a few minutes.

Processing the END keyword is where the real work is done. Up to this point, I'm merely shuffling data around inside my program. However, when I reach the end statement, I'm ready to do something with the database. I begin by incrementing the BookCount value and displaying it to the user, followed by adding the information to the appropriate database tables.

Tip

The number one piece of information everyone wants to know is when will the load be finished. They know (or believe or hope or pray) that the data will be loaded properly, but most database loads run for more than a few seconds. Many run for a few hours, and some will even run for a few days. Adding a counter that periodically displays the number of records loaded does two things. First, it lets you know that the load is still running and is not caught in an infinite loop. Second, it lets you understand how close the load is to completion. This might make the difference between eating junk food from a vending machine and getting a prime rib steak for dinner while you wait for the load to finish.

The first database table I load is Books. It depends only on the Publishers and BindingCodes tables, which contain data I've already loaded by hand. I use the **AddNew** method to create an empty row, and I assign the values from the text boxes on the form to the database fields. I truncate the last digit from the ISBN and truncate the title so that only the first 64 characters are saved. I convert the date value into a Visual Basic **Date** format that can be converted to the database's **DateTime** format. I simply assign constant values to the UserLevel and Discount columns rather than try to randomly create values, but I do create random values for the QuantityOnHand and ReorderPoint fields to make the database more interesting.

After loading the Books table, I load the Reviews table. This is a relatively straightforward process, as you can see in the routine. The only important issue is that I have to remember to set ReviewNumber to zero when the information is loaded so that the information shows up as a description rather than a review or comments.

The next block of code is rather interesting. I construct a file name, which is based on the same directory information that I used to open the data file and the ISBN for the book. This file contains the cover image. I check to see if this file exists by using the **Dir** function. If the file exists, the **Dir** function returns the name of the file; if it doesn't exist, it returns an empty string.

Then I redimension a **Byte Array** variable that I use to hold the image so that it contains the same number of bytes as the image itself. (Remember, Visual Basic assumes arrays start with element zero and the dimension is the relative address of the last element. Thus the dimension value you specify is one less than the number of elements you want in the array.) Then I open the file for **Binary Access** and use the **Get** statement to read the cover image into the **Byte Array** in one chunk.

This process is relatively efficient as long as the image size is reasonable. Most of the images in this database are in the 10,000 to 20,000 byte range. If you want to use this method to load a multimegabyte image, you may want to consider loading the image in smaller chunks. After getting the image into the byte array, it's a simple matter to use the **AppendChunk** method to add the array to the Cover field. One side effect of this method is that you have to go back to the disk to load the image into the **Image** control. I guess I could have made the **Image** control a bound control, but I decided it was too much work for just the one image and I didn't want to restructure the program to put controls for all the fields on the form.

The next block of code is probably the most complex in the subroutine. Since a book can have multiple authors, each author must be extracted from the list and then translated into an AuthorCode value. So to extract the list of authors from the Author value, I use the **Split** function and specify a semicolon and a space as the separator characters. This creates a string array with each element containing a single author. If only one author is found, an array containing one element will be returned.

Then I loop through the array and use the **Filter** method to search for the author's name in the Authors table. However, before I can search, I need to squeeze the spaces from both ends of the string and change all the double quotes to single quotes, since I don't want to store double quotes in the database. (This causes problems when I export information to a CSV file as well as other minor problems.) I also have to change any single quotes in the name to two single quotes, since the value part of the filter expression must be enclosed in single quotes.

If I can't find the author (i.e., **BOF** and **EOF** are both true), I add the author to the table. Note that I don't replace any single quotes with two single quotes since this value is being assigned to the database. Then I use a **MoveFirst** method to get a clean copy of the newly added row. This makes the value that the database automatically assigned to the AuthorCode field available for processing.

After retrieving the author's AuthorCode value or inserting the author for the first time, I can add the AuthorCode and the ISBN values into the AuthorBooks table. I need to also assign a value to the Author-Number column, so I use the index value from the loop. Since the first element of the array is zero, I add one to it, so that the first author has a value of one, the second would have a value of two, etc.

Once I finish adding all the information for the tables, I call **DoEvents** and start the loop all over again. When the loop's finished, I close all the **Recordset** objects and the **Connection** object, after which I close the **TextStream**. Then I send a message to the user indicating how many records were loaded.

> **Tip**
>
> One of the nicest things you can do in your application is to place calls to the **DoEvents** routine any time you have a long running loop. **DoEvents** gives up the processor and lets other tasks run. Without this, your form wouldn't be repainted and all other tasks would be frozen. Note that this is more important on a Windows 9x platform than an NT platform. Windows 9x relies on the applications to give control back to the operating system, while NT can take the processor away to perform other tasks.

The Big Subroutine

The big routine that I just described was built through several iterations. Contrary to what you may believe, large programs are not completely written and then tested; instead, they are written and tested in stages. In this case I started out by building a program that would read the input file and display it in the text boxes on the form. This allowed me to verify that my logic that parsed the input file was correct.

From there I enhanced the program to load the entries in the Books table. This was a relatively straightforward thing to do. I added code to the END keyword processing to add a new record to the table, assign values to the fields, and then **Update** the row. I also added the code to open the database at the start of the routine and close it at the end. While the load ran quickly, I felt that there was some room for improvement.

I decided to take advantage of the **UpdateBatch** method to speed up processing. So I added the BookCount parameter and added an **If** statement after the **Update** statement like the one below.

```
If BookCount Mod 50 Then
    Books.UpdateBatch
End If
```

I also changed the **LockType** to adLockBatchOptimistic. The time to load the database improved. However, since the records already existed in the Books table, I had to erase the table before I ran the program. I used the Query Analyzer to do this using the SQL **Delete** statement. After a couple of times having to switch to the Query Analyzer, I decided to add the statements to allow Visual Basic to do the work for me.

After I loaded the Books table, I tried to load the Reviews table. Then I got a really nice error message stating that errors had occurred. I've found that this error often indicates a constraint or foreign key error, and after a little digging (okay, a lot of digging), I decided that was the problem. Because the **Update** method saves the record locally until the **UpdateBatch** method is used, no rows in the Books table existed when I tried to add the information to the Reviews table. Hence the foreign key error. For this reason, I switched back to the adLockOptimistic cursor and eliminated the extra processing needed for the **UpdateBatch** method. The change in run time at this point wasn't significant, so I wasn't upset about the change.

The most interesting block of code is the code to load the cover image. I computed the image file name from the ISBN value and checked to see if I had a copy of the cover locally. If not, I could acquire it from Prima's

Web site. I used a little routine called GetFile, which allows a programmer to specify the name of a URL and a file name and have the contents of the URL transferred to the file. I've deleted this part of the code in my program, so you can't run it when you run the load program. But I left in the GetFile routine in case you want to see how to download a binary file over the Internet.

Adding the authors proved to be the biggest resource hog, aside from downloading images from the Internet. This is because I used the **Filter** method to determine the author's AuthorCode value. Since there wasn't an index on AuthorName in the Authors table, all the searches were very slow. So I added an index to the table, after which performance improved significantly. Since indexes can be added and removed on the fly, I simply added it before I ran the load program and removed it later.

In hindsight, I should have built an array of AuthorName values and AuthorCode values and searched it to retrieve the AuthorCode value rather than using the **Filter** method. That would have been faster since I then wouldn't need to keep going to the database. However, adding the index improved performance enough to make it not worth the time and effort to rewrite the program.

One final thought—before you try to use your newly loaded database, remember to populate the full-text indexes. Remember, the index updates are scheduled to be run on a daily basis, but you can trigger an update manually by Selecting the Full-Text Catalogs node under the IIS database in the SQL Server Enterprise Manager. Then all you need to do is right-click on each index and select Start Population, Full Population to initialize the indexes.

Testing the Book Information Program

After the data is loaded for the first time, it's time to start using the Book Information program. This program starts by asking for a valid login ID and password for the database (see Figure 12-2). If the login informa-

Figure 12-2
Fill in the form to log in to the Inventory Information Subsystem.

tion isn't valid, you'll get an alternate login information form or an error message asking you to enter the proper information.

After logging onto the database, you will see a form that displays information about a book (see Figure 12-3). Most of the fields relating to a book are directly displayed on this form. The cover is displayed on the Book Cover tab, while the reviews and other text information about the book arc displaycd on thc Rcvicw tab.

Testing the form basically involves pressing every button to verify that each works properly. This has been covered before, so I'll try to focus on the new aspects of testing as they relate to this program. As before, you may want to use the Query Analyzer or SQL Server Enterprise Manager to verify that the actual values in the database have been changed correctly.

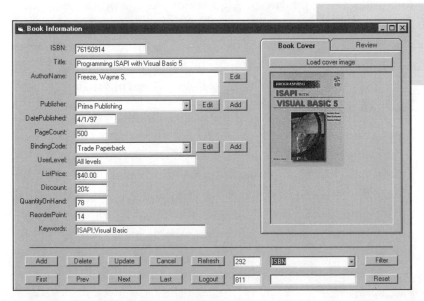

Figure 12-3
View books using the Book Information form.

First you need to make sure that the data that is entered into the fields is processed correctly. Thus the fields like ListPrice and Discount should accept special characters like dollar signs and percent signs. After all, if the value is displayed with the signs, then the user should be free to enter them. This also applies to the DatePublished field.

You also need to verify that the filter function works. However, it may not be as fast as you think. All the fields available for filtering except for ISBN do not have an index. You had better allow a little time for the filter to complete, since the database server has to scan through every row in the recordset.

Tip

When you expect to perform a task for a long time, like using the **Filter** method on a column without a key, you should turn the cursor into an hourglass. To do this, simply declare an integer variable and save the current value of the cursor from the **Screen.MousePointer** property, and then set it to vbHourglass. When you're finished processing, restore the **Screen.MousePointer** property using the temporary integer variable.

Unlike my previous programs, this one includes a lot of specialized forms to edit data in support tables. For example, the other tables such as the Publishers table (see Figure 12-4) provides information that permits a record to be added to the Books table. The more forms and tables you have, the larger the chance of an error. So the more time you spend testing, the less time you'll have users calling you saying that your program died with some strange error message.

In this case, thinking like a user paid off. I found an error in the logic in the Add Publisher function. If the user presses the Add button next to the Publisher field, the publisher form will be displayed, as shown in Figure 12-5. If the user didn't mean to press this button, the natural reaction would be to press the Close button without entering any information. This will cause an error, since the .rsPublishers recordset will be left in adEditAdd mode, while the returning code expects the add to be completed. Listing 12-3 shows the bug, while Listing 12-4 shows how the bug was corrected.

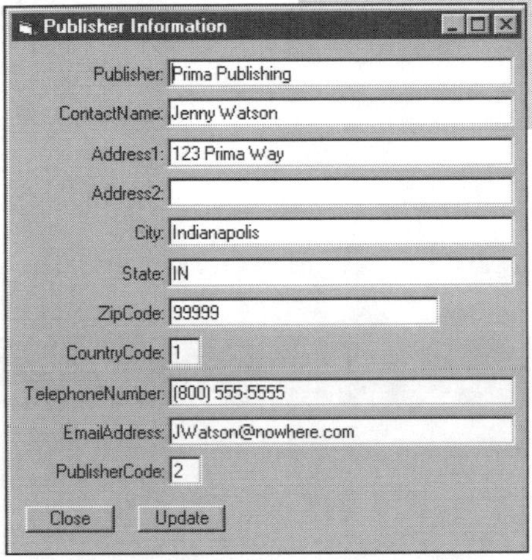

Figure 12-4
Edit information
about a publisher.

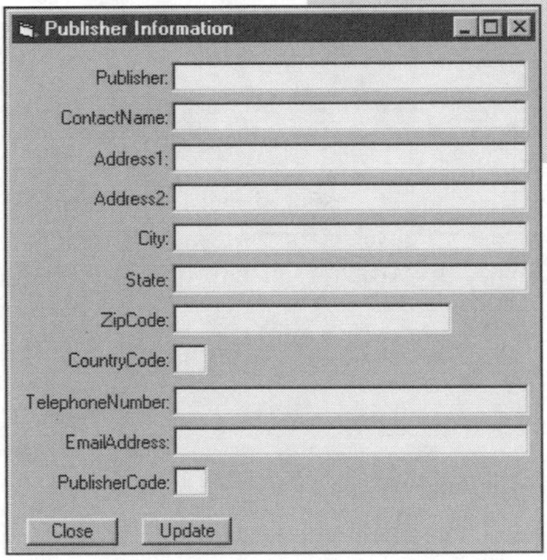

Figure 12-5
A blank form for
adding a new
publisher

The Command15_Click event contains an error:

Listing 12-3

```
Private Sub Command15_Click()

With DataEnvironment1
    .rsPublishers.AddNew
    PubInfo.Show 1
    .rsPublishers.Filter = ""
    .rsPublishers.MoveLast
```

```
    .rsBooks.Fields!publishercode = .rsPublishers.Fields!publishercode
    Set DataCombo2.RowSource = DataEnvironment1
    Set DataCombo2.DataSource = DataEnvironment1

End With

End Sub
```

This version of the Command15_Click event corrects the error:

Listing 12-4

```
Private Sub Command15_Click()

With DataEnvironment1
    .rsPublishers.AddNew
    PubInfo.Show 1
    If .rsPublishers.EditMode <> adEditNone Then
        .rsPublishers.CancelUpdate

    Else
        .rsPublishers.Filter = ""
        .rsPublishers.MoveLast
        .rsBooks.Fields!publishercode = .rsPublishers.Fields!publishercode
        Set DataCombo2.RowSource = DataEnvironment1
        Set DataCombo2.DataSource = DataEnvironment1
    End If

End With

End Sub
```

Testing the WebBooks.com Web Application

This is the key program in the application since it will be used by more people than any other program. So while you should always test everything as thoroughly as possible, programs like this should be tested a little more than the rest. Figure 12-6 shows the main Web page for this program.

I'll give you a hint. There are two bugs, neither of which will generate an error message. Also, no action is required from the user to produce these bugs.

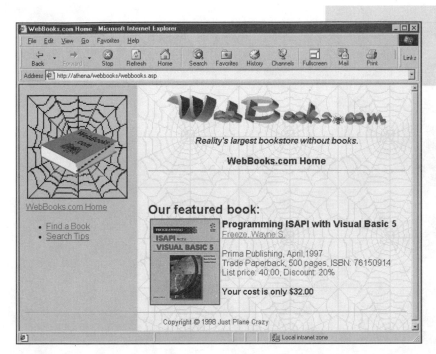

Figure 12-6
Look for errors
in obvious
places.

The ISBN code is not properly formatted. It's displayed as a string of eight digits. A properly formatted ISBN is a string of 10 digits with dashes placed in the appropriate places based on the value of the ISBN. In this case, a leading zero should be include as well as the checksum value at the end, and the dashes need to be properly inserted.

The other error isn't really a true error but a formatting issue that leaves the Web page looking slightly off balance. There is a big gap between the horizontal line in the right-hand column and the top of the book. If you were to look at the Web page in an HTML editor like FrontPage, you'd see that the problem is caused because I display the Web page as a 2-by-2 table. The first row contains the logo on the left and the header on the right. The second row contains the Web links and the main book information. Since the header is shorter than the logo, the logo dictates the height of the row. Thus the left-hand column looks okay, while the right-hand column has the gap in the middle. This can be corrected by converting to a table with only one line and two columns. Then the material will float to the proper places.

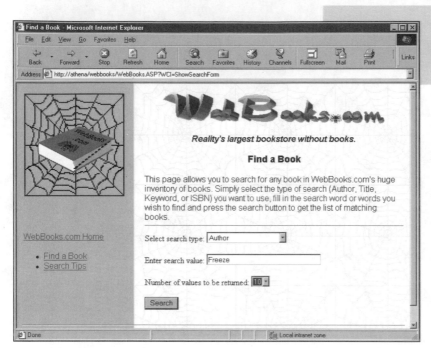

Figure 12-7
Find more
errors on the
Search form.

The search form (see Figure 12-7) has the reverse problem. The links on the left-hand side are further from the logo than they are on the home page. This is because the title section runs a little long due to the amount of text under the heading.

The second error occurs when doing an author search on Freeze. The search will return the list of books, as shown in Figure 12-8. You should notice that Introducing WebTV shows up twice. This is because the search found it once under Wayne S. Freeze and once under Jill T. Freeze. (My wife and I wrote this book together—I wrote the first sentence, she wrote the rest.) Duplicate books like this shouldn't be displayed. It can confuse the customer.

Also, if you scroll further down, the search fields are included (see Figure 12-9). But rather than taking the time to display the values used in the last search, these fields return to their default values. This isn't very user-friendly (is this term still used anymore?), and it really wouldn't take much to correct.

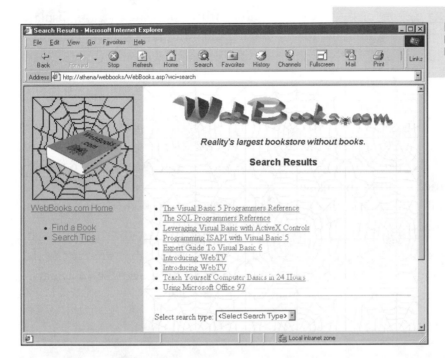

Figure 12-8
Find duplicate
books.

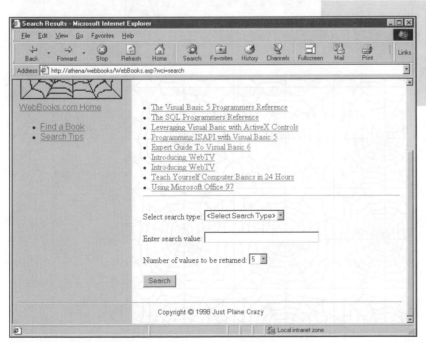

Figure 12-9
It's technically
correct, but it's
also
inconvenient for
the customer.

Selecting one of the books at random from the search results displays the book information form shown in Figure 12-10. Note the same alignment and ISBN formatting problems I've already discussed are here also. This form has only one other minor problem—the ListPrice field doesn't include a dollar sign.

The form to enter a review (shown in Figure 12-11) also has the column layout problem I've discussed in regards to the other forms. And the rating field that I challenged you to implement needs work. It would also be nice to fill in the reader's name and e-mail address as default values. I could get this information from the Customer Information Subsystem if I knew which user was accessing the Web site.

These bugs occur throughout the program. While they are easy to fix, I'm merely going to note them for now and fix them when I enhance the program in the Order Processing Subsystem.

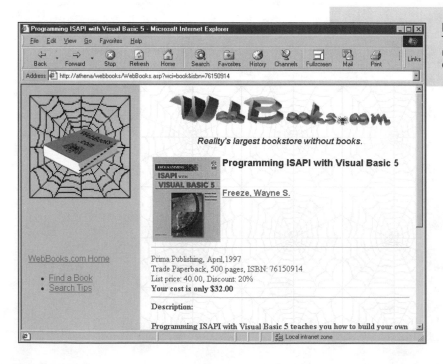

Figure 12-10
There are still minor problems on this form.

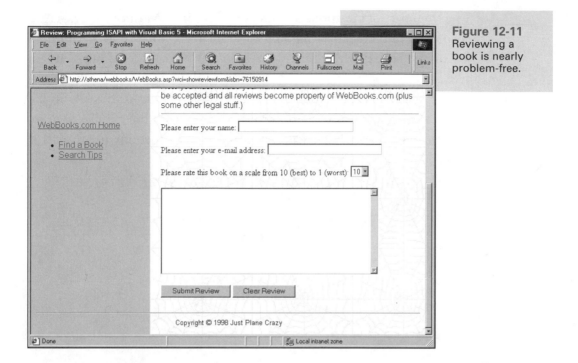

Figure 12-11
Reviewing a
book is nearly
problem-free.

Wrapping Up

The big routine didn't magically appear. It grew from a small routine that opened the data file and displayed the contents in each of the text boxes on the display into the monster shown in Listing 12-1.

If you have the time, you might want to consider modifying the Books table to add new fields for Series and Edition. This information is present in the file I use to load the data, and modifying the load program shouldn't be that difficult. Of course you'd have to modify the other programs to display and edit these fields, but that's a relatively straightforward task also.

The Inventory Information Subsystem client/server program had a few minor bugs that I corrected during the testing phase of this process. These bugs wouldn't happen very often but could occur now and then depending on the person using the application.

The Web part of the application is fairly bug-free. Most of the errors are cosmetic in nature, affecting only how the application looks—not how it works. The rest of the bugs really shouldn't be considered bugs but are areas of the program where a little additional work will make the application much easier to use. These problems will be addressed in the Order Processing Subsystem, when you expand the application by adding the ability to place an order and other functions necessary for processing customer orders.

Project 2 Summary

At the end of this phase of the WebBooks.com project, you should have learned the following:

- How to create a database using the Enterprise Manager
- How to use a full-text index to find information in your database
- How to define a **Data Environment** in Visual Basic
- How to navigate tables using **ActiveX Data Objects**
- How to use bound controls with the **Data Environment**
- How to insert, delete, and update records using the **Data Environment**
- How to build an IIS Application

HANDS ON PROJECT 3

THE ORDER PROCESSING SUBSYSTEM

- ■ Isolate business logic into an ActiveX EXE file
- ■ Send e-mail messages from your application using **CDONTS**
- ■ Use hierarchical **Recordsets** to define complex data relationships
- ■ Print reports with the Data Report Designer

Project Overview

The Order Processing Subsystem teaches you about even more advanced database functions such as hierarchical **Recordsets** and sending e-mail messages from your Web application. You'll learn how to use a hierarchical **Recordset** as input to the Microsoft Data Report to generate professional reports complete with a print preview window.

Also, you will learn how to exploit Visual Basic ActiveX EXE programs to isolate your business logic. This allows you to create a single copy of your business logic that can be accessed by any type of Visual Basic program, including IIS Applications and traditional client/server database processing.

CHAPTER 13

What Is the Order Processing Subsystem?

In the last stage of this project, you'll build on the knowledge gained in the first two phases to complete the WebBooks.com application. The missing piece is the Order Processing Subsystem. As with the previous phases, you'll learn it in terms of the following four steps:

- **Gathering information** for the application
- **Designing** the application
- **Building** the application
- **Testing** the application

This chapter will cover the high-level requirements for the system and its use by the various customers and personnel within WebBooks.com.

Describing the Order Processing Subsystem

The last phase of the WebBooks.com project is to design and build the database tables and programs necessary to process orders from customers. This will involve extending the current Web-based tools available for the customer by including a shopping cart in which customers can place books and a checkout function in which they can pay for the books. Also, tools are needed to print out packing lists and customer invoices.

Database Elements

Everything that is related to an order is managed by this subsystem. Most of this information will be developed in Chapter 14, but at a minimum, the Order Processing Subsystem needs to track the following information:

- List of books ordered
- Customer placing the order
- Shipping information
- Billing information
- Date order was placed

In addition, the Order Processing Subsystem needs to join together with the Customer Information Subsystem and the Inventory Information Subsystem as a complete package, having all the functions required to enable a customer to place an order, so that the three subsystems work seamlessly as a single application.

Application Functions

The Order Processing Subsystem tracks a customer's order from when it's placed to when it's shipped. It contains all the information necessary to process the order, including information that may also be duplicated in other subsystems. To process an order, the Order Processing Subsystem will need to perform these minimum functions:

- Get the order information from a customer
- Track the order's status
- Notify the customer when the order ships
- Produce packing lists
- Reorder and receive books from the publisher
- Generate information on buying patterns

Types of Users

Different users will need different levels of access to various components and data elements in this subsystem. This is done to protect the confidentiality of some data items and to ensure that only the appropriate individual performs the specific task. The five basic types of users for this subsystem are:

- The customer ordering books
- The clerk preparing the order for shipment
- The manager who directs and plans activities
- The computer operator who performs routine functions
- The database administrator

The customer selects books to buy and then enters the payment and shipping information into the computer. Values from the Customer Information Subsystem will be used as default values for most fields, and the customer can override these values if desired. Once the order is placed, the customer can't change anything but can only track the status of the order.

The clerk needs a packing list in order to pull the customer's selected books from the warehouse. At the same time, the shipping information is updated in the database with the shipper's tracking number, and the order is marked as having been sent.

The manager plans activities and performs general administrative tasks, such as data analysis and preparing e-mail messages advertising new books to customers.

The computer operator's main task is to back up the database, and they shouldn't have any more security permissions than what is required to perform the backups.

The database administrator needs complete access to any data element in the database, meaning the ability to read and write any value in any table. This is necessary because the database administrator not only has the responsibility for designing the database but also for resolving any database problems.

Of course this is not a complete application, so one thing you should keep in mind is that the application must be easy to change. You'll update this subsystem later in the book to integrate it with the other subsystems. While it would be better to design the application all at the same time, it rarely happens that way in the real world, so learning how to build an easily-updatable application is very important.

Goals of the Order Processing Subsystem

The main goal of this subsystem is to fill in the missing piece so a customer can order a book. You'll use ActiveX components while building IIS Applications, plus you'll use a few other tools like Microsoft's Data Reporter that you may find useful in your applications.

Determining Data Element Needs

As before, I'm going to start the phase by trying to identify every possible atomic data element that should be in the database. This is important since this information will be used to determine the database design. Once the application has been written, database design changes can be very difficult to make. Adding a field isn't bad, but splitting a table into two pieces can be almost impossible without having to rewrite the application. The better the job you do here, the less likely you are to have these kinds of problems later.

Designing the Database Structures

After determining which elements should be in the database, it's time to understand how they are related to each other. Identifying these relationships allows you to determine how to build the tables. Elements with a one-to-one relationship will usually be grouped in a single table, though not always, as I showed you with the AuthorBiographies table in Chapter 10. Elements with a one-to-many relationship will usually become part of a foreign key, and unrelated elements definitely indicate separate tables will be needed.

Building Programs to Access the Database

Once the database is built, it's time to build the programs. In this case I'm going to expand the capabilities of the IIS Application I built in Chapter 11 by adding the functions required to interact with the customer when placing an order. I'm going to build a DHTML program to let the customer check the status of an order, and finally a traditional client/server program to help the shipping clerk print the packing list and enter the shipping information.

Placing an Order

This function adds a button to the Book form that says Buy It! Pressing this button will add the book to a shopping cart. If the shopping cart doesn't exist, it will be created. From the shopping cart, the customer can delete items and change the quantity. Summary information will automatically be generated so the customer knows how much money has been spent.

Unlike many shopping carts that are implemented on e-commerce sites today, the one included with the Order Processing Module includes a mini-view that is displayed on each and every Web page the customer sees. This allows the customer to see what's in their order while browsing for other books. Also, the WebBooks.com shopping cart allows you to have multiple shopping carts, which you can switch on the fly. This allows a customer to quickly place an order while creating a different order.

Checking Out

This function is started when the customer presses a button in the shopping cart. Pressing this button will display a form containing the shipping address and credit card information. The customer has the option to change any of this information before committing to the purchase.

Checking on the Status of an Order

This function merely reports to the customer if the order has been shipped or not. If the order has been shipped, the date it was shipped and the shipper's tracking information will also be reported.

Packing an Order

This function allows the shipping clerk to print a packing list for the order, after which the clerk can pull the books from the warehouse and pack them into the box for shipment. This function also prints a shipping label that will be placed on the box and generates a tracking number so that the customer can track the package once it is shipped.

Wrapping Up

The Order Processing Subsystem is the final phase of the WebBooks.com application. It builds on the Inventory Information Subsystem to let the customer find books to order and uses information from the Customer Information Subsystem to help the customer process the order. Once the order is placed, the shipping clerk prints a packing list for the order when the order is finally shipped.

By now you should have explored several e-commerce sites to see how they handle shopping carts and other aspects of placing an online order. Perhaps you have even placed some orders using these sites. What you should do now is think about how the other sites handle ordering. What things do you like and what things do you think should be improved? Keep these thoughts in mind as you brainstorm in the next chapter.

Gathering Information for the Order Processing Subsystem

This is the last phase of the WebBooks.com project, where you'll implement the Order Processing Subsystem and clean up any loose odds and ends. As part of the implementation process, you'll have a quick brainstorming session to determine the data elements needed. Then you'll learn the functions needed for this subsystem in more detail.

Determining the Data Elements Needed

Choosing the data elements is essential for any project. However, because this phase of the project builds on an existing design, it is easier to select data elements since you can reuse many of those existing from the other subsystems.

The Brainstorming Session

In this session, you'll identify all the items needed to process a customer book order:

- Customer name
- Order number
- ISBN
- Quantity ordered
- List price
- Discount
- Quantity on hand
- Reorder point
- Quantity on order
- Shipping address information
- Credit card number
- Credit card type

- Credit card approval code
- Shipping method
- Shipping tracking number
- Sales tax
- Purchase order number
- Time to reorder a book
- Number of books back ordered
- Date ordered
- Date shipped
- Shipping cost

Reviewing the Results

Of the databases you've designed so far, this one is the simplest. That's because many of the elements come from the other databases. The rest of the data elements are fairly straightforward, and you probably see them on many other order forms.

The Customer's Order Information

The bulk of the information needed to process an order comes from the customer. This includes the obvious information such as the ISBN of the book they want to order and the quantity to be shipped. The customer also must supply the address where the order should be shipped and the credit card information and has to choose the shipping information.

Since much of this information is already in the Customer Information Subsystem's database, you may be asking why this information needs to be in the Order Processing Subsystem as well. Duplication of data is the curse of the database administrator, but in this case the data is not really duplicated. The customer may want to ship the books to a different address or use a different credit card. The information in the CIS database contains default values so that the customer doesn't have to enter this information again.

Data Elements from the IIS Database

Some more information that is needed to process an order comes from the Inventory Information Subsystem. The IIS database holds the list price of the book and the book's discount, both of which together are necessary to compute the total cost of the book. It also holds the quantity on hand and the reorder point, which is used to determine that the book is in stock and when additional books should be ordered.

New Data Elements

Some of the data elements in the Order Processing Subsystem will be unique to this subsystem. A couple of fields are pretty obvious: the date the order was placed and the date the order was shipped. Since orders will be processed on a first-come first-served basis, both of these data elements should include the time as well.

Also, it is necessary to have a unique value to track the order. This value could be a two-part value that combines the customer ID or order date with a unique counter to form a single value. Or it could merely be a unique value in the database. The primary disadvantage of the two-part fields is that you have to store the seed values somewhere in the database, while SQL Server can automatically generate a single-part value.

Sales tax is collected on book sales at various rates depending on the state the order is shipped to. This implies that I'll have to add an additional item to track the sales tax rate that wasn't included in the data elements from the brainstorming session. The value for sales tax also depends on the customer's tax-exempt status. A tax-exempt organization doesn't have to pay any taxes, including sales tax.

Since part of the process of filling a book order is to reorder books when the supply is low, you need such fields as the time to order books from the publisher, the number of books on order with the publisher, and expected delivery date. Of course any time you place an order, you need to supply some tracking information—thus an element to hold the purchase order number is needed.

Shipping costs are actually based on two main factors: the speed of the delivery (i.e., next day, two days, etc.) and the weight of the package. The distance between the warehouse and the recipient can also be a factor. However, this information requires that you keep track of the weight of each book. Then you also have to calculate the weight of the box the books are shipped in and the weight of the packing material. You should factor in the cost of the box and packing material, plus the money it costs to package the books and deliver them to the shipping company.

This sounds rather complicated. A better idea would be to charge a flat rate for the first book and each additional book. Suppose WebBooks.com charges $3.00 for the first book plus $1.00 for each additional book. This means that a three book order would cost $5.00. Next day delivery might cost $10.00 for the first book and $2.00 for the next book. Other shipping methods would have similar pricing. These values are based on average costs for shipping and are averaged across all orders. Thus about half the time, WebBooks.com will lose money on a shipment, while the rest of the time it will make money. In the long run, it's a win-win situation for both the customers and WebBooks.com since the customers know the shipping costs when they place the order and WebBooks.com doesn't have all the extra work to record and bill the actual shipping costs.

Another key element is the shipping tracking number. With a valid tracking number, you can access the shipping company's database to track the package's location. This gives the customer more information about an order and can prove really useful on books shipped using the standard methods, which could result in the books taking more than a week to arrive.

373

Final Data Elements

Table 14-1 summarizes the data elements discussed, with their preliminary data types and other information. Note that some of these elements already exist elsewhere in the database but are used by this subsystem to process an order.

Table 14-1   Data Element Rules for the Order Processing Subsystem

Data Element	Data Type	Nulls Allowed?	Default Value	Other Edits
ISBN	Numeric	No	—	None
Quantity	String	No	—	None
Customer ID	Numeric	No	—	None
Shipping address1	String	No	" "	None
Shipping address2	String	Yes	" "	None
Shipping city	String	No	" "	None
Shipping state/Province	String	No	" "	Check value if country = "United States"
Shipping ZIP code/ Postal code	String	Yes	" "	Check value if country = "United States"
Shipping country	String	No	"United States"	Must match item in list of specified countries
Shipping telephone number	String	Yes	" "	None
Shipping e-mail address	String	No	" "	None
Date ordered	Date	No	" "	None
Date shipped	Date	No	—	None
Order credit card code	String	No	" "	None
Order credit card number	String	No	" "	None
Order credit card name	String	No	" "	None
Order credit card expiration date	String	No	" "	None
Order tax-exempt status	Boolean	No	False	None

Table 14-1   Data Element Rules for the Order Processing Subsystem (*continued*)

Data Element	Data Type	Nulls Allowed?	Default Value	Other Edits
Number of books back ordered	Numeric	No	—	None
Purchase order number	Numeric	No	—	None
Reorder time	Date	No	—	None
Shipping method	String	No	" "	None
Shipping cost for first book	Money	No	" "	None
Shipping cost for next book	Money	No	" "	None
List price	Money	No	—	None
Discount	Numeric	No	—	None
Sales tax	Numeric	No	0	None
Sales tax rate	Numeric	No	0	None
Quantity on hand	Numeric	No	—	None
Reorder point	Numeric	No	—	None

Determining the Functions Needed

As in the IIS subsystem, you'll develop both Web-based and traditional client/server programs. These functions perform tasks related to processing an order and keeping the customer informed about the order's status.

Adding Books to the Shopping Cart

This function allows a customer to enter information about an order. On a Web page that displays a book, a button will be included to add the book to the shopping cart. When the customer presses this button, the shopping cart will be displayed (if it's not already displayed) and the information added to the form. The customer has the option to choose the number of books ordered and can press the checkout button, which will actually place the order.

The Checkout Process

This function completes the order process by computing the total cost of the order, including discounts, sales tax, and shipping and handling charges. Then it bills the credit card and, if the credit card is approved, makes the appropriate adjustments to the inventory database.

Packing the Books for Shipment

This function takes the order placed by the customer and prints a packing list and assigns a tracking number from the shipping company. It will also generate an e-mail confirmation that indicates when the order is shipped and includes the tracking number.

Reordering Books

This function determines when the supply of books is low and automatically generates a purchase order to the publisher to order more books. It's desirable to use a dynamic process that determines the least number of books that should be ordered to minimize the number of books stored in the warehouse.

Wrapping Up

In this chapter, you went over the process to determine the data elements that need to be in the database and assigned them initial data types and default values. This information will be refined into a complete database design in the next chapter:

You also identified the requirements that the Order Processing Subsystem must meet. It must be capable of:

- Helping the customer to select the books to be purchased
- Collecting payment information from the customer

- Replacing sold books
- Helping the clerk pack the order for shipment

Most of these functions will be available only through the Web. Only the functions used by the packing clerk will be based on client/server technology.

Since this is the final phase of the WebBooks.com application, all of the major functions needed for an e-commerce site should have been identified. However, the functions identified here may not make the Web site complete. Can you identify any other functions that should be implemented? If so, describe those functions and determine what new data elements, if any, will be needed. You can incorporate them into the database tables in the next chapter.

CHAPTER 15

Designing the Order Processing Subsystem

In the last chapter, you identified the data elements needed for the database and the functions needed to support the subsystem. In this chapter, you'll take those data elements and translate them into a database design.

ON THE CD

The complete code for the database design is included on the CD-ROM. Check the \HOSQLSrver7\Chapt15\ops directory for the ops.sql file. Then create an empty database and run the script using the Query Analyzer, as you did in Chapter 5.

Designing the Order Processing Subsystem Database

The first step in designing the Order Processing Subsystem (OPS) database is to take the data elements defined in the last chapter and refine them into a set of tables. Just like in the real world, I found that I needed some additional fields in the existing databases when I designed this database. The changes aren't major, but they are important.

The Order Processing Subsystem Attributes

Many of the fields in this subsystem will be identical to fields in the other subsystems. This is because many of the fields in the Customers table contain default values for a customer. This information is presented to the customer who is allowed to overwrite them if they choose. Thus it is important to choose the same data types to prevent loss of information.

The Order Processing Subsystem Entities

The data elements I listed in Table 14-1 can be grouped into two main tables: the Orders table and the OrderDetails table. The Orders table contains information about the global order. This includes the customer ID, the shipping address, and the customer's credit card number. Each row in the OrderDetails table contains the information about one book in the order. This will contain columns such as ISBN, quantity ordered, etc. In addition, three existing tables in the Customer Information Subsystem will need some changes to accommodate the data needs of the Order Processing Subsystem.

The Orders Entity

The Orders entity is really a catchall table. Any information that is directly related to the order as a whole will be kept here. This includes information about the customer such as the address where the order will be shipped and the credit card that will be billed for the books.

One of the issues I faced when designing this table was what to name some of the fields, such as the address fields. In my brainstorming session I gave them names like Shipping Address1, Shipping City, Shipping ZIP Code, etc. However, there really isn't any difference between the Shipping ZIP Code field and the ZIP Code field from the Customers table. The meaning of the value inside the field is the same no matter what table the field is in, so you should use the same names for the same information.

Tip

> When you design a database, one of your goals should be consistency. You should always try to use the same name for a column no matter where it is located. This prevents confusion on the part of a programmer or an end user who might see two different names for the same information. Hence a ZIP code is a ZIP code is a ZIP code. Not a publisher ZIP code, customer ZIP code, or shipping ZIP code. Occasionally you may need to bend this rule when you require multiple columns in the same table, such as for work telephone number and home telephone number, but even in those cases consistency is the key. Make it easy for the user to understand what is in each field and why they have similar names.

I chose to use a unique value for order number rather than a value combining (or combined with) the customer ID or date. I did this mainly because it made the database design a little bit simpler, since I didn't have to drag the customer ID or date around in the database. It also saves a little space in the database, but that's not really important in the long run.

The Order Status field identifies which step in the process the order is currently in. A value of zero indicates that the order is still open. A value of one means that the customer has placed the order but the order has not been shipped. A value of two means that the order has been shipped to the customer. An order title exists to help the customer choose from the uncompleted orders.

The OrderDetails Entity

The next group of fields contain information about each book the customer wants to order. These fields include such information as the ISBN for the book and the quantity ordered. The list price and discount are also included, as it's possible that one or both of these values may change. Since the customer agreed to purchase the book at the specified price, you need to track these values through the ordering process. Since the customer should always get the lowest possible price for a book, you need to check the current prices before the books are shipped just in case the price drops between the time the customer orders them and the time the books are packed.

Two other columns are required for this table. These make up the primary key. First, you need to include the order number so that you know which order contains this list of books. Then a field for item number is added to make the primary key unique. It also is used to retain the order in which the customer orders the books. Since you'll automatically generate a purchase order based on estimated need, you must track this information in the Purchases Entity

Revisions to PreferredShippingCodes

This table existed originally to translate the PreferredShippingCode value into a string. In the last chapter, I determined that I also needed to keep track of the shipping costs. This meant that I either had to create an additional table to hold this information or add the fields to the PreferredShippingCodes table.

Revisions to StateCodes

This table existed to validate state codes. Since I need to track sales tax values for each state, I decided to add a field for sales tax in this table. I know that I could have added a new table to track this information, but I think that method would make the database more complicated than it needs to be. Any database administrator hates this type of redundancy.

The CountryCodes table existed to validate a country code and translate its value into a string. Now that I need to track sales tax, I decided to add this field, just like I did for state codes.

Revisions to Books

The last table I need to revise is the Books table. This table needs a few more fields to deal with back-ordered books. When the last book in the warehouse has been sold, I need to let the customer know that this book will take longer to deliver than one that's still in stock. Since an order is placed with the publisher when the number of books in the warehouse drops below the reorder point, this shouldn't happen very often.

In case it does happen, I need to let the customer know more than that the book is not in stock. Letting the customer know this is nice, but it's better to tell the customer when the book is expected to be back in stock. To do this, I need to know the expected delivery date from the publisher. I also need to let the customer know when a book is out of print that it may not be available for a long period of time.

Also, I'm going to track some other information to help predict the demand for the book. The new fields are for the quantity on back order, the number of books sold since the last reorder, the date the last reorder was placed, and the expected delivery date.

The Final Database Design

The final database design is shown in Figure 15-1. It consists of three tables: the Orders table (see Table 15-1), the OrderDetails table (see Table 15-2), and the Purchases table (see Table 15-3). The changed tables are PreferredShippingCodes (see Table 15-4), CountryCodes (see Table 15-5), StateCodes (see Table 15-6), and Books (see Table 15-7).

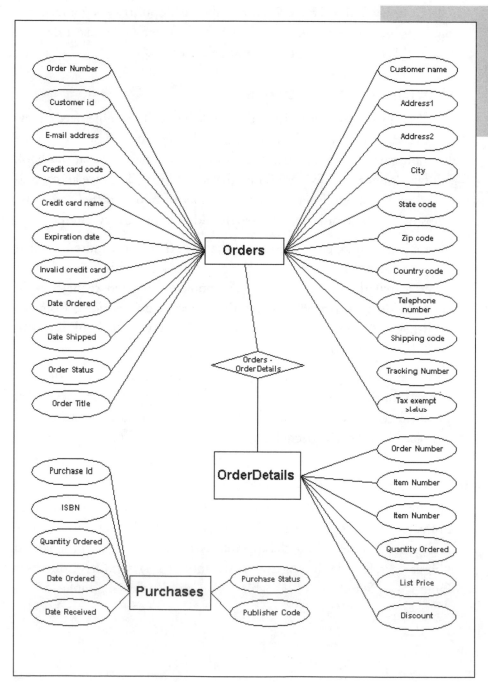

Figure 15-1
An Entity/
Relationship
diagram for
the Order
Entry
Subsystem
database.

Table 15-1   Attributes of the Orders Entity

Data Element	Data Type	Nulls Allowed?	Default Value	Other Edits
Order number	**Int**	No	—	Primary key
Customer ID	**Int**	No	—	None
Customer name	**Varchar**(64)	No	—	None
Company name	**Varchar**(64)	Yes	—	None
Address1	**Varchar**(64)	No	—	None
Address2	**Varchar**(64)	Yes	—	None
City	**Varchar**(64)	No	—	None
State	**Varchar**(64)	No	—	Check value if country code = 1 ("United States")
Zip code	**Varchar**(16)	Yes	—	Check value if country code = 1 ("United States")
Country code	**Smallint**	No	—	Link to country
Telephone number	**Varchar**(24)	Yes	—	None
E-mail address	**Varchar**(64)	No	—	None
Credit card code	**Smallint**	No	—	Link to credit card type
Credit card number	**Varchar**(24)	No	—	None
Credit card name	**Varchar**(64)	No	—	None
Expiration date	**Varchar**(12)	No	—	None
Invalid credit card	**Bit**	No	—	None
Tax-exempt status	**Bit**	No	—	None
Shipping code	**Smallint**	No	—	Link to preferred shipping method
Date ordered	**Datetime**	No	—	None
Date shipped	**Datetime**	No	—	None
Order status	**Smallint**	No	—	None
Order title	**Varchar**(64)	No	—	None
Shipping code	**Smallint**	No	—	None
Tracking number	**Varchar**(64)	No	—	None

Table 15-2   Attributes of the OrderDetails Entity

Data Element	Data Type	Nulls Allowed?	Default Value	Other Edits
Order number	**Int**	No	—	Part of the primary key
Item number	**Smallint**	No	—	Part of the primary key
ISBN	**Int**	No	—	Primary key
Quantity ordered	**Smallint**	No	1	None
List price	**Money**	No	—	None
Discount	**Decimal**(5,2)	No	—	None

Table 15-3   Attributes of the Purchases Entity

Data Element	Data Type	Nulls Allowed?	Default Value	Other Edits
Purchase ID	**Int**	No	—	Primary key
ISBN	**Int**	No	—	None
Quantity ordered	**Smallint**	No	—	None
Date ordered	**Datetime**	No	—	None
Date received	**Datetime**	No	—	None
Publisher code	**Shortint**	No	—	None
Purchase status	**Shortint**	No	—	None

Table 15-4   Attributes of the PreferredShippingCodes Entity

Data Element	Data Type	Nulls Allowed?	Default Value	Other Edits
Preferred shipping code	**Smallint**	No	—	Primary key
Cost for first book	**Money**	No	—	None
Cost for next book	**Money**	No	—	None
Preferred shipping method	**Varchar**(64)	No	—	None

Table 15-5 Attributes of the CountryCodes Entity

Data Element	Data Type	Nulls Allowed?	Default Value	Other Edits
Country	Varchar(64)	No	—	None
Sales tax rate	Decimal(5,2)	No	0	None
Country code	Smallint	No	—	Primary key

Table 15-6 Attributes of the StateCodes Entity

Data Element	Data Type	Nulls Allowed?	Default Value	Other Edits
Country code	Smallint	No	—	Primary key
State code	Char(2)	No	—	Primary key
Sales tax rate	Decimal(5,2)	No	0	None
State	Varchar(64)	No	—	None

Table 15-7 Attributes of the Books Entity

Data Element	Data Type	Nulls Allowed?	Default Value	Other Edits
ISBN	Int	No	—	Primary key
Title	Varchar(64)	No	—	None
Publisher code	Shortint	No	—	Link to publishers
Date published	Datetime	No	—	None
Page count	Int	Yes	0	None
Binding code	Shortint	Yes	—	Link to binding codes
Keywords	Varchar(255)	No	—	None
User level	Shortint	Yes	—	None
List price	Money	No	—	None
Discount	Decimal(5,2)	No	—	None
Out of print	Boolean	No	—	None

Table 15-7	Attributes of the Books Entity *(continued)*			
Data Element	Data Type	Nulls Allowed?	Default Value	Other Edits
Quantity on hand	**Int**	No	—	None
Reorder point	**Int**	No	—	None
Quantity on back order	**Int**	No	—	None
Number sold since last reorder	**Datetime**	No	—	None
Last reorder date	**Datetime**	No	—	None
Expected delivery	**Datetime**	Yes	—	None

Designing the Functions Needed

The programs in this subsystem complete the WebBooks.com application. In the case of the Web-based program used by the customer, I'm going to extend the program I built in Chapter 11 by adding a bunch of new features. Next I'm going to build a program using the DataReporter tool that demonstrates how easy it is to generate paper documents like packing lists using Visual Basic.

Ordering a Book

In the Inventory Information Subsystem, the WebBooks program was designed to help the customer locate a particular book. In the Order Processing Subsystem, I'm going to expand on that logic by adding a button that lets the customer order the book. Before the shopping cart is displayed, the customer has to be logged on to the application. If the customer isn't logged on, a prompt will be given to the customer do so before the shopping cart is displayed.

If there are uncompleted orders, the customer will be given the option of filling the shopping cart with any of those orders or beginning a new order. This allows a customer to begin making an order on one day and continue it on the next without having to reselect any books. The shopping cart will allow the customer to delete any of the items in the cart or change the quantity of the item. It will display a running total cost including sales tax and shipping charges. If the customer isn't registered with WebBooks.com, a registration form is displayed where the customer can enter all the relevant information.

A checkout button in the shopping cart allows the customer to begin the checkout process. This process uses information from the Customer Information Subsystem as the default values for the shipping address and credit card information. The customer can review and change this information, as well as save it back into the Customers table as the new default values.

The checkout form will also have a save button, which allows the customer to save the order information into the database for processing later. The customer can assign a title to the order making it easier to remember what was in the order on the next visit to the Web site.

Pressing the place order button will take all the information and actually place the order. The customer will receive an acknowledgment message when the order has been committed to the database.

Placing the Order

Placing an order for a particular book automatically subtracts the amount in the Quantity Ordered from that in the Quantity on Hand field. If this value becomes negative, it means that the books ordered will be filled from the supply of books that are on back order. Then increment the number of books sold since the last reorder. If the quantity of books plus the number of books on back order drops below the reorder point, then it's time to order some more books. Since I want to minimize the number of books kept in the warehouse, I devised a solution (albeit somewhat complicated) to the problem.

I begin by calculating the average number of books sold per day using the last reorder date and the number sold since the last reorder. Then I figure the number of days to deliver the books from the publisher and add two days to allow for the weekend. I recompute the new value for reorder point based on the average number of books sold per day times the number of days to get the books from the publisher. Then I place an order for the number of books in the reorder point. After placing the order, I add the number of books ordered to the back-ordered column and log the order in the Purchases table.

 Basically I'm ordering enough books to cover the average sales for the books for the time it takes to receive the order. This means that about the time the order arrives, I'll be placing a new order. Thus if it takes a week to get an order of books, I'll keep nine days worth of the books in the warehouse and will probably generate a new order two days before I run out.

Tracking the Order

This Web page displays a list of orders that the customer has placed and indicates order status. If tracking information is available, then it will be displayed to the customer as a hyperlink to another Web site containing the shipping information.

Processing the Order

This traditional client/server program searches the database for the oldest, unfilled order and displays the information on the screen. Pressing the packing list button will generate a packing list that can be used to pick the books to be shipped and will assign a tracking number to the order. An e-mail message indicating that the order has been shipped will be sent to the customer.

Receiving New Books at the Warehouse

Along with processing orders, the staff at the warehouse needs to update the database when shipments of new books are received. When a shipment is received, the number of books received is added to the Quantity on Hand field and subtracted from the Back Ordered field. The entry in the Purchases table is also updated to reflect that the books have been received.

Analyzing the Data for Trends

This program helps the management staff analyze sales information by region. Thus information might be used to help determine how effective a regional ad campaign was or to identify geographic areas that may be candidates for a regional warehouse.

Wrapping Up

In this chapter, I omitted the steps needed to build the database. I've already shown you how to build a database several different ways in Chapters 1, 5, and 10. This time, you're on your own. You may want to try using the Data View window in Visual Basic once you've created the empty OPS database. This utility allows you to create, edit, and view database diagrams, tables, views, and stored procedures just like you can do in the Enterprise Manager. In fact, functions inside the utility look identical to those in the Enterprise Manager. The primary advantage of this utility is that you can create your tables in Visual Basic. You don't need the Enterprise Manager or the Query Analyzer on your system.

The design of this database is relatively basic. Just three tables, one of which stands by itself while the other two form a simple two-level hierarchy. Of course there are some changes to the existing tables in the Customer Information Subsystem, but they aren't difficult. All you need to do is to add a few data elements to some of the existing tables. This type of thing happens all the time in the real world. As designs for new components of an application are finalized, often changes to the existing application are required. The mark of a good design is that when this happens (and it will), the existing programs will continue to run unaffected.

CHAPTER 16

Building the Order Processing Subsystem

Drag out your copy of Visual Basic. It's programming time again. In this chapter, you'll build the final components of this project:

- Allow customers to place orders
- Allow clerks to create packing lists

This chapter will continue to build on the IIS Application program from Chapter 11. However, this time you'll create an ActiveX EXE program to hold some of the application's business logic and share it with programs developed using conventional client/server technology. This allows you to develop true three-tier client/server applications.

In addition to improving the IIS Application, you'll build a whole new program that demonstrates the use of the Microsoft Data Reporter designer. This tool is designed to allow you to build reports quickly and easily. It includes a complete print preview facility that you can integrate into your application, thus giving it a more professional appearance, since users can see what their reports look like before they're printed.

The complete source code for these functions is included on the CD-ROM. Check the \HOSQLSrver7\Chapt16 directory.

ON THE

CD

- **Utility** contains the ActiveX EXE program with some of the business logic.
- **WBIIS** contains the enhanced IIS Application program that runs on the Web server.
- **WBReport** contains the program that demonstrates the Microsoft Data Reporter designer.

Implementing the Ability to Order Books Online

By far the largest block of code in this chapter is contained in the order processing logic. This code builds on the existing IIS Application that I wrote in Chapter 11. However, I decided to make the program slightly more interesting by moving part of the logic into an ActiveX EXE file. This has the advantage of allowing you to shift some of the processing to a different server, thus offloading some of the work from the Web server. It also allows you to write multiple clients (like an IIS Application and a traditional client/server program), but requires you only to write the business logic once.

As I discuss these routines, keep in mind that all the pieces have to work together to form a complete project. All the routines are very tightly coupled. In several cases I was faced with deciding what came first, the chicken or the egg, when it came to discussing the code. Usually I picked the function that involved the least amount of new code, which means that I will describe changes to the existing routines in the application before I start writing new ones. This doesn't mean that they were developed that way, but it serves as a better introduction on how this application works.

The Bug Fixes

There are a few problems that need to be fixed. These include:

- The ISBN is improperly formatted.
- The Web page appears to be off-balance.
- The ListPrice is missing a dollar sign on the book display.
- Book ratings should be implemented to provide additional information to the customer.
- The search form returns duplicate results.
- The search form doesn't retain the previous search values.

I left the task of implementing ratings as a future enhancement for you to add, so I won't discuss that here. Since fixing the List Price bug is trivial (all that's needed is a call to **FormatCurrency** where I output the list price), I'm not going to discuss it here either. Fixing the Web pages' appearance of being off-balance isn't hard—it can be easily implemented with the shopping cart feature I'll discuss later in this chapter, so I'll table that bug for now as well. However, formatting an ISBN is somewhat interesting, as is eliminating the duplicate search results. Retaining the previous search value is easily implemented, so you can add that to your list of assignments.

Fixing the ISBN Format

The ISBN is a number that is unique to a particular book worldwide. Much information can be extracted from this number, such as the country where the book was published, the publisher who published the book, and whether the number itself is valid. The ISBN consists of four parts: the group or country identifier, the publisher identifier, the title identifier, and the check digit. Each part is separated from the others by a dash. The exact placement of the dash depends on a rather complex set of rules.

GROUP OR COUNTRY IDENTIFIERS

The group or country identifier is assigned by the International ISBN Agency headquartered in Berlin. This number is assigned to an ISBN agency in a particular country. From there the local ISBN agency assigns publisher identifiers. A publisher in turn assigns each of its published books a unique ISBN. Once an ISBN is assigned, it can never be reused, even if the book is no longer available.

When a publisher uses all of their assigned title identifiers, the publisher must acquire another publisher identifier from the local ISBN agency. When the local ISBN agency runs out of publisher identifiers, it must request an additional group or country identifier from the International ISBN Agency.

Books in the English language generally have ISBN numbers that begin with 0 or 1. Books in French begin with 2, German with 3, and Japanese with 4. Russian and Chinese books use group or country identifiers of 5 and 7, respectively. Other countries have numbers like 80 for the Czech Republic and 99923 for El Salvador. Table 16-1 shows the distribution of group or country identifiers.

Table 16-1 Ranges of Numbers Available for ISBN Group or Country Identifiers

Number Range	Description
0-7	Single-digit identifiers
80-94	Two-digit identifiers
950-995	Three-digit identifiers
9960-9989	Four-digit identifiers
99900-99999	Five-digit identifiers

PUBLISHER IDENTIFIERS

Publisher identifiers are assigned according to the rules that are set up by each country's local ISBN agency. In the United States, publisher identifiers are assigned in cooperation with the other countries in the English group. Tables 16-2 and 16-3 list the ranges of values available.

Table 16-2 Ranges of Numbers Available for Publishers in ISBN Group or Country Identifier 0

Number Range	Description
00-19	Two-digit identifiers
200-699	Three-digit identifiers
7000-8499	Four-digit identifiers
85000-89999	Five-digit identifiers
900000-949999	Six-digit identifiers
9500000-9999999	Seven-digit identifiers

Table 16-3 Ranges of Numbers Available for Publishers in ISBN Group or Country Identifier 1

Number Range	Description
55000-86979	Five-digit identifiers
869800-998999	Six-digit identifiers
9990000-9999999	Seven-digit identifiers

THE CHECKSUM

Probably the easiest part of formatting an ISBN is placing the dash before the checksum digit. Since the checksum digit is always the last digit in the ISBN, you merely have to insert the dash before the last digit. However, in my situation, it is a little more complex. Since I discarded the checksum digit when I built the database, I have to re-create it.

The actual algorithm sounds relatively simple. Working from left to right, each digit in the 10-digit ISBN number is multiplied by a weighting factor ranging from 10 for the first digit to 1 for the last digit. The sum of these numbers must be zero. The check digit is computed as a modulo 11 value, which returns a number in the 0 to 10 range. Since the number 10 uses two digits, the letter X is substituted.

Sound complicated? Why don't you take a look at an ISBN from a book at random. The ISBN for *Expert Guide to Visual Basic* is 0-7821-2349-X.

Table 16-4 shows the digits of the ISBN, the corresponding weighting factor, the value computed by multiplying the weighting factor by the digit, and the running sum. Note that this ISBN's digit 10 is an X. When 10 is multiplied by a weighting factor of 1, the result is a value of 10, which is correct since X is a placeholder for 10. The sum of all the digits is 209. When you compute 209 modulo 11, you end up with a zero, which means that this ISBN value is correct.

Table 16-4   Analyzing an ISBN's Checksum

Digit	ISBN Digit	Weighting Factor	Value	Running Sum
1	0	10	0	0
2	7	9	63	63
3	8	8	64	127
4	2	7	14	141
5	1	6	6	147
6	2	5	10	157
7	3	4	12	169
8	4	3	12	181
9	9	2	18	199
10	X	1	10	209

IMPLEMENTING FORMATISBN

Taking the above discussion and translating into code results in the function shown in Listing 16-1. First I convert the ISBN value into a string. This will make it easier to insert the dashes at the proper locations. I add leading zeros to the front of the string to make sure that I have a nine-digit number.

Format an ISBN value:

Listing 16-1

```
Private Function FormatISBN(isbn As Long) As String
```

```
Dim i As Long
Dim j As Long
Dim s As String
Dim t As String

s = FormatNumber(isbn, 0, vbTrue, vbTrue, vbFalse)

If Len(s) < 9 Then
    s = String(9 - Len(s), "0") & s
End If

Select Case Left(s, 5)

    Case "00000" To "01999"
        t = Left(s, 1) & "-" & Mid(s, 2, 2) & "-" & Mid(s, 4)

    Case "02000" To "06999"
        t = Left(s, 1) & "-" & Mid(s, 2, 3) & "-" & Mid(s, 5)

    Case "07000" To "08499"
        t = Left(s, 1) & "-" & Mid(s, 2, 4) & "-" & Mid(s, 6)

    Case "08500" To "08999", "15500" To "18697"
        t = Left(s, 1) & "-" & Mid(s, 2, 5) & "-" & Mid(s, 7)

    Case "09000" To "09499", "18698" To "19989"
        t = Left(s, 1) & "-" & Mid(s, 2, 6) & "-" & Mid(s, 8)

    Case "09599" To "09999", "19990" To "19999"
        t = Left(s, 1) & "-" & Mid(s, 2, 7) & "-" & Mid(s, 9)

End Select

j = 0
For i = 1 To 9
    j = j + CInt(Mid(s, i, 1)) * (11 - i)
Next i

i = (11 - (j Mod 11)) Mod 11

If i = 10 Then
    FormatISBN = t & "-X"
Else
    FormatISBN = t & "-" & FormatNumber(i, 0)

End If

End Function
```

Next I use the information in Table 16-2 and 16-3 to build a **Select Case** statement. I normalize the values into five-digit numbers and take advantage of the **Case** clause's ability to specify a range of values. Then in each individual case I insert the first two dashes in the appropriate location. I don't bother with the last dash now, since all I have to do is append it to the end of the string.

Generating the checksum digit is merely a matter of computing the sum of the values and weights like I did in Table 16-4. The only tricky part comes when I have to compute the checksum value itself. I do this by taking the **Mod** of the sum of digits so far and subtract it from 11. This gives me the proper value except in the case where (j **Mod** 11) equals zero. This means that the last digit should be 0 not 11. Using the **Mod** operator again solves that problem. Then all I have to do is append a dash followed by the digit or an X as appropriate.

Eliminating Duplicate Search Results

This problem is very simple to solve if I use the SQL clause called **Distinct**. I show how it fits into the Search_Respond subroutine in Listing 16-2. The **Distinct** keyword fits between the **Select** and **Top** keywords. **Distinct** forces the **Select** statement to return only unique rows. The uniqueness is determined by the data returned in the columns. It doesn't matter what values are in the columns in the base table—a row is only unique when the returned row is unique.

Here is a code fragment from the Search_Respond subroutine that prevents duplicate books from being returned for a particular author:

Listing 16-2

```
Case "Author"
    sel = "Select Distinct Top " & _
        FormatNumber(Request.Form("ResultsReturned"), 0) & _
        " b.ISBN, b.Title " & _
        "From iis.dbo.Authors a, iis.dbo.Books b, " & _
        "iis.dbo.AuthorBooks ab " & _
        "Where a.authorcode = ab.authorcode and " & _
        "ab.isbn = b.isbn and " & _
        "Contains(a.AuthorName, '" & _
        Request.Form("SearchValue") & "')"
```

Caution

One of the reasons I added the **Top** clause to the **Select** statement originally was to limit the amount of work the database server had to do. The **Top** clause stops the query after the specified number of rows have been retrieved. Typically, using the **Distinct** clause forces the server to retrieve all the rows and then sort them to eliminate duplicates. This could cause serious problems if the query were to retrieve a large number of rows.

Approaches to Allowing the Placement of Orders Online

There are two basic approaches to purchasing over the Web. First, you can allow the customer to add a bunch of books to a virtual shopping cart and then ask the customer to log in to the server when it's time to check out. The second is to force the customer to log in before they begin to shop and merely confirm that they wish to purchase the items at the end. Of the two approaches, I prefer the latter approach since you can offer additional services when you know the individual who's shopping.

While I don't penalize the customer for not logging on immediately, I don't create a shopping cart until the customer has successfully logged on. This means that the IIS Application itself must be sensitive to both states. Code needs to be added to ensure that functions are available only to logged-on customers and do not show up on the menu for a customer who is not yet logged on.

To maintain the user's login state, I'm going to use the **Session** object to hold the customer's customer ID and e-mail address values. Then I can test to see if the value for customer ID is valid when I need to know if the customer has logged on to the system.

Implementing the Ability to Log in to the Web Site

The first step in making a purchase over the Web is to log on to the Web site. This process involves collecting the customer's e-mail address and password and verifying them against the database. To make it easier for

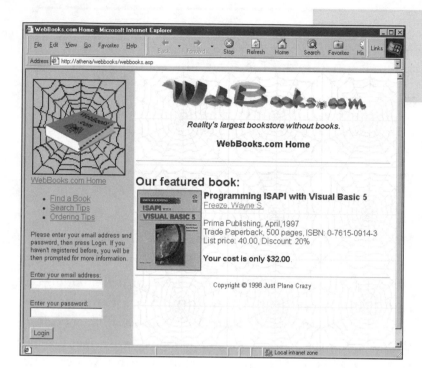

Figure 16-1
The login form is shown on every Web page until the customer logs on.

the customer to log on, I've created a small login form (see Figure 16-1) that fits underneath the list of hyperlinks. All the user needs to do is to fill in the appropriate e-mail address and password and then press Login.

Building the Login Form

The HTML code for the form is relatively straightforward, as you can see in Listing 16-3. This form is added as needed underneath the list of links on each Web page. Pressing the Login button will execute the **Action** clause specified in the **Form** tag that corresponds to the **Login_Respond** event in the IIS Application.

The login form has only two input areas and an input button:

Listing 16-3

```
<form action="WebBooks.asp?wci=Login" method="post" name="login">
Enter your email address:
<input size="20" name="email">
```

```
<p>
Enter your password:
<input size="20" name="password">
<p>
<input type="submit" name="Login" value="Login">
</form>
```

The rest of the form is very straightforward. Two text input fields are used, each 20 characters long, to hold the user's e-mail address and password, and a submit button is used to send the login information to the server for processing.

Responding to the Login Request

When checking the login information, three different conditions can occur. The e-mail address and password can match, the e-mail address matches but the password doesn't match, or the e-mail address doesn't match. When the e-mail address and password match, the user should be logged on to the system. When the e-mail address matches but the password doesn't match, I want to display the password hint and let the customer try again. Finally, when the e-mail address doesn't match anything in the database, I want to prompt the user to register as a new customer.

The code for this routine is shown in Listing 16-4. I begin by retrieving a recordset containing the customer's information. If the recordset is empty, then the customer hasn't registered before. Since I use the **Session** object to hold information about the current login session, I make sure that these variables are cleared. While they shouldn't have a value at this point in time, I don't mind being extra careful here. Once I've cleared these variables, I then show a registration form to the customer, who can enter personal information as required.

The Login_Respond event is triggered when the customer presses the Login button on the Login form:

Listing 16-4

```
Private Sub Login_Respond()

Dim rs As ADODB.Recordset
```

```
With Request
    Set rs = GetCustomer.Execute(, .Form("email"))

End With

If rs.BOF And rs.EOF Then
    Session("email") = ""
    Session("customerid") = ""
    Session("passwordhint") = ""
    ShowRegisterForm_Respond

ElseIf Request.Form("password") <> rs!Password Then
    Session("email") = ""
    Session("customerid") = ""
    Session("passwordhint") = rs!PasswordHint
    If Len(Request.ServerVariables("HTTP_REFERER")) Then
        Response.Redirect Request.ServerVariables("HTTP_REFERER")
    Else
        Response.Redirect "webbooks.asp"
    End If

Else
    Session.Timeout = 10
    Session("email") = Request.Form("email")
    Session("customerid") = rs!customerid
    Session("passwordhint") = ""
    ShoppingCart_Respond

End If

End Sub
```

If the user has entered a bad password for a known e-mail address, I assume that the customer has forgotten the password. So I'll put the contents of the PasswordHint column into the PasswordHint **Session** object variable and redisplay the current form. Redisplaying the form will automatically display the password hint.

To redisplay the current form, I look into the **Request.ServerVariables** property to determine the last displayed URL. I then use the **Redirect** method to send a different Web page back to the browser. Since it's possible that this information may not be available, I'll send the customer back to the WebBooks.com home page.

Finally, if the e-mail address and the password match, I call the **ShoppingCart_Respond** event to display the big shopping cart. This routine

Caution

> You can't use the **Redirect** method after you have started to send a Web page back to the browser, unless you set the **Response.Buffer** property to **True**.

takes care of creating a new order if one doesn't exist and a number of other little details that are related to the login process. All I have to do before I call this routine is to set the e-mail and CustomerId **Session** object variables. Then I make sure that the PasswordHint variable is empty. If this variable has a value, I'll wrongly display another login message with the password hint.

Note that I don't bother to ask the customer to log off. Instead, I set the **Session.Timeout** property to 10 minutes. If the customer hasn't interacted with the Web server in the last 10 minutes, the session automatically closes, and the customer will have to log on again. Since all the order information is stored in the database, nothing would be lost, and the next time logging on to the server, the customer can continue the order process.

Registering a New Customer

Of course the customer can't log on if they don't exist in the database. So entering an e-mail address that doesn't exist in the database will show the register form (Figure 16-2 shows the top half of the form). This form asks for the same basic information as the Edit Customer Information program that I built in Chapter 6 and adds it to the database.

Unlike the Customer Information program in Chapter 6, I don't do a lot of error checking, so entering bad data can generate lots of strange errors. Your mission, should you decide to accept it, is to implement error checking for the fields on this form. There are two basic approaches: first you can check the fields in the IIS Application and return a Web page containing any errors. The other approach would be to add some VBScript to the Web page to check the fields before the data is sent to the server.

Of the two approaches, the VBScript approach is more efficient since the errors would be caught before the form is sent to the server. You can

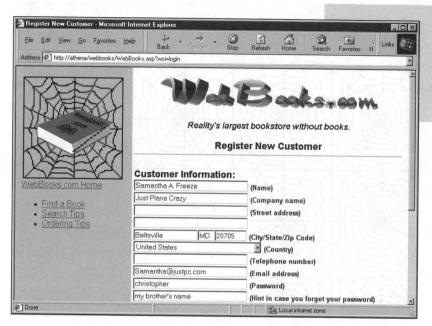

Figure 16-2
The Register New Customer form is shown if a customer doesn't exist in the database.

easily check to see if the required fields are filled in, plus you can do minimal field edits such as verifying that the ZIP code is numeric when the country selected is the United States. This code can be embedded in a template or included directly in the HTML.

Some checks will have to be performed by the IIS Application. These include checking the database return values to make sure that the customer was inserted properly and still doesn't exist. I don't need to worry about allowing the customer to edit this information later, since the customer will have the option to change this information elsewhere in the program.

DISPLAYING THE REGISTER FORM

Displaying the register form is fairly straightforward and would have been included as part of a template like most of the other forms if I had wanted to create a static implementation of the form. However, I wanted to show how you might use a set of database tables to help your users fill out a form.

The ShowRegisterForm_Respond routine (see Listing 16-5) begins by writing the revised header information. (See the section "Understanding the Off-Balanced Web Page Problem" later in this chapter to learn about the changes I made to the header. Note that this is the only routine that doesn't display a shopping cart or a login form. So in place of the call to WriteLittleShoppingCart, I write an end unordered list tag, </ul>.)

The code for the ShowRegisterForm_Respond event generates a registration form for the customer to fill out before being allowed to place an order for the first time:

Listing 16-5

```
Private Sub ShowRegisterForm_Respond()

With Response
    .Write Title("Register New Customer")
    AHeader.WriteTemplate
    .Write "</ul>"
    BHeader.WriteTemplate
    .Write "<p><center><strong><big>Register New Customer"
    .Write "</big></center>"
    .Write "<p><hr><p>"

    .Write "<form action=""WebBooks.asp?wci=register"""
    .Write "method=""post"" name=""register"">"
    .Write "<font size=""+1"">"
    .Write "<b>Customer Information:</b>"
    .Write "<font size=""-1"">"
    .Write "<br><input size=""30"" name=""CustomerName"">"
    .Write " (Name)"
    .Write "<br><input size=""30"" name=""CompanyName"">"
    .Write " (Company name)"
    .Write "<br><input size=""30"" name=""Address1"">"
    .Write " (Street address)"
    .Write "<br><input size=""30"" name=""Address2"">"
    .Write "<br><input size=""16"" name=""City"">"
    .Write "<input size=""3"" name=""State"">"
    .Write "<input size=""7"" name=""ZipCode"">"
    .Write " (City/State/Zip Code)"
    .Write "<br><select name=""Country"" size=""1"">"
    CountryCodes.MoveFirst
    Do While Not CountryCodes.EOF
        .Write "<option value=""" & CountryCodes!CountryCode & """"
        If CountryCodes!CountryCode = 1 Then
```

```
        .Write " selected "
      End If
      .Write ">"
      .Write CountryCodes!Country
      .Write "</option>"
      CountryCodes.MoveNext
  Loop
  .Write "</select> (Country)"

  .Write "<br><input size=""30"" name=""telephone"">"
  .Write " (Telephone number)"
  .Write "<br><input size=""30"" name=""email"" value="""
  .Write Request.Form("email") & """> (Email address)"
  .Write "<br><input size=""30"" name=""password"" value="""
  .Write Request.Form("password") & """> (Password)"
  .Write "<br><input size=""30"" name=""passwordhint"">"
  .Write " (Hint in case you forget your password)"
  .Write "<br><input size=""30"" name=""keyword"">"
  .Write " (List of book keywords.)"

  .Write "<p>"
  .Write "<font size=""+1"">"
  .Write "<b>Credit Card Information:</b>"
  .Write "<font size=""-1"">"
  .Write "<br><input size=""30"" name=""CreditCardNumber"">"
  .Write " (Credit card number)"
  .Write "<br><select name=""Creditcardcode"" size=""1"">"
  CreditCards.MoveFirst
  Do While Not CreditCards.EOF
      .Write "<option value="""
      .Write CreditCards!CreditCardCode & """"
      If CreditCards!CreditCardCode = 0 Then
          .Write " selected "
      End If
      .Write ">"
      .Write CreditCards!CreditCardType
      .Write "</option>"
      CreditCards.MoveNext
  Loop
  .Write "</select> (Credit card type)"
  .Write "<br><input size=""30"" name=""ExpirationDate"">"
  .Write " (Expiration date)"
  .Write "<br><input size=""30"" name=""CreditCardName"">"
  .Write " (Name on the credit card)"

  .Write "<p>"
  .Write "<font size=""+1"">"
  .Write "<b>Shipping Method:</b>"
```

```
.Write "<font size=""-1"">"
.Write "<br>"
.Write "<select name=""ShippingMethod"" size=""1"">"
Shippers.MoveFirst
Do While Not Shippers.EOF
    .Write "<option value="""
    .Write Shippers!preferredshippingcode & """"
    If Shippers!preferredshippingcode = 0 Then
        .Write " selected"
    End If
    .Write ">"
    .Write Shippers!PreferredShippingMethod & "("
    .Write FormatCurrency(Shippers!costoffirstbook) & "/"
    .Write FormatCurrency(Shippers!costofnextbook) & ")"
    .Write "</option>"
    Shippers.MoveNext
Loop
.Write "</select>"
.Write "<p>"
.Write "<input type=""submit"" name=""save"" "
.Write "value=""Save Changes"">"
.Write "<font size=""+1"">"
.Write "</form>"

End With

End Sub
```

For the most part, this form consists of a series of input tags that allow the customer to enter information. At the end of each input tag (or line of input tags), I put a small comment that describes the information the customer should enter. These fields begin with the customer's name and address and continue until the customer selects a default value for shipping. I use the VALUE attribute with the e-mail address and password tags to supply the values that the customer entered on the login form.

There are three exceptions to the standard input fields: country, credit card code, and shipping method. For these three fields, I use a Select tag, which allows the user to choose from a list of entries. The entries are extracted from the database and stored in a recordset when the application is initialized in the **WebClass_Initialize** event. From there it is a simple matter to use a **Do** loop to move through the recordset and create the individual option tags.

One problem with this approach is that retrieving the information from the database can be an expensive operation. In order to minimize the impact, when I initialize the recordset (see Listing 16-6), I specify that a client-side cursor should be used (**CursorLocation** = adUseClient). This means that at least some of the rows will be buffered on the client.

A code fragment from the WebClass_Initialize event creates the CountryCodes recordset:

Listing 16-6

```
Set CountryCodes = New ADODB.Recordset
Set CountryCodes.ActiveConnection = db
CountryCodes.Source = "Select * From cis.dbo.CountryCodes"
CountryCodes.CursorType = adOpenStatic
CountryCodes.CursorLocation = adUseClient
CountryCodes.CacheSize = 250
CountryCodes.LockType = adLockReadOnly
CountryCodes.Open
```

I then set the **CacheSize** property to be larger than the total size of the table so that all the rows can be buffered locally. This means that the IIS Application doesn't have to generate a database request that goes all the way to the database server. Any request for information can be handled locally. This means the application will spend less time waiting for information, which reduces the amount of time necessary to generate the Web page.

Client-side cursors are useful for buffering information locally. As long as the data is in the cache, accessing this information will be much faster than accessing the data from the server. However, if you are really concerned about speed, then you should generate the HTML tags once and save the result in a global string or in a **Session** object. While you may think this will take up a lot of memory, it will probably use less memory than keeping the database objects open with all the locally buffered records. Creating the global string will also save CPU resources in the long run, especially for frequently used tables.

PROCESSING THE INFORMATION FROM THE RESPONSE FORM

Processing this form is very straightforward. Basically I collect all the information and save it into a **Variant** array, which I'll pass on to a stored procedure that does the real work (see Listing 16-7). After the information is added to the database, I go ahead and create a new order for the customer to use by using the InsertNewOrder stored procedure. Then I use the GetOrders stored procedure to get the order number I just generated and save this value in the **Session** variable called order-number. Then I finish this routine by generating a simple message welcoming the user to WebBooks.com.

The Register_Respond event processes the contents of the register form:

Listing 16-7

```
Private Sub Register_Respond()

Dim i As Integer
Dim parms(18) As Variant
Dim rs As ADODB.Recordset

If Len(Request.Form("save")) > 0 Then
    With Request
        parms(0) = .Form("customername")
        parms(1) = .Form("companyname")
        parms(2) = .Form("address1")
        parms(3) = .Form("address2")
        parms(4) = .Form("city")
        parms(5) = .Form("state")
        parms(6) = .Form("zipcode")
        parms(7) = CInt(.Form("country"))
        parms(8) = .Form("telephone")
        parms(9) = .Form("email")
        parms(10) = .Form("password")
        parms(11) = .Form("passwordhint")
        parms(12) = CInt(.Form("creditcardcode"))
        parms(13) = .Form("creditcardnumber")
        parms(14) = .Form("creditcardname")
        parms(15) = .Form("expirationdate")
        parms(16) = Now
        parms(17) = CInt(.Form("shippingmethod"))
        parms(18) = .Form("keyword")
        InsertCustomer.Execute , parms
```

```
        Session("email") = .Form("email")
        Set rs = GetCustomer.Execute(, .Form("email"))
        Session("customerid") = rs!customerid
        Session("passwordhint") = ""
        rs.Close
        InsertNewOrder.Execute , Session("customerid")
        Set rs = GetOrders.Execute(, Session("customerid"))
        Session("ordernumber") = rs!ordernumber
        rs.Close
    End With

    With Response
        .Write Title("Register New Customer")
        AHeader.WriteTemplate
        WriteLittleShoppingCart
        BHeader.WriteTemplate
        .Write "<p><center><strong><big>Register New Customer"
        .Write "</big></center>"
        .Write "<hr>"
        .Write "Thank you for registering to order books from "
        .Write "WebBooks.com. We are the largest virtual bookstore "
        .Write "in reality without books. We appreciate your business."
        FooterForm.WriteTemplate
        .End
    End With

End If

End Sub
```

Adding a Book to the Shopping Cart

Before I get into details about how to view what's in a shopping cart, I want to talk about how to add a book to the shopping cart. This will give you a better feel for operations involved in displaying the information in the shopping cart.

Adding Shopping Carts

The program I built in Chapter 11 helps you find books in the database. However, the goal of this application is to sell books, not find them; thus I need to add a way to select books that a customer wants to purchase. The way most Web sites do this is by creating a shopping cart that customers can add items to. I like doing this a little differently, so I'm going to add two shopping carts to the application. Well, not actually two shopping carts, but two different views of the shopping cart. I call them the big shopping cart and the little shopping cart.

One thing I've noticed when accessing commercial Web sites is that it is hard to see what's in my shopping cart while browsing. Often I may choose to add a book (or CD or Porsche or whatever) to my cart if I only knew what else was in the cart. So knowing how much I've already spent might help me to make up my mind. You can see the little shopping cart in Figure 16-3 and the big one in Figure 16-4.

As you can see, I'm going to add the little shopping cart under the links section of the Web page. This is the same area I used for the login form. Since I can't display the little shopping cart until after the user has logged on to the system, and since I don't need to display the login form after the customer has logged on, it makes sense to reuse this area.

While the shopping carts show the same information, the customer is allowed to have multiple uncompleted orders. Each order has a unique number, plus the customer can assign a title for the order to make it easier to remember what is in the order. This lets the customer prepare multiple orders and hold them on the database server.

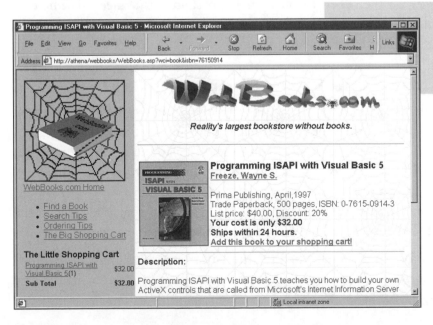

Figure 16-3
The little shopping cart with a single book

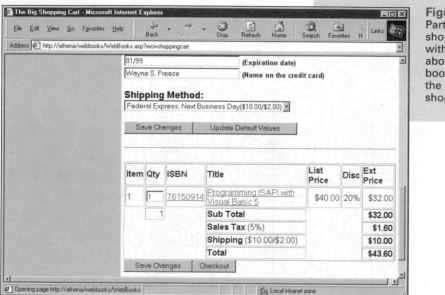

Figure 16-4
Part of the big shopping cart with the details about the same book that's in the little shopping cart.

Also associated with an order is the information about where the customer wants to ship the order and how the customer wants to pay for it. This information is initially pulled from the customer information already on file. Then the customer can change it as needed. The customer can also save the information back to the database to be used as default values for the next order.

Adding the Little Shopping Cart

Adding the little shopping cart and the login form requires changing how I display the information in the left-hand column of the Web page. So I might as well fix the problem with the off-balanced Web page too. The off-balance appearance goes back to my initial setup of the Web page. The Web page is divided into four quadrants: the logo in the upper-left corner, the title information in the upper-right corner, the links in the lower-left corner, and the main body in the lower-right corner.

The problem is caused when the title information is significantly longer or shorter than the logo. When the information displayed in the title area takes up less space than the logo, a gap exists between the end of the title area and the start of the main body. If the information displayed in the title area takes up more space than the logo, the gap exists between the end of the logo and the start of the links.

Since there is no reason to separate the top (the logo area and the title area) from the bottom (the links and the main body), why use two rows? Using only one row makes much more sense.

UNDERSTANDING THE OFF-BALANCED WEB PAGE PROBLEM

Listing 16-8 is pulled from the program I wrote in Chapter 11. It's a very simple routine that illustrates how I built the four-element table. The Title routine initializes the Web page. The HeaderForm template contains the information in the logo and the title areas of the Web page. The **Write** method displays the title of the Web page. Then the Link-Form template displays the information in the lower-left corner of the Web page. The SearchTips template displays the information in the main body and the FooterForm template is used to end the table and display the copyright information at the bottom of the form.

The ShowTips_Respond event sends the SearchTips template to the customer:

Listing 16-8

```
Private Sub ShowTips_Respond()

With Response
    .Write Title("Search Tips")
    HeaderForm.WriteTemplate
    .Write "<p><strong><big><center>Search Tips</center></big></strong>"
    LinkForm.WriteTemplate
    SearchTips.WriteTemplate
    FooterForm.WriteTemplate
    .End

End With

End Sub
```

FIXING THE PROBLEM

Listing 16-9 shows the changes required to handle the new two-element table. The Title function is carried over unchanged from the previous program. But the old Header template has been split into two pieces: the AHeader and the BHeader templates. The AHeader template contains the HTML tags that display the WebBooks.com logo, while the BHeader template contains the HTML tags that display the information at the top of the title area. In between the two header templates I stick a call to the WriteLittleShoppingCart routine, which handles all the new stuff.

The ShowTips_Respond event displays information to help the customer use the search form:

Listing 16-9

```
Private Sub ShowTips_Respond()

With Response
    .Write Title("Search Tips")
    AHeader.WriteTemplate
    WriteLittleShoppingCart
    BHeader.WriteTemplate
    .Write "<p><strong><big><center>Search Tips</center></big></strong>"
    .Write "<p><hr><p>"
    SearchTips.WriteTemplate
    FooterForm.WriteTemplate
    .End

End With

End Sub
```

I still keep the **Write** method that displays the title, but now I have to draw the horizontal line after the title. This was included as part of the LinkForm template, but I decided that it wasn't worth adding another template for that one HTML tag. The SearchTips template and the FooterForm template are unchanged between the two implementations.

THE WRITELITTLESHOPPINGCART

The WriteLittleShoppingCart routine (see Listing 16-10) is somewhat misnamed. It displays the login form, the password hint/login form, or the little shopping cart depending on the login state. One interesting aspect to this routine is that it expects that the unordered list (<UL>) of links is still active. This means that the routine can add other links dynamically to the list of links in the AHeader template. It also means that I have to make sure that the list is always ended properly with a </UL> before sending anything else to the browser.

The WriteLittleShoppingCart displays the login form, the password hint, the login form, and the little shopping cart, depending on the login state:

Listing 16-10

```
Private Sub WriteLittleShoppingCart()

Dim rs As ADODB.Recordset
Dim c As Currency
Dim ct As Currency

With Response
    If Len(Session("passwordhint")) > 0 Then
        .Write "</ul><font size=""-1"">"
        .Write "You entered the wrong password. Here's a hint: "
        .Write Session("passwordhint")
        Session("passwordhint") = ""
        .Write "<br>"
        LoginForm.WriteTemplate
        .Write "<font size=""0"">"

    ElseIf Len(Session("customerid")) = 0 Then
        .Write "</ul><font size=""-1"">"
        .Write "Please enter your email address and password, "
        .Write "then press Login. If you haven't registered "
        .Write ", you will be then prompted for more information."
        .Write "<br>"
        LoginForm.WriteTemplate
        .Write "<font size=""0"">"

    Else
        .Write "<li><a href=""WebBooks.asp?wci=shoppingcart"">"
        .Write "The Big Shopping Cart</a>"
        .Write "</ul>"

        If Len(Session("ordernumber")) > 0 Then
            .Write "<b>The Little Shopping Cart</b>"
```

```
            .Write "<table>"
            Set rs = GetOrderDetails.Execute(, Session("ordernumber"))
            ct = 0
            Do While Not rs.EOF
                .Write "<tr><td><font size=""-1"">"
                .Write "<a href=""WebBooks.asp?wci=book&isbn="
                .Write rs.Fields!isbn & """>"
                .Write rs!Title & "</a>"
                .Write "(" & FormatNumber(rs!QuantityOrdered, 0) & ")"
                .Write "</td><td><font size=""-1"">"
                c = (rs!ListPrice * (1 - rs!Discount) * _
                    rs!QuantityOrdered)
                ct = ct + c
                .Write FormatCurrency(c)
                .Write "</td></tr>"
                rs.MoveNext
            Loop
            .Write "<tr><td><font size=""-1"">"
            .Write "<b>Sub Total</b>"
            .Write "</td><td><font size=""-1"">"
            .Write "<b>" & FormatCurrency(ct) & "</b>"
            .Write "</td></tr>"
            .Write "</table>"
        End If

    End If

End With

End Sub
```

The routine begins by handling the case where I need to display a password hint. This is indicated if the length of the PasswordHint **Session** object variable is greater than zero. I end the unordered list and display a short message containing the password hint to the user. Then I display the LoginForm template. I also make sure that the hint is disabled so that it doesn't display the next time WriteLittleShoppingCart is called.

The second part of the routine displays a message that instructs the user on how to log on to the server and then displays the login form. As in the previous part of this routine, I make sure that the unordered list is properly ended before sending anything new to the browser.

The last part of the routine is the most complicated. I output a hyperlink to the big shopping cart and end the unordered list of links. Then I use the copy of the current order number stored in the **Session** object variable ordernumber to retrieve the list of books in the shopping cart. If the ordernumber variable isn't present, then I simply skip the rest of the code and return to the calling routine.

Note

> Originally when I implemented this part of the program, I always had an order number available. Every time someone logged on to the server, I created a new order. Finally, I decided this wasn't practical due to the large number of empty orders that were created. So I changed the design to only create a new order on request or if no orders already existed. A side effect of this change was that this routine would occasionally be called before an order existed—hence the need to check for a valid order number.

Then I create a simple table containing two columns. The first column contains the title of the book as a hyperlink to the book page that describes it and the number of copies ordered. This information is displayed in parentheses after the title and is not included as part of the hyperlinked text.

The second column contains the extended price, which is computed by multiplying the list price times the quantity times one minus the discount. This value is formatted using the FormatCurrency routine. I also keep a running total that I display after I've processed all the records in the recordset.

Buying Books

Remember the **Book_Respond** routine back in Chapter 11? Its purpose was to display detailed information about a book. Now I need to modify it so that the reader can add the current book to the shopping cart.

MODIFYING THE BOOK_RESPOND EVENT

The modifications to the **Book_Respond** event (see Listing 16-11) are pretty straightforward. I update the logic to fix the off-balance problem and add the little shopping cart. I also insert a call to FormatCurrency to correct the problem where the list price of the book was not properly formatted.

The Book_Respond originally just displayed detailed information about a book; now the customer can order books too:

Listing 16-11

```
Private Sub Book_Respond()

Dim rs As ADODB.Recordset
Dim rs1 As ADODB.Recordset

Set rs = GetBook.Execute(, CLng(Request.QueryString("isbn")))
Set rs1 = GetAuthors.Execute(, CLng(Request.QueryString("isbn")))

If Not (rs.BOF And rs.EOF) Then
    With Response
        .Write Title(rs.Fields!Title)
        AHeader.WriteTemplate
        WriteLittleShoppingCart
        BHeader.WriteTemplate
        .Write "<p><hr><p><table><tr><td>"
        If Len(Session("ordernumber")) > 0 Then
            .Write "<a href=""WebBooks.asp?wci=buy&isbn="
            .Write rs.Fields!isbn & """>"
        End If
        .Write "<img src=""webbooks.asp?wci=cover&isbn="
        .Write Request.QueryString("isbn")
        If Len(Session("ordernumber")) > 0 Then
            .Write """ alt=""Add this book to your shopping cart!""></a>"
        Else
            .Write """ alt=""" & rs!Title & """>"
        End If
        .Write "</td>"
        .Write "<td valign=""top""><strong><big>"
        .Write rs.Fields!Title & "</big>"

        Do While Not rs1.EOF
            .Write "<br><a href=""WebBooks.asp?wci=author&"
            .Write "authorcode=" & rs1.Fields!authorcode & """>"
            .Write rs1!authorname & "</a>"
            rs1.MoveNext
        Loop
        rs1.Close

        .Write "</strong><p>"

        .Write rs.Fields!publisher & ", "
        .Write Format(rs.Fields!DatePublished, "mmmm,yyyy")
        .Write "<br>" & rs.Fields!binding & ", "
```

```
.Write rs.Fields!PageCount & " pages, "
.Write "ISBN: " & FormatISBN(rs.Fields!isbn)
.Write "<br>List price: "
.Write FormatCurrency(rs.Fields!ListPrice, 2)
.Write ", Discount: "
.Write FormatPercent(rs.Fields!Discount, 0)
.Write "<br><Strong>Your cost is only "
.Write FormatCurrency(rs.Fields!ListPrice * _
    (1 - rs.Fields!Discount))
If rs!QuantityOnHand > 0 Then
    .Write "<br>Ships within 24 hours."
ElseIf Not IsNull(rs!expecteddelivery) Then
    .Write "<br>Ships within "
    .Write FormatNumber( _
        DateDiff("d", Now, rs!expecteddelivery), 0)
    .Write " to "
    .Write FormatNumber( _
        DateDiff("d", Now, rs!expecteddelivery) + 2, 0)
    .Write " days."
Else
    .Write "Out of stock."
End If


If Len(Session("ordernumber")) > 0 Then
    .Write "<br><a href=""WebBooks.asp?wci=buy&isbn="
    .Write rs.Fields!isbn
    .Write """>Add this book to your shopping cart!</a>"
End If


.Write "</td></tr></table>"

Set rs1 = GetReviews.Execute(, CLng(Request.QueryString("isbn")))

Do While Not rs1.EOF
    .Write "<hr>"
    Select Case rs1!reviewnumber
        Case 0
            .Write "<strong>Description:</strong>"

        Case 1
            .Write "<strong>Table of Contents:</strong>"

        Case 2
            .Write "<strong>A WebBooks.com review:</strong>"

        Case 3
            .Write "<strong>Comments from the publisher:</strong>"

        Case 4
```

```
                    .Write "<strong>Comments from the author:</strong>"

            Case Else
                .Write "<strong>Reviewed by: " & rs1!reviewername
                .Write "</strong>"

        End Select

        .Write "<p>" & rs1!Review
        rs1.MoveNext

    Loop

    rs1.Close

    .Write "<hr><a href=""WebBooks.asp?wci=showreviewform&"
    .write "isbn=" & rs.Fields!isbn & """>"
    .Write "<p>Click here to add your own review of this book.</a>"

    FooterForm.WriteTemplate
    .End

End With

End If

rs.Close

End Sub
```

Next I add the text "Add this book to your shopping cart!" with a hyperlink reference for "WebBooks.asp?wci=buy", which contains the code to add the book to the shopping cart. I also include this hyperlink reference for the book's cover image, so the customer can click on either the cover or the text to add the book to the shopping cart. I take care to use the hyperlinks only when I have a valid ordernumber variable in the **Session** object. This prevents someone from trying to add a book before being logged on.

Finally, I also try to let the customer know when the book will be shipped. If the book is in stock, WebBooks.com will ship the book within 24 hours. If there is an expected delivery date in the database, I display that information. Otherwise, I let the customer know that the book is out of stock.

ADDING A BOOK TO THE SHOPPING CART

The Buy_Respond event adds a book to the OrderDetails table using the InsertOrderDetail stored procedure (Listing 16-12). Basically all I do is set up the parameters to the stored procedure, the order number, the ISBN of the book, and the number of books the customer wants to order. Note that in this case I only order one copy. After I add the book to the database, I use the **Redirect** trick to redisplay the current Web page.

The Buy_Respond event adds the current book to the shopping cart:

Listing 16-12

```
Private Sub Buy_Respond()

Dim rs As ADODB.Recordset

Dim parms(2) As Variant

With Request
   parms(0) = CLng(Session("OrderNumber"))
   parms(1) = CLng(.QueryString("isbn"))
   parms(2) = CInt(1)
   InsertOrderDetail.Execute , parms

End With

With Response
   If Len(Request.ServerVariables("HTTP_REFERER")) Then
      .Redirect Request.ServerVariables("HTTP_REFERER")
   Else
      .Redirect "webbooks.asp"
   End If

End With

End Sub
```

The InsertOrderDetail stored procedure (see Listing 16-13) is a little more complicated than most of the stored procedures I've written. It takes the three parameters I discussed above: the order number (@on), the ISBN (@isbn), and the number of books ordered (@qty). Then I declare some local variables: the new item number (@i0), the list price of the book (@lp), and the book's discount (@disc).

The InsertOrderDetail stored procedure adds a new entry in the OrderDetails table and automatically determines the appropriate item number:

Listing 16-13

```
CREATE Procedure InsertOrderDetail @on Int, @isbn Int, @qty smallint

As

Declare @i smallint
Declare @lp money
Declare @disc decimal(5,2)

if not exists(select * from ops.dbo.OrderDetails where OrderNumber = @on)
    set @i=0
else
    select @i=max(itemnumber)
        from ops.dbo.OrderDetails where OrderNumber = @on
set @i = @i +1

select @lp=ListPrice, @disc = Discount
    from iis.dbo.books where isbn = @isbn

Insert into ops.dbo.OrderDetails (OrderNumber, ItemNumber, ISBN,
        QuantityOrdered, ListPrice, Discount)
    Values (@on, @i, @isbn, 1, @lp, @disc)
```

The new item number is found by searching for any rows in the OrderDetails table for the specified order number. If none are found, I set @i to zero; otherwise I set @i to the maximum value for ItemNumber in that table. Then I add one to @i to get the next available item number. I use a simple **Select** to retrieve the values for ListPrice and Discount and save them into the @lp and @disc variables. Finally, I use the **Insert** statement to put this information into the database.

Adding the Big Shopping Cart

The big shopping cart contains everything a customer needs to place an order from WebBooks.com. The form is split into three main parts: order management, customer information, and the detailed description of the order. The order management form is included in this routine, while the other two forms are contained in their own subroutines.

WORKING WITH ORDERNUMBERS

This routine (see Listing 16-14) begins by using the GetOrders stored procedure (see Listing 16-15) to get the list of open orders in the database. This information is stored in the rs1 recordset. This stored procedure will return the list in reverse order, so that the most recently created order will be first. If there aren't any open orders for the customer, then a new one will automatically be created and I'll set the **Session** object variable ordernumber to the value of the new order. Note that only those orders with an OrderStatus value that is less than one or **Null** will be selected. Any orders that have gone through the checkout process will be excluded.

The ShoppingCart_Respond subroutine displays the big shopping cart complete with the list of available orders, shipping, and payment information:

Listing 16-14

```
Private Sub ShoppingCart_Respond()

Dim rs As ADODB.Recordset
Dim rs1 As ADODB.Recordset

With Response
    Set rs1 = GetOrders.Execute(, Session("customerid"))
    If Len(Session("ordernumber")) = 0 Then
        If rs1.EOF And rs1.BOF Then
            InsertNewOrder.Execute , Session("customerid")
            rs1.Close
            Set rs1 = GetOrders.Execute(, Session("customerid"))
        End If
        Session("ordernumber") = rs1!ordernumber
    End If
    Set rs = GetOrder.Execute(, Session("ordernumber"))

    .Write Title("The Big Shopping Cart")
    AHeader.WriteTemplate
    WriteLittleShoppingCart
    BHeader.WriteTemplate
    .Write "<p><center><strong><big>The Big Shopping Cart"
    .Write "</big></center>"
    .Write "<hr>"
```

```
    .Write "<form action=""WebBooks.asp?wci=changeorder"""
    .Write "method=""post"" name=""changeorder"">"
    .Write "<font size=""+1"">"
    .Write "<b>Current Order Number: </b><br>"
    .Write "<font size=""-1"">"
    .Write "<select name=""oldorder"" size=""1"">"

Do While Not rs1.EOF
    .Write "<option value=""" & rs1!ordernumber & """"
    If rs1!ordernumber = CLng(Session("ordernumber")) Then
        .Write " selected "
    End If
    .Write ">"
    .Write rs1!ordernumber
    If Len(rs1!ordertitle) > 0 Then
        .Write " (" & rs1!ordertitle & ")"
    End If
    .Write "</option>"
    rs1.MoveNext
Loop
    .Write "</select><br>"
    .Write "<p>"
    .Write "<input type=""submit"" name=""delete"" "
    .Write " value=""Delete Current Order"">"
    .Write "<input type=""submit"" name=""select"" "
    .Write " value=""Select Existing Order"">"
    .Write "<input type=""submit"" name=""new"" "
    .Write " value=""Create New Order"">"
    .Write "</form><p><hr>"

    WriteCustomerInfo rs
    Set rs1 = GetOrderDetails.Execute(, Session("ordernumber"))

    WriteOrderDetails rs, rs1
    FooterForm.WriteTemplate
    .End

End With

End Sub
```

After retrieving the list of orders, I populate the rs1 recordset with the information about the current order. The current order number is found in the **Session** object variable ordernumber. Then I grab the information about the current order from the database and hold it in the rs record-set using the GetOrder stored procedure.

Armed with both recordsets, I begin to generate the Web page. The first step is to write the header information. Even though I'm generating the big shopping cart, I'll go ahead and display the little shopping cart. If I don't want to display the little shopping cart, I can change the call to WriteLittleShoppingCart with the following statement to close the unordered list:

```
.Write "</ul>"
```

After printing the header, I start building the first of three forms on this Web page. This form is relatively simple and is limited to working with the current order. This value is selected from a drop-down list created by using the rs1 recordset created using the GetOrders stored procedure (see Listing 16-15).

The GetOrders stored procedure returns a list of OrderNumber and OrderTitle values for a given CustomerId:

Listing 16-15

```
CREATE Procedure GetOrders @c Int As
Select o.OrderNumber, o.OrderTitle
    From ops.dbo.Orders o
    Where o.CustomerId = @c
        and (o.OrderStatus is Null or o.OrderStatus < 1)
    Order by o.OrderNumber desc
```

I loop through each element and output the order number. Then if there is a value for OrderTitle, I append that to the end of the string. If its value matches the value in the **Session** object variable ordernumber, I mark that value as selected. If there isn't a value in ordernumber, then the most recent value will automatically be selected, since the stored procedure retrieves the values in descending value of OrderNumber.

Using this drop-down list, the customer can select any active order number and perform three different functions. The customer can delete the order, select the order, or create a new order. Each of these functions is controlled by a series of submit buttons that call the Change-Order_Respond event (see Listing 16-16).

The rest of this routine calls two other routines to write out the two other forms: WriteCustomerInfo and WriteOrderDetails. To save resources, I pass the appropriate recordset objects to these routines rather than re-create them.

In Listing 16-16, I respond to the buttons on the form. If the Delete button was pressed, I call the DeleteOrder stored procedure to delete the specified order. If the order I just deleted was the current order, then I clear the ordernumber value stored in the **Session** object. This means that when I display the big shopping cart again, the most recent order number will be selected; or if I just deleted the last order number, I'll create a brand new one.

The ChangeOrder_Respond event performs the action requested by the user:

Listing 16-16

```
Private Sub ChangeOrder_Respond()

If Len(Request.Form("delete")) > 0 Then
   DeleteOrder.Execute , Request.Form("oldorder")
   If Session("ordernumber") = CLng(Request.Form("oldorder")) Then
      Session("ordernumber") = ""
   End If

ElseIf Len(Request.Form("new")) > 0 Then
   InsertNewOrder.Execute , Session("customerid")
   Session("ordernumber") = ""

Else
   Session("ordernumber") = Request.Form("oldorder")

End If

ShoppingCart_Respond

End Sub
```

If the New Order button was pressed, I simply call the stored procedure to create a new order and set the **Session** object variable ordernumber to the empty string. Then when I display the big shopping cart, I'll automatically select the newest order number.

Finally, if the customer selected an existing order number, I simply set the **Session** object's ordernumber variable to the value specified on the form. Once I've processed the buttons, I call the ShoppingCart_Respond subroutine to display the big shopping cart to show the customer the changes I just made.

WORKING WITH CUSTOMER INFORMATION

The second part of the Web page is generated by the WriteCustomerInfo subroutine (see Listing 16-17). This routine works much in the same way as the previous form. It builds a form with each of the individual fields that are in the Orders table. It outputs the current value of each field from the recordset that was passed to this routine.

The WriteCustomerInfo routine draws a form containing customer information:

Listing 16-17

```
Private Sub WriteCustomerInfo(rs As ADODB.Recordset)

With Response
    .Write "<form action=""WebBooks.asp?wci=changecustomerinfo"""
    .Write "method=""post"" name=""scupdate"">"
    .Write "<font size=""+1"">"
    .Write "<b>Order Title: </b><br>"
    .Write "<font size=""-1"">"
    .Write "<input size=""45"" name=""ordertitle"" value="""
    .Write rs!ordertitle
    .Write """>"
    .Write "<p>"
    .Write "<font size=""+1"">"
    .Write "<b>Ship to:</b>"
    .Write "<font size=""-1"">"
    .Write "<br><input size=""30"" name=""CustomerName"" value="""
    .Write rs!customername & """> (Name)"
    .Write "<br><input size=""30"" name=""CompanyName"" value="""
    .Write rs!CompanyName & """> (Company name)"
    .Write "<br><input size=""30"" name=""Address1"" value="""
    .Write rs!Address1 & """> (Street address)"
    .Write "<br><input size=""30"" name=""Address2"" value="""
    .Write rs!Address2 & """>"
    .Write "<br><input size=""16"" name=""City"" value="""
    .Write rs!City & """>"
```

```
.Write "<input size=""3"" name=""State"" value="""
.Write rs!State & """>"
.Write "<input size=""7"" name=""ZipCode"" value="""
.Write rs!ZipCode & """> (City/State/Zip Code)"
.Write "<br><select name=""Country"" size=""1"">"
CountryCodes.MoveFirst
Do While Not CountryCodes.EOF
    .Write "<option value=""" & CountryCodes!CountryCode & """"
    If CountryCodes!CountryCode = rs!CountryCode Then
        .Write " selected "
    End If
    .Write ">"
    .Write CountryCodes!Country
    .Write "</option>"
    CountryCodes.MoveNext
Loop
.Write "</select> (Country)"

.Write "<br><input size=""30"" name=""telephone"" value="""
.Write rs!telephonenumber & """> (Telephone number)"
.Write "<br><input size=""30"" name=""email"" value="""
.Write rs!emailaddress & """> (Email address)"

.Write "<p>"
.Write "<font size=""+1"">"
.Write "<b>Credit Card Information:</b>"
.Write "<font size=""-1"">"
.Write "<br><input size=""30"" name=""CreditCardNumber"" value="""
.Write rs!CreditCardNumber & """> (Credit card number)"
.Write "<br><select name=""Creditcardcode"" size=""1"">"
CreditCards.MoveFirst
Do While Not CreditCards.EOF
    .Write "<option value=""" & CreditCards!CreditCardCode & """"
    If CreditCards!CreditCardCode = rs!CreditCardCode Then
        .Write " selected "
    End If
    .Write ">"
    .Write CreditCards!CreditCardType
    .Write "</option>"
    CreditCards.MoveNext
Loop
.Write "</select> (Credit card type)"
.Write "<br><input size=""30"" name=""ExpirationDate"" value="""
.Write rs!ExpirationDate & """> (Expiration date)"
.Write "<br><input size=""30"" name=""CreditCardName"" value="""
.Write rs!CreditCardName & """> (Name on the credit card)"

.Write "<p>"
.Write "<font size=""+1"">"
```

```
    .Write "<b>Shipping Method:</b>"
    .Write "<font size=""-1"">"
    .Write "<br>"
    .Write "<select name=""ShippingMethod"" size=""1"">"
    Shippers.MoveFirst
    Do While Not Shippers.EOF
        .Write "<option value="""
        .Write Shippers!preferredshippingcode & """"
        If Shippers!preferredshippingcode = rs!shippingcode Then
            .Write " selected"
        End If
        .Write ">"
        .Write Shippers!PreferredShippingMethod & "("
        .Write FormatCurrency(Shippers!costoffirstbook) & "/"
        .Write FormatCurrency(Shippers!costofnextbook) & ")"
        .Write "</option>"
        Shippers.MoveNext
    Loop
    .Write "</select>"
    .Write "<p>"
    .Write "<input type=""submit"" name=""save"" "
    .Write "value=""Save Changes"">"
    .Write "<input type=""submit"" name=""update"" "
    .Write "value=""Update Default Values"">"
    .Write "<font size=""+1"">"
    .Write "</form>"

    Session("salestax") = rs!SalesTax

End With

End Sub
```

After entering all the information, the customer has the option to save the changes to the current order or to save the changes as the customer's default profile. Pressing either button will trigger a response from the ChangeCustomerInfo_Respond event.

The ChangeCustomerInfo_Respond event uses either the UpdateOrder-Info or the UpdateCustomerInfo stored procedure to update the fields in either the Customer Information database or the Order Processing database (see Listing 16-18). These stored procedures require a different number of parameters, so I defined two different parameter variables. Then after determining which button was pressed, I load the parameters and call the stored procedure.

The ChangeCustomerInfo routine updates the database using the information supplied from the customer information form:

Listing 16-18

```
Private Sub ChangeCustomerInfo_Respond()

Dim parms1(16) As Variant
Dim parms2(15) As Variant

With Request
    If Len(Request.Form("save")) > 0 Then
        parms1(0) = CLng(Session("ordernumber"))
        parms1(1) = .Form("customername")
        parms1(2) = .Form("companyname")
        parms1(3) = .Form("address1")
        parms1(4) = .Form("address2")
        parms1(5) = .Form("city")
        parms1(6) = .Form("state")
        parms1(7) = .Form("zipcode")
        parms1(8) = CInt(.Form("country"))
        parms1(9) = .Form("telephone")
        parms1(10) = .Form("email")
        parms1(11) = CInt(.Form("creditcardcode"))
        parms1(12) = .Form("creditcardnumber")
        parms1(13) = .Form("creditcardname")
        parms1(14) = .Form("expirationdate")
        parms1(15) = CInt(.Form("shippingmethod"))
        parms1(16) = .Form("ordertitle")
        UpdateOrderInfo.Execute , parms1

    Else
        parms2(0) = CLng(Session("customerid"))
        parms2(1) = .Form("customername")
        parms2(2) = .Form("companyname")
        parms2(3) = .Form("address1")
        parms2(4) = .Form("address2")
        parms2(5) = .Form("city")
        parms2(6) = .Form("state")
        parms2(7) = .Form("zipcode")
        parms2(8) = CInt(.Form("country"))
        parms2(9) = .Form("telephone")
        parms2(10) = .Form("email")
        parms2(11) = CInt(.Form("creditcardcode"))
        parms2(12) = .Form("creditcardnumber")
        parms2(13) = .Form("creditcardname")
        parms2(14) = .Form("expirationdate")
        parms2(15) = CInt(.Form("shippingmethod"))
```

```
        UpdateCustomerInfo.Execute , parms2

    End If

End With

ShoppingCart_Respond

End Sub
```

I didn't bother to check the various values in the form to make sure that they were correct before updating the database. In the case of the Customers table, there are a number of foreign key references and triggers that should be verified. This includes things like ensuring that the state code is valid if the customer lives in the United States or that the customer name (or any other field that doesn't permit **Null** values) contains useful information.

The stored procedures are very similar. Listing 16-19 shows the Update-OrderInfo stored procedure. This procedure declares the boatload of parameters that correspond to the fields to be updated. Note that not all the fields in the table are supplied, since some key fields, such as CustomerId and OrderStatus, are not included. The CustomerId value is supplied only when the row is inserted into the table, while OrderStatus is only updated when the OrderStatus is changed.

The UpdateOrderInfo stored procedure updates the specified order using the values passed as parameters:

Listing 16-19

```
CREATE Procedure UpdateOrderInfo @on Int, @custname varchar(64),
    @compname varchar(64), @address1 varchar(64), @address2 varchar(64),
    @city varchar(64), @State varchar(64), @ZipCode varchar(16),
    @CountryCode smallint, @telephone varchar(24), @email varchar(64),
    @creditcardcode smallint, @creditcardnum varchar(24),
    @creditcardName varchar(64), @expdate varchar(12),
    @shippingcode smallint, @ot varchar(64)

As

Update ops.dbo.orders
    Set CustomerName = @custname,
```

```
         CompanyName = @compname,
         Address1 = @address1,
         Address2 = @address2,
         City = @city,
         State = @state,
         ZipCode = @zipcode,
         CountryCode = @CountryCode,
         TelephoneNumber = @Telephone,
         EmailAddress = @email,
         CreditCardCode = @creditcardcode,
         CreditCardNumber = @creditcardnum,
         CreditCardName = @creditcardname,
         ExpirationDate = @expdate,
         ShippingCode = @shippingcode,
         OrderTitle = @ot
where OrderNumber = @on
```

WORKING WITH THE ORDER

As the customer adds books to the order, the information is stored in the OrderDetails table. However, clicking the Add the Book to Your Shopping Cart link merely adds one copy of the book to the table. If you need more than one book, you need to work with the big shopping cart.

The third part of the big shopping cart contains the information about the books ordered (see Listing 16-20). These fields include the item number, the number of books ordered, the ISBN, the title of the book, the list price of one book, and the discount. The extended price is also displayed and is computed by multiplying the quantity times the number of books and then by one minus the discount. The ISBN and title are displayed as hyperlinks that will take the customer back to the book information page for that book.

The WriteOrderDetails lists details about the books in the order:

Listing 16-20

```
Private Sub WriteOrderDetails(rs As ADODB.Recordset, _
    rs1 As ADODB.Recordset)

Dim c As Currency
Dim cb As Long
Dim ct As Currency
Dim sh As Currency
Dim st As Currency
```

```
With Response
  .Write "<p><hr><p>"
  .Write "<form action=""WebBooks.asp?wci=changedetails"""
  .Write "method=""post"" name=""changedetails"">"
  .Write "<font size=""-1"">"
  .Write "<p><table valign=""top"" border=""1"">"
  .Write "<tr><td><b>Item</b></td>"
  .Write "<td><b>Qty</b></td>"
  .Write "<td><b>ISBN</b></td>"
  .Write "<td><b>Title</b></td>"
  .Write "<td><b>List Price</b></td>"
  .Write "<td><b>Disc</b></td>"
  .Write "<td><b>Ext Price</b></td></tr>"
   ct = 0
   cb = 0
   Do While Not rs1.EOF
      .Write "<tr><td>"
      .Write FormatNumber(rs1!itemnumber, 0)
      .Write "</td><td align=""right"">"
      cb = cb + rs1!QuantityOrdered
      .Write "<input size=3 name=q" & FormatNumber(rs1!itemnumber, 0)
      .Write " value="""
      .Write FormatNumber(rs1!QuantityOrdered, 0)
      .Write """>"
      .Write "</td><td>"
      .Write "<a href=""WebBooks.asp?wci=book&isbn="
      .Write rs1.Fields!isbn & """>"
      .Write rs1!isbn & "</a>"
      .Write "</td><td>"
      .Write "<a href=""WebBooks.asp?wci=book&isbn="
      .Write rs1.Fields!isbn & """>"
      .Write rs1!Title & "</a>"
      .Write "</td><td align=""right"">"
      .Write FormatCurrency(rs1!ListPrice, 2)
      .Write "</td><td align=""right"">"
      .Write FormatPercent(rs1!Discount, 0)
      .Write "</td><td align=""right"">"
      c = (rs1!ListPrice * (1 - rs1!Discount) * rs1!QuantityOrdered)
      ct = ct + c
      .Write FormatCurrency(c)
      .Write "</td></tr align=""right"">"
      rs1.MoveNext
   Loop
  .Write "<tr><td>"
  .Write "</td><td align=""right"">"
  .Write FormatNumber(cb, 0)
  .Write "</td><td>"
  .Write "</td><td>"
  .Write "<b>Sub Total</b>"
```

```
.Write "</td><td>"
.Write "</td><td>"
.Write "</td><td align=""right"">"
.Write "<b>" & FormatCurrency(ct) & "</b>"
.Write "</td></tr>"

If Session("salestax") > 0 Then
    .Write "<tr><td>"
    .Write "</td><td>"
    .Write "</td><td>"
    .Write "</td><td>"
    .Write "<b>Sales Tax</b> ("
    .Write FormatPercent(Session("salestax"), 0) & ")"
    .Write "</td><td>"
    .Write "</td><td>"
    .Write "</td><td align=""right"">"
    st = ct * Session("salestax")
    .Write "<b>" & FormatCurrency(st) & "</b>"
    .Write "</td></tr>"
End If

.Write "<tr><td>"
.Write "</td><td>"
.Write "</td><td>"
.Write "</td><td>"
.Write "<b>Shipping</b> ("
.Write FormatCurrency(rs!costoffirstbook) & "/"
.Write FormatCurrency(rs!costofnextbook) & ")"
.Write "</td><td>"
.Write "</td><td>"
.Write "</td><td align=""right"">"
If cb > 0 Then
    sh = rs!costoffirstbook + rs!costofnextbook * (cb - 1)
Else
    sh = 0
End If
.Write "<b>" & FormatCurrency(sh) & "</b>"
.Write "</td></tr>"
.Write "<tr><td>"
.Write "</td><td>"
.Write "</td><td>"
.Write "</td><td>"
.Write "<b>Total</b>"
.Write "</td><td>"
.Write "</td><td>"
.Write "</td><td align=""right"">"
.Write "<b>" & FormatCurrency(sh + st + ct) & "</b>"
.Write "</td></tr>"
```

```
        .Write "<font size=""+1"">"
        .Write "</table>"

        .Write "<input type=""submit"" name=""save"" "
        .Write "value=""Save Changes"">"
        .Write "<input type=""submit"" name=""checkout"" "
        .Write "value=""Checkout"">"

        .Write "</form>"

    End With

End Sub
```

This form is created by building a seven-column table containing the values from the OrderDetails table plus the extended price. I begin the process by declaring the table and writing out the header information in separate cells. Then I initialize the variables ct and cb to zero. I'll use the ct variable to keep a running total of the cost and the cb variable to keep track of the number of books ordered.

Then I set up a **Do** loop that retrieves each of the rows from the record-set and then formats them and displays them as the cells in the table. At the start of the loop I start a new row, and at the end of the loop I end the row. In between, I output the values in separate cells. I give each field a name that is formed by converting the item number to a string and appending it to the letter q. This means that the first field will be called q1, the second q2, and so forth. I also compute the extended price of the book using the variable c, and then I add this value to ct. I also add the quantity of books ordered to the variable cb.

After the loop finishes, I check to see if the **Session** object variable salestax contains a value greater than zero. If so, I compute the sales tax based on the tax rate and display the information as a new row in the table. I also add this value to the variable ct. If the sales tax rate is zero, then I don't display anything.

Next I compute the shipping costs based on the rates stored in the database. I use the CostOfFirstBook and CostOfNextBook plus the variable cb to compute the variable sh. Then I display this value in the table and add it to the variable ct.

In the last row of the table, I display the total cost for the order from the variable ct as well as two buttons. The first button allows the customer to make changes in the order. The only real change the customer can make is to change the quantity of a book. Changing the quantity to zero will delete the record from the order. The other button is the Checkout button. Pressing this button will bill the customer's credit card and begin the process to ship the order.

Listing 16-21 contains the ChangeDetails_Respond routine that is triggered whenever the customer presses either the Save Changes or Checkout buttons. When the user presses the Save Changes button, I loop through the form looking for fields that begin with the letter q followed by a number. If the field isn't present, the expression **Request.Form**(s) will return an empty string, which **CInt** will convert into a zero. If I see a quantity of zero, I delete the row from the table using the DeleteOrderItem stored procedure. Otherwise, I change the quantity using the UpdateOrderItem routine. After I finish, I create a new field name beginning with q so that I can check the next field. When I run out of fields, I call with ShoppingCart_Respond event to redraw the shopping cart.

The ChangeDetails_Respond event updates any changes the customer may have made in the order:

Listing 16-21

```
Private Sub ChangeDetails_Respond()

Dim i As Integer
Dim parms1(2) As Variant
Dim parms2(1) As Variant
Dim rs As ADODB.Recordset
Dim s As String
Dim wb As Object

If Len(Request.Form("save")) > 0 Then
    i = 1
    s = "q" & FormatNumber(i, 0)
    Do While Len(Request.Form(s)) > 0
        If CInt(Request.Form((s))) = 0 Then
            parms2(0) = CLng(Session("ordernumber"))
```

```
            parms2(1) = i
            DeleteOrderItem.Execute , parms2
        Else
            parms1(0) = CLng(Session("ordernumber"))
            parms1(1) = i
            parms1(2) = CInt(Request.Form(s))
            UpdateOrderItem.Execute , parms1
        End If
        i = i + 1
        s = "q" & FormatNumber(i, 0)
    Loop

    ShoppingCart_Respond

Else

    Set wb = CreateObject("WebBooksUtility.wbutil", "athena")
    i = wb.PlaceOrder(Session("ordernumber"))
    SendMail wb.returnmsg, Session("email"), _
        "Order Confirmation from WebBooks.com"

    If i > 0 Then
        InsertNewOrder.Execute , Session("customerid")
        Set rs = GetOrders.Execute(, Session("customerid"))
        Session("ordernumber") = rs!ordernumber
        rs.Close
    End If

    With Response
        .Write Title("Order Confirmation")
        AHeader.WriteTemplate
        .Write "</ul>"
        BHeader.WriteTemplate
        .Write "<p><center><strong><big>Order Confirmation"
        .Write "</big></center>"
        .Write "<hr>"
        .Write "<pre>"
        .Write wb.ReturnMsg
        .Write "</pre>"
        FooterForm.WriteTemplate
        .End
    End With

End If

End Sub
```

Responding to the Checkout button is a bit more complicated than most of the other processing I've done so far. I'm going to use an ActiveX EXE program to perform the details of processing the order. As part of the processing, the ActiveX EXE program will generate a formatted document containing the details of the order. I will take this information and return it to the customer as a Web page and also e-mail it to the customer. I'll also take the time to create a new order for the customer so that the order will be ready when the customer tries to order more books.

The **CreateObject** function is used to create a new instance of the ActiveX EXE object. Then I use the **PlaceOrder** method to instruct the object to perform the tasks related to placing an order. The method will return the estimated number of days to deliver the books or minus one, if the order can't be placed for some reason. The **ReturnMsg** property contains a formatted document containing such information as availability of the books, the total amount charged to the credit card, and the list of books ordered. I'll cover the workings of this object in a lot more detail later in this chapter. This is a very important concept that you may want to use when developing database applications.

After the **PlaceOrder** method completes, I take the results in **Return-Msg** and call a subroutine called SendMail that will send the customer an e-mail message confirming the order. If the order is successful (I will have a value greater than zero), I create a new order; otherwise I leave the current order alone. Finally, I print the **ReturnMsg** for the user. Note that I use the <Pre> tag since the text is already formatted.

Building Utility Functions

When the customer presses the Checkout button, the IIS Application uses an object in an ActiveX EXE to actually place the order. While this program is resident on the same system as the Web server, this isn't a requirement. The machine where this program resides is called an *application server*.

There are many advantages to using an application server. First, the work can be isolated from both the database server and the Web server.

This means that if you are close to capacity on one machine, you can move part of your application to another machine. Second, by using the ActiveX technology, you can access objects on the application server from Visual Basic IIS Applications, DHTML Applications, and traditional client/server applications, as well as programs written in C, C++, and Java.

Using ActiveX Technology

You should be familiar with the ActiveX controls that come with Visual Basic. These controls provide useful facilities and extensions to Visual Basic that help you develop your programs more quickly and effectively. However, you are not limited to using the ActiveX tools that are provided with Visual Basic. You can write your own. There are three different types of ActiveX programs: the ActiveX control, the ActiveX DLL, and the ActiveX EXE. Each of these has its own characteristics and uses.

USING ACTIVEX CONTROLS

As a Visual Basic programmer, you've already come to know and love the ActiveX control. The control has a visual component that must be placed in a container. (Even though some controls aren't visible on your screen at run time, they are visible at design time.) A container may be a Visual Basic form, a Visual Basic Picture control, or an Internet Explorer Web page. An ActiveX control is always run as part of its parent's process (known as *running in process*).

USING ACTIVEX DLLS

The ActiveX DLL is also an in-process component and shares its parent's address space. This type of ActiveX program is designed for unattended operation. It is used to store objects created through the Visual Basic Class facility. Unlike an ActiveX control, it doesn't have a visual component. IIS Applications are created using an ActiveX DLL.

USING ACTIVEX EXES

The ActiveX EXE is an out-of-process component. It runs in a totally separate address space and may even run on a different computer. This is the way that programs such as Microsoft Word and Excel are created. Like Word and Excel, the ActiveX EXE may have a visual interface, but that is not required. You can run the program in the background and never know it is being used. Running in a different address space (out of process) is a little slower than being in process, but it does protect your program, in that crashing a user program will not affect the ActiveX EXE and it can be easily shared among many different types of programs.

Using Your Own Objects in Visual Basic

ActiveX EXEs (and ActiveX DLLs, for that matter) are really a collection of Visual Basic classes. Each class corresponds to a single object. An object has a collection of properties and methods. A property can be either a simple module-level variable or it can be a special function or subroutine called **Property Get, Property Set,** or **Property Let.** Methods are merely functions or subroutines. For any of these things to be used outside the project, they must be declared as **Public.** You can also declare **Events** that you can trigger from within your object, just like a regular Visual Basic control.

Every class object has two standard events: **Class_Initialize** and **Class_Terminate.** As you might expect from their names, these routines are called when the object is created and when the object is destroyed. Running the program not only calls the **Class_Initialize** event, but it registers the program with the system so that other programs can reference the objects it contains. Then the next time you run that program, the information on how to locate the program is already in the registry and Windows will automatically start it for you.

Note

While an ActiveX EXE can register itself with the operating system, ActiveX DLLs must be explicitly registered using a special utility. Simply run RegSvr32 followed by the name of the DLL file. This will add the information about the DLL file into the system registry, including its location on disk. Then any program can reference the objects in the DLL without having to know where the file is located.

Looking at the WebBooks.com Utility Program

There are three different classes in the Utility ActiveX EXE. The first class is CreditUtil and contains all the credit card processing interface. The second class is PubUtil and contains the logic and handles the interactions with a publisher. The last class is WBUtil and contains the business logic needed for processing an order.

Keep in mind that the application I'm building in this book is meant to show you different programming techniques by building a complex application. I didn't want to spend a lot of time trying to build interfaces into other applications. The CreditUtil and PubUtil classes are designed to handle the interface with companies outside WebBooks.com. Rather than making these routines realistic, I built them as stubs. The stubs let me test the rest of the application now while deferring work on the stubs until later. Since I don't know how to electronically access the credit card vendors, nor the various computer book publishers, I'm leaving the stubs in the program. If you find out how to do this (and don't get arrested while testing your code), please let me know.

Tip

I often run into situations where I need to perform a specific function but I don't want to write it at that time. In these cases I create a dummy function or subroutine called a **stub**. Sometimes the stub contains no code. Other times the code inside the stub simply returns a constant value. Later when I'm ready to write that function, I simply replace the stub with the real subroutine. This lets me write and test the calling program before I have to worry about how to write and test the stub.

The CreditUtil Class

The CreditUtil class is the interface between WebBooks.com and the credit card companies. All transactions that bill a credit card use this class to perform the actual work. Each credit card company will have its own way to process a charge in real time. To make it easy to use, I choose to build a common routine that will figure out which credit card is being billed and then take the appropriate action.

The CreditUtil object contains only one member, the CheckCreditCard method (see Listing 16-22). Since this routine is a stub, I merely check each of the fields to see if there is any data. If there isn't, I return **False**. I also check the credit card number (ccnum) to see if the last digit ends with a 9. If it does, I'll also return **False**. This feature lets me supply complete information with a bad credit card number so that I can test the bad credit card logic in the calling program.

The CheckCreditCard method returns **True** if the credit card information is accepted and **False** if it is not accepted:

Listing 16-22

```
Public Function CheckCreditCard(cctype As Integer, _
    ccnum As String, ccname As String, ccexpdate As String, _
    ccamount As Currency) As Boolean

If cctype = 0 Then
    CheckCreditCard = False

ElseIf Len(ccname) = 0 Then
    CheckCreditCard = False

ElseIf Len(ccexpdate) = 0 Then
    CheckCreditCard = False

ElseIf Right(ccnum, 1) = "9" Then
    CheckCreditCard = False

Else
    CheckCreditCard = True
End If

End Function
```

The PubUtil Class

Like the CreditUtil class, the PubUtil class is really a stub with the purpose to let me test the rest of the application. There are two methods in this class. The Deliver method (see Listing 16-23) returns the number of days to receive a particular book from the publisher, while the Reorder method (see Listing 16-24) places an order for the specified number of copies of a particular book and returns the estimated delivery time.

The Deliver method returns the amount of time required to get a book from a publisher:

The Deliver method returns the amount of time required to get a book from a publisher:

Listing 16-23

```
Function Deliver(isbn As Long) As Integer

Deliver = 5

End Function
```

The Reorder method orders a book from a publisher:

Listing 16-24

```
Function Reorder(isbn As Long, qty As Integer) As Integer

Reorder = Deliver(isbn)

End Function
```

The WBUtil Class

While the other two classes contained nothing but stub routines, this one is different. It is typical of the type of code you might want to implement for an application server. While there is only one method and one property associated with this class, the method performs a fairly complex set of database calls and the property returns details constructed by the method.

THE PLACEORDER METHOD

The PlaceOrder method is called in the ChangeDetails_Respond event of the WebBooks.com IIS Application. In very simple terms, this routine takes the order number and performs all the work necessary to purchase the order. It must compute the total dollar amount and bill the credit card company. Then assuming that the credit card information is approved, it adjusts the inventory levels of the books and generates the confirmation message that will be returned in ReturnMsg.

Listing 16-25 shows the PlaceOrder method, which performs each of the steps necessary to transform the contents of the customer's shopping cart into a set of paid-for books. It begins by opening records for the Orders, OrderDetails, Books, CreditCardCodes, PreferredShipping-Codes, StateCodes, and CountryCodes tables. Where possible, I narrow the results to only those records I need, such as in the Orders and OrderDetails tables.

The PlaceOrder method bills the credit card company, adjusts the inventory levels in the database, and prepares an order confirmation message:

Listing 16-25

```
Public Function PlaceOrder(OrderNumber As Long) As Integer

Dim Books As ADODB.Recordset
Dim Cards As ADODB.Recordset
Dim Countries As ADODB.Recordset
Dim Details As ADODB.Recordset
Dim c As Currency
Dim cb As Integer
Dim cc As New CreditUtil
Dim ct As Currency
Dim ed As Integer
Dim maxed As Integer
Dim Order As ADODB.Recordset
Dim sh As Currency
Dim Shippers As ADODB.Recordset
Dim st As Currency
Dim States As ADODB.Recordset
Dim t As String

Set Order = New ADODB.Recordset
Set Order.ActiveConnection = db
Order.Source = _
    "Select * From ops.dbo.Orders Where OrderNumber=" & _
    FormatNumber(OrderNumber, 0, , vbFalse, vbFalse)
Order.CursorType = adOpenStatic
Order.CursorLocation = adUseClient
Order.LockType = adLockOptimistic
Order.Open

Set Details = New ADODB.Recordset
Set Details.ActiveConnection = db
Details.Source = _
    "Select * From ops.dbo.OrderDetails Where OrderNumber=" & _
```

```
         FormatNumber(OrderNumber, 0, , vbFalse, vbFalse)
     Details.CursorType = adOpenStatic
     Details.CursorLocation = adUseClient
     Details.CacheSize = 50
     Details.LockType = adLockOptimistic
     Details.Open

     Set Shippers = New ADODB.Recordset
     Set Shippers.ActiveConnection = db
     Shippers.Source = _
         "Select * From cis.dbo.PreferredShippingCodes " & _
         "Where PreferredShippingCode=" & _
         FormatNumber(Order!Shippingcode, 0, , vbFalse, vbFalse)
     Shippers.CursorType = adOpenStatic
     Shippers.CursorLocation = adUseClient
     Shippers.LockType = adLockOptimistic
     Shippers.Open

     Set Cards = New ADODB.Recordset
     Set Cards.ActiveConnection = db
     Cards.Source = "Select * From cis.dbo.CreditCardCodes " & _
         "Where CreditCardCode=" & _
         FormatNumber(Order!CreditCardCode, 0, , vbFalse, vbFalse)
     Cards.CursorType = adOpenStatic
     Cards.CursorLocation = adUseClient
     Cards.LockType = adLockOptimistic
     Cards.Open

     Set States = New ADODB.Recordset
     Set States.ActiveConnection = db
     States.Source = "Select * From cis.dbo.StateCodes " & _
         "Where StateCode='" & Order!State & "'"
     States.CursorType = adOpenStatic
     States.CursorLocation = adUseClient
     States.LockType = adLockOptimistic
     States.Open

     Set Countries = New ADODB.Recordset
     Set Countries.ActiveConnection = db
     Countries.Source = "Select * From cis.dbo.CountryCodes " & _
         "Where CountryCode=" & _
         FormatNumber(Order!CountryCode, 0, vbFalse, vbFalse, vbFalse)
     Countries.CursorType = adOpenStatic
     Countries.CursorLocation = adUseClient
     Countries.LockType = adLockOptimistic
     Countries.Open

     Set Books = New ADODB.Recordset
     Set Books.ActiveConnection = db
```

```
Books.Source = "Select * From iis.dbo.Books"
Books.CursorType = adOpenStatic
Books.CursorLocation = adUseClient
Books.LockType = adLockOptimistic
Books.Open

Order!DateOrdered = Now

Msg = Order!OrderTitle & "("
Msg = Msg & FormatNumber(Order!OrderNumber, 0, vbFalse, vbFalse, vbFalse)
Msg = Msg & ")" & vbCrLf
Msg = Msg & "This order was placed on " & FormatDateTime(Order!DateOrdered)
Msg = Msg & vbCrLf & vbCrLf
Msg = Msg & "Ship to:" & vbCrLf
Msg = Msg & "    " & Order!customername & vbCrLf
Msg = Msg & "    " & Order!address1 & vbCrLf
Msg = Msg & "    " & Order!address2 & vbCrLf
Msg = Msg & "    " & Order!city & " " & Order!State & " "
Msg = Msg & Order!zipcode & vbCrLf
Msg = Msg & "    " & Countries!Country & vbCrLf
Msg = Msg & vbCrLf
Msg = Msg & "Credit card information:" & vbCrLf
Msg = Msg & "    Credit card number: " & Order!creditcardnumber & vbCrLf
Msg = Msg & "    Credit card type: " & Cards!creditcardtype & vbCrLf
Msg = Msg & "    Name on credit card: " & Order!creditcardname & vbCrLf
Msg = Msg & "    Expiration date: " & Order!expirationdate & vbCrLf
Msg = Msg & vbCrLf
Msg = Msg & "Books Ordered:" & vbCrLf

Details.MoveFirst
ct = 0
cb = 0
Do While Not Details.EOF
    c = (Details!listprice * (1 - Details!discount) * _
        Details!QuantityOrdered)
    ct = ct + c
    cb = cb + Details!QuantityOrdered
    Books.Filter = "ISBN=" & _
        FormatNumber(Details!isbn, 0, vbFalse, vbFalse, vbFalse)

    Msg = Msg & FormatNumber(Details!itemnumber, 0, vbFalse, _
        vbFalse, vbFalse)
    Msg = Msg & ": " & Books!Title & vbCrLf
    Msg = Msg & "    ISBN: " & FormatISBN(Details!isbn) & vbCrLf
    Msg = Msg & "    List Price: " & FormatCurrency(Details!listprice)
    Msg = Msg & vbCrLf
    Msg = Msg & "    Discount: " & FormatPercent(Details!discount, 0)
    Msg = Msg & vbCrLf
    Msg = Msg & "    Quantity: "
```

```
        Msg = Msg & FormatNumber(Details!QuantityOrdered, 0, vbFalse, _
            vbFalse, vbFalse)
        Msg = Msg & vbCrLf
        Msg = Msg & "   Your cost: " & FormatCurrency(c) & vbCrLf
        Msg = Msg & vbCrLf


    Details.MoveNext

Loop

Msg = Msg & "Subtotal: " & FormatCurrency(ct) & vbCrLf
Msg = Msg & vbCrLf

If States!Salestax > 0 Then
    If Not Order!TaxExemptStatus Then
        st = ct * States!Salestax
        ct = ct + st
        Msg = Msg & "Sales tax: " & vbCrLf
        Msg = Msg & "   Tax rate for " & States!State & " is "
        Msg = Msg & FormatPercent(States!Salestax) & "." & vbCrLf
        Msg = Msg & "   Sales tax for this order is "
        Msg = Msg & FormatCurrency(st) & vbCrLf
    Else
        Msg = Msg & "Sales tax: " & vbCrLf
        Msg = Msg & "   Your order was tax exempt." & vbCrLf
    End If
End If

sh = Shippers!costoffirstbook
If cb > 1 Then
    sh = sh + Shippers!costofnextbook * (cb - 1)
End If

ct = ct + sh

Msg = Msg & vbCrLf
Msg = Msg & "Shipping and handling charges: " & vbCrLf
Msg = Msg & "   Using " & Shippers!preferredshippingmethod & vbCrLf
Msg = Msg & "   First book costs "
Msg = Msg & FormatCurrency(Shippers!costoffirstbook)
Msg = Msg & ", each additional books costs "
Msg = Msg & FormatCurrency(Shippers!costofnextbook) & vbCrLf
Msg = Msg & "   Total charge for " & FormatNumber(cb, 0)
Msg = Msg & " books is " & FormatCurrency(sh) & "."

Order!invalidcreditcard = Not cc.CheckCreditCard(Order!CreditCardCode, _
    Order!creditcardnumber, Order!creditcardname, Order!expirationdate, ct)

Msg = Msg & vbCrLf
Msg = Msg & "Total amount charged was " & FormatCurrency(ct) & "." & vbCrLf
```

```
If Not Order!invalidcreditcard Then
    Details.MoveFirst
    maxed = 1

    Do While Not Details.EOF
        Books.Filter = "ISBN=" & _
            FormatNumber(Books!isbn, 0, vbFalse, vbFalse, vbFalse)

        ed = OrderBook(Books, Details!isbn, Details!QuantityOrdered)
        If ed > maxed Then
            maxed = ed
        End If

        Details.MoveNext
    Loop

    If maxed = 1 Then
        Msg = Msg & "Your order should be shipped in 24 hours."

    Else
        Msg = Msg & "Your order should be shipped in "
        Msg = Msg & FormatNumber(maxed, 0, vbFalse, vbFalse, vbFalse)
        Msg = Msg & " days." & vbCrLf

    End If

    Order!OrderStatus = 1

Else
    Msg = Msg & "Your credit card was declined. " & vbCrLf

    Order!OrderStatus = -1
    maxed = -1

End If

Order.Update

Order.Close
Details.Close
Shippers.Close
States.Close
Cards.Close
Books.Close

Set Order = Nothing
Set Details = Nothing
Set Shippers = Nothing
```

```
Set States = Nothing
Set Cards = Nothing
Set Books = Nothing

PlaceOrder = maxed

End Function
```

Then I set the DateOrdered field in the Orders Table to **Now**. Any time I need to know when the order was processed, all I have to do is refer to this value. If I used the **Now** function here and then later in the routine, there would be a slight difference in time. While most likely it wouldn't cause any problems; all it would take is one highly improbable situation that could cause all kinds of problems.

One problem I've run across many times over the years is when a programmer uses the **Now** function (or its equivalent) when performing some task. Consider the case of a programmer who would submit a batch job to print a report that started before midnight and finished after midnight. Each page would print the current date using the **Now** function. Then when the date changes at midnight, the printed date on the report would also change. This would cause confusion among users who weren't sure on which date the report was run. I always recommend getting the date and time at the start of a program and using this value throughout the program.

After I get the current date and time, I begin building the return message in the local variable msg. I add information about the date and time the order was placed and where the order will be shipped, as well as information from the credit card. Then I loop through the OrderDetails rows I retrieved to compute the cost of the books. At the same time, I append the information about the specific books to msg, including the book's title, ISBN, list price, discount, quantity ordered, and extended price.

Next I compute the sales tax and append that information to msg only if the state where the order is being shipped collects sales tax. Then I compute the cost of shipping and append that information to msg.

At this point, I've computed all the costs related to the order and I'm ready to bill the credit card company. I do this using the CheckCredit-Card stub I created. If the credit card company accepts the charges, I'll update the database for each of the ordered books. If not, I'll inform the user that the credit card was declined and update the status of the order accordingly.

I begin to order the books by moving the cursor for the OrderDetails table back to the first row and using the OrderBook routine to actually place the order. This function returns the number of days required to prepare the book for shipment. If the book is in stock, this value should be one. Otherwise, this represents the number of days to get the book from the publisher. I then track the maximum amount of time for the books to become available, since the order can't ship until all the books are available. At the end of this process I'll append to msg the estimated time to ship the order and mark the order as being ready for shipping. I end this routine by updating the Orders table, closing all the recordsets I used, and setting each of those objects to **Nothing**. Before I return from the function, I set its value to the maximum number of days for estimated delivery (maxed).

THE ORDERBOOK ROUTINE

The OrderBook routine (see Listing 16-26) adjusts the inventory level and returns the estimated delivery time for a particular book in the order. WebBooks.com will always ship a book even if it has to order more copies from a publisher to fulfill the order. With that in mind, the first step in this process is to determine if I need to order any additional books. I do this by seeing if the number of books I have on hand plus the number of books I've ordered from the publisher less the quantity of books that the customer ordered is less than my reorder point. If it isn't, then I merely subtract the quantity of books from the quantity on hand, add the quantity to the number of books sold since the last reorder, and return the estimated delivery date.

The OrderBook method adjusts inventory levels for book orders and places an order if the total number of books on hand is below the reorder point:

Listing 16-26

```
Private Function OrderBook(b As ADODB.Recordset, isbn As Long, _
    qty As Integer) As Integer

Dim abpd As Integer
Dim ed As Integer
Dim nrp As Integer
Dim Publisher As New PubUtil
Dim PubOrder As ADODB.Recordset

If (b!QuantityOnHand + b!QuantityonBackorder - qty) < _
      b!ReorderPoint Then
    abpd = b!NumberSoldSinceLastReorder / _
      DateDiff("d", Now, b!LastReorderDate)
    nrp = abpd * (Publisher.Deliver(isbn) + 2)
    ed = Publisher.Reorder(isbn, nrp)
    b!ExpectedDelivery = DateAdd("d", ed, Now)
    b!QuantityonBackorder = b!QuantityOnBack0rder + nrp
    b!ReorderPoint = nrp
    b!LastReorderDate = Now
    b!NumberSoldSinceLastReorder = 0

    Set PubOrder = New ADODB.Recordset
    Set PubOrder.ActiveConnection = db
    PubOrder.Source = "Select * From ops.dbo.Publisher"
    PubOrder.CursorType = adOpenStatic
    PubOrder.CursorLocation = adUseClient
    PubOrder.LockType = adLockOptimistic
    PubOrder.Open
    PubOrder.AddNew
    PubOrder!isbn = isbn
    PubOrder!QuantityOrdered = nrp
    PubOrder!DateOrdered = Now
    PubOrder!PublisherCode = b!PublisherCode
    PubOrder!PurchaseStatus = 0
    PubOrder.Update
    PubOrder.Close
    Set PubOrder = Nothing

End If

b!QuantityOnHand = b!QuantityOnHand - qty
b!NumberSoldSinceLastReorder = b!NumberSoldSinceLastReorder + qty
```

```
If IsNull(b!EstimatedDelivery) Then
    OrderBook = 1
Else
    OrderBook = b!EstimatedDelivery
End If

b.Update

End Function
```

If I have to reorder books, I want to try to reorder the smallest quantity I can. So to compute this quantity, I begin by calculating the average number of books sold per day (abpd) using the NumberSold-SinceLastReorder field and the LastReorderDate. Then I multiply this value by the number of days to get an order from the publisher plus two to get a new reorder point (nrp). If the expected delivery date from the publisher is three days, then I want to order enough books to cover the next five days.

After computing the new reorder point, I place the order with the publisher using the PubUtil object. This object returns the number of days to deliver the additional books. From there I add this value to the current date to create the new ExpectedDelivery date. I add the number of books I have just ordered to the QuantityOnBackorder field, since I may have one or more books on back order already. Then I can update ReorderPoint with the new value, change LastReorderDate to today, and set NumberSoldSinceLastReorder to zero.

The last step of this process is to update the PubOrder table with the specifics of this order. I create a new recordset and then use the **AddNew** method. Then I update each of the fields in the recordset with the current values, update the row to commit the changes, and close the recordset.

Using CDONTS to Send Mail

The last book I wrote for Prima (*Programming ISAPI with Visual Basic 5*) discussed how to use OLEISAPI2 to write Internet programs. The IIS Applications in Visual Basic 6 are a much improved and enhanced version of OLEISAPI2. The number two request from readers of that book was how to send e-mail from their application. (The number one request was how to access SQL Server.) I found a tool called the

Collaboration Data Objects for NT Server (**CDONTS** for short) that let me generate mail from inside an IIS Application.

CDONTS and IIS

By default, **CDONTS** is installed with the NT 4 Option Pack. It is included as part of the IIS SMTP service. It provides support for sending and receiving Internet mail. Only the inbox and outbox folders are supported. These folders are mapped into local folders in the \Inet-Pub\mailroot directory. Message transfer is quick, so typically there will be no messages in either the inbox or the outbox.

Incoming mail is read from either a standard Microsoft Exchange inbox or a standard Internet POP3 mailbox. Incoming mail is stored locally and then made available based on the e-mail address you specify in the **LogonSMTP** method. Outgoing mail is routed through the IIS SMTP service, which maintains its own message store facility. If a message can't be sent immediately, it is queued for sending at a later time.

The CDONTS Object Model

CDONTS is modeled after the Collaboration Data Objects (**CDO**) used by Outlook 98 and Exchange Server, but is simplified for use on the Internet. It is not designed for use with an interactive client interface, but instead is targeted for use with Visual InterDev programs. This makes it a natural for Visual Basic IIS Applications. It is designed to send and receive mail using the SMTP and POP3 Internet mail protocols.

The **CDONTS** contain many of the same objects found in the **CDO**, so using them is just like using the **CDO**.

- The **Session** Object
- The **Folder** Object
- The **Messages** Collection and the **Message** Object
- The **Recipients** Collection and the **Recipient** Object
- The **Attachments** Collection and the **Attachment** Object
- The **AddressEntry** Object
- The **NewMail** Object

The **Session** object contains a link between the application and the mail server. The **Folder** object contains the inbox or outbox. The **Messages** collection contains the set of all messages in a **Folder**, while the **Message** object contains a single e-mail object. The **Message** object also contains a reference to a **Recipients** collection and an **Attachment** collection. The **Recipients** collection holds the set of **Recipient** objects, each of which holds information about a single recipient of the mail message. An **Attachments** collection contains the set of **Attachment** objects associated with an e-mail message. The **AddressEntry** object contains information about the person sending the note. The **NewMail** object provides a quick way to send an e-mail message.

> **Note**
>
> The **CDONTS** objects are a subset of the **CDO** objects. All the properties and methods found in the **CDONTS** work the same as those found in the **CDO** library with the exception of the **LogonSMTP** method. This method corresponds to the **CDO Logon** method.

THE SESSION OBJECT

The **Session** object is the root object of the **CDONTS**. Tables 16-5 and 16-6 describe the key properties and methods of this object. It provides access to the **Inbox** and **Outbox Folder** objects, which are used to let your program read and send e-mail. The **MessageFormat** property determines if the mail you send is sent in MIME (Multipurpose Internet Mail Extensions) format or in a raw format. The **Application** and **Class** properties provide information about the object library itself. The **Version** property returns the current version of the object library, which is 1.2. The **Class** object returns an **Integer** value that uniquely identifies the object. The **Parent** property returns **Nothing** for the **Session** object, but for other objects the **Parent** property will return an object reference to the object's parent object. The **Session** object always returns a reference to the root **Session** object. The **Application**, **Class**, **Parent**, and **Session** properties are common to all the objects in the **CDONTS** library.

Table 16-5	Properties of the **Session** Object
Property	**Description**
Application	Returns a string containing the name of the library.
Class	Returns a value indicating the type of object.
Inbox	Returns an object reference to the **Folder** object containing the inbox.
MessageFormat	Determines if the message is sent in MIME format or in plain text.
Name	Contains the sender's name.
Outbox	Returns an object reference to the **Folder** object containing the outbox.
Parent	Returns an object reference of this object's parent, or **Nothing** for the **Session** object.
Session	Returns a reference to the **Session** object.
Version	Returns a string containing the version of the object library.

The **LogonSMTP** method is used to initialize the e-mail session by supplying values for the sender's name ("Wayne S. Freeze") and the sender's e-mail address ("WFreeze@JustPC.com"). This information will be used when your application sends e-mail messages. The **Logoff** method closes the **Session** object, while the **GetDefaultFolder** method sets the default folder to either your Inbox or your Outbox folder.

Table 16-6	Selected Methods of the **Session** Object
Method	**Description**
GetDefaultFolder	Sets either the inbox or outbox as the default folder.
Logoff	Closes the **Session** object.
LogonSMTP	Initializes the **Session** object.

THE FOLDER OBJECT

The **Folder** object contains several properties (see Table 16-7), but only the **Messages** property (which returns an object reference to the collection of messages in the folder) and the **Name** property (which contains the name of the folder) are important. The remaining properties in this object are those that are common to all the objects in this collection.

Table 16-7 Selected Properties of the **Folder** Object	
Property	**Description**
Messages	Returns an object reference to a **Messages** collection containing the e-mail messages.
Name	Contains the name of the **Folder** object.

THE MESSAGES COLLECTION AND MESSAGE OBJECT

The **Messages** collection contains all the messages in the folder, while the **Message** object contains the information about a single message. The **Count** and **Item** properties in the **Messages** collection return, respectively, the number of messages and the object reference for a specific message in the collection (see Table 16-8).

Table 16-8 Selected Properties of the **Messages** Collection	
Property	**Description**
Count	Returns the number of **Message** objects in the folder.
Item	Returns a particular **Message** object.

The methods in the **Messages** collection allow you to create new messages, delete messages, and navigate through the messages in the collection (see Table 16-9). The **Add** method allows you to create a new message using the specified subject line and message body. The **Delete** method erases all the messages from the collection. The **GetFirst, Get-Last, GetNext,** and **GetPrevious** methods allow you to step through the **Message** objects in the **Messages** collection. If the previous or next message doesn't exist, then **Nothing** will be returned.

Table 16-9	Methods of the **Messages** Collection
Method	**Description**
Add	Adds a new message to the collection.
Delete	Deletes all the **Message** objects in the collection.
GetFirst	Returns an object reference to the first **Message** object in the collection.
GetLast	Returns an object reference to the last **Message** object in the collection.
GetNext	Returns an object reference to the next **Message** object in the collection.
GetPrevious	Returns an object reference to the previous **Message** object in the collection.

The **Message** object contains all the information about a particular message (see Table 16-10). The **Attachments** property returns an object reference to the **Attachments** collection. The **Recipients** property returns the list of people who will receive (or have received) this message. The **Sender** object returns information about the person who sent the mail. The **Subject** property contains the message's subject line. The **HTML-Text** and **Text** properties contain the body of the message in HTML or plain text format, respectively. The **TimeReceived** and **TimeSent** return the time the message was received and sent, respectively. Both values are expressed in terms of the local machine's time.

Table 16-10 Selected Properties of the **Message** Object	
Property	**Description**
Attachments	Returns an object reference to the **Attachments** collection.
ContentBase	Sets or returns the Content-Base MIME header.
ContentId	Returns the Content-ID MIME header.
ContentLocation	Sets or returns the Content-Location MIME header.
HTMLText	Contains the HTML-formatted version of the mail message.
Importance	Contains the relative importance of a mail message.
MessageFormat	Determines if the message was sent in MIME format or in plain text.
Recipients	Returns an object reference to the **Recipients** collection.
Sender	Returns an **AddressEntry** object containing information about who sent the message.
Size	Returns the approximate size of the message in bytes.
Subject	Sets or returns the subject of the message.
Text	Contains the plain-text version of the mail message.
TimeReceived	Contains the date and time the message was received.
TimeSent	Contains the date and time the message was originally sent.

The **MessageFormat** property instructs the **CDONTS** to send the message either as a MIME-encoded message or as an unformatted message. The **ContentBase, ContentId,** and **ContentLocation** properties return or set the corresponding MIME headers. The **Importance** property determines the relative priority of the message (Low, Normal, or High). The **Size** property returns the approximate size of the message in bytes.

There are only two methods for a message (see Table 16-11): **Send,** which saves the changes to your message and moves it to your outbox, and **Delete,** which removes the message from the folder. A message that has been sent will automatically be deleted from the outbox.

Table 16-11   Methods of the Message Object

Method	Description
Delete	Deletes the message.
Send	Saves the new changes to the message and sends it to the list of recipients.

THE RECIPIENTS COLLECTION AND RECIPIENT OBJECT

The **Recipients** collection contains the list of people who will receive the message, while the **Recipient** object contains information about a specific person. The **Count** and **Item** properties in the **Messages** object return, respectively, the number of recipients and the object reference for a specific recipient in the collection (see Table 16-12).

Table 16-12   Selected Properties of the Recipients Collection

Property	Description
Count	Returns the number of **Recipient** objects in the folder.
Item	Returns a particular **Recipient** object.

The **Add** and **Delete** methods allow you to create new **Recipient** objects and remove all the existing **Recipient** objects from the **Recipients** collection (see Table 16-13).

Table 16-13   Methods of the Recipients Collection

Method	Description
Add	Adds a new **Recipient** object to the collection.
Delete	Deletes all the **Recipient** objects in the collection.

The **Recipient** object contains three basic properties (see Table 16-14). The **Name** property contains the name of the person who will receive the message. The **Address** property contains the person's e-mail address. The **Type** property indicates if the recipient will be listed as To, CC, or BCC. The **Delete** method (see Table 16-15) removes the **Recipient** from the collection

Table 16-14 Selected Properties of the Recipient Object

Property	Description
Address	Sets or returns the e-mail address of the person receiving the message.
Name	Contains the name of the person receiving the message.
Type	Indicates if the recipient was listed as To, CC, or BCC on the message.

Table 16-15 Method of the Recipient Object

Method	Description
Delete	Deletes the specific **Recipient** object.

THE ATTACHMENTS COLLECTION AND ATTACHMENT OBJECT

The **Attachments** collection contains the list of attachments to an e-mail message. The **Count** and **Item** properties return the number of attachments to the message and the object reference to a particular attachment (see Table 16-16). The **Add** and **Delete** methods create a new attachment or delete all attachments in the collection (see Table 16-17).

Table 16-16 Selected Properties of the Attachments Collection

Property	Description
Count	Returns the number of **Attachment** objects in the folder.
Item	Returns a particular **Attachment** object.

Table 16-17	Methods of the Attachments Collection
Method	**Description**
Add	Adds a new **Attachment** object to the collection.
Delete	Deletes all the **Attachment** objects in the collection.

The **Attachment** object can be either another message or the contents of a file. This information is described in the **Type** property (see Table 16-18). The **Source** property contains an object reference to another **Message** object. This applies only when the **Type** property specifies that the attachment is a **Message** object. Otherwise, the **Source** property is not used. The **Name** property contains the name that will be displayed for the attachment. The **ContentBase**, **ContentId**, and **ContentLocation** properties return information from the corresponding MIME headers.

Table 16-18 Selected Properties of the Attachment Object	
Property	**Description**
ContentBase	Returns the Content-Base MIME header.
ContentId	Returns the Content-ID MIME header.
ContentLocation	Returns the Content-Location MIME header.
Name	Contains the visible name for an attachment.
Source	Contains an object reference to another **Message** object.
Type	Describes if the attachment is another **Message** object or is an embedded file.

The **Delete** method (see Table 16-19) removes the attachment from the **Attachments** collection. The **ReadFromFile** method loads the specified attachment from a disk file, while the **WriteToFile** method saves the attachment to a disk file. The **ReadFromFile** and **WriteToFile** methods work only when the attachment is a file attachment. Using these methods to attach other messages doesn't work and will cause an error.

Table 16-19	Methods of the Attachment Object
Method	**Description**
Delete	Deletes the specific **Attachment** object.
ReadFromFile	Loads an attachment from a disk file.
WriteToFile	Saves an attachment to a disk file.

THE ADDRESSENTRY OBJECT

The **AddressEntry** object contains three basic properties (see Table 16-20). The **Name** property contains the name of the person who sent the message. The **Address** property contains the sender's e-mail address, while the **Type** property always returns "SMTP".

Table 16-20 Selected Properties of the AddressEntry Object	
Property	**Description**
Address	Sets or returns the e-mail address of the person sending the message.
Name	Contains the name of the person sending the message.
Type	Always contains "SMTP".

THE NEWMAIL OBJECT

The **NewMail** object provides a quick way to send an e-mail message. You don't have to create a **Session** object and use the **LogonSMTP** method, nor do you use the **Logoff** method. All the properties, except for **Version**, are write-only.

Table 16-21 lists the properties of the **NewMail** object. The **Bcc, Cc,** and **To** properties contain the list of e-mail addresses that will receive the message. Semicolons must separate multiple addresses in a single property or **CDONTS** may not correctly parse the addresses. The **From** property contains the e-mail address of the sender. Note that more than one address in this property will cause an error. The **Body** and **Body-**

Format properties determine the content of the message and its format. The **Subject** property contains the subject of the message. The **Value** property allows you to create additional SMTP mail headers in your message such as Keywords or Reply-To.

Table 16-21 Properties of the NewMail Object	
Property	**Description**
Bcc	Contains a list of e-mail addresses that will receive the message as a blind carbon copy recipient.
Body	Contains the body of the message.
BodyFormat	Describes the body of the message as either HTML or plain text.
CC	Contains a list of e-mail addresses that will receive the message as a carbon copy recipient.
ContentBase	Returns the Content-Base MIME header.
ContentId	Returns the Content-ID MIME header.
ContentLocation	Returns the Content-Location MIME header.
From	Contains the e-mail address of the person sending the message.
Importance	Contains the relative importance of the message.
MailFormat	Determines if the message is sent in MIME format or in plain text.
Subject	Contains the subject of the message.
To	Contains a list of e-mail addresses that will receive the message as a To recipient.
Value	Creates additional mail headers in a message.
Version	Returns a string containing the version of the object library.

Caution

The **NewMail** object can be used to send only one message. If you want to send a second message, you must create a new instance of the object.

The **NewMail** object contains methods (see Table 16-22) for attaching files and URLs to the message. Once the message is complete, you can use the **Send** method to send it.

Table 16-22	Selected Methods of the NewMail Object
Method	**Description**
AttachFile	Loads the specified file as an attachment to the message.
AttachURL	Attaches the specified URL to the message.
Send	Sends the message.

By specifying values for From, To, Subject, and Body on the **Send** method, you can create and send an e-mail message in only three statements:

```
Set msg = CreateObject("CDONTS.NewMail")
msg.Send "WFreeze@JustPC.com", "Readers@Nowhere.com", _
   "Three statements", "This message was sent with only
three statements."
Set msg = Nothing
```

Using the SendMail Function

A simple application of **CDONTS** is shown in Listing 16-27. This routine begins a new **CDONTS** session by first creating a new **CDONTS.Session** object and then using the **LogonSMTP** method. Then it adds a new message to the outbox using the specified subject line and message body. Next it adds the list of **To** recipients to the message using the **Recipients.Add** method. You could also add a list of **CC** recipients and attachments to the message at this point. I use the **Send** method to commit the changes and start the message on its way, using the **Logoff** method to close the **Session** object.

The SendMail subroutine constructs and sends an e-mail message using the specified message body, recipient list, and subject:

Listing 16-27

```
Private Sub SendMail(m As String, r As String, s As String)

Dim ms As CDONTS.Session
Dim msg As CDONTS.Message

Set ms = New CDONTS.Session
ms.LogonSMTP "WebBooks.com", "Orders@WebBooks.com"
Set msg = ms.Outbox.Messages.Add(s, m)
msg.Recipients.Add , r, CdoTo
msg.Send
ms.Logoff

End Sub
```

Performing Warehouse Functions

The last step of the process of ordering a book is for the warehouse to assign a tracking number and print a packing list. The easiest way to print the packing list is to use the Microsoft Data Report Designer. The warehouse also has to receive books from the publisher and update the inventory records.

The Microsoft Data Report Designer

The Microsoft Data Report Designer is a tool that works with the Data Environment Designer to help you build reports quickly and easily. Reports are built visually by creating a **Command** object in the Data Environment and then dragging the individual fields onto the Data Report Designer.

The basic report (see Figure 16-5) consists of a series of bands across it. Each band can contain an assortment of visual report controls (see Table 16-23). The two primary controls are the **RptTextBox** and **RptLabel**. These controls correspond to the **TextBox** and **Label** controls normally found in Visual Basic. The **RptTextBox** control is used to display data

Figure 16-5
The Data Report
Designer starts with
a blank report.

from the database, while the **RptLabel** control is used to display constant information such as titles or column headings. The **RptImage** control allows you to place a graphic image on the report, though it won't display a graphic from the database. The **RptLine** and **RptShape** controls draw various lines and shapes on the report. The **RptFunction** is a powerful control that allows you to perform various calculations on the information displayed in the report, making it easy to create total lines on the report.

Table 16-23   Controls That Can Be Used with the Data Report Designer

Control	Description
RptFunction	Performs a function such as sum, min, max, count, standard error, or standard deviation on fields listed in the inner band.
RptImage	Displays an image on the report.
RptLabel	Displays a constant block of text on the report.
RptLine	Draws a line on the report.
RptShape	Draws a shape (such as a rectangle, square, oval, circle, rounded rectangle, or rounded square) on the report.
RptTextBox	Displays information from a database.

Creating the Data Environment Command

The key to using the Data Report Designer is creating a Data Environment **Command** object with child commands. This is known as a hierarchical recordset. You might think of this as a recordset where one of the fields in a particular row is really just another recordset. These recordsets can be nested as many times as necessary to describe the data for the report. The nested **Command** object is known as a Child Command.

Consider the diagram shown in Figure 16-6. The recordset generated by the **Command1** object returned three rows with two fields in each row,

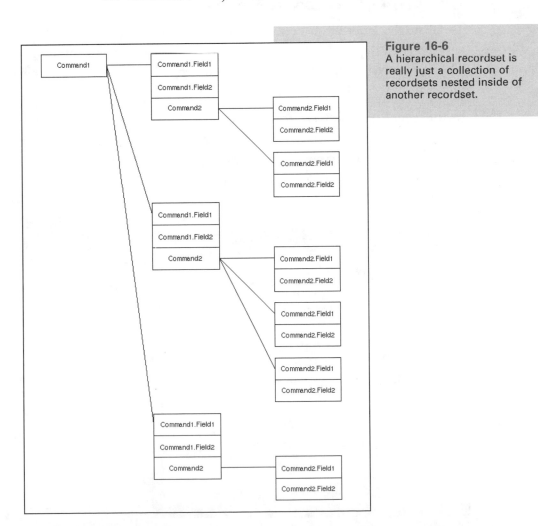

Figure 16-6
A hierarchical recordset is really just a collection of recordsets nested inside of another recordset.

plus another recordset generated by the **Command2** object. In the first row of the **Command1** recordset, the **Command2** recordset generated two rows. In the second row it generated three rows, while the last row in the **Command1** recordset had only one row in the **Command2** object.

Figure 16-7 shows a typical packing list from the WebBooks.com Warehouse Manager utility. The Command1 object returned only one row of information from the Orders table, while the Command2 child command returned three rows of information from the OrderDetails and Books tables.

Creating the Data Report

To create the report, you need to add the Data Environment Designer and the Data Report Designer to the Project menu's list of menu items. Then you need to use the Data Environment Designer to create the hierarchical recordset you want to use as input to the report.

In this case I use the GetOrder stored procedure to retrieve the information for a particular order number (see Figure 16-8). Then I add a child command underneath the Command1 object that executes the query shown in Listing 16-28. This query generates a recordset con-

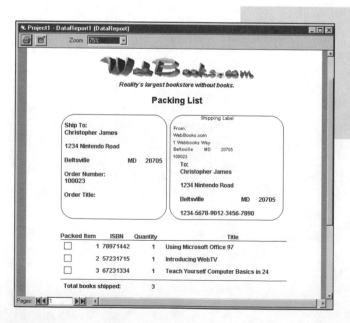

Figure 16-7
Here is a sample report generated by the Data Report Designer using a hierarchical recordset.

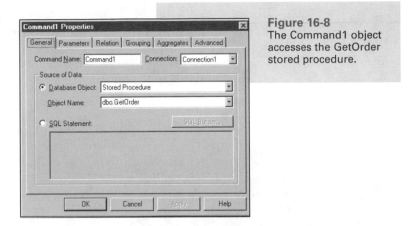

Figure 16-8
The Command1 object accesses the GetOrder stored procedure.

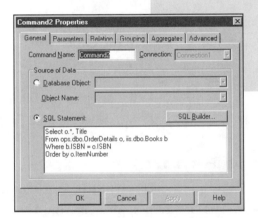

Figure 16-9
The Command2 object returns information about the books ordered.

taining all the detail information for an order (see Figure 16-9).

Generate rows for the Command1 object:

Listing 16-28

```
Select o.*, Title
From ops.dbo.OrderDetails o, iis.dbo.Books b
Where b.ISBN = o.ISBN
Order by o.ItemNumber
```

If you look carefully, you'll see that the Command2 object does not restrict the query based on OrderNumber. So as the query stands, it will retrieve information about all the books ordered in the OrderDetails table. However, since this is a child command, you must specify a rela-

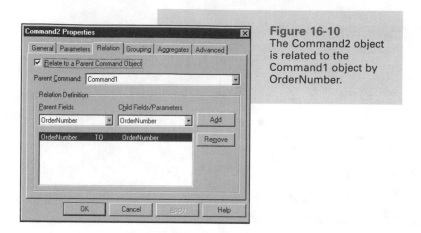

Figure 16-10
The Command2 object is related to the Command1 object by OrderNumber.

tionship to the parent command object. In this case the OrderNumber field of the parent command is related to the OrderNumber field of the child command (see Figure 16-10). This means that the Command2 object will contain only those rows having the same value of Order-Number as found in the Command1 object. This gives me the hierarchical recordset I need to produce the report (see Figure 16-11).

Designing the Report

Once you have created the hierarchical recordset, you should then create the skeleton report. The first step is to define the **DataSource** and **DataMember** properties of the report. The **DataSource** property should be set to the Data Environment you created. In my case it is DataEnvironment1. The **DataMember** property is set to the **Command** object that contains the hierarchical recordset, which is Command1 in this application.

Then I right-click on the report and select Retrieve Structure from the pop-up menu. This command synchronizes the bands on the report skeleton with the levels of hierarchy in the hierarchical recordset.

Each band in the report is printed in a specific order or in a specific position on the page (see Table 16-24). You can't specify database information in the report and page bands (both header and footer). The group bands can only contain information from the Command1 object, while the detail band can display information from the Command2 and Com-

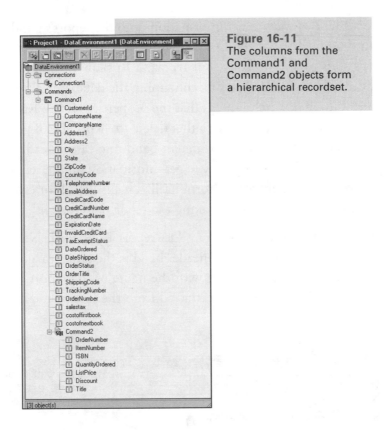

Figure 16-11
The columns from the Command1 and Command2 objects form a hierarchical recordset.

mand1 objects. The only exception to these rules is that the group footer and report footer bands can include an **RptFunction** control that calculates a value based on the information contained in the inner bands.

Table 16-24 Specific Functions of Report Bands

Band	Description
Report Header	Printed one time at the start of the report
Page Header	Printed at the top of each page
Group Header	Printed for each row in the Command1 object
Detail	Printed for each row in the Command2 object
Group Footer	Printed for each row in the Command1 object
Page Footer	Printed at the top of each page
Report Footer	Printed one time at the end of the report

There are two ways to get information onto the report's bands. First, you can drag fields from the Data Environment description onto the band. This adds two controls to your report: a **RptLabel** containing the name of the field and a **RptTextBox** containing the database value. The advantage of using this technique is that the properties for the **RptTextBox** are already properly set. You can either delete the **RptLabel** if you don't need it or you can drag it onto a different band to create a header that is only printed once. The second way to get information on the report is to draw the controls directly on the form itself. This is useful for creating header and footer information or making the report look better.

Figure 16-12 shows the Packing List report I designed. Note that at the top of the report in the page header band is the same image I used at the top of each Web page, along with the name of the report. In the group header band is information extracted from the Command1 object. Note

Figure 16-12
Use the Data Report Designer to design the Packing List report.

that I printed the address information twice, since the address information on the right will be used as a shipping label on the outside of the box.

At the very bottom of the group header band is a series of labels that will serve as headers for the fields in the detail band. The detail band contains fields from the Command2 object. I also include a small check box on the left edge of the report so that the packer can check off the books as they are packed.

In the group footer band I total up the books in this order using the **RptFunction** control. Then at the bottom of the page I leave a space for the warehouse employee to sign the order. If enough books are ordered so that a second page is needed, the page header and page footer bands will be repeated, but the group header will only appear on page one and the group footer will only appear on the last page.

Running the Report

Running the report is a fairly straightforward matter (see Listing 16-29). I verify that the recordset associated with the Command1 object is closed by checking its **State** property. If it isn't, then I explicitly close it. Then I set the parameter "o" to the value of the order number the warehouse employee entered in the Text3 text box and use the **DataReport1.Show** method. This method will display the preview screen for the report.

Generate rows for the Command1 object:

Listing 16-29

```
Private Sub Command2_Click()

With DataEnvironment1
    If .rsCommand1.State = adStateOpen Then
        .rsCommand1.Close
    End If
    .Commands("Command1").Parameters("o") = Text3.Text
    DataReport1.Show

End With

End Sub
```

> **If you don't need to see a preview of the report before sending it to the printer, you can replace the Show method with the Print method. This will send the output directly to the printer. You can optionally specify a dialog box to select which pages are printed or specify the page range as a parameter on the Print method.**

Note that unless I close the recordset after it's been opened, changing the parameter will have no effect. Thus the report would contain the data from the previous recordset.

Wrapping Up

The Order Processing Subsystem uses the facilities built in the Customer Interface Subsystem and the Inventory Information Subsystem to finish the WebBooks.com application. In building this phase of the application, I've continued working on the IIS Application I wrote in Chapter 11. But since the database is not limited to processing Web pages, I've also shown you the basics of several other technologies, such as ActiveX programming, DHTML Applications, and Data Report. With the sample code I've written, you should be able to incorporate these technologies into your own applications without a lot of difficulty.

As you can probably tell, I'm a big believer in the IIS Application. It is an efficient and easy way to implement the server side of a Web-based application. However, it need not be used by itself. Using this technology along with an ActiveX EXE is a powerful combination. You can implement your business logic in the ActiveX EXE and share it with both your Web-based applications and your traditional client/server applications. You can choose to implement the applications on the same server as the Web server or database server or you can implement them on a dedicated application server. This is a key element that allows your applications to scale up in size.

The Data Report Designer is an easy alternative to writing your own printing program. Although creating your own reports without the Data Report Designer isn't very hard to do in Visual Basic, it is somewhat time-consuming. It's very much like developing your own Web pages using Notepad. While it is possible to do it this way, using a high-level tool like FrontPage is much more efficient. Of course the Data Report Designer can't build every type of report imaginable. However, with the trend to eliminate paper wherever possible, you might want to consider not implementing some types of reports, especially those that you can't implement using the Data Report Designer.

I've identified and fixed several problems with the WebBooks.com application. However, the new code I've added leaves the door open for other problems. In the meantime, you should implement book ratings and modify the program to hold the last search value. The database design is already set up to implement ratings, and holding the last search value is merely a matter of adding a **Session** object variable that holds the last search value. Then you can include it on the Web page by using the VALUE attribute of the <INPUT> field that holds the search value.

CHAPTER 17

Testing the Order Processing Subsystem

Just like in the previous subsystems, testing this subsystem involves verifying that all the features and functions of the programs work properly. Unlike the other two subsystems, all the necessary data is already in the database. Also unlike the other subsystems, it's not immediately apparent whether the program worked properly or not, so the database will have to be examined directly to see if the information was properly updated.

Testing the WebBooks.com Application

Half of the WebBooks.com application was developed in Chapter 11. In Chapter 16, I added a lot of code to perform new functions while fixing some of the previous problems that I found while testing the application in Chapter 12. So now I want to verify that I didn't break any of the old code while adding the new code. After I'm satisfied that the old code works properly, then I'll test the new code.

Verifying the Old Application

Because I made so many changes to the existing parts of the Web-Books.com application, I need to verify that they work properly. This is good practice even if I haven't made any changes to that part of the program. Sometimes it's possible that a change in one part of the program will adversely affect another part of the program, even if you're positive that you haven't changed that part of the program.

Figure 17-1 shows the default home page for WebBooks.com. The first thing you should notice is that the login form is included under the links section on the left-hand side of the page. The second thing you might notice is that the Web page no longer looks off-balance. There are no gaps because the information didn't line up properly. If you look closer at the form, you'll notice that the ISBN is now properly format-ted and a new link was added called Ordering Tips.

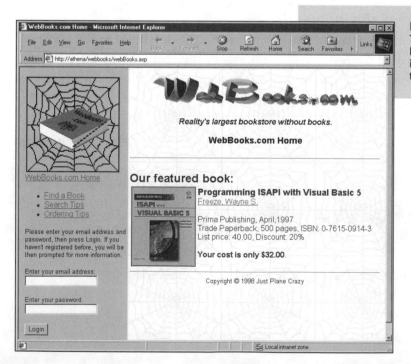

Figure 17-1
The WebBooks.com home page now includes a form to let the customer log in.

Clicking on the book takes me to the book form (see Figure 17-2). Again note that the login form is present, along with the new links on the left side of the Web page. On the right side of the form, notice that there's now another phrase included: "Ships within 24 hours." To verify that this information is correct, I need to verify that the value of QuantityOnHand is greater than zero.

There are two ways to do this. I could use the Enterprise Manager and open the Books table. That's a very useful tool, but the table holds more than 800 rows of information, and I don't want to search through each one looking for a particular book. So I use the Query Analyzer to search for the particular information I want (see Figure 17-3). As you can see

Tip

The Query Analyzer is a very useful tool when you want to look for a particular piece of information in the database. You simply enter a SQL statement and execute it. The results will be displayed in the bottom half of the display. You can even execute stored procedures in addition to the regular SQL statements.

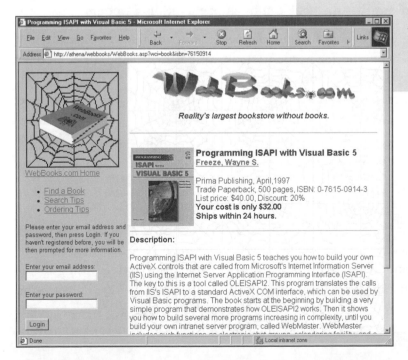

Figure 17-2
The WebBooks.com book form shows the detailed information about a book.

Figure 17-3
You can use the Query Analyzer to determine how many copies of the book are available.

from the results, the number of copies on hand is greater than zero, which means that the book can be shipped within 24 hours.

Clicking on the author name displays the list of books written by the author. Again the form doesn't look off-balanced, and all the books appear to be listed properly (see Figure 17-4). From this screen, I do an author search on Freeze (see Figure 17-5). Since both Jill T. Freeze and Wayne S. Freeze wrote *Introducing WebTV,* this book is only listed once. In the previous version of the program, it was listed twice, once for Jill and once for Wayne.

Verifying the Login Process

Now that I'm satisfied that the old application works the same or better than it did before, I'm going to verify the login process. Since this will work from any screen, I'll log on from my current screen using the e-mail address Chris@nowhere.com and the password cj. Pressing the Login button displays the Web page shown in Figure 17-6. The login process takes me to the big shopping cart. Since this is my first visit to

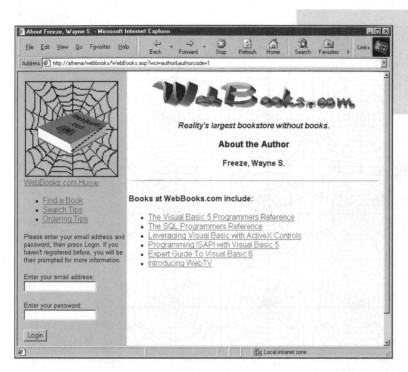

Figure 17-4
WebBooks.com can easily create a listing of all of the books written by Wayne S. Freeze.

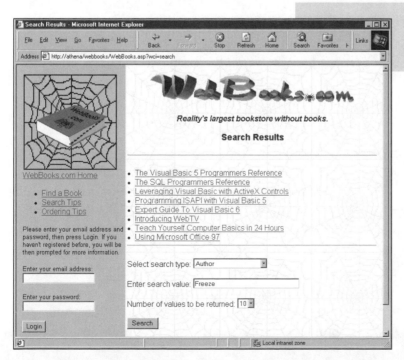

Figure 17-5
Listing the books written by Freeze.

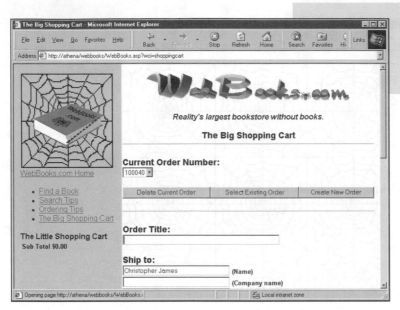

Figure 17-6
Log on to
WebBooks.com and
view the big shopping
cart.

the Web site, I've been assigned a brand new order number, and of course I have nothing in my shopping cart.

After I log on, I want to verify that I can log off properly. Since the customer can't explicitly log off the server, I just have to wait for 20 minutes without accessing the Web site. The server is set to keep the current **Session** object around for only 20 minutes. After that, the object is destroyed and with it the variables that I use to identify the current session. Clicking on The Big Shopping Cart link should refresh this form.

The error message in Figure 17-7 doesn't provide any clear information about the error, but after thinking about it for a while and looking at the code, I realized I made an obvious mistake. The **ShoppingCart_Respond** event assumes that the customer is logged on to the system. However, after the program has timed out, this won't be the case. To fix this problem, I need to see if the customer is logged on and if not, redirect the customer to a different form. The code fragment in Listing 17-1 will take care of this. This fix will have to be installed in the Buy_Respond, the ChangeCustomerInfo_Respond, the **ChangeDetails_Respond**, the **ChangeOrder_Respond**, and of course the **ShoppingCart_Respond** events.

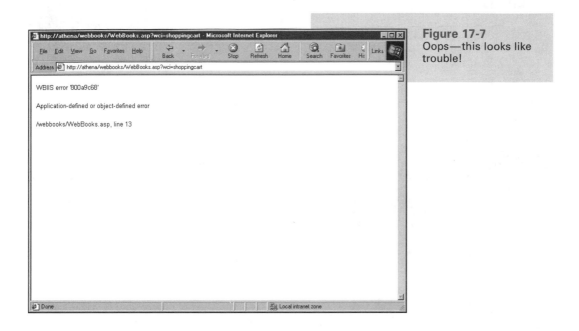

Figure 17-7
Oops—this looks like
trouble!

Ensure that only users who are logged on can execute this routine:

Listing 17-1

```
If Len(Session("customerid")) = 0 Then
    Response.Redirect "webbooks.asp"
    Exit Sub
End If
```

Now that I've corrected this problem, it's time to finish testing the login process. If I enter an incorrect password for a valid e-mail address, I should get a hint to help me remember my password. You can see that this works properly in Figure 17-8. Note that I didn't display the e-mail address on purpose. I felt it wasn't fair to display the e-mail address and the hint at the same time, since it makes it too easy for someone to try to guess a password.

Registering for the First Time

Entering an e-mail address that doesn't exist in the system will display the Register New Customer form shown in Figure 17-9. Note that the values for e-mail address and password are already filled in with the

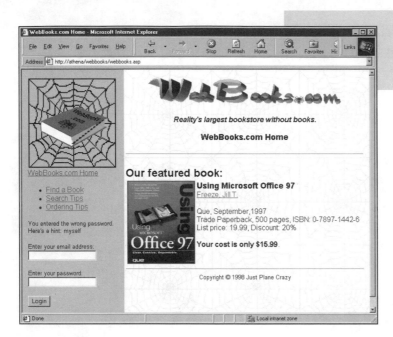

Figure 17-8
Entering a bad password means that I'll get a hint for the correct one.

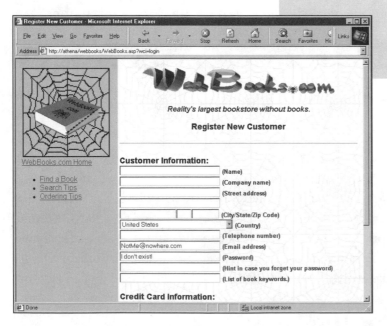

Figure 17-9
Enter registration information for a new customer.

values from the login form. From here, all I need to do is enter the information on the registration form, and then I can shop for books.

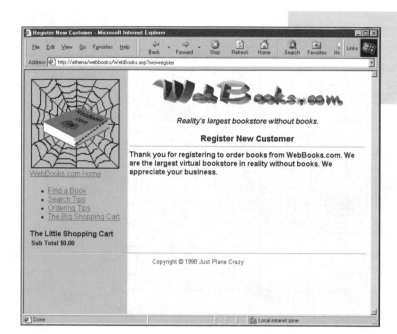

Figure 17-10
After submitting the
registration form, the
customer will see a nice
thank-you message.

After filling out the registration form and pressing the Save Changes button, the information will be saved to the database. If the information is valid, the customer will see the Web page shown in Figure 17-10. Notice that the small shopping cart is displayed on the left-hand side of the page. This means that an order has been created for the new customer and is ready for shipment.

Ordering a Book

Ordering a book is a simple process. Simply find the book you want to order and click on the book's cover or the link Add This Book to Your Shopping Cart! And the book will appear in the shopping cart. Now that I've logged on to the Web site, the book information page (see Figure 17-11) appears different than the one from before I logged on (see Figure 17-2).

Clicking on the book's cover adds the book to the shopping cart (see Figure 17-12). You can see that the book's title and price are now in the little shopping cart.

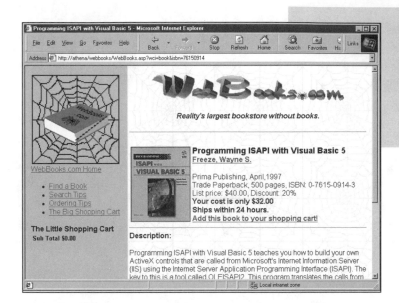

Figure 17-11
The WebBooks.com book form has been revised to show the detailed information about a book, an empty shopping cart, plus the hyperlinks to add the book to the shopping cart.

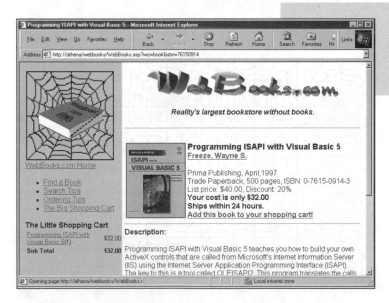

Figure 17-12
The WebBooks.com book form now shows the shopping cart containing one copy of the book.

Viewing the Big Shopping Cart

After adding a couple books to the shopping cart, I'm ready to check out. So I go to the Big Shopping Cart form. There are three main areas on this Web page. The top area allows me to create, select, and delete orders. So the first step is to create another order and try to add some books to it. Next I switch back to the original order, and then I delete the newest order. This leaves me with the original order.

On the middle part of the form is the shipping and billing information. At the bottom of this form are two buttons: one to update the current order and the other to save the information to the Customer Information Subsystem. To verify that the Save Changes button works, I give the order a different title and press the button. The title is now part of the information at the top of the form as well as the Order Title field (see Figure 17-13).

When I originally registered, I didn't enter any credit card information. So next I enter the credit card information on the form (see Figure 17-14) and press the Update Default Values button to update the information in the Customer Information Subsystem. There are two ways to verify that this information updates properly. The first way is to use the Query Analyzer and examine the information in the Customers table. The other way is to delete all of my orders. Then a new blank order will automatically be created using the default information.

The really interesting information is shown at the bottom of the form (see Figure 17-15). This section holds the details about which books are

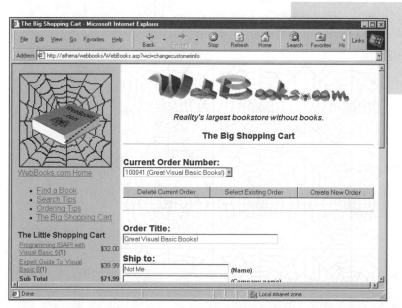

Figure 17-13
The top of the big shopping cart lets you switch to another order.

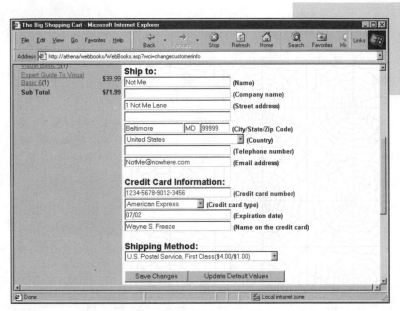

Figure 17-14
The shipping information can be changed in the big shopping cart.

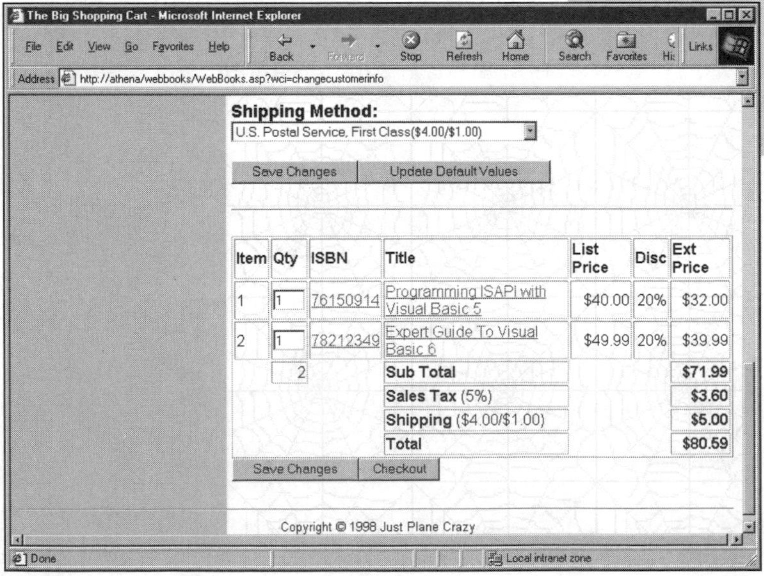

Figure 17-15
The Big Shopping Cart contains detailed information about the books ordered.

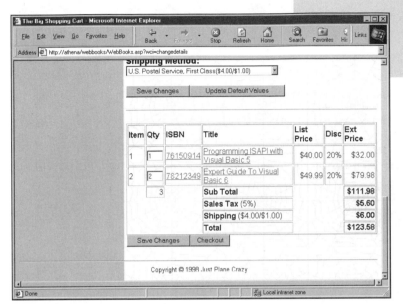

Figure 17-16
You can easily add a
second copy of a
book to the order.

being ordered and, more importantly, how much the order is going to cost. This section also allows me to change the quantities of each book. So changing the number of copies from one to two and pressing the Save Changes button should update the information so that a total of three books are ordered—and all the dollar figures should be adjusted accordingly as well (see Figure 17-16).

Once I'm satisfied with the order, I press the Checkout button to pay for the books. The system processes it and returns the Order Confirmation report shown in Figure 17-17 and Listing 17-2. Not only will I receive this report as a typical Web page, but I will also receive it as an e-mail message.

The full confirmation note lists all of the details about the order:

Listing 17-2

```
Great Visual Basic Books! (100041)
This order was placed on 12/14/98 8:21:13 PM
```

```
Ship to:
    Not Me
    1 Not Me Lane

    Baltimore MD 99999
    United States

Credit card information:
    Credit card number: 1234-5678-9012-3456
    Credit card type: American Express
    Name on credit card: Wayne S. Freeze
    Expiration date: 07/02

Books Ordered:
1: Programming ISAPI with Visual Basic 5
    ISBN: 0-7615-0914-3
    List Price: $40.00
    Discount: 20%
    Quantity: 1
    Your cost: $32.00

2: Expert Guide To Visual Basic 6
    ISBN: 0-7821-2349-X
    List Price: $49.99
    Discount: 20%
    Quantity: 2
    Your cost: $79.98

Subtotal: $111.98

Sales tax:
    Tax rate for Maryland is 5.00%.
    Sales tax for this order is $5.60

Shipping and handling charges:
    Using U.S. Postal Service, First Class
    First book costs $4.00, each additional books costs $1.00
    Total charge for 3 books is $6.00.
Total amount charged was $123.58.
Your order should be shipped in 24 hours.
```

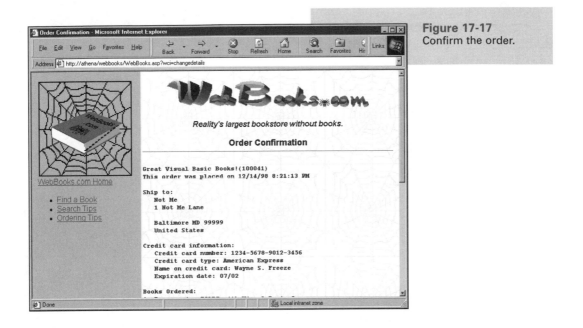

Figure 17-17
Confirm the order.

Assigning a Tracking Number and Printing the Packing List

After the order has been placed, the warehouse shipping clerk needs to assign a tracking number to the order and print the packing list. This is done with the WebBooks.com Warehouse Manager utility (see Figure 17-18). Before testing this program, you need to ensure that you have a completed order and its order number to process. Entering this information pressing the Get Tracking Number button will assign a tracking

Figure 17-18
Enter an order number to get tracking information and to create the packing list.

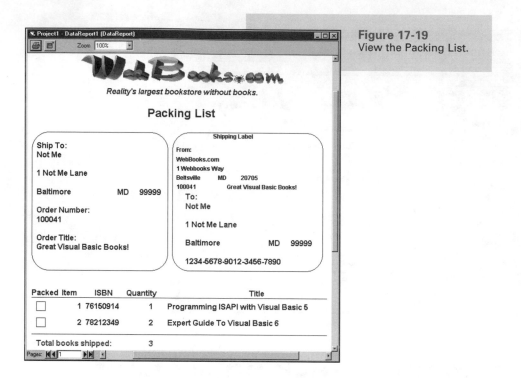

Figure 17-19
View the Packing List.

number from the shipper to the database information and will also set the date shipped. Then pressing the Show Packing List button will display the report window shown in Figure 17-19, and pressing the printer icon will send the report to the printer.

Wrapping Up

Testing the final subsystem in the WebBooks.com application really tests much more than the Order Processing Subsystem. In order for this subsystem to work properly, the previous subsystems must have done their jobs properly. Only one serious bug was encountered in this subsystem, which occurred when a customer would attempt to refresh their shopping cart after their session had been logged off. This bug was easily patched once the source of the problem was identified. The rest of the testing process just verified that the functions worked as designed.

Project 3 Summary

At the end of this phase of the WebBooks.com project, you should have learned the following:

- How to add new fields to an existing database table without disrupting existing programs
- How to create an ActiveX EXE program to provide a middle tier of processing between the Web server and the database server
- How to send e-mail messages from an IIS Application
- How to retrieve data from a database using a hierarchical **Recordset**
- How to create printed reports using the Microsoft Data Report Designer

18

Beyond WebBooks.com

Now that you've finished building the WebBooks.com application, does this mean there's nothing left to do? Of course not. There are several interesting adjustments that you can make to the WebBooks.com application to improve it. Plus there are lots of interesting technologies that can be investigated.

Improving WebBooks.com

By now you should have lots of ideas about how to improve the Web-Books.com application. Some of the ideas affect the basic design of the application, while others are merely cosmetic. All are aimed at improving the application.

Using Keywords and Categories

The keyword string in the Customers table isn't useful in today's version of the WebBooks.com application; however, it is a very useful concept. Imagine receiving information about a new book. After entering the information, a clerk could run a database search that would create a mailing list of people who had the keyword included in their customer profile. Then the clerk could prepare an e-mail message (or a snail-mail message, for that matter) that would let the customer know about the new book.

Also, you could modify the search form by adding a button that would append the search words to the customer's profile. This would make it easier for the customer to build the profile. Of course it would be nicer to intelligently add the keywords that aren't already present in the profile.

Alternate Ways to Find Books

There's one area that is totally missing from the WebBooks.com application when compared with other places where users can order books via the Web. Books should be organized by a hierarchy. A potential reader looking for a book might start out by looking at a general list of categories. For instance, this book might be classified both as Computers > Programming > Databases > SQL Server and as Computers > Programming > Languages > Visual Basic.

A book hierarchy could easily be implemented by adding one or more classifications like I used above for each book. Then I would also create a Classifications table containing the classification and a short text description of the material. Then it would be a simple matter to work my way down the classification chain displaying the text associated with the classification and any subclassifications that may be available. The titles of the books with that classification would follow. Then the customer would merely click on the book title in order to go to the book information page.

More Use of E-mail

One of the tools I developed is the SendMail subroutine. It is a very easy-to-use subroutine that makes it practical to send e-mail from your Web server. It is a great tool for sending e-mail messages about new books being added to the inventory. I can also use the same subroutine to send notes when an order has been shipped in addition to when an order has been placed. I can even send a note a few days after the order should have arrived at the destination to make sure that everything is fine. To categorize the message, I could use the tool with which I built SendMail to read new messages from customers and scan them for keywords and phrases. Then the mail would be redirected to the person assigned the task of reviewing and responding to that category of mail.

Ratings and Rankings

One problem with ordering books over the Internet is that the customer doesn't have the opportunity to physically hold the book and flip through it. While you can compensate somewhat by adding such information as the table of contents or a sample chapter, the more information you can give a potential customer, the better. Customer reviews help, but so do customer ratings. I've added the database fields and left room in the appropriate forms to allow reviewers to rate the various books. All you have to do is add a little code in the right places.

Another interesting way to help customers choose books is by implementing a WebBooks.com best-sellers list. Most bookstores have a wall with the top 10 best-selling books.

Although WebBooks.com can't arrange its books on a wall by best-seller number, it can do something even better. How about listing the books in order of sales rank within particular categories?

All the information needed to determine sales rank is available. In the Books table I had a field called NumberSoldSinceLastReorder and another called LastReorderDate. From these two fields I can compute a temporary field that contains the average number of books sold per day. Then it's a simple matter to build a query that will retrieve the information I want. Then I can use the **Order By** clause on this temporary field and print the records in the order in which they were retrieved.

A Complex Database

In some respects, the WebBooks.com application is too complex. The three separate subsystems often make for confusing references to tables, since they are implemented in different databases. This is also true for the stored procedures. Putting all the tables in one database would also simplify certain administrative functions.

However, placing all the tables in one database or a handful of databases could impact performance. For WebBooks.com, the database is small enough that it shouldn't matter much. But if your database has hundreds of thousands of records, you might benefit by placing individual tables into different databases. Then you could allocate the space for each database on different physical disk drives to better manage the I/O.

Application Design Philosophies

WebBooks.com was designed and built using a number of various approaches to give you a feel for the different ways to build SQL Server programs. However, while I tried to give you a taste of many different technologies, you probably want to review your options and pick the one that's most appropriate for your situation.

Client/Server Applications vs. IIS Applications vs. DHTML Applications

There are three main ways to create a Visual Basic database application: the traditional client/server application, the IIS Application, and the DHTML Application. Each has its own advantages and disadvantages, but I tend to prefer the IIS Application approach over the other two.

For any of these approaches to work, the client computer needs to be connected to the database server using some sort of network connection. However, in the case of the client/server application and the DHTML Application, some or all of the application must be installed on the client's computer. This can make it difficult to ensure that the client has the most current version of the application.

IIS Applications, on the other hand, are stored on the Web server and downloaded as needed. Since the client doesn't keep a copy of the application locally, it is always using the most up-to-date version. You can use nearly any browser as the client environment for an IIS Application, since you don't need to worry about the ability to call an ActiveX control.

However, if deploying applications isn't a major problem (perhaps you only have a handful of PCs that will be running the application), there are many advantages to using the traditional client/server approach. You can create a more powerful application because of the more advanced ActiveX controls available, plus the ability to handle events like Change, Click, and MouseMove. Also, using bound controls on your forms makes you a more efficient programmer because you don't have to worry about moving the data back and forth between the form and the database record.

Stored Procedures vs. Application Server vs. Client Application

In this book, much of the business logic was divided between stored procedures and the ActiveX EXE on the application server and in the client application itself. I did this deliberately since I wanted you to be familiar with all three approaches. However, in the real world, using all three approaches probably isn't a good idea. It confuses the developers and leads to problems. When you implement a routine in code and then copy it to a dozen programs, over time you'll end up with a dozen different implementations. This can easily lead to inconsistencies and a lot of other problems.

It is far better to choose one strategy and stick with it. Based on my experience, I would focus on building an ActiveX EXE that contained the business rules. I probably wouldn't use stored procedures, since that approach compiles SQL statements on the fly and keeps the compiled code around for a while in case the same program used the same statement again. This negates much of the benefit of stored procedures. However, I would use stored procedures when I have a sequence of operations that can be performed totally on the server. This avoids a data transfer between the database server and the application server, which is one of the traditional bottlenecks when using a database server.

I'd also try to limit the amount of code in the application itself. Any code beyond the code required to maintain the user interface should be moved to the application server. I would even consider moving some common user interface functions into the ActiveX EXE, if they spanned multiple program files.

Exploiting Other Tools and Technologies

There are a lot of other tools and technologies that can be used to improve the WebBooks.com application. All of these tools are designed to work with SQL Server and/or Visual Basic and can add value to any application.

Using VBScript in the Client

Another area in which you can easily improve the WebBooks.com application would be to add VBScript code to Web page forms to verify that the information is entered properly. This would include checks like verifying that numeric fields contain only numbers and that fields that should contain a value aren't blank. Of course you really can't perform checks that access information not on the Web page, but if you can detect and correct errors before they get to the database, the data in your database is more accurate and reliable.

Using a Secure Server

While I designed the WebBooks.com application, I assumed that I would always be using a secure Web server. Well, I was and I wasn't. The Internet Information Server has everything it needs to support secure transactions except for one thing. It needs a server certificate that has been issued by a recognized certificate authority. Once that is in place, you can do transfers using the Secure Sockets Layer (SSL) and using the HTTPS protocol. Then you have to convert all of your code so that it will use SSL transfers.

This isn't as complicated as you might think. All you have to do is replace any reference to HTTP with HTTPS. That's the extent of the conversion.

You may want to consider installing a second Web server that would contain only secure Web pages. Then you can restrict the server so that it accepts only secure communications. This will make your server a little more secure since it won't respond to regular HTTP requests. Of course you'll still need a regular Web server for unsecured requests.

Using Office Components

Microsoft Office contains a very powerful set of tools. All of these tools can be accessed as a series of objects. Thus you can write a Visual Basic program that can directly manipulate objects in Word and Excel to custom documents, spreadsheets, and charts.

Excel is a very powerful tool for analyzing data. Given that the Data Transformation Services can read and write Excel spreadsheets, it becomes very easy to exploit that capability to periodically create reports containing information that management personnel needs to know. This may help them recognize potential trouble spots, determine the effectiveness of their advertising, or identify books that are climbing the charts.

You've seen how Microsoft Excel can be a useful tool, but you may want to look at some of the other tools in Office. Word has the ability to create a form letter that can be combined with a list of names, addresses, and other information to produce custom letters. This process is known as a Mail Merge. You could write a small Visual Basic program that would generate the list of information that you want to merge with the form letter. This technique could be used to generate letters to specific groups of customers or to confirm orders placed with publishers.

While the other tools may not appear to be as useful as Excel and Word, remember that it might be useful to synchronize Outlook contact lists from the data in the Publishers table. Also, some of the charts and tables generated by Excel could easily find their way into PowerPoint presentations. You might even want to output data from the database using the Access format to allow some power users the ability to analyze data from the database on their own computers where it wouldn't interfere with the production database server.

Analyzing Information with OLAP

Perhaps one of the key features of SQL Server 7 is support for Online Analytical Processing (OLAP). This tool helps you to identify trends in your data by allowing you to view the data as a multidimensional cube. You can rotate the cube in different directions to aggregate data or to drill down to see the details. SQL Server OLAP Services handle the database side of managing the data, while a tool like Excel can be used as a front end to view the data using pivot tables.

In the case of WebBooks.com, this might help identify sales trends. You could view sales data by publisher, location, and size of sale to determine how to improve service to the customers. This is also a natural for tuning inventory levels, since you can look for situations where the standard reordering policy may not be working.

Using Microsoft Transaction Server

Microsoft Transaction Server (MTS) manages ActiveX EXE and DLL programs that are designed to run under MTS. You build your programs as a set of objects designed to be used by a single user, and MTS will handle all the issues like how to handle multiple users, security, and threading. MTS also provides transaction services that allow multiple objects to be grouped together into a package. Then the package either executes completely or not at all. You don't have to worry about what happens if the transaction dies in the middle.

MTS would be extremely helpful in providing scalability for the ActiveX objects that contain the business logic. It would let the programmers focus on implementing the business rules without worrying about how to handle concurrency issues.

Creating Help Files

Every application needs documentation, even if it isn't much more than a brief description of the application and how it works. Currently there are two types of help files: Windows Help and HTML Help. Windows Help files are created by building a rich text format document in Microsoft Word using special tags and fields.

HTML Help files are created with the HTML Help Workshop. These files are the same as those supplied with Windows 98, Windows 2000, and Office 2000. They provide more robust services than found in previous help files since you can take full advantage of the HTML language and use features like your own ActiveX controls or embedded VBScript programs.

This is an area that is really lacking in WebBooks.com. Since the purpose of the application was to teach you about SQL Server and Visual Basic, I skipped the documentation. After all, you have the option to read the code and you have this book to explain what is happening. But anyone who uses this application would appreciate additional information about how to use it.

Microsoft Agent

If you've used Microsoft Office 97, you'll likely remember the cute little characters that popped up in a window on the screen and tried to offer you advice on how to use the application. More often than not, you probably disabled the character (since it wasn't very useful) and thought that if Microsoft would give you the APIs you could do a much better job. Well, enter Microsoft Agent.

If you took those characters out of their windows, gave them the ability to move around on the screen, and let them talk to you and even listen to your commands, you would have Microsoft Agent. Featured in the new Office 2000 applications, Microsoft Agent is a completely new generation of programmable characters with more animations and better performance than ever before.

Microsoft Agent is fairly easy to use. You can program it from most programming languages including Visual Basic and VBScript. This means that it is easy to incorporate into Web pages or in applications that run natively in Windows. Starting with Windows 2000 (formerly known as Windows NT 5), Microsoft has decided to make Microsoft Agent a part of the operating system. Once installed, it can't be removed. Microsoft Agent will also be included as a standard feature as will any major updates to Windows 9x.

Imagine building a tutorial for the WebBooks.com Web site that has an agent character moving around the screen, pointing out fields that should be filled out and buttons that should be pressed. Or having the agent pop up from time to time recommending alternate books when a selected book is out of stock. Of course the true power of the agent might simply be in providing a personality for the Web site. Despite the agent's limited speech recognition capabilities, it might attract customers to the Web site for the sheer novelty. And anything that attracts customers to a Web site can't be all bad.

Wrapping Up

WebBooks.com was designed to illustrate many different concepts about how to combine SQL Server 7 and Visual Basic 6 to create a realistic application. However, a realistic application probably wouldn't be a combination of so many different technologies. A better approach would be to focus on a core set of technologies and use them as much as possible.

I'm a big believer in the IIS Application. Were I to build WebBooks.com for real, I would abandon the conventional client/server Visual Basic application in favor of the IIS Application coupled with the ActiveX EXE, possibly with Microsoft Transaction Server. This avoids the problem of distributing the application to each computer that will use it and doesn't take a powerful PC on the client side. The server side is a different story, and depending on the workload, I would use up to three PCs, one for each server type.

Now it's your turn. I've given you an introduction into how to design and build applications using SQL Server and Visual Basic. The more effort you put into it, the more you're going to learn. Everything you need to try some of the ideas I've suggested in this chapter is on the book's CD-ROM, including a demo version of SQL Server 7. Go ahead and try it. You'll have fun.

CHAPTER 19

Building DHTML Programs

After spending most of this book looking at the server side of developing Web-based applications, the following is a quick introduction of client-side programming using Visual Basic's DHTML programming model and the WebBooks.com application.

ON THE CD

The complete code for this program is included on the CD-ROM. Check the \HOSQLSrver7\Chapt19\WBHTML directory for the complete program.

What Is a DHTML Application?

A DHTML Web page is a composite of an ActiveX DLL and a Web page that is written in DHTML. The ActiveX DLL supplies code that will be called when various events on the Web page occur. Unlike using VBScript in the Web page, the ActiveX DLL can exploit nearly any feature available in Visual Basic.

While programming DHTML Applications is significantly different than Visual Basic programs, many concepts carry over. The Visual Basic form corresponds to the Web page. Text boxes correspond to input fields. Command buttons correspond to input buttons. Both contain events that are called when various situations are encountered, such as a button being pressed.

Writing DHTML Applications is significantly different than writing traditional Visual Basic programs. The user interface is completely different, and many of events and controls you are accustomed to will not be present. However, many of the fundamental concepts remain the same since DHTML is an event-driven program like a regular Visual Basic program. As the user interacts with the form, events will be triggered to perform various tasks on behalf of the user.

Building the DHTML Program

There are two basic parts to this program: the DHTML source code for the form and the Visual Basic function Button1_onclick. The form contains fields for the customer e-mail address and password and a button

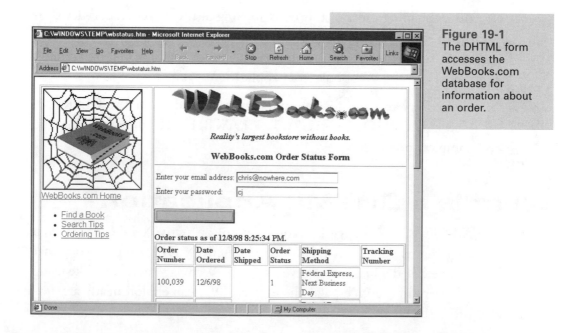

Figure 19-1
The DHTML form accesses the WebBooks.com database for information about an order.

that, when pressed, will retrieve the status for all of the customer's orders from the database and format it, as shown in Figure 19-1.

The DHTML Form

The DHTML form is a relatively simple form containing two input fields and an input button (see Figure 19-2). These objects are placed on the standard WebBooks.com Web page that I've built many times before. One nice aspect of creating these forms is that in addition to using the DHTML designer to draw the Web page, I can export the page to any Web page editor. So to create this form, I open the Web page using Notepad and copy the source from one of the other Web-Books.com Web pages. When I close Notepad, the DHTML Designer lets me know that the Web page has changed and asks me if I want to save the changes. I say Yes and most of the design work is done for me.

I then use the interactive features to create a two-column table that holds the two input fields and their description. I also add the input button interactively. Listing 19-1 contains the source code for the body of the new Web page.

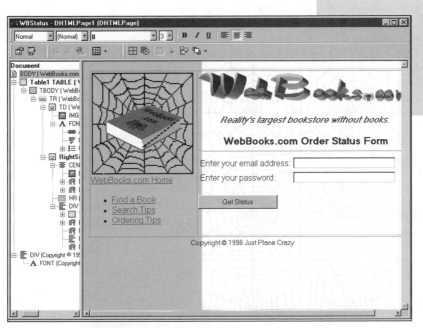

Figure 19-2
You can easily design the WebBooks.com form in the DHTML Designer.

This is the DHTML source code for the body of the WebBooks.com Order Status Form:

Listing 19-1

```
<BODY background="background.gif">
<TABLE border=1 id=Table1 name = Table1>
<TR><TD width=216 vAlign=top>
<IMG align=top alt="WebBooks.com logo" height=200
            src="http://athena/webbooks/logo.gif" width=200>

<FONT face=Arial>
<A href="http://athena/webbooks/webbooks.asp">WebBooks.com Home</A><BR>
<UL>
<LI><A href="http://athena/webbooks/WebBooks.ASP?WCI=ShowSearchForm">
Find a Book
</A>
<LI><A href="http://athena/webbooks/WebBooks.ASP?WCI=ShowTips">
Search Tips
</A>
<LI>
<A href="http://athena/webbooks/WebBooks.ASP?WCI=ShowOrderTips">
Ordering Tips
</A>
</UL>
</TD>
<TD align=left vAlign=top id=RightSide>
<CENTER>
<IMG align=bottom alt=WebBooks.com height=60
   src="http://athena/webbooks/webbooks.gif" width=426>
<P>
<STRONG><EM>Reality's largest bookstore without books.</EM></STRONG>
<P>
<BIG><STRONG>WebBooks.com Order Status Form</STRONG></BIG>
</CENTER>
<hr>
<DIV align=left>
<TABLE border=0 id=Table2 name = Table2>
<TR>
<TD>
Enter your email address:
</TD>
<TD>
<INPUT id=TextField1 name=TextField1
   style="HEIGHT: 22px; LEFT: 431px; TOP: 247px; WIDTH: 201px">
</TD>
</TR>
<TR>
```

```
<TD>
Enter your password:
</TD>
<TD>
<INPUT id=TextField2 name=TextField2
    style="HEIGHT: 22px; LEFT: 431px; TOP: 247px; WIDTH: 201px">
</TD>
</TR>
</TABLE>
<P>
<INPUT id=Button1 name=Button1 type=button value="Get Status"
    style="HEIGHT: 27px; LEFT: 242px; TOP: 296px; WIDTH: 156px" >
<p>
<DIV id="Results"></DIV>
<P>
</TD>
</TR>
</TABLE>
<DIV align=center>
<FONT face="" size=2>Copyright &copy; 1998 Just Plane Crazy</FONT>
</DIV>
</BODY>
</HTML>
```

The DHTML Designer automatically generates the header for this Web page (see Listing 19-2). It exists primarily to reference the ActiveX DLL compiled by the designer.

The header information generated by the DHTML Designer:

Listing 19-2

```
<!—METADATA TYPE="MsHtmlPageDesigner" startspan—>
<object id="DHTMLPage1"
    classid="clsid:13983F2F-891C-11D2-9A33-0080C79E9D8F"
    width=0 height=0></object>
<!—METADATA TYPE="MsHtmlPageDesigner" endspan—>
```

The Button1_onclick Event

The Button1_onclick event is triggered when the customer presses the Get Status button. It uses the values from the input fields, which were named TextField1 and TextField2. It then uses standard ADO objects to access the Orders table to determine the latest status of the customer's order.

> When you reference a field in your program, you use the ID attribute, not the Name attribute. Thus it doesn't matter which value you enter for the Name attribute. To make it easier, use the same value for both Name and ID.

The routine begins by opening a **Connection** object to the database (see Listing 19-3). Then it creates a **Command** object that references the GetOrderStatus stored procedure. Then it uses the values from both text fields to call the stored procedure. This returns a recordset containing the list of orders that have been placed by the customer.

The Button1_onclick event is triggered by pressing the Get Status button:

Listing 19-3

```
Private Function Button1_onclick() As Boolean

Dim db As ADODB.Connection
Dim cmd As ADODB.Command
Dim parms(1) As Variant
Dim rs As ADODB.Recordset
Dim s As String

Set db = New ADODB.Connection
db.Open _"provider=sqloledb;data source = athena;initial catalog=iis", _
    "sa", ""

Set cmd = New ADODB.Command
Set cmd.ActiveConnection = db
cmd.CommandText = "GetOrderStatus"
cmd.CommandType = adCmdStoredProc

parms(0) = TextField1.Value
parms(1) = TextField2.Value
Set rs = cmd.Execute(, parms)

s = "<b>Order status as of " & FormatDateTime(Now) & ".</b>" & _
    "<Table id=""Results"" border=""1"">" & _
    "<TR><TD><STRONG>Order Number</STRONG></TD>" & _
    "<TD><STRONG>Date Ordered</STRONG></TD>" & _
    "<TD><STRONG>Date Shipped</STRONG></TD>" & _
```

```
            "<TD><STRONG>Order Status</STRONG></TD>" & _
            "<TD><STRONG>Shipping Method</STRONG></TD>" & _
            "<TD><STRONG>Tracking Number</STRONG></TD></TR>"

Do While Not rs.EOF
    s = s & "<tr><td>" & FormatNumber(rs!OrderNumber, 0) & "</td>" & _
        "<td>" & FormatDateTime(rs!DateOrdered, vbShortDate) & "</td>" & _
        "<td>" & FormatDateTime(rs!DateShipped, vbShortDate) & "</td>" & _
        "<td>" & rs!OrderStatus & "</td>" & _
        "<td>" & rs!PreferredShippingMethod & "</td>" & _
        "<td>" & rs!TrackingNumber & "</td></tr>"

    rs.MoveNext
Loop

s = s & "</table>"

Results.innerHTML = s

rs.Close
Set rs = Nothing
Set cmd = Nothing
db.Close
Set db = Nothing

End Function
```

After retrieving the recordset, I begin building the response to the customer in a temporary string. I append the current date and time so the customer knows when the information was retrieved. Then I start building a table. I initialize the header row with the titles Order Number, Date Ordered, Date Shipped, Order Status, Shipping Method, and Tracking Number. I loop through the recordset and append one row for each record. I create cells for each field and format its entry. When I'm finished I close the row, and at the end of the loop I close the table.

Now for the tricky part. If you look near the end of Listing 19-1, you will see a <DIV> tag labeled "Results". This tag appears in my program as the **Results** object. Then all I need to do is assign the temporary string holding my formatted table to Results.innerHTML. This effectively replaces whatever HTML statements appear inside the <DIV> </DIV> pair with my table. If the customer were to press the Get Data button again, the current table would be replaced with the new one.

After that, all I need to do is close the recordset and database objects and assign them to **Nothing**. Then I can safely end this routine.

The GetOrderStatus stored procedure is shown in Listing 19-4. The really interesting part about this one is that I use the **Exists** clause to determine if the e-mail address and password combination is valid. Only if it's valid do I search the database for the fields that I want to report.

The GetOrderStatus stored procedure retrieves the status of all the orders for a customer:

Listing 19-4

```
CREATE Procedure GetOrderStatus @email varchar(64), @password varchar(16)

As

if (exists(select * from cis.dbo.customers
      Where EmailAddress = @email and Password = @password ))
   Select o.OrderNumber, o.DateOrdered, o.DateShipped, o.OrderStatus,
         o.TrackingNumber, s.PreferredShippingMethod
      From ops.dbo.Orders o, cis.dbo.PreferredShippingCodes s
      Where emailaddress=@email
         and o.ShippingCode = s.PreferredShippingCode
         and o.OrderStatus > 0
      Order by o.ordernumber desc
```

Testing the DHTML Application

After placing the order, the customer has the option to sit and wait for their books to arrive, or the customer can use the WebBooks.com Order Status Form to request information about the order (see Figure 19-3). This utility requests the customer's e-mail address and password and checks the database for all the customer's outstanding orders. These orders will then be displayed in a table containing the key information about when the order was shipped (see Figure 19-4). If the date shipped and tracking number information isn't available, the relevant fields will be blank.

Figure 19-3
Check on the order's status.

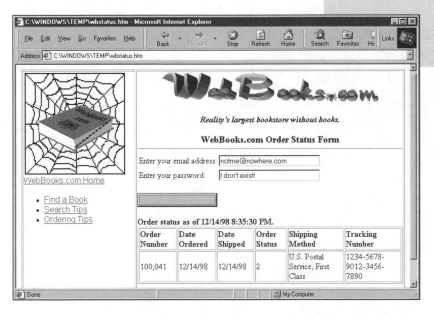

Figure 19-4
View the order's status.

Wrapping Up

This is a bonus chapter that introduces you to a different way to use SQL Server 7 with Visual Basic 6. DHTML Applications are programs that operate entirely on the client machine. The only time they need a Web server is to load the Web page itself. From then on, a DHTML program doesn't interact with the Web server unless you need another Web page or want to submit a form back to the server. With the database code embedded in the client application, the client can interact directly with the database server.

APPENDIX

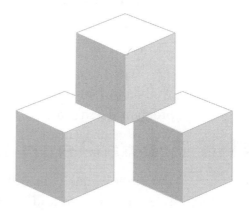

What's On the CD-ROM?

The CD that accompanies this book contains the example projects from the book and an evaluation edition of Microsoft SQL Server 7. The example projects are also located on Prima Tech's Web site at www. prima-tech.com/hosql7vb6.

Running the CD

To make the CD more user-friendly and take up less of your disk space, no installation is required. This means that the only files transferred to your hard disk are the ones you choose to copy or install.

> **Caution** ▶ **This CD has been designed to run under Windows 95/98 and Windows NT 4. Neither the CD itself nor the programs on the CD will run under earlier versions of Windows.**

Windows 95/98/NT4

Since there is no install routine, running the CD in Windows 95/98/NT4 is a breeze, especially if you have autorun enabled. Simply insert the CD in the CD-ROM drive, close the tray, and wait for the CD to load.

If you have disabled autorun, place the CD in the CD-ROM drive and follow these steps:

1. From the Start menu, select Run.
2. Type **D:\CDInstaller.exe** (where D:\ is the CD-ROM drive).
3. Select OK.

The Prima Tech License

The first window you will see is the Prima Tech License Agreement. Take a moment to read the agreement and click the "I Agree" button to accept the license and proceed to the user interface. If you do not agree with the license, click the "I Decline" button to close the user interface and end the session.

The Prima Tech User Interface

Prima Tech's user interface is designed to make viewing and using the CD contents quick and easy. The opening screen contains a two-panel window with three buttons across the bottom. The left panel contains the structure of the programs on the disc. The right panel displays a description page for the selected entry in the left panel. The three buttons across the bottom of the user interface make it possible to install programs, view the contents of the disc using Windows Explorer, and view the contents of a help file for the selected entry. If any of the buttons are grayed out, they are unavailable. For example, if the Help button is grayed out, it means that no Help file is available.

Resizing and Closing the User Interface

As with any window, you can resize the user interface. To do so, position the mouse over any edge or corner, hold down the left mouse button, and drag the edge or corner to a new position.

To close and exit the user interface, either double-click on the small button in the upper left corner of the window, or click on the exit button (marked with a small "x") in the upper right corner of the window.

Using the Left Panel

The left panel of the Prima Tech user interface works very much like Windows Explorer. To view the description of an entry in the left panel, simply click on the entry. For example, to view the general information about Prima Publishing, click on the entry "Prima Tech."

Some items have subitems that are nested below them. Such parent items have a small plus (+) sign next to them. To view the nested subitems, simply click on the plus sign. When you do, the list expands and the subitems are listed below the parent item. In addition, the plus (+) sign becomes a minus (-) sign. To hide the subitems, click on the minus sign to collapse the listing.

 You can control the positon of the line between the left and right panels. To change the position of the dividing line, move the mouse over the line, hold down the mouse button (the mouse becomes a two-headed arrow) and drag the line to a new position.

Using the Command Buttons

The right panel displays a page that describes the entry you choose in the left panel. In addition to a general description, the page may provide added information and hyperlinks. By clicking the buttons below the left panel, you can obtain additional information and install the programs to your hard drive.

Install. Use this button to install the program corresponding to your selection onto your hard drive.

Explore. Use this button to view the contents of the CD using the Windows Explorer.

Help. Click on this button to display the contents of the Help file provided with the program.

Pop-Up Menu Options

Install. If the selected title contains an install routine, choosing this option begins the installation process.

Explore. Selecting this option allows you to view the folder containing the program files using Windows Explorer.

View Help. Use this menu item to display the contents of the Help file provided with the program.

The Software

This section gives you a brief description of the shareware and evaluation software you'll find on the CD.

The software included with this publication is provided for your evaluation. If you try this software and find it useful, you must register the software as discussed in its documentation. Prima Publishing has not paid the registration fee for any shareware included on the disc.

SQL Server 7 Evaluation Edition. The evaluation edition of Microsoft's SQL Server 7 is provided on the disc. You can install this software and use it to try out the various book projects. Pay particular attention to the system requirements necessary to run SQL Server 7, as discussed in the installation program screens. For example, if you are running NT, you must have Service Pack 4 (not included with this disc). You can download Service Pack 4 from Microsoft's Web site at www.microsoft.com/ntserver.

The Sample Programs

The complete source code for all of the sample programs and sample data used in this book is included on the CD. You can easily use the Prima Tech User Interface to install the sample software on your computer. The material for each chapter is stored in a separate directory.

CHAPTER 5: CREATING THE CIS DATABASE

- \HOSQLSrver7\Chapt05\CIS

Use the SQL Server Enterprise Manager to create an empty database called CIS. Then use the Query Analyzer to load the cis.sql file and run it. This will create the CIS database.

CHAPTER 6: RUNNING THE CUSTINF PROGRAM

- \HOSQLSrver7\Chapt06\CustInf

Before you can run this program, you need to create data link files for the ADO Data Controls. Right-click on the ADODC1 control and select ADODC Properties. Press the Browse button associated with the Use Data Link File entry. Right-click on the file area and select New, Microsoft Data Link. Right-click on the file and select Open. On the Provider tab, choose Microsoft OLE DB Provider for SQL Server. On the Connection tab, enter the name of your database server, your user name (this is really your login name), and password, and then select the CIS database you created in Chapter 5. Press the Test connection button to verify that you can connect to the database server.

For the remaining ADODC controls, you can just right-click on the control, select ADODC Properties, and choose the name of the file you just created. The first time you load the form, you'll get error messages like "Data source name not found." Don't worry about these messages. Defining the data link file in this fashion will correct the problem.

CHAPTER 7: LOADING THE SAMPLE DATA

- \HOSQLSrver7\Chapt07\Data

Use the SQL Server Enterprise Manager to create a Data Transformation Services package to load each of the files as instructed in Chapter 7. Note that you will have to load the Customers table last.

CHAPTER 10: CREATING THE IIS DATABASE

- \HOSQLSrver7\Chapt10\IIS

Use the SQL Server Enterprise Manager to create an empty database called IIS. Then use the Query Analyzer to load and run the iis.sql file.

This will create the IIS database. Once the database has been defined, you will need to create the full-text indexes covered in Chapter 10.

CHAPTER 11: RUNNING THE BOOKINFO PROGRAM

- \HOSQLSrver7\Chapt11\BookInfo

In this program, you define the data link information for the Data Environment's Connection1 object. Simply show the Data Environment window, right-click on the Connection1 object, and select properties. On the Provider tab, choose Microsoft OLE DB Provider for SQL Server. On the Connection tab, enter the name of your database server and IIS database you created in Chapter 10. Do not fill in the user name and password information, since this will be collected from the user when the program first starts. Press the Test connection button to verify that you can connect to the database server.

CHAPTER 11: RUNNING THE WBIIS PROGRAM

- \HOSQLSrver7\Chapt11\WebBooks

This program requires an IIS Web server. You will need to modify the call to db.Open in the WebClass_Initialize event to make this program run properly. Change *athena* to the name of your database server and change *sa* to the name of your database login. The parameter that follows *sa* is the password. If your password isn't empty, you'll need to insert the password parameter.

Once you fix the code, you need to compile the code and save it into a directory in your IIS Web server where you have to execute permissions. You'll need to copy all of the GIF files and the HTML files into this directory along with the ASP, EXP, LIB, and DLL files.

CHAPTER 12: RUNNING THE LOADER PROGRAM

- \HOSQLSrver7\Chapt12\Data
- \HOSQLSrver7\Chapt12\Loader

You will need to make the same changes in the Command1_Click event's call to db.Open as you made in the WBIIS program. Specifically you need to change the server name from *athena* to your database server's name, change the login id *sa* to your login id, and add the correct password. Before running this program, you need to make sure that all of the tables in the IIS database are empty. This means that if you choose to run this program again, you'll need to erase the various tables to insure that the program runs properly.

There is a space at the top of the form where you must specify the directory containing the sample data files. You need to change it to reflect where the data was stored on your system. Don't expect this program to run in the blink of an eye, since there is a lot of data to load. After loading the database, you'll need to populate the full-text indexes so that the search feature in the WBIIS program works properly.

CHAPTER 15: CREATING THE OPS DATABASE

- \HOSQLSrver7\Chapt15\OPS

Use SQL Server Enterprise Manager to create an empty database called OPS. Then use the Query Analyzer to load and run the ops.sql file. This will create the OPS database.

CHAPTER 16: CREATING THE UTILITY PROGRAM

- \HOSQLSrver7\Chapt16\Utility

In the Class_Initialize event of the WBUtil class, you'll need to include the name of your database server and your login id and password in the call to db.Open. The program itself is self registering, so all you need to do is run it, and any program that references it will be able to find it. However, you will have to adjust the system name for any program that references this program.

CHAPTER 16: CREATING THE WBIIS PROGRAM

- \HOSQLSrver7\Chapt16\WBIIS

While this program is an enhanced version of the program found in Chapter 11, all of the files necessary to compile and run it are stored with this program. You don't need any of the files from Chapter 11. As a consequence of this, you need to make the same changes to this program that you made to the version in Chapter 11. This includes changing the call to db.Open in the WebClass_Initialize event to insert your database server name, plus the login and password needed to access the database. You'll also need to copy the same files into the appropriate directory in your IIS Web server. In my testing, I used the same directory for both sets of programs; however, there is no reason why you can't use different directories.

This program also references the objects in the Utility program. Since the Utility program can run on a different system than the database server, you will need to find the reference to the CreateObject function in the ChangeDetails event and change the name of the computer that is running the Utility program. In this sample program, I expected to find the Utility program on the same computer as my database server, *athena*.

CHAPTER 16: CREATING THE WBREPORT PROGRAM

- **\HOSQLSrver7\Chapt16\WBReport**

The WBReport program uses a Data Environment just like the Book-Info program in Chapter 11. So, you'll need to define the Data Link properties just like you did for the BookInfo program. The only difference is that you'll need to include the user name and password on the Connection tab, since I didn't include the Login form as I did in the BookInfo program.

This program also references the Utility program, though I used it on my local machine, *mycroft*. You can find references in the Command1_Click and Command3_Click events in Form1.

CHAPTER 19: CREATING THE WBDHTML PROGRAM

- **\HOSQLSrver7\Chapt19\WBDHTML**

Like most of the other programs in this book, the WBDHTML program uses the ADO objects to access the database. To make this program work, you need to change the name of the database server from *athena* to the name of your database server. You also need to change the login id and password to reflect the ones you use to access your database.

Glossary

ActiveX: A set of technologies that allow you to build and use *objects* created using the *Component Object Model* (COM) and *Distributed Component Object Model* (DCOM).

ActiveX Controls: Compiled software components developed with ActiveX technology that run on client computers.

ActiveX Data Objects (ADO): A collection of ActiveX objects that provide an interface to data objects such as a SQL Server database or an Excel spreadsheet.

ADO: See *ActiveX Data Objects*.

ANSI SQL: A standard for the *SQL* language from the American National Standards Institute (ANSI). The current version of the standard is referred to as SQL-92.

API: See *Application Programming Interface*.

Application: A collection of programs and *databases* that solve a problem.

Application Programming Interface (API): A well-defined set of rules and calling conventions that describe how a programmer can invoke the services of another application or the operating system.

Atomic Field: A *field* whose contents can't be broken down any more. (For example, a date is not atomic since it can be broken down into day, month, and year, while a month is atomic since it can't be broken into smaller pieces.)

Authentication: The process of verifying a user's identity to the database.

Authorization: The rights granted to a particular user to perform certain functions or access specific data.

Backup: A copy of a file or *database* taken at a point in time.

Base Table: The *table* that is used to derive a *view*.

Batch Job: A process where a noninteractive program is executed, typically at a time when no one is around to control its execution.

Binary Large Object (BLOB): A *column* containing information such as an *image* that can exceed the size of a normal binary column. It often requires special handling when compared to a normal column.

BLOB: See *Binary Large Object*.

BMP: An *image* file format developed by Microsoft. It supports many different formats, but files are usually larger than with other image formats such as *GIF* and *JPEG*.

Browser: A program that is designed to translate *HTML* tags into a visible document.

Business Logic: The set of rules used to operate a business.

Business Rule: A set of instructions that implement a business procedure. For example, the steps to place an order for a book is considered a business rule.

Cache: A buffer in memory where database information is kept to reduce the number of *physical I/Os* by changing them into *logical I/Os*.

Client/Server: A programming technique where a client program makes requests of a server program. In the case of SQL Server, the client program running on the user's computer generates requests for information or supplies commands to the *database server,* which processes them and returns the results back to the calling application.

Clustered Index: Used to determine the physical order of the rows in a table. A database table can only contain one clustered index.

Column: An attribute of a *table* that contains information. The concept of a column is similar to a *field* in a record.

COM: See *Component Object Model.*

Compile Time: Refers to activities performed and events that occur while compiling a program.

Component Object Model (COM): A technology used to create and access *objects* from a *Windows* program.

Composite Field: A *field* that can be broken into smaller parts. A date is an example of a composite field since it can be broken into year, month, and day.

Composite Key: A *key* containing more than one *column.*

Concatenation: The process of combining multiple *strings* into a single string by appending one string after another.

Concurrency: Occurs when multiple users share a resource; often requires *locks* to ensure that the sharing is done in an orderly fashion.

Connection: A link between the client program and the SQL Server *database server.*

Connection String: A *string* containing the parameters necessary to connect to the *database server.*

Constraint: A restriction placed on a *column* or set of columns that any value entered into the column must meet. Some examples of constraints are *foreign key, primary key,* and *unique.*

Container: A *control* that can contain other controls.

Control: An *object* that can be placed on a Visual Basic form or report to provide a specific function or to interact with the user. Some examples of controls are text boxes where the user can enter and edit text *strings,* labels that display test values, and buttons that can be pushed by the user.

Cookie: A set of data that is maintained by a user's *browser* and is available for processing by Web server-based *applications.*

Current Record: The single row pointed to by the *cursor.* The current record can be changed by moving the cursor to a different row.

Cursor: Used by an application program to point to a specific *row* in a *table* or *recordset.* This row is then considered the *current record.*

Data Access Objects (DAO): An obsolete way to access a *database* from Visual Basic. *ActiveX Data Objects* have replaced this technology.

Data-Bound Controls: A way of linking a *control* in a Visual Basic program to a *column* in a *recordset.* Whenever the value in the column changes, it will automatically be displayed in the control. Changing the value in the control will change the value in the *database.*

Data Control: A Visual Basic *control* that links other controls on a form to a *database.* This control supports scrolling through a *recordset* one record at a time and displaying the contents of the recordset on the linked controls. You can also use the data control to insert new records, update existing records, or delete existing records.

Data Element: Another name for a *column.*

Data Environment: A tool in Visual Basic that simplifies database programming. It allows you to define and design your access methods to the *database.*

Data Transformation Services (DTS): A component of SQL Server 7.0 that allows you to *import* and *export* data to and from a *database*.

Database: A collection of *tables, indexes,* and other *database objects* that are used by one or more *applications* stored inside a *database server*.

Database Log: A place where the *database* records information about *transactions* that have been completed.

Database Object: A *table, column, index, trigger, view, constraint, rule, stored procedure,* or *key* in a *database*.

Database Owner (DBO): The *username* of the person who is responsible for the *database*.

Database Server: A special program that manages the collection of *databases*.

DBO: See *Database Owner*.

DCOM: See *Distributed Component Object Model*.

Design Time: Refers to activities performed and events that occur while writing a program.

Distributed Component Object Model (DCOM): A superset of the Component Object Model (COM) that allows the distribution of objects over a local area and wide area network.

DLL: See *Dynamic Link Library*.

DTS: See *Data Transformation Services*.

Dump: See *backup*.

Dynamic Link Library (DLL): A file containing compiled code that can be shared by multiple programs at *run time*.

Event: An external subroutine called by an *object* when a specific situation is encountered. This allows the program using the object to supply additional information to the object or take a specific action based on information supplied by the object.

EXE: See *Executable File*.

Executable File (EXE): Contains a compiled version of a program that can be loaded into memory and executed.

Export: The process of copying data from a *database* to a file. This is the opposite of *import*.

Field: Another name for *column* or *data element*.

Filter: A set of criteria that reduces the number of records in a *recordset* without repopulating the recordset. Eliminating the filter criteria restores the full contents of the recordset, while changing the criteria will result in a different set of records selected from the original recordset.

Foreign Key: A *column* or set of columns whose values must match that of the *primary key* of another *table*. This is a way to implement *referential integrity*.

Full-Text Query: A *query* that searches for one or more words or phrases in a *column*.

GIF: See *Graphics Interchange Format*.

Graphics Interchange Format (GIF): A file format (which uses technology owned by Unisys Corporation) that is commonly used to store graphic *images* typically with 256 colors or fewer. Users whose *applications* use GIF images may have to license the technology.

Globally Unique Identifier (GUID): A 128-bit (16-byte) value that is generated by an algorithm that guarantees that the value will be unique. The algorithm that generates this value can be used at the rate of one new GUID per second for several centuries and never duplicate a value on your local computer nor any other computer.

GUID: See *Globally Unique Identifier*.

Hierarchical Recordset: A *recordset* in which a *column* in a particular *row* can contain another recordset.

HTML: See *Hypertext Markup Language*.

HTTP: See *Hypertext Transport Protocol*.

HTTP User Agent: A unique *string* that identifies the name and version of a Web *browser*. From this value you can deduce its capabilities.

Hypertext Markup Language (HTML): A simple language used to create a hypertext document consisting of tags to define formatting options and hypertext links.

Hypertext Transport Protocol (HTTP): A stateless object-oriented protocol used by Web clients and servers to communicate.

Identity Column: A column in a table that contains a system-generated, monotonically-increasing value that is guaranteed to be unique within the table.

IIS: See *Internet Information Server.*

Image: A graphical picture. Many different image formats are available, such as *BMP, GIF,* and *JPEG.*

Import: The process of copying data from a file to a *database.* This is the opposite of *export.*

Index: A database facility that stores details about the location of records containing a specified key value. This database object allows the database server to retrieve rows from a table faster than without using the index. Indexes are usually created based on typical searches performed by users to increase performance.

Integrity Constraint: See *rule.*

Interface: A way to access the services supplied by an *object.* A *COM*-based object can contain zero or more *properties,* zero or more *methods,* or zero or more *events.*

International Standard Book Number (ISBN): A 10-digit number that uniquely identifies a book.

Internet: An international network that permits computers to communicate among one another using the TCP/IP suite of protocols.

Internet Information Server (IIS): Microsoft's high-performance Web server that runs on a *Windows NT Server* system.

Internet Server Application Programming Interface (ISAPI): A programming *interface* that permits a programmer direct access to facilities inside Microsoft *Internet Information Server.*

Intrinsic Controls: *Controls* available in Visual Basic that are included with the run-time library. They are usually limited to performing relatively simple functions.

ISAPI: See *Internet Server Application Programming Interface.*

ISBN: See *International Standard Book Number.*

JPEG: See *Joint Photographic Experts Group.*

Joint Photographic Experts Group (JPEG): An *image* file format optimized for 24-bit color images. It uses a compression scheme where data that may not be noticed by the user is thrown away and results in very small images.

Key: A *column* or set of columns whose contents identify a *row* or rows. See *primary key, foreign key,* and *index.*

Locking: A process where a user is granted exclusive access to a particular *database object.* This prevents other users from changing the object until the first user has finished.

Logical I/O: An *I/O* request from the *database server* that may or may not be satisfied by information already in memory.

Login: An identifier that gives an individual access to a *database server.* A login is mapped to a particular *username* when accessing a specific *database.*

Many-to-Many Relationship: A relationship between two *data elements* where a particular value for one *field* implies that the other field can have a particular range of values, while that field implies that the first field may also have a range of values. For example, an author may write many books, while a book may be written by many authors.

MAPI: See *Messaging Application Programming Interface.*

Master Database: The *database* used by the *database server* to manage all the other databases on the server.

Messaging Application Programming Interface (MAPI): An interface developed by Microsoft to provide functions that developers could use to create mail-enabled applications.

Metadata: Information about a *database object.* For example, the metadata for a *column* would include its data type, its name, the *table* it is located in, whether **Nulls** are allowed, its default value, etc.

Method: A way to access a subroutine or function to perform a specific task within an *object.*

Microsoft Transaction Server (MTS): A server that manages distributed application *objects.*

Model Database: A *database* that contains all the default *tables* and supporting information that must exist in an empty database.

MTS: See *Microsoft Transaction Server.*

Normalization: The process of designing a *database* according to a set of well-defined rules that minimize duplication of information.

Null: A condition that exists when a *column* doesn't have a value. This should not be confused with an empty *string,* whose value is a string of characters with a length of zero.

Object: A software component that contains one or more *interfaces* that can be used to request information or perform functions.

ODBC: See *Open Database Connectivity.*

OLAP: See *Online Analytical Processing.*

OLE-DB: An object-oriented programming *interface* to access a *database* or other data source that supports Microsoft's *COM* technology.

OLE-DB Consumer: A program that requests information from a data source using the *OLE-DB* programming *interface.*

OLE-DB Provider: A *database* or other source of data that supplies data to an *OLE-DB consumer.*

One-to-Many Relationship: A relationship between two *data elements* where a particular value for one *field* implies that the other field can have a particular range of values, while that field implies that the first field can have only one value. For example, there is a one-to-many relationship between a mother and her children. A mother may have many children, while a child has only one mother.

One-to-One Relationship: A relationship between two data elements where a particular value for one *field* implies that the other field will have a particular value, and vice versa. For example, there is a one-to-one relationship between a person and that person's social security number.

Online Analytical Processing (OLAP): A database technology that allows you to use multidimensional *views* of the *database* for data analysis.

Open Database Connectivity (ODBC): Microsoft's *API* that permits *Windows* programs to access different database systems. ODBC has been superseded by *OLE-DB.*

Page: The fundamental unit of physical database storage. All *tables, indexes,* and other database information are mapped onto one or more pages, which are transferred as needed between disk and memory. In SQL Server 7.0, one page equals 8K bytes worth of data, 128 pages is 1 megabyte.

Permission: The ability to perform a specific function inside a *database*. The Grant and Revoke *SQL* statements manage permissions associated with a *username*.

Personal Web Server (PWS): A lightweight Web server designed for use with *Windows 9x* and *Windows NT Workstation*.

Physical I/O: An input or output request that results in a physical transfer of data from or to a disk drive or other hardware device. This differs from a *logical I/O,* where the information may be buffered in memory and no physical transfer may take place.

Primary Key: The *column* or columns in a *table* that will uniquely define a *row*.

Property: A way to access a data attribute stored inside an *object*. A property may be read/write, read-only, or write-only.

Protocol: A set of rules that define how two or more computers communicate with each other.

PWS: See *Personal Web Server*.

Query: A *database* request that retrieves, inserts, updates, or deletes information in a database.

Query Optimizer: A part of the *database server* that analyzes a database *query* to determine the most efficient way to execute the query.

RDBMS: See *Relational Database Management System*.

RDO: See *Remote Data Objects*.

Recordset: A collection of records retrieved from a *database*.

Recovery: The process of rebuilding a *database* based on database *backups* and *transaction logs*.

Referential Integrity: A way to ensure that the information in the *database* is valid by only permitting values to be entered into a *table* if the value in the *foreign key* is found in the *primary key* of another table.

Registry: The area in *Windows* that holds configuration information about the operating system and application programs.

Relational Database: A *database* that appears to the user as a simple collection of *tables,* where each table consists of a series of *columns* or *fields* across the top and a series of *rows* or records down the side. The underlying data structures used to hold the data are totally invisible to the user.

Relational Database Management System (RDBMS): A collection of *relational databases* on a single *database server*.

Remote Data Objects (RDO): A technology that allows a program running on *Windows* to access a SQL Server database. This technology has been superseded by *ActiveX Data Objects*.

Repeating Group: A variable that contains multiple occurrences of information. This is similar to an array with dynamically defined bounds. An example of a repeating group would be book authors, where book authors might hold one, two, three, or more authors, depending on the particular book.

Replication: A way of keeping two *databases* with the same information in sync.

Role: A predefined set of *permissions* in the *database*. When a *login* ID is assigned to a role, it inherits all the permissions associated with the role.

Row: A collection of *columns* that are stored in a *table*. The concept of a row is similar to a record in a file.

Rule: A way to verify a value entered in a *column*. It's created by adding an *Integrity Constraint* to a table. You can specify a list of permitted values or other limits on the particular values.

Run Time: When the program is being executed, as opposed to *design time* (when the program is being written) or *compile time* (when the program is being compiled).

SA: See *System Administrator.*

Schema: A description of the *database* using a database language such as *SQL.*

Secondary Key: A *column* or set of columns that can be used to identify a *row* in a *table.* Unlike the *primary key,* a secondary key need not be unique.

Source File: Contains the programming language statements that a compiler will translate into an *executable file,* which can be loaded into memory and run.

SQL: See *Structured Query Language.*

Stored Procedure: A set of *SQL* statements that are executed on the *database server* and can optionally return a result to the database client program. Using stored procedures is usually more efficient than trying to perform the same function directly on the database client because they are precompiled and may also be contained in the server's memory.

String: A sequence of characters that can be stored in a *database* or manipulated by a program. Strings can contain ASCII characters or *Unicode* characters.

Structured Query Language (SQL): A language originally developed by IBM in the 1970s that has become the standard language for accessing *databases.*

System Administrator (SA): The *login* associated with the individual responsible for the *database server.* The system administrator is exempt from all security rules and is treated as the *database owner* of whatever *database* is being used.

System Catalog: The *tables* found in the *Master Database* used to store information on the other databases and system configuration.

System Databases: Consists of the *Master Database, Temporary Database (tempdb), and Model Database.* These *databases* are required to operate the *database server.*

System Table: A *table* required by the *database server* to hold information about itself. This includes such information as *user databases, tables, columns, indexes,* etc.

Table: The only database structure that contains the business data. It provides a view of this data by a series of *columns* and *rows.* Each column of data corresponds to a field, while a row is also known as a record.

Temporary Database: A *database* that holds temporary information such as temporary tables and other temporary storage needs. All temporary tables are stored in this database no matter which database the user is accessing. In SQL Server the temporary database is called "tempdb".

Thread: An execution path through the same instance of a program.

Transact-SQL: The name of the *SQL* language implemented in SQL Server. It consists of many extensions to the ANSI standard including local variables, assignment statements, **If** statements, and other control flow statements that help you build *stored procedures.*

Transaction: A logical unit of work that consists of one or more changes to the *database.* Either all of the steps in a transaction are completed or none of them. The classic example of a transaction is transferring money from one account to another, where the funds are subtracted from the source account and then added to the destination account. If only half of the transaction is completed, the database will be in error.

Transaction Log: A file containing a list of changes made to the *database.* This information can be used to undo changes made to the database or it can be combined with a *backup* file to recover *transactions* made after the backup was made.

Trigger: A special type of *stored procedure* that is called whenever a *row* is inserted in, deleted from, or updated in a *table*. If a severe error is encountered while running the trigger, the *transaction* will automatically be rolled back. It is used primarily for ensuring that new data is valid or to cascade changes from one table to another. For example, you may include a trigger on an order entry table that ensures that the customer ID exists in the customer table before an order is placed.

UDL File: See *Data Link File*.

Unicode: A way to store international characters in a 16-bit character. This makes it easier for processing multilingual data.

Unique Index: An *index* that ensures that two or more *rows* can't have the same value. The *primary key* always has a unique index.

User Database: A *database* where user information is kept.

Username: An identifier associated with a *login* that is used to determine an individual's *permissions* inside a *database*.

View: A virtual *table* that is created through the use of a *SQL* **Select** statement. A view appears to the user exactly as a table for all read operations and some write operations, depending on how the view was created.

Web Page: A document typically written in *HTML* that is made available over the *Internet*.

Windows: An operating system from Microsoft that usually refers to either Windows 95 or Windows 98 (collectively known as *Windows 9x*) but also may refer to *Windows NT Workstation* or *Windows NT Server*.

Windows 9x: An operating system designed to support interactive processing. The 9x refers to either Windows 98 (the most current version) or Windows 95 (the predecessor to Windows 98).

Windows NT Server: An operating system designed to support various servers, such as a *database server* or Web server.

Windows NT Workstation: An operating system designed to support interactive processing, typically used by power users.

Index

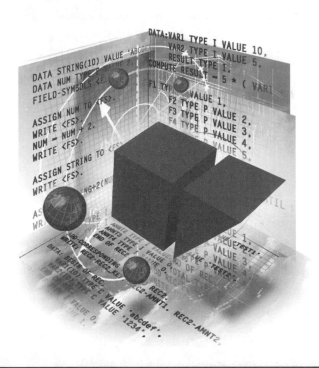

License Agreement/Notice of Limited Warranty

By opening the sealed disk container in this book, you agree to the following terms and conditions. If, upon reading the following license agreement and notice of limited warranty, you cannot agree to the terms and conditions set forth, return the unused book with unopened disk to the place where you purchased it for a refund.

License:

The enclosed software is copyrighted by the copyright holder(s) indicated on the software disk. You are licensed to copy the software onto a single computer for use by a single concurrent user and to a backup disk. You may not reproduce, make copies, or distribute copies or rent or lease the software in whole or in part, except with written permission of the copyright holder(s). You may transfer the enclosed disk only together with this license, and only if you destroy all other copies of the software and the transferee agrees to the terms of the license. You may not decompile, reverse assemble, or reverse engineer the software.

Notice of Limited Warranty:

The enclosed disk is warranted by Prima Publishing to be free of physical defects in materials and workmanship for a period of sixty (60) days from end user's purchase of the book/disk combination. During the sixty-day term of the limited warranty, Prima will provide a replacement disk upon the return of a defective disk.

Limited Liability:

THE SOLE REMEDY FOR BREACH OF THIS LIMITED WARRANTY SHALL CONSIST ENTIRELY OF REPLACEMENT OF THE DEFECTIVE DISK. IN NO EVENT SHALL PRIMA OR THE AUTHORS BE LIABLE FOR ANY OTHER DAMAGES, INCLUDING LOSS OR CORRUPTION OF DATA, CHANGES IN THE FUNCTIONAL CHARACTERISTICS OF THE HARDWARE OR OPERATING SYSTEM, DELETERIOUS INTERACTION WITH OTHER SOFTWARE, OR ANY OTHER SPECIAL, INCIDENTAL, OR CONSEQUENTIAL DAMAGES THAT MAY ARISE, EVEN IF PRIMA AND/OR THE AUTHOR HAVE PREVIOUSLY BEEN NOTIFIED THAT THE POSSIBILITY OF SUCH DAMAGES EXISTS.

Disclaimer of Warranties:

PRIMA AND THE AUTHORS SPECIFICALLY DISCLAIM ANY AND ALL OTHER WARRANTIES, EITHER EXPRESS OR IMPLIED, INCLUDING WARRANTIES OF MERCHANTABILITY, SUITABILITY TO A PARTICULAR TASK OR PURPOSE, OR FREEDOM FROM ERRORS. SOME STATES DO NOT ALLOW FOR EXCLUSION OF IMPLIED WARRANTIES OR LIMITATION OF INCIDENTAL OR CONSEQUENTIAL DAMAGES, SO THESE LIMITATIONS MAY NOT APPLY TO YOU.

Other:

This Agreement is governed by the laws of the State of California without regard to choice of law principles. The United Convention of Contracts for the International Sale of Goods is specifically disclaimed. This Agreement constitutes the entire agreement between you and Prima Publishing regarding use of the software.